EARNING
and
LEARNING

EARNING
and
LEARNING

How Schools Matter

SUSAN E. MAYER
and
PAUL E. PETERSON
Editors

BROOKINGS INSTITUTION PRESS
Washington, D.C.

RUSSELL SAGE FOUNDATION
New York, N.Y.

Copyright © 1999

BROOKINGS INSTITUTION PRESS   RUSSELL SAGE FOUNDATION

Earning and Learning: How Schools Matter may be ordered from :
Brookings Institution Press
1775 Massachusetts Avenue, N.W.
Washington, D.C. 20036
Tel. 1-800-275-1447 or (202) 797-6258
Fax: (202) 797-6004
www.brook.edu

Library of Congress Cataloging in Publication Data

Earning and learning : how schools matter / Susan E. Mayer and
Paul E. Peterson, editors.
    p.   cm.
Includes bibliographical references and index.

ISBN 0-8157-5528-7 (cloth : perm. paper)
ISBN 0-8157-5529-5 (pbk. : perm. paper)
    1. Education—Economic aspects—United States.   2. Academic
achievement—Social aspects—United States.   3. Educational
equalization—United States.   4. School improvement programs—United
States.   5. Class size—United States.   6. School choice—United
States.   I. Mayer, Susan E. II. Peterson, Paul E., 1936– .
    LC66 .E23 1999
    306.43'2—dc21   99-6383
                                                            CIP

9 8 7 6 5 4 3 2 1

The paper used in this publication meets minimum requirements of the
American National Standard for Information Sciences—Permanence of Paper for
Printed Library Materials, ANSI Z39.48-1984.

Typeset in Adobe Garamond

Composition by
R. Lynn Rivenbark
Macon, Georgia

Printed by
R.R. Donnelley and Sons
Harrisonburg, Virginia

Contents

Acknowledgments   vii

PART ONE
Schooling, Cognitive Skills, and Future Earnings

1   From Learning to Earning   3
Susan E. Mayer

2   Aptitude or Achievement: Why Do Test Scores
Predict Educational Attainment and Earnings?   15
Christopher Jencks and Meredith Phillips

3   Economic Success and the Evolution of Schooling
and Mental Ability   49
Christopher Winship and Sanders D. Korenman

4   Does the Timing of School Affect How Much
Children Learn?   79
Susan E. Mayer and David Knutson

v

PART TWO

Improving Schooling

5 School Reforms: How Much Do They Matter?   105
Paul E. Peterson

6 How Does Class Size Relate to Achievement in Schools?   117
Frederick Mosteller

7 The Evidence on Class Size   131
Eric A. Hanushek

8 The Effects of Math and Math-Related Courses
in High School   169
Robert H. Meyer

9 Do Hard Courses and Good Grades Enhance
Cognitive Skills?   205
Jay R. Girotto and Paul E. Peterson

10 Nerd Harassment, Incentives, School Priorities,
and Learning   231
John H. Bishop

11 The Effects of School Choice on Curriculum
and Atmosphere   281
Caroline M. Hoxby

12 The Effects of School Choice in New York City   317
Paul E. Peterson, David E. Myers, William G. Howell,
and Daniel P. Mayer

13 The Costs and Benefits of School Reform   341
Susan E. Mayer and Paul E. Peterson

Contributors   355

Index   357

Acknowledgments

NEARLY EVERYONE agrees that schools should do more than simply increase children's cognitive test scores. But few deny that a central purpose of schools is to enhance opportunities for children to learn to read, write, and calculate—capacities that enhance the cognitive skills necessary to perform well in contemporary life. The effects of cognitive skill on productivity, as measured by the wages and earnings individuals receive, can now be estimated with greater precision than ever before; these estimates suggest that the capacities learned in school have significant economic consequences later in life. Some schools and some school districts do better jobs than others at facilitating the opportunities of young people to acquire these cognitive abilities and, by implication, their eventual earnings.

In this book we pull together much of the evidence on these questions and identify school reforms that seem to have the potential for making schools better. The first half of the book tries to better estimate the effect of schooling on cognitive test scores and on wages. The second tries to demonstrate how effective a variety of educational policies are likely to be at increasing such scores.

The book concludes on an ironic note. School reforms that are likely to yield the highest payoff are politically the most controversial. The payoff from more popular reforms is often high enough to make them worthwhile, but the benefit-cost ratio from these reforms is much lower than this ratio appears to be for more controversial proposals.

This project began with a year-long faculty seminar on "Meritocracy and Inequality," organized at the University of Chicago by Christopher Jencks and Susan Mayer in 1995. The seminar was sponsored by the Irving B. Harris School of Public Policy Studies and the Russell Sage Foundation. The seminar was organized partly in response to the provocative findings of Richard Herrnstein and Charles Murray's *The Bell Curve* (Free Press, 1994). It brought together experts from many academic disciplines with long-standing interests in the relationships among cognitive skills, schooling, and economic and social well-being. *The Black-White Test Score Gap* (Brookings, 1998), edited by Jencks and Meredith Phillips, emerged in part from the work of that seminar, as well as from a day-long workshop, also organized by Jencks and Mayer, on the gap in cognitive skills between blacks and whites in the United States.

Through the efforts of Paul Peterson, the seminar was expanded to Harvard University in 1996. With financial assistance from the Russell Sage Foundation and the Rockefeller Foundation, Mayer and Peterson organized a conference on "Meritocracy and Inequality" at Harvard University in September 1996. The work of many of the participants in that conference appears in this volume.

We would like to thank the Russell Sage Foundation and the Rockefeller Foundation for financial assistance for this project. We also thank all the participants in the original conference, who, besides the authors in this book, include the following: Joseph Altonji, Orley Ashenfelter, Leesa Boeger, Margaret Braatz, John Cawley, David Cohen, Yves Duhaldeborde, Greg Duncan, Rachael Dunifon, Curtis Frazier, Claudia Goldin, Adam Gamoran, Peter Gottschalk, Zvi Griliches, Min-Hsiung Huang, Robert Hauser, James Heckman, Lawrence Katz, Frank Levy, Richard Murnane, Robert Putnam, Derek Neal, Cecilia Rouse, Edward Vytlacil, and John Willett.

We would also like to thank others who helped make this book possible. Sara Miller Acosta organized the original seminars at the University of Chicago. Becky Contreras and Shelley Weiner assisted with the conference and seminars at Harvard and with preparation of the manuscript. Finally, Nancy Davidson, who has now retired from the Brookings Institution Press, attended the Harvard conference and remained enthusiastic about this project throughout its long genesis. We are grateful to her and to the many others at Brookings who have assisted in the production of this volume.

SUSAN E. MAYER
PAUL E. PETERSON

EARNING
and
LEARNING

PART I

Schooling, Cognitive Skills, and Future Earnings

SUSAN E. MAYER

1

From Learning to Earning

N O   O N E   D O U B T S that adults with a lot of schooling earn more than adults with less schooling. In 1996 the average working-age male who had completed high school earned $28,878, while the average working-age male college graduate earned about $50,000. Employers appear to want workers with more skills and to be willing to pay for those skills. In addition, the returns to education have been increasing. In 1973 college graduates earned 46 percent more than high school graduates. By 1989, the difference was 53 percent and it has risen since.[1]

Not everyone agrees about why schooling improves economic well-being. Some people believe that schooling is associated with higher wages mainly because students who are smart to begin with get more schooling, and employers are willing to pay for such "smarts." Others believe that employers value what students learn in school. This is an important distinction. If employers are willing to pay for what children learn in school, policies that increase the length or quality of schooling could increase wages, at least as long as demand for highly educated workers remains strong. But if employers are willing to pay for students' ability to learn rather than what they have learned in school, and if schooling has a relatively small effect on students' ability to learn, it is less clear how social policy can help. The essays

1. Murnane, Willett, and Levy (1995).

in the first part of this book address this controversy. Combined with other evidence, they provide strong support for the argument that how much students learn affects how much they earn.

Aptitude and Achievement

In this chapter I use the term *achievement* to refer to what people have learned. I use the term *aptitude* to denote the ability to learn. Aptitude is the result of both genetic endowment and other factors, such as lead poisoning or illness, that have long-term effects on children's ability to learn. Some psychologists might prefer to call achievement "crystallized intelligence" and to call aptitude "intelligence," "generalized intelligence," or "fluid intelligence." I avoid the terms intelligence and IQ mainly because they have acquired emotional and political overtones that can complicate a discussion.

I use the term *cognitive skills* to denote scores on tests of cognitive skill. The chapters in this book use a variety of tests of cognitive skill. None of these were designed to test general intelligence. Almost everyone agrees that scores on these tests are the result of some combination of ability to learn and opportunity to learn, although there is less agreement about the relative importance of aptitude and achievement to cognitive test scores, and hence to future economic success.

Cognitive test scores are associated with both schooling and wages. Most people think that schooling affects wages mainly because it affects test scores. Therefore much of the debate over how schooling affects wages is really over how schooling affects cognitive skills. Those who think that schooling is associated with higher wages because smart people get more schooling tend to think that cognitive test scores are primarily the result of children's aptitude. Those who think that schooling mainly affects wages because children with a lot of schooling have learned a lot tend to think that cognitive test scores primarily reflect achievement.

In the late 1950s and early 1960s Theodore Schultz, Jacob Mincer, Gary Becker, and other economists developed the theory of human capital.[2] According to this theory, human capital is a function of endowments and investment and, like physical capital, is amenable to accumulation

2. See Becker (1964); Mincer (1962, 1974); Schultz (1963, 1971).

and growth. Educational institutions are the chief mechanism by which such accumulation takes place. Endowments include both genetic factors, such as sex and eye color, and cultural factors, such as language. Investments include both parental investments of time and money in their children and children's own efforts in acquiring human capital. These investments can include both how much schooling a child gets and how hard the child works in school. By emphasizing the role of investments in the accumulation of human capital, this model emphasizes the importance to employers of what students have learned in school. It parallels psychological theories that predict that schooling increases both achievement and aptitude.[3]

Building on human capital theory, social scientists produced a large body of empirical work showing that the longer people remain in school, the higher their future income, and presumably the greater their contribution to the economic wealth of society. The federal Great Society intitiative was largely based on this argument. The intent was to fight poverty and inequality with a wide variety of educational and training programs: Head Start, compensatory education, employment and training programs, and Pell grants to low-income college students, to name only a few.[4]

As America's commitment to education edged to its high-water mark, doubt began to be cast on the usefulness of a wide range of educational and social interventions for increasing cognitive test scores. In the mid-1960s, the Coleman report provided an influential scientific challenge to the notion that school quality affects children's cognitive test scores.[5] James Coleman found that differences in expenditures, classroom size, and teacher training had little impact on the amount pupils learned. He concluded that the experience, habits, and values that children acquire from their families and the environments in which they live have more influence on what they learn in school than do school resources. Work by Christopher Jencks seemed to confirm that school quality had little effect on school achievement or educational success.[6] Evaluations of the compensatory education programs and Head Start produced conflicting evidence about their ability to improve either cognitive test scores or

3. See, for example, Cattell (1987); Ceci (1991).

4. While the rhetoric of the Great Society and the "war on poverty" depended on human capital arguments, relatively little money was spent on such programs.

5. Coleman and others (1966).

6. Jencks and others (1972).

economic outcomes. A number of studies seemed to indicate that early improvements in children's cognitive skills "faded out" within a few years.[7]

In addition, some economists argued that the number of years a person remains in school affects their future earnings in part because employers rely on diplomas and credentials as "signals" that enable them to sort job applicants with high aptitude from those with low aptitude. According to this view, more able children get more schooling, giving the appearance that schooling enhances ability. Employers are willing to pay for more able workers, but ability is largely determined either by heredity or by prenatal or very early environmental influences. Very able children learn a lot in school. But the fact that they know algebra or have a large vocabulary is important to employers mainly as an indicator of their aptitude or their ability to learn something new. Neither schooling nor other social interventions have much effect on aptitude. A less radical version of the signaling model holds that while aptitude is mainly hereditary, employers do value the specific skills that students learn in school, such as math and reading. Thus schooling signals both that students have learned these things and that they have a high aptitude for learning new skills in the work place.

This view was bolstered in the mid-1980s by Eric Hanushek's review of research on the effect of school characteristics on achievement.[8] Hanushek concluded that, like the Coleman report, this research showed that no measured characteristic of schools consistently improved students' cognitive test scores. Although recent meta-analyses of the same research show that some school characteristics do have positive effects, these effects are not large.[9]

The economists' signaling model was not the first to emphasize the importance of initial ability to economic success. Some research by psychologists suggests that employers value aptitude and that aptitude is primarily genetically determined.[10]

In *The Bell Curve*, Richard Herrnstein and Charles Murray contend that the United States is becoming increasingly meritocratic.[11] They argue, as

7. See Lee and Loeb (1995); Lazar and Darling (1982, 1989); Haskins (1989); McKey and others (1985); Spitz (1986). See Barnett (1995) for a review of the research literature on early childhood programs.

8. Hanushek (1986).

9. See Hedges, Laine, and Greenwald (1992); Card and Krueger (1992); and for a review, Card and Krueger (1994). For explanations of the divergent findings in the research literature, see Burtless (1996); Loeb and Bound (1995).

10. See Hartigan and Wigidor (1989). See also Jencks (1998) for a review of this research.

11. Herrnstein and Murray (1994).

had others before them, that in a meritocratic society family background plays a minor role in economic success, whereas initial aptitude—or IQ—plays a large role. IQ influences economic success by affecting both the quantity and the quality of schooling that children get. Some children simply will not be able to learn as much as others. This inequality in aptitude will inevitably result in economic inequality. To bolster this argument, Herrnstein and Murray point out that although today Americans get more schooling and at higher cost than ever before, the verbal and quantitative test scores of students have changed little over the past two decades, and economic disparities have increased, not decreased. In this view the role of schools is to sort students by their ability to learn new material, and then to help them efficiently achieve the level of learning that is right for them.

Because so much controversy remains about the relative importance of aptitude and achievement to economic success, the chapters in this book reexamine the question using new methods that try to separate the effects of aptitude from ability. These chapters combined with earlier research provide strong evidence that what children learn in school affects their economic success.

The Evidence on the Effect of Achievement

The central methodological issue that arises in virtually every chapter in the first section of this book is selection bias. No one disputes that there are correlations between test scores and earnings and between test scores and years of schooling.[12] The question is why one observes such correlations. Imagine two men who are the same age. Joe graduated from college and earns $25 per hour. Bob graduated from high school and earns $10 per hour. Some people would argue that Joe earns more than Bob because he got more schooling, and hence learned more. Others would say that Joe earns more because he was smarter to start with, which resulted in his both getting more schooling and earning a higher wage. To see whether schooling affects wages, one must control both men's aptitude before they began school. Otherwise, some of the benefit that is attributed to more schooling

---

12. The correlation between measured intelligence and schooling is quite high. Herrnstein and Murray (1994) estimate that for white males it is about 0.60. Stephen Ceci (1991) reviews sixteen studies and finds estimates ranging from 0.50 to 0.90. The correlation between test scores and years of schooling is also high. For example, Jencks and Phillips show in chapter 2 below that the correlation between twelfth grade math scores and years of schooling is 0.517.

might really be caused by initial aptitude—put another way, students who get a lot of schooling will be "selected" on their initial aptitude.

The selection issue arises not only in estimating the effects of additional years of schooling, but also in assessing the impact of specific school policies on children's outcomes. For example, studies find that students who take more challenging academic courses subsequently score higher on tests of cognitive skill. This could be because they learned more in the challenging courses. Or it could be that more able students are more likely to choose challenging courses. Because few data sets include both a measure of children's aptitude before they began school and a measure of their wages as adults, researchers have had to develop ways to overcome the problem of omitting (or not controlling) initial aptitude. The chapters in this volume are valuable for the care that they take to overcome the selection problem.

Several recent studies have tried to determine the relative contribution of aptitude and achievement to economic well-being. Most of these have been done by economists interested in estimating the economic returns to a year of schooling.[13] Researchers have used various techniques to overcome the selection problem. For example, some have compared the wages of identical twins who had different amounts of schooling to see if more schooling is associated with higher wages among people who are genetically identical.[14] Most of these studies find that schooling increases wages, holding constant initial aptitude. This implies that what children learn in school pays off in the labor market. Other studies have tried to determine whether additional schooling or particular aspects of schooling increase children's cognitive test scores.[15] These studies tend to show that additional schooling does increase cognitive skill. But because all of these studies are flawed in one way or another, controversy over the importance of achievement remains.

In chapter 2, Christopher Jencks and Meredith Phillips ask whether what children learn between tenth and twelfth grades affects their future educational attainment and wages—or whether the apparent effects on education and wages of cognitive test scores measured in the twelfth grade

13. For a review of this literature see Ashenfelter and Rouse (1999), as well as the chapters in this volume.

14. For a summary of studies that have tried to estimate the effect of ability bias in studies of the returns to schooling, see Ashenfelter and Rouse (1999). See also Blackburn and Neumark (1993).

15. For a review of this literature see Ceci (1991), as well as the individual papers in this volume.

are really due to aptitude. Jencks and Phillips use the High School and Beyond (HS&B) survey to estimate how much students gained on tests of math and verbal ability between their tenth and twelfth years in high school. They find, surprisingly, that gains in test scores did not depend on students' tenth grade scores. Therefore Jencks and Phillips argue that these gains do not reflect initial aptitude, but instead reflect learning.

They then use these gains to estimate how much what students learned in school between the tenth and twelfth grade affects their eventual education and wages. Their results show that learning one item on the HS&B math test (the mean gain is 1.52 items) is associated with an additional 0.14 year of school and 2.5 percent greater earnings at ages twenty-seven to twenty-eight. A fifth of the wage gain is attributable to the fact that students who learn more math items get more schooling. Verbal scores have a smaller effect than math scores on education and wages, and gains in verbal scores have almost no effect on additional schooling.

If learning affects educational attainment and wages, it is important to know what affects learning. Jencks and Phillips find, not surprisingly, that students who stay in school learn more than students who drop out. Students who take more math classes learn more math, as do students who do more homework. This suggests that between tenth and twelfth grade, learning is responsive to environmental influences and individual effort, rather than simply depending on aptitude.

In chapter 3, Christopher Winship and Sanders Korenman estimate the effects of schooling and test scores on economic well-being. They find that, holding education constant, a 15 point (one standard deviation) increase in scores on the Armed Forces Qualification Test (AFQT), a test of cognitive skill, increases the family income of twenty-five to thirty-two-year-olds by 18.5 percent and the wages of the same age group by 16.9 percent. Holding AFQT score constant, a one year increase in schooling increases family income by 6.2 percent and wages by 7.9 percent. But, like other researchers, Winship and Korenman find that as people get smarter they get more schooling, and as people get more schooling they get smarter. Each increase in schooling increases cognitive test scores, which in turn increases schooling, until the increments are small. This feedback means that holding test scores constant when estimating the returns to schooling understates the total effect of schooling, and holding schooling constant when estimating the economic payoff to test scores understates the importance of test scores. Taking into account this feedback loop, the composite effect of a year of education on family income is 13.4 percent. The composite effect on earnings is 14.9 percent.

In estimating these feedback effects, Winship and Korenman also find that the effects of schooling and test scores on economic well-being are roughly equal. This implies that the claim that employers are only interested in workers' aptitude is as wrong as the claim that employers care only about workers' achievement. Test scores are a function of more or less equal measures of aptitude and achievement, as is economic success.

If one could design an experiment in which students were randomly assigned to groups that got different amounts of schooling, one could compare the eventual wages of these groups to see if the amount of schooling affects wages. While one cannot conduct such an experiment, random variation in the timing of children's enrollment in school arguably provides a rough approximation. In chapter 4, David Knutson and I take advantage of the fact that most states require children to enter first grade if they reach a compulsory school age, usually six years old, by a particular date, such as September 1. As a result, children born in the months immediately following the cut-off date begin school at a later age than those born in the months just before the cut-off date. The difference in age can be nearly one year. States also require children to stay in school until they reach a particular age, usually sixteen years, rather than until they finish a particular grade. Consequently, children who start school when they are younger, because of their birth date, get more schooling than children who start when they are older. This variation in amount of schooling is more or less random.

Like other researchers, we find that beginning first grade at an early age improves adult economic success. Starting school a year earlier increases future wages by 2.7 percent. Some of this increase in wages is due to the fact that children who start school earlier get more schooling. But the timing of schooling also affects cognitive test scores and wages among children with the same amount of schooling.

We find that among children with the same amount of schooling, beginning school at age five rather than at age seven is associated with a 0.64 standard deviation increment in verbal test scores and a 0.44 standard deviation increment in math scores. These effects decline somewhat as children progress through school, but the effect of early enrollment on verbal ability remains substantial at the end of elementary school. If the timing of schooling affects test scores, and the increase in test scores results in higher wages, the implication is that employers are willing to pay for what students learn in school.

This finding also has important implications for compulsory school laws. Currently, the age at which states require children to enter school varies from five years to eight years. Although increasing the length of schooling is expensive, changing the timing of schooling without changing the length is likely to be relatively inexpensive. In fact, if starting school at younger ages improves children's outcomes, shifting the years of compulsory school attendance down by one year could save money, because it generally costs less to educate young children than to educate older children. In addition, working parents with preschool-age children must find someone else to care for them.

The chapters presented in this volume suggest that an additional year of schooling increases cognitive test scores by about one-fifth of a standard deviation, holding constant initial aptitude. Cognitive test scores appear to increase wages among young adults by 10 to 20 percent. If so, an additional year of schooling would increase wages by 2 to 4 percent, net of the effect of aptitude.[16]

The chapters in this book examine the relationship between cognitive test scores and economic success. But cognitive test scores alone do not determine economic success. As the chapters in this book show, cognitive test scores explain only a modest amount of the overall variation in schooling and wages. Most of the variation in wages can be attributed either to factors other than cognitive skills or to cognitive skills not measured by conventional tests. Employers say they want workers who are not only skilled but are also reliable, creative, confident, and honest. But social scientists have devoted little effort to measuring such characteristics, so one cannot tell how important they are to wage differences.[17] One also cannot tell when a school is doing a better or a worse job of fostering these attributes. In contrast, for over a hundred years social scientists have been developing and refining tests of cognitive skills. These tests still have serious

16. Cawley and Heckman (1998) note that the relationship between schooling and wages may vary with cognitive ability and the relationship between test score gains and wages also may vary with initial test score. See Ashenfelter and Rouse (1999) for counterevidence.

17. Murnane and others (1997) and Duncan and others (1997) assess the relationship between noncognitive characteristics—such as early behavioral problems, self-esteem, and self-efficacy—and wages. Unfortunately, most measures of noncognitive characteristics are weak and poorly motivated by theory about how they affect economic success.

problems, especially for assessing the cognitive skills of individuals as opposed to mean skill levels of groups. Nonetheless it is not surprising that researchers try to evaluate schools on the factors that we can measure best, even while it is surprising how little effort has been spent on trying to understand other attributes that employers, parents, teachers, and policy-makers seem to think are important.

The fact that cognitive tests imperfectly measure only one important attribute of children does not imply that one should abandon efforts to improve average test scores or reduce inequalities in test scores. Parents and policymakers agree that increasing how much children know is a central goal of schooling, and when all other factors are equal, employers prefer someone who knows more to someone who knows less. Furthermore, economic success is not the only rationale for improving children's cognitive skills. Improving test scores is likely to improve other outcomes besides children's eventual wages. Children with high cognitive skills are less likely to become teenage parents or unwed parents, or to engage in crime.[18] Thus by focusing only on wages, the chapters in this book no doubt understate the overall social benefit of raising children's cognitive skills.

The studies in part 1 of the volume provide strong evidence that what children learn in school affects their economic success. The studies in part 2 try to determine whether particular aspects of schooling or the ways schools are organized affect how much children learn.

References

Ashenfelter, Orley, and Cecilia Rouse. 1999. "Schooling, Intelligence, and Income in America: Cracks in the Bell Curve." Working Paper 6902. Cambridge, Mass.: National Bureau of Economic Research (January).

Barnett, W. Steven. 1985. "Long-Term Effects of Early Childhood Programs on Cognitive and School Outcomes." *Future of Children* 5(3): 25–50.

Becker, Gary S. 1964. *Human Capital: A Theoretical and Empirical Analysis with Special Reference to Education.* New York: National Bureau of Economic Research.

Blackburn, McKinley L., and David Neumark. 1993. "Omitted-Ability Bias and the Increase in the Return to Schooling." *Journal of Labor Economics* 11(3): 521–44.

Bronfenberger, Uri, and others. 1996. *The State of Americans.* Free Press.

Burtless, Gary. 1996. *Does Money Matter? The Effect of School Resources on Student Achievement and Adult Success.* Brookings.

18. Bronfenberger and others (1996); Herrnstein and Murray (1994); Yoshikawa (1995).

Card, David, and Alan Krueger 1992. "Does School Quality Matter? Returns to Education and the Characteristics of Public Schools in the United States." *Journal of Political Economy* 100(1): 1–40.

————. 1994. "The Economic Returns to School Quality: A Partial Survey." Working Paper 334. Princeton University, Industrial Relations Section.

Cattell, Raymond B. 1987. *Intelligence: Its Structure, Growth and Action*. Amsterdam: Elsevier.

Cawley, John, and James Heckman. 1998. "Three Observations on Wages and Measured Cognitive Ability." Unpublished paper. University of Chicago.

Ceci, Stephen. 1991. "How Much Does Schooling Influence General Intelligence and Its Cognitive Component?" *Developmental Psychology* 27(5): 703–22.

Cicarelli, V. G., J. W. Evans, and J. S. Schiller. 1969. *The Impact of Head Start: An Evaluation of the Effects of Head Start on Children's Cognitive and Affective Development*. Athens, Ohio: Westinghouse Learning Corporation and Ohio University.

Coleman, James S., and others. 1966. *Equality of Educational Opportunity*. Government Printing Office

Duncan, Greg, Rachael Dunifon, and David Knutson. 1997. "Long-Run Effects of Motivation and Social Capital on Success." Unpublished paper. Northwestern University.

Hanushek, Eric A. 1986. "The Economics of Schooling: Production and Efficiency in Public Schools." *Journal of Economic Literature* 24(September): 1141–77.

Hartigan, John, and Alexandra Wigidor, eds. 1989. *Fairness in Employment Testing: Validity, Generalization, Minority Issues, and the General Aptitude Test Battery*. Washington: National Academy Press.

Haskins, Ronald. 1989. "Beyond Metaphor: The Efficacy of Early Childhood Education." *American Psychologist* 44: 274–82.

Hedges, Larry, Richard Laine, and Rob Greenwald. 1992. "Does Money Matter? Meta-Analyses of the Effect of Differential School Inputs on Student Outcomes." *Educational Researcher* 23(3): 5–14.

Herrnstein, Richard J., and Charles Murray. 1994. *The Bell Curve: Intelligence and Class Structure in American Life*. Free Press.

Jencks, Christopher. 1998. "Racial Bias in Testing." In *The Black-White Test Score Gap*, edited by Christopher Jencks and Meredith Phillips. Brookings.

Jencks, Christopher, and others. 1972. *Inequality*. Basic Books.

Lazar, Irving, and Richard Darlington. 1982. *Lasting Effects of Early Education: A Report from the Consortium for Longitudinal Studies*. Monographs for the Society for Research in Child Development Series 195, 47(2–3).

Lee, Valerie E., and Susanna Loeb. 1995. "Where Do Head Start Attendees End Up? One Reason Why Preschool Effects Fade." *Educational Evaluation and Policy Analysis* 17(1): 62–82.

Loeb, Susanna, and John Bound. 1995. "The Effect of Measured School Inputs on Academic Achievement: Evidence from the 1920s, 1930s, and 1940s Birth Cohorts." Unpublished paper. University of Michigan.

McKey, Ruth H. and others. 1985. *The Impact of Head Start on Children, Families and Communities*. Washington: CSR, Inc.

Mayer, Susan E. 1996. *What Money Can't Buy: Family Income and Children's Life Chances*. Harvard University Press.

Mincer, Jacob. 1962. "On-the-Job Training: Costs, Returns and Some Implications." *Journal of Political Economy* 70(October).

————. 1974. *Schooling, Experience and Earnings.* Columbia University Press.

Murnane, Richard J., John B. Willett, and Frank Levy. 1995. "The Growing Importance of Cognitive Skills in Wage Determination." *Review of Economics and Statistics* 77(2): 251–66.

Murnane, Richard J., and others. 1997. "Does the Self-Esteem of High School–Aged Males Predict Labor Market Success a Decade Later?" Unpublished paper. Harvard University.

Schultz, Theodore W. 1963. *The Economic Value of Education.* Columbia University Press.

————. 1971. *Investment in Human Capital: The Role of Education and of Research.* Free Press.

Spitz, H. H. 1986. *The Raising of Intelligence: A Selected History of Attempts to Raise Retarded Intelligence.* Hillsdale, N.J.: Erlbaum.

Winship, Christopher, and Sanders Korenman. 1997. "Does Staying in School Make You Smarter? The Effect of Education on IQ in *The Bell Curve.*" In *Intelligence, Genes, and Success: Scientists Respond to The Bell Curve*, edited by Bernie Devlin and others. New York: Springer-Verlag.

Yoshikawa, Hirozaku. 1995. "Long-Term Effects of Early Childhood Programs on Social Outcomes and Delinquency." *Future of Children* 5(3): 51–75.

CHRISTOPHER JENCKS
MEREDITH PHILLIPS

2

Aptitude or Achievement: Why Do Test Scores Predict Educational Attainment and Earnings?

IN 1971 RICHARD HERRNSTEIN wrote a controversial article in the *Atlantic Monthly* arguing that scores on cognitive tests are more or less stable over an individual's lifetime, that most of the variation in such scores is genetic in origin, and that these scores predict labor market success because they measure skills that are essential in most high-level jobs.[1] In 1994 Herrnstein and Charles Murray revived this argument in *The Bell Curve*, arguing that cognitive tests predict life chances largely because they measure a collection of stable abilities that psychologists often call *g* (for "general" intelligence), and that variation in *g* is primarily (though not exclusively) attributable to genetic factors.[2] The most important ability measured by *g*, according to many psychologists, is the ability to learn new things quickly and easily. We refer to all such stable, biologically based cognitive traits as aptitudes.

We would like to thank Zvi Griliches, Robert Hauser, James Heckman, Michael Hout, Caroline Minter Hoxby, Susan Mayer, Paul Peterson, and seminar participants at the University of Chicago, Harvard University, and the University of Wisconsin–Madison, for helpful comments on previous drafts. We are especially grateful to Hauser for many hours of advice on how to estimate the seemingly intractable LISREL models that we used in the early stages of this research. All remaining errors are our own.

1. Richard J. Herrnstein, "I.Q.," *Atlantic Monthly*, September, 1971, pp. 43–64.
2. Herrnstein and Murray (1994).

What we call the aptitude model of cognitive development assumes that test scores correlate with economic success because they measure how quickly and easily people learn, and because people who learn quickly and easily are considerably more useful to their employers than people who learn more slowly or with greater difficulty. This model also assumes that test scores correlate with the amount of schooling individuals complete because students who learn new things quickly and easily get better grades and are more inclined to stay in school than students who find learning difficult. In its most extreme form, the aptitude model implies that the entire school curriculum is a prolonged aptitude test, and that the specific skills and knowledge taught in school have no economic value whatever. The pure aptitude model implies, for example, that people who do well at Latin should earn as much as people who do well at algebra, because the ability to master Latin measures g about as well as the ability to master algebra does.

Many economists, educators, and ordinary citizens reject the aptitude model in favor of what we call the achievement model. In the achievement model what counts is what you know or what you can do, not how hard you have to work to learn it. Math scores predict wages because employers value workers who can solve math problems or reason mathematically, not because math scores are a proxy for workers' ability to learn something else. Likewise, fluency in formal written English predicts economic success because employers in English-speaking countries need workers who can understand and write complex English prose. Fluency in other languages is an equally good proxy for g but is not valuable to most employers in English-speaking countries.

The achievement model does not deny that aptitude influences adult success. But the achievement model assumes that academic aptitude influences adult success largely by affecting academic achievement. Imagine two groups of adults with the same average score on a conventional math achievement test. One group has relatively poor math training but very favorable genes (and hence high aptitude). The other group has better math training but less favorable genes (and hence lower aptitude). The achievement model predicts that the two groups will earn the same average wage. The aptitude model predicts that the high-aptitude group will earn substantially more than the low-aptitude group, even though the two groups currently have the same math skills.[3]

3. The contrast between the achievement and aptitude models is in many respects similar to the contrast between human capital theory and signaling theory in economics. Human capital theory

Figure 2-1. *Possible Effects of Aptitude and Achievement on Adult Success*

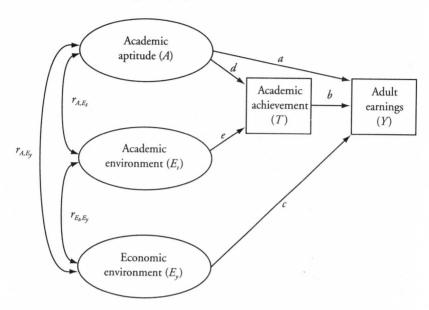

Source: Authors' model as described in text.

Figure 2-1 shows the causal connections among the variables that concern us. The three variables on the far left are theoretical constructs that one cannot measure directly. We define these as follows:

—Academic aptitude (A) measures the cumulative effect of all the genes that lead individuals to learn different amounts when they have been exposed to identical environments. Since no two individuals have identical environments, we can never measure aptitude directly.

—Academic environment (E_t) measures the cumulative effect of all the experiences and circumstances that influence test performance. We can measure some components of academic environment, but we can never hope to measure them all.

—Economic environment (E_y) measures the cumulative effect of all the experiences and circumstances that influence earnings, independent of

---

assumes that people spend time, effort, and money to acquire verbal and mathematical skills because these skills make them more productive. Signaling theory assumes that people spend time, effort, and money to acquire such skills because this is a good way of proving that they have the stable aptitudes and motivations that employers value.

academic aptitude and achievement. Again, we can measure some of these experiences and circumstances but not all of them. Because some of the environmental factors that influence academic achievement also have a direct effect on earnings with achievement controlled, economic environment and academic environment are correlated.

The two remaining variables in figure 2-1 are academic achievement (T) and adult success (Y). We can measure these variables directly, albeit with some error. For our purposes, academic achievement means an individual's score on one or more cognitive tests. For heuristic purposes we equate adult success with annual earnings. Later, we will also consider the effects of aptitude and achievement on years of school completed. This change has no effect on the basic model.

The letters a to e on the causal arrows in figure 2-1 designate coefficients that measure the effect of a one-unit change in the causal variable on the outcome at the end of the arrow. Each of these coefficients is estimated holding constant the other variables in the model. Our goal in this chapter is to determine the relative size of the coefficients that measure the direct effects of aptitude and achievement on adult outcomes, namely a and b. We expect both a and b to be positive, because we expect employers to value both a new worker's initial competence and the worker's ability to acquire new skills quickly and easily. Intuition does not tell us whether the direct effect of aptitude will be larger or smaller than the direct effect of achievement. Advocates of the achievement model tend to assume that a is negligible. Advocates of the aptitude model, including Herrnstein and Murray, assume that a is large, and hence that b is relatively small. Empirical evidence on this issue is almost nonexistent.[4]

Resolving the conflict between the aptitude and achievement models is critical if we want to assess the value of policies that raise test scores. Suppose, for example, that cutting the average size of high school math classes from twenty-five to twenty-two students raises the math scores of high school seniors by a tenth of a standard deviation. If we want to know how much this change will boost adult earnings, we need an unbiased estimate of b. If mathematical aptitude affects both math scores and earnings and we fail to control aptitude, we will overestimate the economic value of

---

4. Failure to measure and control all the components of E_t and E_y can obviously yield upwardly biased estimates of both a and b. Many early criticisms of *The Bell Curve* stressed this problem, but Korenman and Winship (forthcoming) find that this bias is relatively small. If the environmental determinants of achievement and earnings are identical, and if their relative weights are the same, $r_{E_y E_t} = 1$ and we cannot distinguish the effects of T from the effects of A and E.

smaller math classes. If math scores predict earnings solely because they serve as a proxy for mathematical aptitude, reducing class sizes will probably be a waste of money. Indeed, if we follow this line of argument to its logical conclusion, *any* investment in schooling is likely to be a waste of money, because schooling cannot improve the gene pool.

One key question about figure 2-1 is whether variation in academic achievement mainly reflects variation in genetically determined aptitudes or variation in the people's experiences and circumstances. We do not know the answer to this question. There is a vast literature on the "heritability" of test performance, but this literature does not tell us much about the effects of aptitude as we have defined it, because our definition of aptitude (A) is not the same as the conventional definition of genotype (G) in behavioral genetics.[5] Behavioral geneticists who estimate the heritability of test performance normally treat both the individual's genes and the individual's environment as exogenous. This means that when individuals' genes affect their environment, these effects are attributed to genetic rather than environmental variation. Our definition of aptitude, in contrast, requires that we estimate the effect of genetic aptitude with all aspects of the environment held constant, including those that are influenced by genes.

We can illustrate the difference between these two approaches by considering a simple measure of the explanatory power of genes, namely the correlation between the test scores of identical twins reared apart. Suppose these twins are separated at birth and assigned to random homes.[6] Suppose, too, that schools assign fast and slow learners to different math classes, and that these assignments depend partly on genetically determined aptitudes. In such a world, identical twins adopted by randomly selected families are likely to take somewhat similar math courses. If twins assigned to fast classes learn more math, the correlation between their school experiences will increase the correlation between their math scores. Traditional heritability estimates will attribute this correlation entirely to its ultimate cause, namely the twins' genetic resemblance. Our model, in contrast, attributes part of the correlation to the fact that separated twins have similar academic environments.

---

5. The use of G to denote genotype should not lead readers to assume that genotype is the same as g, general intelligence. The relationship between G and g is an empirical question.

6. Separated identical twins are not assigned to homes randomly. In practice, therefore, studies of separated twins usually try to show that their home environments were no more alike than those of randomly selected individuals.

Although traditional heritability estimates are useful for studying corn and cattle, they are less useful for assessing educational policies, many of which seek to alter the correlation between genetic advantages and environmental advantages. High school tracking and academically selective colleges tend to give genetically advantaged students more demanding classes. Programs for students with learning disabilities, in contrast, often assign genetically disadvantaged students to unusually small classes, where they get more individual attention. Because society can exert considerable control over the correlation between genes and environment, heritability estimates that confound genes' effect on children's experiences with genes' effect on how much children learn when they have the same experiences do not tell us about what educational policy can and cannot achieve. To answer that question, we need to know how much achievement would vary if we treated all children alike, and how assigning children with different genotypes to different environments would alter the variance of achievement.

Behavioral geneticists can estimate the correlation between genotype and achievement from data on relatives who share different percentages of their genes. But we cannot estimate the correlation between aptitude and achievement from such data. We know, for example, that the achievement scores of adopted siblings are less alike than the scores of natural siblings, and we have fairly strong evidence that this is partly because adopted siblings are less alike genetically. But no one knows to what extent the greater cognitive differences among adopted siblings reflect the fact that they learn different amounts even when they are treated alike, and to what extent greater genetic differences between adopted siblings lead people to treat adopted siblings differently.[7] All we can say is that if people's genes have *any* effect on their environment, the correlations between aptitude and environment (r_{A,E_t} and r_{A,E_y}) are likely to be positive. If that is the case, aptitude, as we have defined it, will explain less of the variation in test performance than genes explain in traditional heritability models.

Aptitude, Achievement, and Age of Testing

Several studies have tried to separate the effects of aptitude and achievement by analyzing correlations between measures of adult success and test

---

7. We assume that both processes are at work. The unanswered question is their relative importance.

scores obtained at different ages. This approach is useful if—and only if—academic aptitude is fixed, while academic achievement changes in response to changes in the environment.[8] If employers pay for current skills rather than past skills or aptitude, then when we control a measure of current skill and correct for measurement error, no earlier measure of the same skill should have any effect on an individual's current wage. Furthermore, since the correlation between two measures of a given skill tends to fall as the interval between the two measurements lengthens, the achievement model implies that the correlation between current earnings and test performance should fall steadily as one looks at increasingly early tests.

The aptitude model has quite different implications. If g is stable over time, if test performance predicts success largely because it is a proxy for g, and if tests administered at different ages are equally good proxies for g, then tests administered at different ages should predict adult success equally well.

We have found four studies that bear on this issue. In 1975 Christopher Jencks and Marsha Brown analyzed data collected by Project Talent in the 1960s.[9] They found that ninth and twelfth grade scores on vocabulary and social studies tests were equally good predictors of students' educational attainment and occupational status five years after high school. This finding seems to support the aptitude model. But the vocabulary and social studies tests were not very reliable, only a third of the Talent sample returned the follow-up questionnaire, and adult success was measured only five years after high school graduation.

In 1979 James Crouse compared the correlation between test performance and later success in four different American surveys, each of which tested people at a different age.[10] He found that sixth grade scores predicted adult success about as well as later scores did. This finding again seems to support the aptitude model. But none of the four surveys that Crouse examined retested the same respondents at different ages, so differences in age of testing are confounded with differences between the tests, the samples, and the ages at which the surveys measured adult success.

---

8. Although an individual's genes do not change with age, their impact on achievement can change over time. This is obvious when the measure of achievement changes with age. The aptitudes required for accurate arithmetic computation in fourth grade can obviously differ from the aptitudes required to solve college-level calculus problems. Even when one uses the same measure of achievement at different ages, however, the impact of specific genes may change over the life course. This issue deserves closer attention in future work.

9. Jencks and Brown (1975).

10. Crouse (1979).

Ingemar Fagerlind studied Swedish males tested at the ages of ten and twenty.[11] He found that test scores at age twenty predicted labor market success much better than test scores at age ten. This seems to support the achievement model. Fagerlind's data were better than the data used by either Crouse or Jencks and Brown, but the two tests that he used were quite different from each other. The second test might have been a better predictor of economic success not because achievement is more important than aptitude, but because the second test was more reliable than the first test or was a better measure of aptitude.

In 1994 John Bishop reported an analysis similar to Fagerlind's, using the National Longitudinal Survey of Youth (NLSY).[12] The NLSY gave almost all respondents the Armed Services Vocational Aptitude Battery (ASVAB) in 1980, when they were between the ages of fifteen and twenty-three. It also retrieved any earlier IQ scores from their school records. Bishop found that ASVAB scores predicted adult earnings much better than earlier IQ scores. He therefore concluded that adult achievement, not aptitude, determines labor market success. But Bishop's analysis has several limitations. First, some of the IQ tests that the NLSY retrieved from respondents' high school records were administered *after* the ASVAB.[13] Second, and more important, the ASVAB is more reliable than most of the IQ tests that schools administer. Thus the ASVAB may predict job performance better than earlier IQ tests because the ASVAB is a better measure of stable aptitudes, not because learning the material tested on the ASVAB actually raises earnings.

One can avoid some of the problems that make the findings of Crouse, Fagerlind, and Bishop hard to interpret by using data on students who took the same test twice, as Jencks and Brown did. But even then, one cannot be sure that the two tests are equally good proxies for aptitude. As children grow older, their potential environment expands beyond their home, and they are freer to choose their actual environment in accord with their own preferences. They can read books that develop their mental powers,

11. Fagerlind (1975).

12. Bishop (1994).

13. Jencks and Phillips (1996) analyze the same data as Bishop, interacting the age at which respondents took each test with scores on the test to see whether the effects of test performance rise with age. Because the sample is small, these interactions are often only marginally significant. Since all respondents were tested in 1980, those who took the AFQT when they were younger also reached maturity later. The age at which respondents took the AFQT is thus confounded with secular trends in returns to skill.

books that merely entertain them, or no books at all. They can watch television programs that expand their vocabulary, television programs that never use unfamiliar words, or no television at all. They can do their school work or not do it, take demanding high school courses or easy courses, and make intellectual or anti-intellectual friends. Young people's genes are quite likely to have some influence on such choices. As a result, people's genes probably exert more influence on their environment as they get older. Whether for this or other reasons, twin studies suggest that the correlation between test performance and genotype rises with age.[14] That need not mean that the correlation between test performance and academic aptitude rises with age, but that is certainly a possibility. Thus if one wants to estimate returns to academic achievement independent of aptitude, one needs to consider other approaches to the problem.

Aptitude Bias and Ability Bias

The problem we seek to resolve is similar to the problem of "ability bias" in the literature on economic returns to schooling. The debate over ability bias was motivated by the observation that while workers with more schooling typically earn more money than those with less schooling, this correlation need not be causal. Earnings could be correlated with schooling because both earnings and schooling depend on ability, broadly conceived. Economists have used three methods to eliminate this kind of bias from their estimates of the returns to schooling: (1) controlling scores on a test that claims to measure ability; (2) comparing genetically identical twins who get different amounts of schooling; and (3) studying natural experiments that raise the schooling of randomly selected groups. The first method is not useful for eliminating aptitude bias from estimates of the returns to academic achievement, but the second and third methods could be quite useful.

PROBLEMS WITH CONTROLLING MEASURED ABILITY. Economists' earliest approach to eliminating ability bias from estimates of the returns to schooling was to compare the earnings of students who had the same score

---

14. For an overview of evidence on age-related changes in traditional estimates of heritability, see Plomin and Petrill (1997).

on some standardized test when they were in school, but who subsequently got different amounts of schooling.[15] The difficulty with this approach is that no test (or battery of tests) measures genetic aptitude at all precisely. Even the Educational Testing Service (ETS), which developed the Scholastic Aptitude Test (SAT), has never claimed that this test measures genetic potential per se. It has long argued that the SAT "measures the verbal and mathematical abilities students have developed over many years, both in and out of school."[16] Indeed, all tests, no matter how they are labeled, measure developed abilities (achievement), and no test correlates perfectly with genotype, even after correcting for random measurement error. It follows that even when individuals have the same score on an aptitude test, they are likely to have somewhat different genetic aptitudes. Furthermore, when two students with the same aptitude score get different amounts of schooling, this may well reflect a difference in their academic aptitude. If academic aptitude also has a direct effect on earnings, independent of schooling, comparing students with the same aptitude scores will overestimate the effect of schooling per se.

When we try to estimate returns to academic achievement, these problems all recur, but with new complications. Now controlling performance on an aptitude test can bias our estimates in either direction. This can happen because all tests measure achievement as well as aptitude. Any experience that raises a student's achievement is therefore likely to raise the student's scores on conventional academic aptitude tests as well. Thus if a student takes both an aptitude test and an achievement test at the same time, controlling aptitude will yield a downwardly biased estimate of the returns to achievement. Fagerlind and Bishop tried to solve this problem by controlling scores on an aptitude test administered many years before the achievement test. But as we have already noted, an achievement test administered in late adolescence or adulthood may be a better proxy for genetic aptitude than an aptitude test administered in early or middle childhood. If that is the case, controlling only an early aptitude test may yield upwardly biased estimates of the returns to academic achievement per se.

---

15. If one estimates returns to schooling by controlling scores on a test given while all students are still in school, it does not matter whether the test measures aptitude or achievement. Either way, test performance is causally prior to the educational experiences whose consequences we want to estimate. Olneck (1979) presents data from several surveys that allowed him to control early test scores when estimating returns to schooling.

16. To avoid the implication that the SAT measures genetic potential, ETS renamed the test in 1995. It is now officially called the Scholastic Assessment Test.

DIFFERENCES BETWEEN IDENTICAL TWINS. Economists have also used data on identical twins reared together to eliminate ability bias from their estimates of the returns to schooling.[17] Because identical twins have exactly the same genes, differences in the length of time that identical twins spend in school cannot reflect differences in genetic aptitude. Thus when such twins get different amounts of schooling, the difference between their subsequent earnings cannot be inflated by differences in genetic aptitude.

This logic applies with equal force to differences in the achievement scores of identical twins. If one twin knows more math than the other and earns more money, we cannot be sure that math expertise explains the difference, but we can be sure that the difference is not a by-product of differences in genetic aptitude. Unfortunately, we have not found any research that uses this method.[18]

NATURAL EXPERIMENTS. Economists have also tried to eliminate ability bias from estimates of the returns to schooling by studying natural experiments in which a randomly selected treatment group is somehow induced to get more schooling than an initially similar control group. Joshua Angrist and Alan Krueger, for example, have exploited the fact that most states require students to stay in school until they reach a specific birthday.[19] As a result, students born during the summer have usually completed one more year of school when they become eligible to drop out than have students born earlier in the calendar year. Angrist and Krueger show that men born during the summer not only complete slightly more schooling, but earn slightly more money as adults. Since men's genes are unlikely to correlate with the quarter in which they are born, this difference in earnings provides an estimate of the monetary returns of additional schooling that is not subject to aptitude bias. The estimate may, however, be biased by failure to control other economically significant effects of birth quarter.

Quarter of birth affects the age at which children start school as well as the age at which they leave. Susan Mayer and David Knutson show in this volume that when one tests children with the same amount of schooling, those who started school younger because of their quarter of birth have higher scores.[20] This effect appears to persist into adulthood. This poses a

17. See Taubman (1976); Ashenfelter and Rouse (1998). Data on identical twins reared apart would, in some ways, be even better than data on twins reared together, but such data are scarce.
18. For a partial exception see Jencks and Brown (1977).
19. Angrist and Krueger (1991).
20. See chapter 4 below.

problem for Angrist and Krueger's argument, since it implies that what looked to them like returns to staying in school may really have been returns to higher test scores. In principle, Mayer and Knutson's findings might also provide a way of estimating the effects of academic achievement on earnings with aptitude controlled, but they do not present such estimates.

Another way to estimate returns to academic achievement independent of aptitude would be to follow up participants in educational experiments that assigned randomly selected students to a treatment that raised their academic achievement. If assignment was truly random, the treatment and control groups should have the same aptitude but different levels of achievement. In principle, one could follow both groups to see how this difference in achievement affected their subsequent educational attainment and earnings. Unfortunately, large educational experiments aimed at raising achievement are quite rare. Large experiments with sizable sustained effects on achievement are even rarer. And as far as we know, no one has collected data on the adult earnings of participants in such an experiment. But the Tennessee class size experiment described by Frederick Mosteller in this volume will soon provide an ideal opportunity to do this.[21]

Estimating the Effect of Test Score Gains

In the absence of true experimental data, we have tried to eliminate aptitude bias from estimates of the returns to academic achievement by analyzing a special kind of natural experiment. More than thirty years ago, Benjamin Bloom's classic study *Stability and Change in Human Characteristics* argued that gains on a wide range of tests were uncorrelated with initial scores.[22] Bloom believed that this was true at all ages. His argument implied that cognitive growth was a random walk, in which the factors that influenced growth during one period had no influence in later periods. Taken literally, this cannot be true. To see why, imagine that we were to measure children's vocabulary every day and compute the gain or loss since

21. See chapter 6 below. One complication in any such analysis is that if an intervention raises test scores, it may well have other positive effects. Some preschools, for example, appear to have a positive long-term impact on achievement (Barnett, 1995). But preschools also seem to reduce the frequency of adolescent behavior problems. Thus even if one had experimental data showing that preschool alumni earned more than a matched control group, one would not know whether this was because preschools raised academic achievement or because they produced other behavioral changes.

22. Bloom (1964).

the previous day. A twenty-year-old's vocabulary would then be the sum of more than 7,000 small gains and losses. If cognitive growth on any given day were uncorrelated with cognitive growth on previous days, all twenty-year-olds would have roughly the same vocabulary. In reality, twenty-year-olds' vocabulary varies dramatically. It follows that vocabulary growth in successive periods must to some extent reflect stable underlying influences.

Although Bloom's model cannot be literally correct, his empirical findings require some explanation. Many psychometricians have dismissed his findings as an inevitable by-product of random measurement error.[23] But random measurement error cannot be the whole story, because the correlation between initial scores and gain scores is often close to zero even *after* correcting for random errors.[24] How can this be? David Rogosa and John Willett provide a plausible answer.[25] They show that the relationship between initial scores and gain scores depends on two factors: the shape of individual growth curves for a particular skill or piece of knowledge and the age at which researchers measure that skill or knowledge. Whether the correlation between initial scores and gain scores is positive, negative, or zero depends on what the test measures and when the people taking the test normally learn whatever the test covers.

Suppose, for example, that one gives a first year algebra test at the end of eighth grade. One would expect high-aptitude eighth graders to do well on the test, because high-aptitude students often study first year algebra in eighth grade. Low-aptitude students will do worse, both because they have lower aptitude and because they are less likely to have studied algebra. Now

23. To see why measurement error can create a negative correlation between initial scores and gains, define an individual's true score as the mean of the scores he or she would get on an infinite number of tests, all of which used items drawn randomly from the same item pool. An individual's observed score on any given test will then be the sum of his or her true score, a random error term that reflects familiarity with the specific items that happened to be on the version of the test that the individual took, and another random error term that reflects the influence of circumstances peculiar to the day the individual took this particular test. If one measures gain scores by subtracting observed time 1 scores from observed time 2 scores, positive random errors in the time 1 score will appear with positive signs in the time 1 scores and with negative signs in the gain scores. This can create a negative correlation between initial scores and gains.

24. Werts and Hilton (1977), who argued that gains and initial scores should be positively correlated, reported correlations between true seventh grade scores and gains between seventh and ninth grade. Although these correlations were generally positive, they ranged from 0.45 to −0.45, depending on the test. Phillips obtained similar results in unpublished analyses of elementary school test performance in data from Prospects: The Congressionally Mandated Study of Educational Growth and Opportunity.

25. Rogosa and Willett (1985).

suppose one repeats the test at the end of ninth grade. Many lower aptitude students will now have studied first year algebra, so their scores will rise. Many higher aptitude students will have spent ninth grade studying geometry. This experience may improve their ability to do first year algebra, but the effect will probably be smaller than the effect of studying first year algebra was. Ninth grade gains in first year algebra may therefore turn out to be uncorrelated with any plausible indicator of math aptitude. Indeed, the correlation may be negative.[26]

Situations of this kind are frequent in school systems where high- and low-aptitude students study the same material. In such systems, high-aptitude students tend to learn many things sooner than low-aptitude students. But this very fact ensures that high-aptitude students also learn less in many areas later on. If tests measure the full range of facts or skills taught at different ages, the correlation between aptitude and gains should remain positive. But if a test emphasizes a circumscribed range of facts or skills, as most tests do, the correlation between aptitude and gains in a specific period may be negligible. To put the same point slightly differently, one can say that while long-term increases in achievement appear to be strongly correlated with aptitude, short-term increases on many tests appear to be almost uncorrelated with aptitude. Our estimates of returns to achievement exploit this fact.

The High School and Beyond Data

Increases in individual achievement over short periods of time are hard to measure, because the true gain over a short period is usually small relative to random measurement errors. This means that we need a large sample to estimate the effects of short-term gains on adult earnings with precision. High School and Beyond (HS&B) is the only large American survey that has both tested students more than once and followed a representative sample of these students into adulthood.[27]

26. Readers may find it helpful to think about this example using the notation in figure 2-1. For a test that measures mastery of first year algebra, ninth grade is organized in such a way that students with low values of A have high values of E_i, whereas students with high values of A have somewhat lower values of E_i. If we gave a test that measured mastery of geometry, however, the correlations would probably be reversed.

27. Project Talent tested some students twice and followed some of them up eleven years after high school graduation, but the response rate in the follow-ups was low. The National Education

HS&B tested a nationally representative sample of tenth graders in 1980 and retested them using the same tests in 1982.[28] It also collected data on respondents' highest degree and earnings in 1992, when most of them were twenty-seven or twenty-eight years old.[29] The HS&B tests covered math, vocabulary, reading comprehension, science, writing, and civics. Donald Rock and his colleagues have shown that a math factor and a verbal factor explain more than 85 percent of the reliable variance in these six tests.[30] This is true in both tenth and twelfth grades. We therefore limited our analysis to the math, vocabulary, and reading tests. After some experimentation, we further simplified our analysis by summing students' vocabulary and reading scores to create a single "verbal" score.[31] While the HS&B data do not allow us to examine the effects of achievement before tenth grade or after twelfth grade, they can tell us quite a lot about the payoff to certain kinds of achievement in high school.[32]

Table 2-1 shows correlations between test scores in tenth and twelfth grade. The correlations below the diagonal, which are not corrected for

---

Longitudinal Study (NELS) tested eighth graders in 1988, retested them in 1990 and 1992, and is planning to follow them into adulthood. At this writing, however, NELS respondents are too young to provide a reliable estimate of their economic success as adults.

28. Sophomores who graduated early, transferred to another school, or dropped out were subsampled, located, and given the second round of tests in small groups. Ninety percent of the out-of-school participants (including transfer students) and 94 percent of participants who remained in the same schools took the second round of tests (Rock and others, 1985).

29. We recoded highest degree completed in 1992 to approximate the number of years of schooling required to earn this degree. We did not measure the actual number of years students spent earning their degrees. Furthermore, since HS&B interviewed respondents in the middle of 1992, we do not have annual earnings for that year. To construct our earnings measure, we averaged annual earnings in 1990 and 1991 and took the natural log of the mean. We excluded respondents who reported no earnings in either 1990 or 1991. We recoded respondents who reported earnings averaging more than $250,000 a year to $250,000.

30. Rock and others (1985).

31. Our math test is the sum of thirty-eight math items. Our verbal test is the sum of twenty-one vocabulary items and nineteen reading items. (There are actually twenty reading items in the test, but one has no right answer and is excluded.) We combined vocabulary and reading into a verbal test after running analyses for the two tests separately and obtaining results in which a correct reading item had almost the same effect as a correct vocabulary item. The twelfth grade writing and civics tests have substantial ceiling effects, making them unsatisfactory for our purposes.

32. A well-known result from HS&B is that the mean gain between tenth and twelfth grade is very small relative to the variability of initial scores. Table 2-1 shows, for example, that twelfth graders typically knew only 1.5 more math items (out of thirty-eight) and 2.8 more verbal items (out of forty) than tenth graders. Individuals also differ considerably in how much they learn between tenth and twelfth grade: the true standard deviation of the gain is about 3.0 items for both tests. As a result, some students had lower true scores in twelfth grade than in tenth grade.

Table 2-1. *Correlations between Test Scores and Adult Outcomes in the High School and Beyond Survey*[a]

Variable	1	2	3	4	5	6	7	8
1. 10th grade math	1	0.920	0.799	0.775	0.045	0.117	0.504	0.231
2. 12th grade math	0.832	1	0.765	0.818	…	…	0.546	0.253
3. 10th grade verbal	0.697	0.678	1	0.921	0.112	0.021	0.476	0.197
4. 12th grade verbal	0.686	0.735	0.835	1	…	…	0.496	0.211
5. Math gain	−0.150	0.424	0.070	0.191	1	…	…	…
6. Verbal gain	0.073	0.193	−0.164	0.407	0.225	1	…	…
7. Educational attainment	0.470	0.517	0.445	0.471	0.153	0.105	1	…
8. ln Average annual earnings	0.216	0.240	0.184	0.200	0.075	0.053	0.208	1
Summary statistic								
Mean	19.57	21.09	20.79	23.60	1.52	2.82	13.42	9.75
Standard deviation	7.35	8.02	7.45	8.04	4.50	4.49	2.09	0.75
Reliability	0.870	0.897	0.874	0.899	0.450	0.446	…	…

Source: Authors' calculations.

a. Correlations above the diagonal have been corrected for attenuation. All estimates are for 8,235 respondents with complete data.

measurement error, show that students' observed scores on the tenth and twelfth grade HS&B tests correlate 0.832 for math and 0.835 for the verbal composite (vocabulary plus reading).[33] The correlations above the diagonal show that correcting for measurement error raises both correlations to about 0.92. Yet even after correcting for measurement error, the estimated correlation between true tenth grade math scores and true gains between tenth and twelfth grade is only 0.045.[34] For verbal scores, the analogous correlation is 0.021. Thus if tenth grade verbal and math scores are strongly related to aptitude, gains on these tests between tenth and twelfth grade cannot be strongly related to aptitude.

To check this conclusion, we can look at the correlation between tenth grade scores on one test and subsequent gains on the other test. This strategy prevents errors in measuring tenth grade scores from appearing with their signs reversed in the gain score. Since observed scores on the verbal and math tests correlate 0.799, both should be fairly good proxies for g. Thus if tenth grade verbal scores are uncorrelated with subsequent math gains, and if tenth grade math scores are uncorrelated with subsequent verbal gains, verbal and math gains are probably uncorrelated with g.

Table 2-1 shows that math gains correlate 0.070 with initial verbal scores, while verbal gains correlate 0.073 with initial math scores. After correcting for measurement error, these correlations become 0.112 and 0.117, respectively. These correlations are somewhat higher than the estimated correlations between true tenth grade scores and true gains on the same test, but they are still extremely low. We conclude that *in the domains covered by the HS&B tests*, the amount that students learn between tenth and twelfth grade is almost uncorrelated with the aptitudes that affect tenth grade scores.

One possible explanation for this finding is that gains on the HS&B tests involve skills that the "average" student learns between tenth and twelfth grade. High-aptitude students might already have these skills in tenth grade, moderate-aptitude students might acquire them between tenth and twelfth grade, and low-aptitude students might never acquire them. Were that the case, gains would be greatest for students in the middle of the tenth grade distribution. To examine this possibility, figure 2-2 plots math gains against

33. We limited our analytic sample to respondents with valid data on the math, reading, and vocabulary tests in both tenth and twelfth grade and with data on educational attainment, occupational status, and earnings in 1992. We weighted all our analyses with the fourth follow-up weight.

34. See appendix 2A for details on our calculation of the correlation between true initial scores and true gains.

Figure 2-2. *Relationship of Observed Gains between Tenth and Twelfth Grade to Observed Initial Scores in HS&B*

Math gains and initial verbal scores

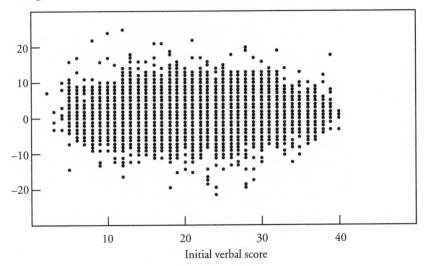

Verbal gains and initial math scores

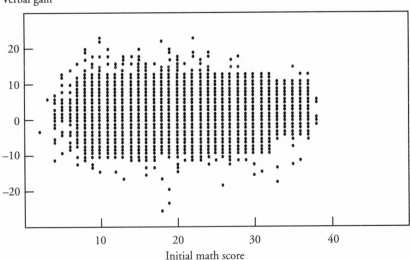

Source: Authors' calculations.

tenth grade verbal scores and verbal gains against tenth grade math scores. There is no obvious relationship. This reinforces our conclusion that math and verbal gains in HS&B are unrelated to aptitude.[35]

The Analytic Model

A conventional estimate of returns to academic achievement might take the form

$$(2\text{-}1) \qquad Y = B_0 + B_{M12}M_{12} + B_{V12}V_{12} + e,$$

where Y is adult earnings (or educational attainment), M_{12} is a student's twelfth grade math score, V_{12} is a student's twelfth grade verbal score, and e is a random error term. In such an equation, B_{M12} estimates the average earning gap between two students whose twelfth grade math scores differ by one point and whose verbal scores do not differ at all. B_{V12} estimates the gap between students whose verbal scores differ by one point and whose math scores do not differ at all. Unfortunately, such estimates are usually biased.

Failure to correct for random measurement error in the math and verbal tests usually biases B_{M12} and B_{V12} downward. Because the HS&B tests contain only thirty-eight or forty items, they yield imprecise estimates of the scores students would earn if they took a longer test. We can estimate the average size of this discrepancy from the correlations among the items on the HS&B tests.[36] Using that information, we can correct the estimates of B_{M12} and B_{V12} using conventional methods. All our estimates are corrected for errors of this kind.

A second possible source of error in equation 2-1 is failure to take account of the fact that the environmental determinants of academic

35. This result is not a by-product of ceiling effects on the twelfth grade tests. Only 0.7 percent of the twelfth graders in our sample obtained perfect scores on the math test, and only 0.4 percent obtained perfect scores on the verbal test. Had the HS&B tests included more of the material that high-aptitude students study between tenth and twelfth grades, the correlation between initial scores and gain scores might have been larger. But the fact that students with low initial scores gain as much as students with moderate initial scores suggests that the weak relationship between initial scores and gains is not just an artifact of curriculum design. The fact that the pattern holds for verbal as well as math tests also suggests that the relationship is not a simple by-product of the curriculum.

36. If the items in a test correlate perfectly, adding more items from the same pool will not alter individuals' relative performance. If the items do not correlate at all, adding more items from the same pool may change students' relative performance dramatically.

achievement can also have a direct effect on earnings, independent of achievement.[37] In principle, one can eliminate some of this bias by comparing siblings reared in the same family. One can eliminate the rest by measuring all the environmental factors that affect both academic achievement and adult success. But HS&B did not collect much data on students' home environment, so we do not try to estimate the effects of this source of bias.[38]

A third possible source of error in equation 2-1 is the fact that academic aptitude may have a direct effect on earnings, independent of academic achievement. If genetic aptitudes affect academic achievement, and if these same genetic aptitudes also affect earnings independent of achievement, B_{M12} and B_{V12} will overestimate the payoff to raising achievement. To assess the magnitude of this bias, we estimate the effects of math and verbal gains between tenth and twelfth grade. We denote these gains as M_G and V_G. In a further effort to control for possible aptitude bias, we control true tenth grade scores (M_{10} and V_{10}) when we estimate the effect of true gains. Thus we estimate the coefficients B_{MG} and B_{VG} in

$$(2\text{-}2) \qquad Y = B_0 + B_{M10}M_{10} + B_{V10}V_{10} + B_{MG}M_G + B_{VG}B_G + e \, .$$

We cannot estimate equation 2-2 directly from the data because the HS&B scores contain random measurement error. Nor can we make a conventional correction for unreliability, because errors in estimating true tenth grade scores appear twice: first in the observed tenth grade score and then in the observed gain (with their signs reversed). But when we compare people with the same tenth grade scores, any difference in their twelfth grade scores must, by definition, reflect a difference in their gain (or loss) between tenth and twelfth grade. Thus we can capture the effect of gains between tenth and twelfth grade by estimating

$$(2\text{-}2') \quad Y = B'_0 + B'_{M10}M_{10} + B'_{V10}V_{10} + B'_{M12}M_{12} + B'_{V12}B'_{12} + e \, .$$

Because equation 2-2' controls tenth grade scores, the coefficients of twelfth grade scores (B'_{M12} and B'_{V12}) are identical to the coefficients of the math and verbal gains in equation 2-2 (B_{MG} and B_{VG}).[39] Furthermore, if

---

37. Figure 2-1 represents this potential source of error by assuming $r_{E_t, E_y} > 0$.

38. See, for example, Korenman and Winship (forthcoming). For a somewhat different reading of the same data, see Fischer and others (1996).

39. If we replace M_{12} in equation 2-2' with $M_{10} + M_G$, and replace V_{12} with $V_{10} + V_G$, equation 2-2' becomes

$$Y = B'_0 + B'_{M10}M_{10} + B'_{V10}V_{10} + B'_{M12}(M_{10} + M_G) + B'_{V12}(V_{10} + V_G) + e \, .$$

Rearranging,

errors in tenth and twelfth grade scores are independent, we can estimate B'_{M12} and B'_{V12} using a conventional correction for measurement error.[40]

Since HS&B gains between tenth and twelfth grades are almost uncorrelated with tenth grade scores, estimates of B'_{M12} and B'_{V12} from equation 2-2' should not suffer from much aptitude bias. Comparing B'_{M12} and B'_{V12} in equation 2-2' with B_{M12} and B_{V12} in equation 2-1 should therefore indicate whether aptitude bias appreciably distorts uncorrected estimates of the returns to academic achievement.

Figure 2-3 provides a visual representation of our causal model.[41] The notation follows the conventions of path analysis. For reasons already discussed, this figure does not include proxies for E_t or E_y, the environmental variables in figure 2-1.

Results

Table 2-2 shows the coefficients of true math and verbal scores in various models.[42] Equation 1 is identical to equation 2-1. It shows the association

---

$(2\text{-}2'')$ $\qquad Y = B'_0 + (B'_{M10} + B'_{M12})\, M_{10} + (B'_{V10} + B'_{V12})\, V_{10} + B'_{M12} M_G + B'_{V12} V_G + e\,.$

Comparing equations 2-2'' and 2-2, one can see that $B'_{M10} + B'_{M12} = B_{M10}$ and that $B'_{M12} = B_{MG}$. The same logic applies to the coefficients of verbal scores.

40. Errors on the same item may well be correlated over time. We return to this issue below.

41. As noted in appendix 2A, the model allows for correlations not only between true tenth and twelfth grade scores (a_M and a_V) but also between tenth and twelfth grade errors (g_M and g_V). We allow for correlated errors by allowing each item in the tenth grade test to be correlated with the identical item in the twelfth grade test, independent of the correlation between true tenth and twelfth grade scores.

42. We estimated the models in table 2-2 using maximum likelihood in LISREL 7; see Joreskog and Sorbom (1988). LISREL 7 does not correct the standard errors for design effects. In the fourth follow-up, HS&B reports a mean root design effect of 1.43, with a standard deviation of 0.08 (Zahs and others, 1995). Readers should multiply the LISREL 7 standard errors by about 1.5 in order to estimate the true standard errors. Coefficients that are significant at the 0.05 level in our tables will then be significant at about the 0.10 level.

We estimated the models in two parts. First, we used all the test items and the tests' internal consistency reliabilities to estimate the true correlation (a) between the tests. We then calculated the correlations among the errors using the formula $r_{o10,o12} = (g)(d)(f) + (a)(c)(e)$, where $r_{o10, o12}$ is the observed correlation between tenth and twelfth grade scores and g is the correlation between the errors in observed tenth and twelfth grade scores due to repeating the same items. Paths c and e equal the square roots of the internal consistency reliability estimates for the two tests. Paths d and f are identified because in combination with paths c and e they must explain all of the variance in the two observed scores. Since $d^2 + c^2 = 1$ and $f^2 + e^2 = 1$, and since c and e are known, we can solve for d and f. We then estimated the model shown in figure 2-3, setting g at the calculated values and the error variances of the tests at $(1 - \text{reliability})(\text{observed variance})$.

Figure 2-3. *Effects of True Gains on Adult Success*

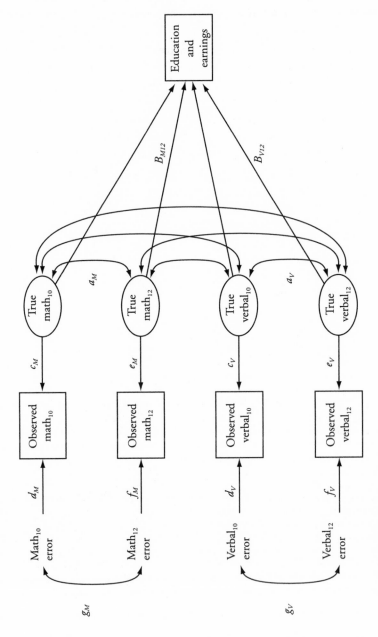

Source: Authors' model as described in text.

Table 2-2. *Effects of True Math and Verbal Gains between Tenth and Twelfth Grade on Educational Attainment and Annual Earnings in HS&B*[a]

Independent variable	Educational attainment		ln Annual earnings		
	1	2	1	2	3
12th grade math					
B	0.116	0.132	0.024	0.025	0.021
	(0.006)	(0.014)	(0.002)	(0.006)	(0.006)
Beta	0.423	0.478	0.243	0.257	0.209
12th grade verbal					
B	0.041	0.012	0.001	0.001	0.000
	(0.006)	(0.014)	(0.002)	(0.006)	(0.006)
Beta	0.150	0.043	0.012	0.007	0.003
10th grade math					
B		−0.021		−0.002	−0.001
		(0.015)		(0.006)	(0.006)
Beta		−0.069		−0.016	−0.009
10th grade verbal					
B		0.038		0.001	−0.001
		(0.015)		(0.006)	(0.006)
Beta		0.125		0.006	−0.006
Educational attainment					
B					−0.001
					(0.006)
Beta					−0.006
Summary statistic					
R^2	0.305	0.307	0.064	0.064	0.071

Source: Authors' calculations.

a. Data are weighted with the fourth follow-up weight (*FU4WT*). Estimates are corrected for measurement error in the test scores and for correlated errors. "Educational attainment" is years of school completed by 1992, estimated from the highest degree completed. "ln Annual earnings" is the natural log of the average annual earnings reported for 1990 and 1991. All estimates are for 8,235 respondents with complete data. Standard errors are in parentheses.

of true twelfth grade scores with educational attainment and annual earnings when we do not control tenth grade scores. Equation 2 includes true tenth grade scores and is identical to equation 2-2′. When earnings are the dependent variable, we also estimate equation 3, which controls educational attainment. This equation shows the extent to which verbal and math skills influence earnings through their effects on educational attainment. The crucial comparison, however, is between the coefficients of twelfth grade scores in equations 1 and 2. This comparison indicates whether aptitude bias is a serious problem in conventional estimates of the returns to academic achievement.

EFFECTS ON SUBSEQUENT SCHOOLING. Table 2-2 suggests that the relationship between twelfth grade math scores and educational attainment is not much affected by aptitude bias. A one-point gain in achievement between tenth and twelfth grades has slightly *more* impact on educational attainment than a one-point difference in overall twelfth grade scores (0.132 versus 0.116).

We can express this result in another way that may seem more intuitively understandable. Equation 2 in table 2-2 shows that each math item a student learns between tenth and twelfth grade is associated with a 0.13 year increase in the amount of schooling the student is likely to complete. This effect is almost identical to the effect of knowing an extra math item in tenth grade (results not shown). Learning a math item between tenth and twelfth grades is thus worth as much as learning it before tenth grade. If knowing an HS&B item in tenth grade is strongly correlated with aptitude, while learning the item between tenth and twelfth grade is not, aptitude bias cannot be important.

Equation 1 shows that HS&B verbal scores (reading comprehension plus vocabulary) have far less impact on educational attainment than math scores do. Equation 2 shows that verbal scores may also suffer from more aptitude bias than math scores. The initially weak effect of twelfth grade verbal scores on educational attainment drops almost to zero when we control tenth grade scores. This means that when we hold math scores constant, vocabulary and reading gains between tenth and twelfth grade are not associated with staying in school longer—a quite surprising result.

EFFECTS ON EARNINGS. Our results for annual earnings resemble those for educational attainment. We find no evidence of aptitude bias in the estimated monetary returns to math skills. Each math item that students learn between tenth and twelfth grade increases expected earnings a decade later by about 2.5 percent. Only a fifth of this increase can be traced to the fact that people who learn more math between tenth and twelfth grade also get more schooling.[43]

When we control math scores, verbal scores do not appear to have any direct effect on earnings, but this result turns out to be somewhat misleading. When we analyze the data for women and men separately (results not shown), we find that twelfth grade verbal scores do affect women's earnings even after controlling twelfth grade math scores, tenth grade math scores, and tenth grade verbal scores. We do not find consistent gender differences in the extent to which the apparent effects of twelfth grade scores are biased by aptitude.

We also investigated the possibility that aptitude bias differed for high and low scorers. If aptitude bias were larger among low scorers, the payoff to improving their achievement might be smaller than linear models imply. Our estimates (not shown) suggest that the relationship between twelfth grade scores and outcomes is, in fact, slightly more "aptitude-biased" among low scorers than among high scorers, but the difference is small and is not statistically reliable.[44]

What Factors Influence Gains on the HS&B Tests?

If we could identify the specific experiences that influence learning between tenth and twelfth grade, our claim that academic achievement between tenth and twelfth grade affects adult success would become considerably more policy relevant. Using the HS&B data, we regressed students' gains between tenth and twelfth grade on whether they were enrolled in school between the two tests, the courses they took, how they spent their time outside school, and the type of school they attended. All these estimates controlled tenth grade scores on the other test, as well as several other variables. Table 2-3 shows our results.

Students who stayed in school rather than dropping out learned about 0.6 more math items and 0.8 more verbal items between tenth and twelfth grade, independent of their family background, the math classes they took, the amount of homework they did, and the type of school they attended.

43. Crouse (1979) found that educational attainment explained a much larger fraction of the association between test scores and earnings in his sample of earlier surveys than it does in our HS&B analyses. We do not know whether this represents a secular trend or a peculiarity of the HS&B data.

44. Separate estimates by gender and by initial test score are available from Phillips on request.

Table 2-3. *Determinants of Math and Verbal Gains between Tenth and Twelfth Grade in HS&B*[a]

Independent variable	Math gain		Verbal gain	
	B	Standard error	B	Standard error
High school dropout[b]	−0.615	0.236	−0.814	0.243
Math coursework[c]				
Prealgebra	0.412	0.201	0.322	0.198
Algebra I	0.204	0.148	0.064	0.154
Geometry	0.571	0.175	0.645	0.172
Algebra II	0.714	0.167	0.036	0.174
Advanced math	0.950	0.194	0.432	0.217
Calculus	0.099	0.266	−0.049	0.310
Advanced placement credits[c]				
English + history	−0.147	0.206	−0.033	0.206
Math + science	0.363	0.168	−0.074	0.157
Time spent outside school on[d]				
Reading	0.036	0.036	0.078	0.036
Homework	0.060	0.021	0.034	0.024
Type of school in 10th grade[e]				
Catholic	−0.162	0.259	0.445	0.257
Private	−0.130	0.480	0.869	0.388

(Continued)

This estimate implies that even if students took no math and did no homework, they learned more math (or forgot less) if they stayed in school.

Students who took more math classes also learned more math than those who took fewer math classes. Those who stopped taking math after geometry learned 1.8 fewer math items between tenth and twelfth grade than students who took the entire math sequence, including calculus. Students also gained about a third of a point on the math test for every advanced placement math or science class they took.[45] Math courses even

45. Of the 332 people in our sample who had a calculus credit on their high school transcripts, 101 also had an advanced placement calculus credit.

Table 2-3. *Determinants of Math and Verbal Gains between Tenth and Twelfth Grade in HS&B[a] (Continued)*

Independent variable	Dependent variable			
	Math gain		Verbal gain	
	B	Standard error	B	Standard error
School characteristics[f]				
Offered at least one advanced placement class	0.262	0.146	0.203	0.150
Percent of students who go to college	0.006	0.005	−0.005	0.004
District per-pupil expenditure in $100s	0.010	0.014	0.011	0.012
Summary statistic				
R^2	0.059		0.031	

Source: Authors' calculations.

a. Cases are weighted with *FU4WT.* Standard errors are corrected for the nonindependence of observations within schools. The equation also controls tenth grade score on the other test; student's gender and ethnicity; urbanism of school; region; student's family structure and number of siblings; parents' occupations, education, income, and possessions; student's educational expectations in tenth grade; and dummy variables for missing data. All estimates are for 8,235 respondents with complete data.

b. High school dropout is coded 1 if a student dropped out between tenth and twelfth grade, 0 otherwise.

c. Data for coursework and advanced placement (AP) credit variables come from student transcripts. Coursework variables are coded 1 if a student had one or more Carnegie units in the subject, 0 otherwise. For advanced placement, English + history is the sum of credits in English and U.S. and world history; math + science is the sum of credits in calculus, biology, chemistry, and physics.

d. Reading is measured as the approximate number of days per week that students read for pleasure. Homework is measured as the approximate number of hours per week spent on homework.

e. Public is the omitted category.

f. Data on advanced placement offerings are based on school officials' reports during the tenth grade survey. Percent of students going to college and district per-pupil expenditure are the averages of officials' reports in 1980 and 1982.

appear to enhance verbal skills. Students who took geometry and advanced math (trigonometry) gained 1.1 more points on the verbal test between tenth and twelfth grade than students who did not take advanced math. This could be because math textbooks are verbally challenging (indeed, some would say incomprehensible), but a more likely explanation is that students who took advanced math classes also took more demanding English and history classes, in which they read more difficult material.[46]

All else equal, students who read for pleasure every day learned about half an additional verbal item between tenth and twelfth grade. Students who did fifteen hours of homework a week also learned about one more math item between tenth and twelfth grade than students who did no homework at all. These results suggest that what students do outside school has some effect on their test performance.

Conclusion

Our findings suggest that gains between tenth and twelfth grade on the HS&B math and verbal tests are not appreciably correlated with the genetic aptitudes that affect tenth grade scores. Nonetheless, a one-point gain in math performance between tenth and twelfth grade has the same impact on subsequent educational attainment and earnings as a one-point difference in tenth grade scores. This suggests that conventional estimates of returns to math achievement are not greatly biased by failure to control mathematical aptitude. The verbal skills measured on the HS&B tests do not appear to have much payoff for men once we control math skills. Gains in verbal achievement between tenth and twelfth grade do, however, have some payoff for women.

Students' behavior influences how much they learn between tenth and twelfth grade. Students who take more math classes and do more home-work learn more math. Students who read a lot in their spare time increase their vocabulary and improve their reading comprehension. Students who drop out of school learn fewer math and verbal skills than those who stay in school.

But while learning in high school pays off, the effects are not large. Table 2-2 suggests that students would need to learn eight extra math items between tenth and twelfth grade to raise their expected educational attainment by one year. Hardly anyone improves his or her math score

46. Robert Meyer also shows in chapter 8 below that math and science coursework influenced math gains on the HS&B tests. Altonji (1995) used the National Longitudinal Study of the High School Class of 1972 (NLS-72) to estimate the effects of coursework in tenth through twelfth grade on stu-dents' future educational attainment and wages. He found almost no relationship, but because the NLS-72 did not test students in tenth grade, he could not estimate the effect of coursework on test scores. Altonji's findings suggest that the payoff to academic achievement may be lower than we claim, but they do not provide direct evidence on this issue.

that much between tenth and twelfth grade: the average student gains only 1.5 points (about a fifth of a standard deviation). Table 2-2 suggests that a 1.5 point gain raises a student's expected educational attainment by only a fifth of a year and raises earnings by only 4 percent.

The HS&B data provide no direct evidence about the effects of learning prior to tenth grade, but we can make some crude indirect estimates. We first need an estimate of how much math students learn between first and twelfth grade. If we assume that first graders could not do any of the HS&B items and did not guess, their scores would fall 2.78 standard deviations below those of the average twelfth grader (using the twelfth grade standard deviation).[47] We can check this estimate using the data collected in the National Assessment of Educational Progress (NAEP), which tests students at the ages of nine, thirteen, and seventeen, and then uses item response theory to convert these scores to a common metric. The NAEP shows that in 1982 the average nine-year-old scored 2.45 standard deviations below the average seventeen-year-old.[48] These estimates seem roughly consistent.

If the effects of math gains were linear, and if gains at earlier ages were no more subject to ability bias than gains between tenth and twelfth grades, table 2-2 would imply that HS&B students who had learned no math between first and twelfth grade but made average gains on the verbal test would have earned about 40 percent less in 1992 than students who had made average gains on both tests.[49] This is a huge difference. We suspect, however, that math gains at earlier ages are more correlated with genetic aptitude than math gains between tenth and twelfth grade.[50] Alternatively,

---

47. Table 2-1 implies that the true standard deviation of the twelfth grade HS&B math test is $(8.02)(0.897)^{0.5} = 7.60$ points. If the first graders had guessed randomly, they would have earned a mean score of 8.75, which is $(21.09 - 8.75)/7.6 = 1.62$ standard deviations below the twelfth grade mean. But the twelfth grade mean is presumably also inflated by guessing. If we were to correct for this, the true gain would be less than 1.62 standard deviations.

48. NAEP did not test the 1982 cohort of seventeen-year-olds in 1974, so we cannot estimate this cohort's mean gain between the ages of nine and seventeen. It did test a cohort of nine-year-olds in 1982 and retested them in 1990. This cohort gained 2.8 standard deviations. A cohort of nine-year-olds tested in 1986 and retested in 1994 gained 2.7 standard deviations. One reason these gains are larger than the cross-sectional difference between nine- and seventeen-year-olds in 1982 is that seventeen-year-olds' math scores rose faster than those of nine-year-olds after 1982.

49. The estimate in the text reflects the fact that $e^{(-21.09)(0.025)} = 0.59$. If we were to take account of guessing on the twelfth grade test, the estimated effect on earnings would be smaller.

50. The estimate in the text assumes that the HS&B math test has linear effects on the log of earnings. When we investigated nonlinear effects, we got inconsistent results with large standard errors. But while the payoff to knowing more math may well be nonlinear, we would expect the slope to be concave downward. In the absence of ability bias, therefore, estimates of returns to gains between tenth and twelfth grades should tend to understate returns to gains at earlier ages.

math gains may be proxies for other important types of learning that are not captured by the HS&B vocabulary or reading tests.

Nonetheless, our findings suggest that Herrnstein and Murray may well have exaggerated when they claimed that "for many people, there is nothing they can learn that will repay the cost of the teaching."[51] Our findings indicate that enhancing student achievement can yield substantial benefits, regardless of aptitude. Whether these benefits will repay the cost of the teaching is harder to say, because neither we nor Herrnstein and Murray have any data on what it costs to raise student achievement. Acquiring verbal skills by reading for pleasure is cheap. Acquiring math skills by taking four years of math in high school is more expensive—although it may not cost significantly more than taking four years of something else that yields lower benefits.

Readers should also bear in mind that we have probably underestimated the long-term economic payoff to learning the skills that the HS&B tests measure. The impact of adolescent achievement on adult earnings tends to increase with age. Our estimates cover workers in their late twenties. When these workers are a decade older, the earnings gap between high and low scorers will probably be somewhat higher. There is also some evidence that the effects of adolescent test performance on adult earnings have increased since the early 1980s.[52] If that is the case, the payoff to academic achievement for more recent cohorts of high school graduates may be higher than it was for the class of 1982. Finally, and perhaps most important, we have estimated the effect of academic achievement on only two adult outcomes: educational attainment and earnings.[53] As Herrnstein and Murray emphasize in *The Bell Curve*, the cognitive skills of teenagers also predict many other adult outcomes, ranging from unwed motherhood to criminal behavior. We have not investigated whether these correlations reflect the influence of academic achievement or academic aptitude. But we feel fairly confident that a more complete accounting would significantly increase the estimated benefits of raising academic achievement.

51. Herrnstein and Murray (1994, p. 520).

52. See Grogger and Eide (1995); Jencks and Phillips (1996); Murnane, Willett, and Levy (1995).

53. We also analyzed the determinants of occupational status, but the results were not sufficiently different from the results for education and earnings to justify presenting them here.

Appendix 2A
Estimating the Correlation between
True Tenth Grade Scores and True Gains

To estimate the correlation between true tenth grade scores and true gains $(r_{T10,TG})$, we proceed as follows. We denote true gains as G_T, true scores in tenth and twelfth grade respectively as T_{10} and T_{12}, and the correlation between observed tenth and twelfth grade scores as $r_{o10,o12}$. By definition

$$(2A\text{-}1) \qquad T_{12} = T_{10} + G_T .$$

Taking the variance of both sides yields

$$(2A\text{-}2) \qquad s^2{}_{T12} = s^2{}_{T10} + s^2{}_{GT} + 2(s_{T10})(s_{GT})(r_{T10,GT}) .$$

The only unknowns in equation 2A-2 are $r_{T10,GT}$ and s_{GT}. But we also know that

$$(2A\text{-}3) \qquad G_T = T_{12} - T_{10} .$$

Taking variances yields

$$(2A\text{-}4) \qquad s^2{}_{GT} = s^2{}_{T12} + s^2{}_{T10} - 2(s_{T10})(s_{T12}) \, (r_{T10,T12}) .$$

Since all the quantities on the right-hand side of equation 2A-4 are known, we can solve for $s^2{}_{GT}$. Substituting into equation 2A-2, we can then solve for $r_{T10,GT}$.

The reliability corrections used in these calculations and elsewhere also require some explanation. Standard reliability corrections assume that test items are randomly selected from a larger pool of items. A student's true score is then the average of the scores that the student would get if he or she took an infinite number of such tests, each of which involved an independent sample of the items in the underlying item pool. The estimated correlation between observed and true scores is $(r_{AB})^{0.5}$, where r_{AB} is the correlation between two tests administered at the same time but composed of different items from the same pool. The formula for correcting the observed correlation between tenth and twelfth grade scores is then $r_{T10,T12}$ = $r_{o10,o12}/(r_{AB}r_{CD})^{0.5}$, where $r_{T10,T12}$ is the true correlation, $r_{o10,o12}$ is the observed correlation, r_{AB} is the correlation between alternate forms of the test in tenth grade, and r_{CD} is the correlation between alternate forms in twelfth grade.

We cannot apply the standard reliability correction to the correlation between tenth and twelfth grade HS&B scores, because students took exactly the same test in both tenth and twelfth grade. Even if two students know exactly the same percentage of words in the underlying item pool, we expect a student who by chance knew more of the words on the tenth grade test to know more of them in twelfth grade also. For example, a student who happened to know the meaning of "superfluous" in tenth grade is still likely to know it in twelfth grade, and a student who did not know it in tenth grade is unlikely to have learned it, even if the two students have the same total vocabulary at both times. To minimize this source of bias, our estimates of the true correlation between tenth and twelfth grade scores exclude any stability created by students' ability (or inability) to answer the same item correctly in both tenth and twelfth grade. Instead, we estimate stability in true scores by looking at the degree to which students' twelfth grade performance on a given item depends on their tenth grade performance on all *other* items in the tenth grade test. We did these calculations in LISREL 7 by allowing the errors of identical test items to correlate over time.[54]

References

Altonji, Joseph. 1995. "The Effects of High School Curriculum on Education and Labor Market Outcomes." *Journal of Human Resources* 30: 409–38.

Angrist, Joshua, and Alan Krueger. 1991. "Does Compulsory School Attendance Affect Schooling and Earnings?" *Quarterly Journal of Economics* 106: 979–1014.

Ashenfelter, Orley, and Cecilia Rouse. 1998. "Income, Schooling, and Ability: Evidence from a New Sample of Identical Twins." *Quarterly Journal of Economics* 113:253–84.

Barnett, Stephen. 1995. "Long-Term Effects of Early Childhood Programs on Cognitive and School Outcomes." *The Future of Children* 5(3): 25–50.

Bishop, John H. 1994. "Schooling, Learning and Worker Productivity." In *Human Capital Creation in an Economic Perspective*, edited by R. Asplund, 14–67. Heidelberg: Physica-Verlag.

Bloom, Benjamin. 1964. *Stability and Change in Human Characteristics*. John Wiley.

Crouse, James. 1979. "The Effects of Academic Ability." In *Who Gets Ahead? The Determinants of Economic Success in America*, by Christopher Jencks and others, 85–121. Basic Books.

Fagerlind, Ingemar. 1975. *Formal Education and Adult Earnings: A Longitudinal Study on the Economic Benefits of Education*. Stockholm: Almqvist & Wiksell International.

Fischer, Claude, and others. 1996. *Inequality by Design: Cracking the Bell Curve Myth*. Princeton University Press.

---

54. On LISREL 7, see Joreskog and Sorbom (1988).

Grogger, Jeffrey, and Eric Eide. 1995. "Changes in College Skills and the Rise in the College Wage Premium." *Journal of Human Resources* 30: 280–310.

Herrnstein, Richard J., and Charles Murray. 1994. *The Bell Curve: Intelligence and Class Structure in American Life*. Free Press.

Jencks, Christopher, and Marsha Brown. 1975. "The Effects of High Schools on Their Students." *Harvard Educational Review* 45: 273–324.

————. 1977. "Genes and Social Stratification." In *Kinometrics: Determinants of Socioeconomic Success within and between Families*, edited by Paul Taubman, 169–223. New York: North-Holland.

Jencks, Christopher, and Meredith Phillips. 1996. "Does Learning Pay Off in the Job Market?" Paper prepared for the Meritocracy and Inequality Conference. Harvard University, September 26–27.

Joreskog, Karl G., and Dag Sorbom. 1988. *LISREL VII: A Guide to the Program and Applications*. Chicago: SPSS, Inc.

Korenman, Sanders, and Christopher Winship. Forthcoming. "A Reanalysis of *The Bell Curve*: Intelligence, Family Background, and Schooling." In *Meritocracy and Society*, edited by Kenneth Arrow, Samuel Bowles, and Stephen Durlauf. Princeton University Press.

Murnane, Richard J., John B. Willett, and Frank Levy. 1995. "The Growing Importance of Cognitive Skills in Wage Determination." *Review of Economics and Statistics* 77(2): 251–66.

Olneck, Michael. 1979. "The Effects of Education." In *Who Gets Ahead: The Determinants of Economic Success in America*, by Christopher Jencks and others, 159–190. Basic Books.

Plomin, Robert, and Stephen Petrill. 1997. "Genetics and Intelligence: What's New?" *Intelligence* 24(1): 53–77.

Rock, Donald A., and others. 1985. *Psychometric Analysis of the NLS and the High School and Beyond Test Batteries. A Study of Excellence in High School Education: Educational Policies, School Quality, and Student Outcomes*. Washington: National Center for Education Statistics.

Rogosa, David A., and John B. Willett. 1985. "Understanding Correlates of Change by Modeling Individual Differences in Growth." *Psychometrika* 50(2): 203–28.

Taubman, Paul. 1976. "Earnings, Education, Genetics, and Environment." *Journal of Human Resources* 11: 447–61.

Werts, C. E., and T. L. Hilton. 1977. "Intellectual Status and Intellectual Growth, Again." *American Educational Research Journal* 14(2): 137–46.

Zahs, Daniel, and others. 1995. *High School and Beyond Fourth Follow-Up Methodology Report*. NCES 95-426. U.S. Department of Education (February).

CHRISTOPHER WINSHIP
SANDERS D. KORENMAN

3

Economic Success and the Evolution of Schooling and Mental Ability

ONE OF THE MORE ENDURING controversies of social policy has been whether education can reduce inequality and improve the lot of the poor in America. In his 1972 book, *Inequality*, Christopher Jencks argued that since the effects of education on economic success are modest relative to overall inequality, equalizing educational attainment in the United States would only modestly reduce differences in economic success.[1] As a result, although education has important effects on success, it is not, as some on the political left had argued, a panacea for reducing social inequality.

More recently, Charles Murray and the late Richard Herrnstein have taken an even more pessimistic position. In their controversial book *The Bell Curve*, they claim that education has few, if any, direct effects on social and economic success, and that the apparent effects of education mainly represent the indirect effects of "intelligence." They further argue that formal education and other types of educational interventions do little to increase intelligence: "Taken together, the story of attempts to raise intelligence is one of high hopes, flamboyant claims, and disappointing results. For the foreseeable future, the problems of low cognitive ability are not going to be solved by outside interventions to make children smarter."[2]

---

1. Jencks and others (1972).
2. Herrnstein and Murray (1994, p. 389).

Others, however, take an opposing view. In *Inequality by Design*, a book-length response to *The Bell Curve* based on analysis of the same data, Claude Fischer and coauthors contend that the Armed Forces Qualifications Test (AFQT), which Herrnstein and Murray use to measure intelligence, is predominantly determined by educational attainment: "In some ways, the AFQT might be a good measure of instruction, but not one of native intelligence. What it captures best is how much instruction people encountered and absorbed."[3] They go on to argue that education has both direct effects on success and indirect effects through its effect on cognitive skills. In another critique William Dickens, Thomas Kane, and Charles Schultze point out that if cognitive skills are as important in determining success as Herrnstein and Murray claim, then even if education's effect on cognitive skills is modest, its indirect effects on social and economic success through such skills may be substantial.[4]

Certainly the controversy over the importance of education as a means of reducing inequality and poverty is enduring. Within the current debate, the nature of the interrelationship between education and cognitive skills and their effects on economic success are contested. The present paper seeks to shed light on these controversies. Our purpose is to present and estimate a model for the interrelationships among schooling, cognitive skills, and economic success. Our model is simple and should be regarded as a starting point for exploring these issues. With this model, we investigate a number of hypotheses.

We examine whether there is a reciprocal relationship between schooling and cognitive skills. We then focus on the implications of this relationship for understanding the mutual effects of schooling and cognitive skills on economic success, in particular, family income and earnings. We present evidence that schooling and cognitive skills affect each other; that they both have important effects on social and economic success; and that these effects are in part direct and in part indirect, working through one another. Greater recognition of the possibility that schooling and cognitive skills reinforce each other may further progress toward consensus in the literature.

We begin by presenting our basic model. Following a brief discussion of previous research, we describe our data, the National Longitudinal Survey of Youth (NLSY)—used also by Herrnstein and Murray, Fischer and co-authors, and Dickens, Kane, and Schultze. Our subsequent analysis falls

---

3. Fischer and others (1996, p. 62).
4. Dickens, Kane, and Schultze (forthcoming).

into three subsections. First, we examine the mutual effects of schooling and cognitive skills. We show that individuals with greater early cognitive skills are likely to get more schooling, and that schooling increases an individual's later cognitive skills. We find reciprocal effects of schooling and cognitive skills that are comparable in size. Second, we estimate the direct effects of cognitive skills and schooling on economic success. Third, we combine results from the two previous subsections and describe the different components of the effects of schooling and cognitive skills on economic success. We find that about half of each variable's effects on economic success are direct and independent of the other variable, but half are indirect and related to their mutually reinforcing relationship.[5] Finally, we review our findings and discuss their implications.

The Basic Model

Figure 3-1 presents the path model for interrelationships among schooling, cognitive skills, and family income that are the main interest of this paper. It has several components. First are the possible effects of family background on schooling, cognitive skills, and economic success (a_2, b_2, c_3). Our previous paper, as well as a host of studies in sociology and economics, have estimated these effects.[6] The effects of family background, however, are not at issue in the present paper: it is only important that we control for family background in estimating the effects of schooling and cognitive skills on each other and on economic success. In the analyses presented below, we also control for demographic characteristics, including age, race and ethnicity, and gender.

Second, the path diagram in figure 3-1 indicates that there is a possible reciprocal relationship between schooling and cognitive skills—that is, greater cognitive skills should lead to higher schooling attainment (a_1), and schooling should increase cognitive skills (b_1). The question of whether a_1 or b_1 is zero or nearly so, or schooling and cognitive skills instead have substantial mutual effects, is critical to understanding how these variables

---

5. Throughout the paper we measure economic success around 1990, when individuals in the sample are in their late twenties and early thirties. Cawley and others (1997) argue that the effect of education on wages measured at relatively young ages may dramatically overstate lifetime effects, and partly reflects the greater tendency of young high-ability individuals to invest in education when the economic return to "skill" rises, as it did in the 1980s.

6. Korenman and Winship (forthcoming).

Figure 3-1. *Path Model for Interrelationships among Schooling,*
Cognitive Skills, and Family Income

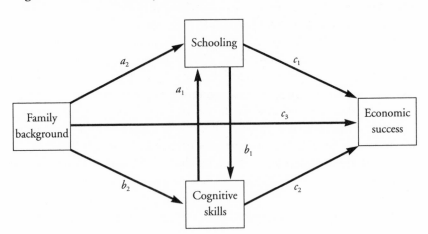

Source: Authors' model as described in text.

affect economic success. Finally, the path diagram indicates possible direct
and independent effects of schooling and cognitive skills on economic success. The independent effect of schooling on success is denoted by c_1,
which indicates the amount by which a one-unit increase in schooling
increases success, holding constant cognitive skills and family background.
The independent effect of cognitive skills on success is denoted by c_2,
which indicates the amount by which a one-unit increase in cognitive skill
increases success, holding constant schooling and family background. The
equations corresponding to figure 3-1 are given in appendix 3A.

Our model can be used to describe a variety of hypotheses that appear
in the literature. Jencks's argument about the inability of schooling to
reduce inequality essentially concerns the magnitude of the direct and indirect effects, or total effect, of schooling.[7] Formulas for these effects are
given in appendix 3A. The square of the effect of a one standard deviation
change in schooling is equal to the proportion of the variance in success
that is due independently to schooling. It thus tells one by how much
equalizing schooling across individuals might reduce inequality, as measured by the variance of success.

---

7. Jencks and others (1972).

Herrnstein and Murray's argument that schooling does not affect cognitive skills is equivalent to b_1 being essentially zero and a_1 being relatively large, large enough to explain most of the variance in schooling.[8] Fischer and coauthors argue the reverse, that is, that the AFQT measures educational attainment and what an individual has learned in school.[9] This implies that a_1 should be relatively small and b_1 should be large, sufficiently so to explain most of the variance in cognitive skills. Herrnstein and Murray's claim that education should not be included in models predicting economic success can be seen either as an argument that schooling has no direct effect on economic success—that is, c_1 is zero or nearly so—or that the effect of cognitive skills on schooling (a_1) is so substantial that there is little variation in schooling independent of cognitive skills. Finally, Dickens, Kane, and Schultze's observation is that even if the effect of schooling on cognitive skills is small, because the effect of cognitive skills on economic success is large schooling's effect on economic success may nonetheless be large, due to its indirect effect through cognitive skills.[10] This is equivalent to saying that even if b_1 is small, because c_2 is large the product of b_1 and c_2 maybe still be substantial.

Previous Research

Different literatures are relevant to the various components of the path diagram in figure 3-1. Little attention has been paid to the effects of cognitive skills on schooling (a_1), though the finding that individuals with better cognitive skills are likely to have higher educational attainment is well documented.[11] Jencks and coauthors provide an extensive array of analyses involving multiple data sets. They report that cognitive skill, as measured by the first principal component of scores on a set of thirty tests, explains 34.2 percent of the variance in schooling. The thirty test scores together explain only 37.1 percent.

The figure indicates that both schooling and cognitive skills directly affect economic success. The extent to which schooling affects economic success has been perhaps the most thoroughly examined issue in labor economics

8. Herrnstein and Murray (1994).
9. Fischer and others (1996).
10. Dickens, Kane, and Schultze (forthcoming).
11. See, for example, Jencks and others (1979); Duncan, Featherman, and Duncan (1972); Herrnstein and Murray (1994); Winship and Korenman (1997).

in the past several decades. The main concern has been the market valuation of additional years of schooling. In estimating such returns to schooling, a major preoccupation has been how to control for the fact that individuals with more cognitive skill are likely to get more schooling.

In a recent review, Orley Ashenfelter and Cecilia Rouse discuss a vast literature demonstrating that schooling leads to higher wages among individuals with comparable cognitive skills.[12] In fact, the issue in labor economics has not been whether schooling affects earnings net of ability—the evidence is overwhelming that it does—but rather, how to obtain a precise estimate of the effect. Ashenfelter and Rouse review a number of the more recent analytic strategies. In order to control for genetic differences and differences in family background, some authors have compared fathers and sons, siblings, or identical twins.[13] Researchers have also taken advantage of natural experiments to study the effects of plausibly exogenous variation in schooling, including compulsory school laws, sex of siblings, distance to the nearest college, and differences in birth weight.[14] All of these studies find significant effects of schooling on earnings, typically in the range of 4 to 10 percent.

Ashenfelter and Rouse also examine whether returns to schooling differ by race, sex, social class, or cognitive skills. They find little difference in the return to schooling by race or sex. Individuals from lower socioeconomic backgrounds and individuals with lower cognitive skills have somewhat higher returns to schooling. In short, across various demographic groups and different samples, and using different methods, economists have consistently found significant and substantial effects of schooling on earnings, net of differences in cognitive skills.

In the past several decades there has also been considerable and acrimonious debate about the effects of schooling on cognitive skills, particularly as to whether additional years of schooling raise an individual's "intelligence." This debate was reignited with the publication of *The Bell Curve* by

12. Ashenfelter and Rouse (forthcoming).

13. On fathers and sons, see Ashenfelter and Zimmerman (1993). On siblings, see Altonji and Dunn (1995); Ashenfelter and Zimmerman (1993); Corcoran, Jencks, and Olney (1976); Chamberlain and Griliches (1975, 1977); as well as Griliches (1979) for a review of earlier work. On identical twins, see Ashenfelter and Krueger (1994); Ashenfelter and Rouse (forthcoming); Behrman, Rosenzweig, and Taubman (1994); Miller, Mulvey, and Martin (1995).

14. On compulsory school laws, see Angrist and Krueger (1991); also Mayer and Knutson in chapter 4 below. On siblings, see Butcher and Case (1994); Kaestner (1997). On distance to the nearest college, see Card (1993). On differences in birth weight, see Berhman, Rosenzweig, and Taubman (1994).

Herrnstein and Murray's controversial claim that schooling has little or no effect on cognitive skills. In a recent paper, we review the literature on this subject and replicate Herrnstein and Murray's analysis.[15] We focus on twelve studies that attempt to estimate the magnitude of the effect of schooling on cognitive skills. Stephen Ceci provides a broader review.[16] Estimates of the effect of a year of schooling on cognitive skills range from one-fifteenth to nearly one-half of a standard deviation of cognitive skills.[17] Most studies, however, have found that a year of school produces an increase of about one-fifth of a standard deviation in cognitive skills. The studies that produce the more extreme estimates appear to have method-ological problems. In our replication of Herrnstein and Murray's analysis, we find that they had not adequately handled missing data on schooling and had failed to include an important control variable. In particular, they included seven cases in their analysis where schooling was missing and coded as −5. Also, they did not include as a control variable the age at which the earlier test of cognitive skills was taken, although in the book they stated that they had done so. Correction of these two errors results in an estimated effect of schooling more than twice as large as that reported in *The Bell Curve*. We have carried out further analyses, most important, including a control for family background and corrections for measure-ment error. From these, our preferred estimate is that a year of schooling increases cognitive skills by about 0.18 standard deviation.[18]

A smaller literature has examined the effects of cognitive skills on eco-nomic success. Researchers have examined the effects of cognitive skills on job performance and criminal behavior.[19] The economics literature on the returns to schooling establishes that cognitive skills affect economic suc-cess, but has been relatively unconcerned with the size of this effect. In the 1970s a vast sociological literature based on path analysis examined the

15. Winship and Korenman (1997).

16. Ceci (1991).

17. For the smaller estimate, see Herrnstein and Murray (1994) and Jencks and others (1972); for the larger, see Green and others (1964).

18. In an incomplete study based on the same data as *The Bell Curve* but using quite different methods, Lillard and Kilburn (1997) find much smaller schooling effects: about 0.08 standard devia-tion per year of schooling for men, and 0.06 for women. Interestingly, they find that the graduate equivalency diploma (GED) has substantial effects: about one-fifth of a standard deviation of cogni-tive skills for men and women.

19. On performance, see Gottfredson (1986), Hartigan and Wigdor (1989); on criminality, see Gordon (1976, 1980).

effects of cognitive skills on economic success, culminating in *Who Gets Ahead?* by Jencks and coauthors.[20] Using data from seven different studies, Jencks and coauthors estimate that a one standard deviation increase in cognitive skills increases earnings from 3 to 27 percent.

Herrnstein and Murray revisit this question in *The Bell Curve*. They conclude that for a host of different measures of economic and social success, intelligence is far more important than socioeconomic background, and is the dominant determinant of individual success. For example, they show that a one standard deviation increase in the AFQT, which they use to measure cognitive skills, increases family income by about $7,000 (in 1990 dollars), whereas a one standard deviation increase in an individual's socioeconomic background increases income only by about $4,600. A peculiarity of their study that has been noted by others and is germane to this paper is their decision to exclude schooling from most analyses.[21]

We have replicated Herrnstein and Murray's analysis using more extensive measures of family background.[22] Specifically, we use a variety of observed measures of family characteristics and we compare siblings, whose family backgrounds are presumably more similar than among unrelated adolescents. We find that estimates of the effect of cognitive skills are only modestly affected by using better controls or better methods of controlling for family background. For example, we find that a one standard deviation increase in AFQT score results in a $5,600 increase in family income. Our results differ from Herrnstein and Murray's in the finding that the importance of family background is comparable to that of cognitive skills. For example, we find that a one standard deviation increase in a very inclusive composite measure of family background increases family income by $6,100.

Furthermore, throughout our analyses we find that when we control for schooling, the effect of cognitive skills on success is substantially reduced. For example, including schooling as a control reduces the effect of a one standard deviation increase in AFQT score on family income from nearly $7,000 to about $4,100. And schooling has a comparable effect on family income: a one standard deviation increase in schooling (2.45 years) increases family income by about $4,600. Our results are similar for other measures of economic and social success. But none of the studies discussed

20. Duncan (1968); Jencks and others (1972); Duncan, Featherman, and Duncan (1972); Sewell and Hauser (1975); Hauser and Daymont (1977); Jencks and others (1979).

21. See, for example, Hauser (1995); Heckman (1995).

22. Korenman and Winship (forthcoming).

above explicitly considers the reciprocal relationship between schooling and cognitive skills. As a result, they may misrepresent the effects of schooling and cognitive skills on economic success.

Data and Methods

Our empirical analyses are based on data from the National Longitudinal Survey of Youth. The NLSY is an ongoing longitudinal study of a national sample of 12,686 individuals who were between the ages of fourteen and twenty-one on January 1, 1979.[23] The survey contains extensive information on labor market, schooling, and family formation histories. For the present purpose, the importance of the NLSY is that it contains a high-quality measure of cognitive skills, the Armed Services Vocational Aptitude Battery (ASVAB), which was administered to nearly the whole sample in April 1980. The ASVAB consists of ten tests aimed at measuring both general cognitive skills and knowledge of specific topics. Our measure of cognitive skills is an equally weighted combination of four of the items that collectively constitute the Armed Forces Qualifications Test (AFQT): word knowledge, paragraph comprehension, arithmetic reasoning, and mathematical knowledge. The AFQT's reliability is quite high, probably 0.95 and certainly higher than 0.9.[24]

Whether the AFQT is a measure of "innate intelligence" has been debated in the recent literature.[25] Fischer and coauthors claim that the AFQT is essentially a measure of educational achievement (we return to this point below).[26] Research is needed to examine whether schooling influences other components of the ASVAB, as well as the possible effects of these components on different measures of social and economic success. A recent study by Jill Corcoran is an effort in this direction.[27] The question of whether intelligence is appropriately conceptualized as a one-dimensional variable has also been highly contentious.[28] Psychometricians typically believe that intelligence is unidimensional and that it is

23. Center for Human Resources Research (1994).
24. Bock and Moore (1986).
25. See Herrnstein and Murray (1994); Cawley and others (1997).
26. Fischer and others (1996).
27. Corcoran (1996).
28. See Brody (1992); Carroll (1992).

well measured by IQ tests.[29] Others, most notably Robert Sternberg and Howard Gardner, have argued that intelligence is multidimensional.[30] Until there is further research on different cognitive skills and the degree to which they may be measured by the various ASVAB and other tests, one is in the unfortunate position of having to choose a measure of cognitive skills arbitrarily. The AFQT is a convenient choice as a measure cognitive skills, whether innate or acquired.

The NLSY is suited to our research objectives for an additional reason. For a small subsample (1,408 cases), an additional and earlier measure of cognitive skills is available. This allows us to estimate the effect of schooling on cognitive skills, while controlling for earlier cognitive skills. Many studies have used a similar design. Unfortunately, in the case of the NLSY the earlier measures of cognitive skills were taken at different ages and with different tests. The reliabilities of these measures are unknown. Typically, such tests have reliabilities over 0.9. Given that the scores for the NLSY subsample come from school administrative records and are based on a variety of tests, treating them as a single variable may well result in a lower reliability, possibly as low as 0.8.

In estimating the effects of cognitive skills and schooling, we control for an individual's family background with Herrnstein and Murray's index of socioeconomic status (SES), which is a simple combination of family income, mother's and father's schooling, and head of household's occupation. We do not use more elaborate measures since, as discussed above, in most cases more extensive controls for family background or the use of sibling comparisons did not substantially change estimates of the effect of AFQT or schooling on success.[31]

The other key variable in our analysis is completed schooling, measured in 1980 and 1990. The reliability of the schooling variable in the NLSY is unknown. Other research is of some help. Examining a variety of different sources, Jencks and coauthors provide estimates of its reliability ranging from 0.854 to 0.933. Ashenfelter and Alan Krueger's work on twins suggests a reliability of 0.9 for schooling.[32]

---

29. See Linda S. Gottfredson, "Mainstream Science on Intelligence," *Wall Street Journal,* December 13, 1994.

30. Sternberg (1985, 1990); Gardner (1983). For recent discussions, see Hunt (1997); Carroll (1997).

31. Korenman and Winship (forthcoming).

32. Jencks and others (1979, table A2.14); Ashenfelter and Krueger (1994).

Analysis

In this section, we first examine the reciprocal effects of schooling and cognitive skills. We then report estimates of the direct effects of schooling and cognitive skills on family income and annual earnings for year-round workers. Finally, we attempt to integrate these findings in order to examine the overall effects of schooling and cognitive skills on economic success. Table 3-1 presents summary statistics for the variables used in the analysis.

We estimate the effect of schooling and cognitive skills on each other, family income, or annual earnings. Both schooling and cognitive skills are measured with error. Since they are also highly related in the NLSY, with correlations as high as 0.65, assumptions about the measurement error in each variable substantially affect both its own effect and that of the other variable.

In the tables below, we first present estimates under the assumption that all variables have reliability of one; that is, they are measured perfectly. We then check the sensitivity of estimates to different assumptions about reliability. As our preferred values, we choose estimates with an intermediate set of reliabilities: 0.95 for AFQT, 0.9 for early cognitive skills, and 0.9 for schooling. All our models include controls for socioeconomic background, age, race or Hispanic origin, and gender. We assume that the reliabilities of these variables are equal to one.[33] In order to compare the size of the effects of schooling and cognitive skills, we present standardized as well as unstandardized estimates. Readers may find it easiest to think about schooling in unstandardized units, that is, a year of schooling; and cognitive skills in standardized units, one standard deviation equal to fifteen points.

The Reciprocal Relationship between Schooling and Cognitive Skills

What is the effect of cognitive skills on schooling? Specifically, if one could increase an individual's cognitive skill, holding all other variables constant, how much more schooling would he or she be likely to get? Table 3-2 presents both standardized and unstandardized estimates of the effects of an

---

33. The reliability of our measure of SES is almost certainly less than one. However, we have investigated the effects of measurement error in parental SES. As noted, our measure of SES is a combination of mother's education, father's education, occupational status of the head of household, and family income. Jencks and others (1979) report reliabilities for these component variables ranging from 0.72 to 0.96. Thus the reliability of our measure of SES will be higher. In general, we find that different assumptions about the reliability of SES have little impact on our estimates of the effects of schooling and cognitive skills.

Table 3-1. *Summary of Variables Used in the Analysis of the National Longitudinal Survey of Youth*[a]

Variable	Mean	Number of observations	Description
Family income	34,345 (27,080)	7,977	Total net family income in 1989, 1990 dollars. Excludes persons not working because of school in 1989 or 1990.
Annual earnings	24,225 (16,083)	4,974	Year-round workers.
Schooling in 1980 (*Ed80*)	11.07 (1.95)	12,844	Years of school completed in 1980.
Schooling in 1990 (*Ed90*)	12.76 (2.46)	10,506	Years of school completed in 1990.
AFQT	101.31 (15.02)	12,038	Armed Forces Qualifying Test.
Early cognitive skills	100.3 (15.2)	1,216	Test score from school transcript.
Age in 1990	29.10 (2.27)	10,585	. . .
Black	0.2483 (0.432)	12,846	. . .
Latino	0.1565 (0.363)	12,486	. . .
Other race	0.045 (0.207)	12,846	. . .
Female	0.495 (0.500)	. . .	. . .
SES	−0.348 (1.07)	12,036	Equally weighted combination of parents' income and education, and occupation of head of household.
Years between tests	6.12 (2.74)	1,216	Number of years between initial school-based test and AFQT.

a. Standard deviations are in parentheses.

individual's educational attainment in 1980 and AFQT score in 1980 on educational attainment in 1990, holding constant SES and demographic characteristics.[34]

For the full cross-sectional NLSY sample, table 3-2 indicates that a one-year increase in schooling in 1980 is associated with an increase of 0.72 year in schooling in 1990. A one-point increase in the AFQT score is associated with an increase of 0.063 year in schooling in 1990. Equivalently a one standard deviation increase in the AFQT score increases schooling by 0.39 year. Different assumptions about the reliability of schooling and the AFQT score have substantial effects on the estimates. The effect of a one-year increase in schooling in 1980 on years of schooling in 1990 ranges from about 0.66 to 1.5 years, and the effect of a one-point increase in AFQT score on schooling ranges from 0.022 to 0.079 years.[35]

However, the full NLSY sample comprises respondents aged between fifteen and twenty-two in 1980. A number of respondents had completed their schooling by this time, and including them in the sample may overstate the effect of current schooling on future schooling. Table 3-2 also reports the results from running the same models with the sample of individuals who were less than eighteen years old in 1980, and thus were likely to still be in school. In this sample, a year of schooling in 1980 is associated with an additional 0.58 year of schooling in 1990, a reduction of about 20 percent from the full-sample estimate, while a one-point increase in the AFQT score is associated with 0.081 additional years of schooling, an increase of nearly 30 percent. Again, the estimated effects of schooling in 1980 and AFQT score vary with the assumptions about reliability. The effect of a one-year increase in 1980 on schooling in 1990 ranges from 0.49 year to 0.96 year, and the effect of a one-point increase in AFQT score ranges from 0.072 year to 0.099 year. Our preferred estimate is model 6, where the reliabilities of AFQT and schooling in 1980 are assumed to be 0.95 and 0.90, respectively. In this case, the effect on schooling in 1990 of a one-year increase in schooling in 1980 is 0.675 year, and the effect of a one-point increase in the AFQT score is 0.085 year. Put

---

34. Estimates are from the following equation:

$$Ed90 = \alpha_0 + (Ed80)\alpha_1 + (AFQT)\alpha_2 + \text{controls}.$$

The standardized coefficients are derived by scaling the dependent variable (schooling in 1990) and the independent variables (schooling in 1980 and AFQT) to have variance 1.

35. In Korenman and Winship (forthcoming) we find that the use of sibling comparisons reduces the effect of AFQT score on schooling by approximately 25 percent.

Table 3-2. *Effects of Cognitive Skills on 1990 Educational Attainment in the NLSY*[a]

Model	Full sample[b]					Less than 18 years old in 1980[c]				
	Unstandardized		Standardized		Reliability	Unstandardized		Standardized		Reliability
	Ed80	AFQT	Ed80	AFQT		Ed80	AFQT	Ed80	AFQT	
1	0.719	0.063	0.584	0.386	Ed80 = 1.00	0.582	0.081	0.473	0.499	Ed80 = 1.00
	0.012	0.000	0.010	0.009	AFQT = 1.00	0.043	0.003	0.035	0.018	AFQT = 1.00
2	1.458	0.029	1.185	0.182	Ed80 = 0.80	0.822	0.089	0.669	0.551	Ed80 = 0.80
	0.023	0.000	0.019	0.012	AFQT = 0.90	0.071	0.004	0.058	0.024	AFQT = 0.90
3	1.486	0.025	1.208	0.155	Ed80 = 0.80	0.899	0.080	0.731	0.491	Ed80 = 0.80
	0.022	0.002	0.018	0.011	AFQT = 0.95	0.067	0.004	0.057	0.022	AFQT = 0.95
4	1.507	0.022	0.123	0.135	Ed80 = 0.80	0.960	0.072	0.781	0.443	Ed80 = 0.80
	0.021	0.002	0.017	0.009	AFQT = 1.00	0.069	0.003	0.056	0.020	AFQT = 1.00
5	0.905	0.067	0.735	0.394	Ed80 = 0.90	0.614	0.095	0.499	0.588	Ed80 = 0.90
	0.017	0.002	0.014	0.012	AFQT = 0.90	0.054	0.004	0.043	0.022	AFQT = 0.90
6	0.943	0.056	0.767	0.344	Ed80 = 0.90	0.675	0.085	0.549	0.527	Ed80 = 0.90
	0.016	0.002	0.013	0.010	AFQT = 0.95	0.053	0.003	0.043	0.020	AFQT = 0.95
7	0.973	0.049	0.791	0.305	Ed80 = 0.90	0.725	0.077	0.589	0.478	Ed80 = 0.90
	0.016	0.002	0.013	0.009	AFQT = 1.00	0.053	0.003	0.043	0.019	AFQT = 1.00
8	0.656	0.079	0.533	0.489	Ed80 = 1.00	0.490	0.099	0.398	0.610	Ed80 = 1.00
	0.013	0.002	0.011	0.011	AFQT = 0.90	0.043	0.004	0.035	0.022	AFQT = 0.90
9	0.691	0.070	0.562	0.432	Ed80 = 1.00	0.541	0.089	0.440	0.549	Ed80 = 1.00
	0.013	0.002	0.010	0.010	AFQT = 0.95	0.043	0.003	0.035	0.020	AFQT = 0.95

Source: Authors' calculations as described in text. In this and subsequent tables, underlying source for NLSY data is Center for Human Resources Research (1994).
a. Controls include socioeconomic status (SES) of family, age, race or ethnicity, and gender.
b. N = 10,033.
c. N = 3,014.

another way, a one standard deviation increase in schooling in 1980 is associated with a 0.549 standard deviation increase in schooling in 1990, and a one standard deviation increase in the AFQT score is associated with a 0.527 standard deviation increase in schooling in 1990. This suggests that schooling in 1980 and the AFQT in 1980 are of approximately equal importance in determining schooling in 1990.

What effect does schooling have on cognitive skills? Specifically, if schooling increases by one year, holding all other variables constant, how much does cognitive skill increase? To answer this question, we estimate the effect of schooling in 1980 and earlier tests of cognitive ability on AFQT score in 1980, controlling family background and demographic characteristics. We report these results in table 3-3.[36] In this case, the sample is small because only a small portion of the NLSY sample has an early measure of cognitive skill.

The first model in table 3-3 reports estimates of the effect of schooling and early cognitive skills on AFQT scores, assuming reliabilities of 1. An additional year of schooling increases an individual's AFQT score by 2.46 points. This effect is significant. A one-point increase in score on a test of early cognitive skills is associated with an additional 0.60 point on the AFQT. The effect of a one standard deviation increase of schooling (0.40) is two-thirds of that of early cognitive skills. This suggests that AFQT score responds both to schooling, as argued by Fischer and coauthors, and to early cognitive skills, as argued by Herrnstein and Murray, though early skills are approximately 50 percent more important than schooling.[37]

Models 2 through 9 in table 3-3 report estimates for the effects of schooling and early cognitive skills on the AFQT for different assumptions about the reliabilities of these variables. The effect of schooling on AFQT ranges from 1.63 points to 5.47 points per year of school completed. The effect of early skills ranges from 0.52 point to 0.89 point. Our preferred estimates are those of model 6, where the effect of schooling is 2.95 and the effect of early skills is 0.69. As in model 1, the effect of a one standard deviation increase in schooling (0.48) is approximately 70 percent as large as that for early skills (0.69).[38]

---

36. Estimates are from the following equation:

$$AFQT = (Ed80)\theta_1 + (early\ cognitive\ skills)\theta_2 + controls.$$

37. Fischer and others (1996); Herrnstein and Muray (1994).

38. These estimates are somewhat higher than those in Winship and Korenman (1997) because in the present paper we use a more extensive set of demographic controls.

Table 3-3. *Effects of Schooling on Cognitive Skills in the NLSY*[a]

	Unstandardized		Standardized		
Model	Ed80	Early skills	Ed80	Early skills	Reliability
1	2.464	0.601	0.404	0.601	Ed80 = 1.00
	0.207	0.020	0.034	0.020	Skills = 1.00
2	3.793	0.814	0.622	0.814	Ed80 = 0.80
	0.375	0.026	0.061	0.026	Skills = 0.80
3	4.816	0.637	0.789	0.637	Ed80 = 0.80
	0.409	0.023	0.067	0.022	Skills = 0.90
4	5.473	0.523	0.897	0.523	Ed80 = 0.80
	0.425	0.021	0.070	0.021	Skills = 1.00
5	2.283	0.869	0.374	0.869	Ed80 = 0.90
	0.235	0.024	0.039	0.024	Skills = 0.80
6	2.954	0.693	0.484	0.693	Ed80 = 0.90
	0.263	0.022	0.043	0.022	Skills = 0.90
7	3.399	0.577	0.557	0.577	Ed80 = 0.90
	0.279	0.020	0.046	0.020	Skills = 1.00
8	1.634	0.893	0.268	0.893	Ed80 = 1.00
	0.171	0.023	0.028	0.023	Skills = 0.80
9	2.131	0.718	0.349	0.718	Ed80 = 1.00
	0.194	0.022	0.032	0.022	Skills = 0.90

Source: Authors' calculations as described in text.

a. Sample comprises individuals with measures of early cognitive skills (N = 1,215). Controls include family SES, age, race or ethnicity, gender, and number of years between tests.

In these models schooling in 1990 and AFQT score are the dependent variables, and schooling in 1980 and early cognitive skills have been used simply as controls. It is of interest, however, to ask how the reciprocal effects of schooling and cognitive skills compare in size. To do this, we compare estimates for the effect of AFQT score on schooling in 1990 for the smaller sample in table 3-2, with the effect of schooling in 1980 on AFQT score in table 3-3. Focusing on standardized estimates for model 6, we find that the effect of AFQT score on schooling is 0.527, and the effect of schooling in 1980 on AFQT score is 0.484. The effects are of approximately equal size.

In additional analyses (not shown), we have explored whether schooling raises AFQT score more among those with higher or lower early cognitive skills by adding an interaction term between schooling and early skills to the models reported in table 3-3. The interaction term has a negative sign and is statistically significant in all models, which suggests that those with lower cognitive skills benefited most, in terms of their future AFQT score, from additional years of schooling. This result contrasts with the hypothesis that the brightest students gain the most from additional years of schooling, at least for the ages represented in the sample.

The Direct Effects of Schooling and Cognitive Skills on Economic Success

In this section we examine the independent effects of schooling and of cognitive skills on family income and the earnings of year-round workers. We ask how additional schooling is related to success, holding other variables constant, including cognitive skills. Holding AFQT score constant, schooling may affect earnings either by developing skills not measured by the AFQT (for example, noncognitive skills such as specialized training) or by increasing earnings independent of cognitive skills (for example, through qualification for a professional license). Analogously, we ask how higher cognitive skills are related to economic success, holding other variables constant, including schooling.[39]

Table 3-4 reports estimates of the effects of schooling and cognitive skills on the log of family income. Because the dependent variable is in log form, the unstandardized coefficients can be interpreted as indicating that a one-unit increase in an independent variable produces a percentage change in the dependent variable equal to approximately 100 times the coefficient. The standardized coefficients (which involve standardization of the independent variables) multiplied by 100 approximately indicate the percentage change in the dependent variable for a one standard deviation change in the independent variable. Table 3-4 shows that the effect of schooling on the log of family income is 0.054, or that one additional year

39. Estimates are from the equation

$$\textit{Economic success} = (\textit{Ed90})\gamma_1 + (\textit{AFQT})\gamma_2 + \text{controls.}$$

Table 3-4. *Effects of Schooling and AFQT Score on Log of 1989 Family Income in the NLSY*[a]

Model	Unstandardized		Standardized		
	Ed90	AFQT	Ed90	AFQT	Reliability
1	0.054	0.012	0.130	0.180	Ed90 = 1.00
	0.005	0.001	0.013	0.015	AFQT = 1.00
2	0.074	0.012	0.177	0.182	Ed90 = 0.80
	0.001	0.002	0.024	0.023	AFQT = 0.90
3	0.082	0.010	0.198	0.151	Ed90 = 0.80
	0.009	0.001	0.021	0.020	AFQT = 0.95
4	0.089	0.009	0.212	0.129	Ed90 = 0.80
	0.008	0.001	0.020	0.017	AFQT = 1.00
5	0.054	0.015	0.129	0.217	Ed90 = 0.90
	0.007	0.001	0.017	0.020	AFQT = 0.90
6	0.062	0.013	0.148	0.185	Ed90 = 0.90
	0.007	0.001	0.016	0.017	AFQT = 0.95
7	0.067	0.011	0.161	0.161	Ed90 = 0.90
	0.006	0.001	0.015	0.015	AFQT = 1.00
8	0.042	0.016	0.102	0.237	Ed90 = 1.00
	0.006	0.001	0.014	0.018	AFQT = 0.90
9	0.049	0.014	0.118	0.205	Ed90 = 1.00
	0.005	0.001	0.013	0.016	AFQT = 0.95

Source: Authors' calculations as described in text.

a. Full cross-sectional sample ($N = 7,984$). Controls include family SES, age, race or ethnicity, and gender. 1989 income is in 1990 dollars.

of schooling increases family income by about 5.4 percent. An increase of one standard deviation in schooling increases family income by approximately 14.8 percent. The effect of AFQT score is 0.012, or equivalently, that a one standard deviation increase in AFQT score (fifteen points) increases family income by 18.5 percent.

The effects of schooling and AFQT score on family income vary widely, depending on the assumptions about reliability. The effect of schooling on family income ranges from 4.2 to 8.9 percent. The effect of a one standard deviation increase in AFQT score on family income ranges from 12.9 to

21.7 percent. We prefer model 6, in which reliabilities for schooling and AFQT score are 0.9 and 0.95, respectively. Accordingly, the effect of a year of schooling on family income is approximately 6.2 percent, and the effect of a standard deviation change in AFQT score is approximately 18.5 percent.[40]

Table 3-5 presents estimates of the effects of schooling and AFQT score on the log of annual earnings for year-round workers. The ordinary least squares estimate of the effect of schooling is 0.068, or approximately 6.8 percent, which lies within the range of estimates found in the labor economics literature.[41] The effect of AFQT is .012. The effect of a one standard deviation increase in AFQT score is approximately 17.1 percent, while the effect of a one standard deviation increase in schooling is approximately 16.2 percent.

As in the other analyses, the effects of schooling and the AFQT vary depending on the assumptions about reliabilities. The effect of a one-year change in schooling on earnings ranges from 5.7 percent to 11.0 percent. The effect of a one standard deviation increase in AFQT score ranges from 10.9 percent to 22.4 percent. We prefer model 6, which, with reliabilities for schooling and AFQT score of, respectively, 0.9 and 0.95, produces estimates of 7.9 percent for each additional year of school and 16.9 percent for a one standard deviation increase in AFQT score.[42]

---

40. An important objection to the models we estimate in table 3-4 is that AFQT score is measured in 1980 rather than in 1990. Since our analyses above show that AFQT score is affected by schooling, one would expect 1990 AFQT score to be more highly correlated than 1980 score with schooling in 1990. One might also expect that 1990 AFQT score would be more highly correlated than 1980 score with economic success, if current rather than past cognitive skills determine economic success. Unfortunately, 1990 AFQT scores are not available for our sample. The net impact of using 1980 AFQT score instead should be to overstate the effect schooling and understate the effect of cognitive skills. In analyses not presented here, we have investigated this issue for family income and annual earnings. We create a predicted 1990 AFQT score based on the results from model 6 in table 3-3. We then use this predicted AFQT instead of 1980 AFQT as the regressor in a two-stage least squares procedure. Our estimates of the effect of AFQT score change only modestly. In the case of family income, the ordinary least squares estimate of family income is 0.054 and the two-stage least squares estimate is 0.050; the effects of AFQT score are, respectively, 0.0122 and 0.0105—a decrease, the opposite of what would be predicted. In the case of annual earnings, the coefficients for schooling are, respectively, 0.068 and 0.060; and for AFQT score they are, respectively, 0.012 and 0.011. Jencks and coauthors (1997) report similar findings from using an earlier as opposed to a current measure of cognitive skill to predict earnings. Since using the predicted variable adds substantial complications to the analysis and the discussion and yields only modest changes in the estimates, we use AFQT score in 1980 as the dependent variable.

41. Ashenfelter and Rouse (forthcoming).

42. There are no significant or large interaction effects between education and AFQT scores in the models of income or wages that we have analyzed.

Table 3-5. *Effects of Schooling and AFQT Score on Log of Annual Earnings in the NLSY*[a]

Model	Unstandardized		Standardized		Reliability
	Ed90	AFQT	Ed90	AFQT	
1	0.068	0.012	0.162	0.171	Ed80 = 1.00
	0.006	0.001	0.015	0.018	AFQT = 1.00
2	0.098	0.010	0.234	0.152	Ed80 = 0.80
	0.012	0.002	0.028	0.028	AFQT = 0.90
3	0.105	0.009	0.250	0.127	Ed80 = 0.80
	0.011	0.002	0.026	0.024	AFQT = 0.95
4	0.110	0.007	0.262	0.109	Ed80 = 0.80
	0.100	0.001	0.024	0.020	AFQT = 1.00
5	0.072	0.013	0.172	0.197	Ed80 = 0.90
	0.009	0.002	0.021	0.024	AFQT = 0.90
6	0.079	0.011	0.188	0.169	Ed80 = 0.90
	0.008	0.001	0.019	0.021	AFQT = 0.95
7	0.084	0.010	0.200	0.147	Ed80 = 0.90
	0.008	0.001	0.018	0.018	AFQT = 1.00
8	0.057	0.015	0.136	0.224	Ed80 = 1.00
	0.007	0.002	0.016	0.022	AFQT = 0.90
9	0.063	0.013	0.151	0.194	Ed80 = 1.00
	0.007	0.001	0.016	0.019	AFQT = 0.95

Source: Authors' calculations as described in text.

a. Sample comprises full-year workers ($N = 6,780$). Controls include family SES, age, race or ethnicity, and gender.

The Compound Effects of Schooling and Cognitive Skills on Economic Success

We have shown, first, that schooling and cognitive ability appear to affect each other; and second, that they both have important and *independent* effects on family income and wages. In terms of figure 3-2, estimates for the log of family income taken from tables 3-2 (smaller sample), 3-3, and 3-4 yield the following standardized coefficients: $a_1 = 0.527$, $b_1 = 0.484$, $c_1 = 0.148$, and $c_2 = 0.185$.

Figure 3-2. *Path Model for Interrelationships among Education,*
Mental Ability, and Family Income in Standardized Coefficients

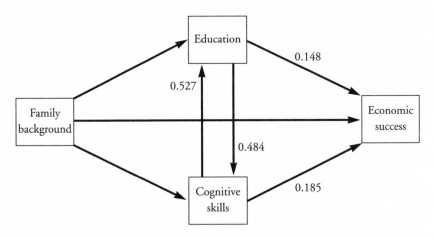

Source: Authors' model as described in text.

We would now like to estimate how the indirect and direct effects of cognitive skills combine to determine economic success. To do so, we must assume that one can meaningfully use the estimates from tables 3-2 (smaller sample), 3-3, and 3-4 in a single analysis. This raises several problems. First, it would require a common time unit—for example, one year—over which to measure the interaction between schooling and skills. One would therefore need data on each individual's schooling and cognitive skills at each successive year. While we have a measure of schooling for each year after 1979, cognitive skill is measured only in 1980 for most of the sample, and for a small portion of the sample also prior to 1979, albeit poorly.

Second, our model assumes that schooling and cognitive skills adjust to each other dynamically and finally arrive at an equilibrium. The implication is that as a child gets a year of schooling, his cognitive skills increase, as a result of which he gets more schooling, and so on; but that these mutual increases diminish over time, until they disappear. The model lacks any clear specification of how schooling and cognitive skills evolve in relation to each other from year to year. Attempting to provide such specification introduces a difficult set of modeling issues. For example, there may be nonlinear increases in cognitive skills at particular years of schooling, for example, in the first year of college.

We leave these problems to future research. As a result, our estimates are crude, and probably biased. The absence of several repeated measures of cognitive skills and schooling may lead us to overstate the reciprocal effects of these variables. Nevertheless, it is worthwhile to illustrate roughly how the different components of figure 3-1 might interact as a system.

Consider the possible ways in which an increase in schooling might increase family income. First, there are direct effects. Our analysis suggests that a year of schooling increases income by 6.2 percent, or equivalently, that a one standard deviation increase in schooling (2.45 years) increases family income by 14.8 percent. This estimate is based on holding everything else, including cognitive skills, constant. That is, it indicates how much income increases when schooling increases for individuals who are similar in all other relevant respects, with equivalent family backgrounds and *equal levels of cognitive skill*.

Alternatively, imagine that the length of compulsory schooling were increased by one year. This would represent an exogenous increase in schooling that would raise cognitive skills. Thus schooling affects family income both directly and indirectly by increasing cognitive skills. The indirect effect is equal to the effect of schooling on cognitive skills multiplied by the effect of cognitive skills on family income. With unstandardized coefficients, this is $(2.95)(0.013) = 0.038$. The one-year increase in compulsory schooling would directly increase family income by 6.2 percent and indirectly increase it, through schooling's effect on cognitive skills, by an additional 3.8 percent. Table 3-6 reports these combined effects.

In the standard theory of path analysis reciprocal effects are not allowed, and the sum of a variable's direct and indirect effects is known as its total effect. As we discuss below, in the present model the reciprocal relationship between schooling and cognitive skills means that there are additional effects beyond each variable's direct and indirect effects. Therefore for clarity we refer to the combination of a variable's direct and indirect effects in our model as its composite effect.

The composite effect of schooling on the log of family income is 0.100, indicating that one year of schooling increases family income by approximately 10 percent: directly by 6.2 percent and indirectly, through AFQT score, by 3.8 percent. Thus one of the ways in which schooling increases income is to make one smarter, which in turn raises family income.

If an increase in schooling results in an increase in cognitive skill, this increase in cognitive skills could also increase schooling. The increase in schooling will then result in an additional increase in cognitive skill, lead-

Table 3-6. *Decomposition of Effects of Schooling and AFQT Score in the NLSY*[a]

| | Log of income | | | | Log of annual earnings | | | |
| | Unstandardized | | Standardized | | Unstandardized | | Standardized | |
Type of effect	Ed90	AFQT	Ed90	AFQT	Ed90	AFQT	Ed90	AFQT
Direct	0.062	0.013	0.148	0.185	0.079	0.011	0.188	0.169
Indirect	0.038	0.005	0.090	0.078	0.032	0.007	0.082	0.099
Composite	0.100	0.018	0.238	0.263	0.111	0.018	0.270	0.268
Multiplier	1.335	1.335	1.335	1.335	1.335	1.335	1.335	1.335
Overall	0.134	0.024	0.317	0.351	0.149	0.024	0.360	0.358

Source: Authors' calculations based on estimates for model 6 in tables 3-2 (smaller sample) through 3-5.

ing to a further increase in schooling, and so on. This is a common situation in models with lag structures. Essentially, there is a repeated feedback loop. This process may either explode or converge. In the present case, equilibrium will be reached if the product of the effect of AFQT score on schooling (0.085) and the effect of schooling on AFQT score (2.95) is less than one. In fact, it is 0.251, indicating that the process will converge.

As a result of the feedback process through cognitive skills, the effect of schooling on a given outcome is multiplied by a constant (see appendix 3A for derivation and formulas). From our estimates of the reciprocal effects of AFQT score and schooling, the multiplier is 1.335. Therefore the overall effect of schooling on the log of family income is its composite effect multiplied by (0.100)(1.335) = 0.1335. This estimate is more than twice as large as that of the direct effect of schooling on the log of family income (0.062). Thus, schooling's overall effect on the log of family income in part comes from its independent effect (0.062), but also in part from its interrelationship with AFQT score.

One can perform a similar analysis for the effect of AFQT score. For ease of interpretation we focus on the standardized effects in table 3-6. A one standard deviation increase in AFQT score, holding all other variables constant, increases the log of family income by 0.185, or increases family income by approximately 18.5 percent. If we allow the AFQT score to increase schooling, it has an additional indirect effect of 0.078, or an approximately 7.8 percent increase in family income. The combination of the direct and indirect effects of AFQT score is 0.263. Allowing for the feedback effects between AFQT score and schooling increases this combined effect by approximately 33.5 percent, resulting in an overall effect of 0.317, or approximately 31.7 percent—more than twice the size of the direct effect of AFQT score on family income. Thus for both schooling and AFQT score, somewhat less than half of the overall effect on family income is direct and somewhat more than half is the result of their mutually reinforcing relationship.

One can consider figure 3-1 in terms of the log of annual earnings. Table 3-6 breaks down the effects of schooling and AFQT score on the log of earnings. The direct effect of a year of schooling is to increase earnings by 7.9 percent; its indirect effect through AFQT score is 3.2 percent, and its overall effect is 14.9 percent. The direct effect of a one standard deviation increase in AFQT score is a 16.9 percent increase in earnings; its indirect effect through schooling is 8.2 percent, and its overall effect is 31.7 percent. As for family income, for both schooling and AFQT score, approximately half of the effect on log earnings is direct and half results from their mutually reinforcing relationship.

Conclusion

The picture that our model and parameter estimates offer is considerably at variance with many, though not all, of the claims in the existing literature. Our results appear to support Jencks's contention that equalizing schooling would only modestly reduce economic inequality.[43] The overall standardized effect of schooling on family income is 0.317, and on annual earnings is 0.360. Squaring these coefficients and multiplying by 100 indicates that 10.0 percent of the variance in family income and 12.3 percent of the variance in annual earnings is due to schooling.

Dickens, Kane, and Schultze's claim that education may be important because of indirect effects through cognitive skills receives mixed support from our results.[44] Table 3-6 shows that schooling has strong direct effects on both family income and annual earnings: one year of schooling increases them by 6.2 percent and 7.9 percent, respectively. Schooling also

43. Jencks and others (1979).
44. Dickens, Kane, and Schultze (forthcoming).

has important indirect effects: one year of schooling increases family income and annual earnings by 3.8 percent and 3.2 percent, respectively. It is the combination of these direct and indirect effects with the multiplier, however, that produces large overall effects: a 13.4 percent increase in family income and a 14.9 percent increase in earnings. Thus the effect of schooling on economic success is important because of, first, its direct effect; second, its indirect effects through cognitive skills; and third, the interaction of the two through the multiplier.

Our results fly in the face of Herrnstein and Murray's claim that schooling should not be controlled in a model predicting economic outcomes, since it represents only the effects of intelligence.[45] Squaring the standardized coefficient for AFQT—$(0.527)^2 = 0.278$—indicates that 27.8 percent of schooling can be attributed to AFQT score. Thus most of the variance in years of schooling is unrelated to AFQT score. Even if we estimate our model without controls for earlier schooling, we find that the standardized coefficient for AFQT is 0.620, the square of which is 0.384. As noted, our results also demonstrate that among individuals with the same AFQT score, differences in schooling lead to differences in economic success. These findings imply that Herrnstein and Murray's failure to control for schooling leads them to overstate the effect of intelligence on social and economic success.[46]

Nor do our model and estimates support Fischer and coauthors' claim that AFQT score is primarily a function of education.[47] While schooling does affect cognitive skills, the reverse is also true, with the effect of cognitive skills on schooling being somewhat larger. The analyses reported in table 3-3 indicate that the effect of early cognitive skills on AFQT score is 50 percent larger than the corresponding effect of schooling.

Ultimately, our model and its estimates characterize schooling, cognitive skills, and their effects on economic success as follows. Schooling and cognitive skills affect each other, and each has substantial independent and direct effects on economic success. However, it is also possible that schooling and cognitive skills could substantially reinforce each other's effect on economic success. The direct effect of each could be as much as doubled by this mutual reinforcement. Neither schooling nor cognitive skills is clearly dominant in determining economic success. Rather, their roles appear to be roughly symmetrical, both in reinforcing each other and in determining economic success.

45. Herrnstein and Murray (1994).
46. See also Heckman (1995); Hauser (1995); Korenman and Winship (forthcoming).
47. Fischer and others (1996).

Appendix 3A
The Calculation of Different Effects

The path model in figure 3-1 is equivalent to the following three equations:

(3A-1) $$E = Ca_1 + Fa_2 + e_1$$

(3A-2) $$C = Eb_1 + Fb_2 + e_2$$

(3A-3) $$S = Ec_1 + Cc_2 + Fc_3 + e_3,$$

where E is education or schooling, C is cognitive skills, F is family background, and S is economic success.

Consider the effect of an exogenous increase in education on economic success. An exogenous increase in education is equivalent to increasing e_1. To calculate the effect on S of changing e_1, we differentiate equation 3A-3 with respect to e_1:

(3A-4) $$\partial S/\partial e_1 = (\partial E/\partial e_1)c_1 + (\partial C/\partial e_1)c_2 .$$

From equation 3A-1,

(3A-5) $$\partial E/\partial e_1 = (\partial C/\partial e_1)a_1 + 1 .$$

We then ask what is the effect of increasing e_1 holding cognitive skills (C) constant—that is, we assume that $\partial C/\partial e_1 = 0$. From equations 3A-5, $\partial E/\partial e_1 = 1$, and substituting this into equation 3A-4,

(3A-6) $$\partial S/\partial e_1 = (\partial E/\partial e_1)c_1 = c_1 .$$

In the language of path analysis, this is the direct effect of education on success.

Now consider allowing education to affect success both directly and indirectly, through cognitive skills. From equation 3A-2,

(3A-7) $$\partial C/\partial e_1 = \partial E/\partial e_1 \, b_1 .$$

For the moment, we allow education to increase only by a fixed amount δe_1, that is, we allow no feedback; or equivalently, we set $\partial E/\partial e_1 = 1$. Substituting into equation 3A-7, we get $\partial C/\partial e_1 = b_1$. Further substituting into equation 3A-4,

(3A-8) $$\partial S/\partial e_1 = c_1 + c_2 \, b_1.$$

In the language of path analysis, this is the total effect. In our model, how-ever, there are additional effects due to the potential self-reinforcing effect of education through cognitive skills. In order to avoid confusion, we call the effect in equation 3A-8 the composite effect.

If we allow feedback, neither $\partial E/\partial e_1$ nor $\partial C/\partial e_1$ are fixed, and both need to be solved for from equations 3A-5 and 3A-7:

(3A-9) $\partial E/\partial e_1 = 1/(1 - a_1 b_1)$

(3A-10) $\partial C/\partial e_1 = b_1 (1 - a_1 b_1)$.

Substituting into equation 3A-4 and rearranging terms,

(3A-11) $\partial S/\partial e_1 = c_1 [1 + (a_1 b_1)/(1 - a_1 b_1)] +$
                    $c_2 b_1 [1 + (a_1 b_1)/(1 - a_1 b_1)]$.

Consider the components of equation 3A-11: c_1 is the direct effect of education on success, $c_2 b_1$ is the indirect effect of education on success through cognitive skills, and their sum is the composite effect. Finally, $1 + (a_1 b_1)/(1 - a_1 b_1)$ is the feedback multiplier, the amount by which an ini-tial exogenous increase in education leads to a further increase in educa-tion, due to its feedback through cognitive skill. We term the entire right-hand side of equation 3A-11 the overall effect of education on success.

Using an analogous derivation, one can break down the effect of cogni-tive skills on success, as follows:

c_2 Direct effect

$c_1 b_2$ Indirect effect through education

$c_2 + c_1 b_2$ Composite effect

$1 + (a_1 b_1)/(1 - a_1 b_1)$ Feedback multiplier

$c_1 b_2 [1 + (a_1 b_1)/(1 - a_1 b_1)] +$
    $c_2 [1 + (a_1 b_1)/(1 - a_1 b_1)]$ Overall effect.

References

Altonji, Joseph, and Thomas Dunn. 1995. "Estimating the Returns to Schooling by Social Class and School Quality." Working Paper 5072. Cambridge, Mass.: National Bureau of Economic Research.

Angrist, Joshua D., and Alan B. Krueger. 1991. "Does Compulsory Schooling Affect Schooling and Earnings?" *Quarterly Journal of Economics* 106(4): 979–1014.

Ashenfelter, Orley, and Alan B. Krueger. 1994. "Estimates of the Economic Return to Schooling from a New Sample of Twins." *American Economic Review* 84(5): 1157–73.

Ashenfelter, Orley, and Cecilia Rouse. Forthcoming. "Schooling, Intelligence, and Income in America: Cracks in the Bell Curve." In *Meritocracy and Society*, edited by Kenneth Arrow, Samuel Bowles, and Stephen Durlauf. Princeton University Press.

Ashenfelter, Orley, and David Zimmerman. 1993. "Estimates of the Return to Schooling from Sibling Data: Fathers, Sons, and Brothers." Working Paper 4491. Cambridge, Mass.: National Bureau of Economic Research.

Behrman, Jere R., Mark R. Rosenzweig, and Paul Taubman. 1994. "Endowments and the Allocation of Schooling in the Family and in the Marriage Market: The Twins Experiment." *Journal of Political Economy* 102(6): 1131–74.

Bock, R. Darrell, and Elise G. J. Moore. 1986. *Advantage and Disadvantage: A Profile of American Youth*. Hillsdale, N.J.: Erlbaum.

Brody, Nathan. 1992. *Intelligence*, 2d ed. San Diego, Calif.: Academic Press.

Butcher, Kristin F., and Anne Case. 1994. "The Effect of Sibling Sex Composition on Women's Education and Earnings." *Quarterly Journal of Economics* 109(3): 531–63.

Card, David. 1993. "Using Geographic Variation in College Proximity to Estimate the Return to Schooling." Working Paper 4483. Cambridge, Mass.: National Bureau of Economic Research.

Carroll, John B. 1992. "Cognitive Abilities: The State of the Art." *Psychological Science* 3(5): 266–70.

————. 1997. "Theoretical and Technical Issues in Identifying a Factor of General Intelligence." In *Intelligence, Genes, and Success: Scientists Respond to The Bell Curve*, edited by Bernie Devlin and others. New York. Springer-Verlag.

Cawley, John, and others. 1997. "Cognitive Ability, Wages, and Meritocracy." In *Intelligence, Genes, and Success: Scientists Respond to The Bell Curve*, edited by Bernie Devlin and others. New York. Springer-Verlag.

Ceci, Stephen. 1991."How Much Does Schooling Influence General Intelligence and Its Cognitive Components? A Reassessment of the Evidence." *Developmental Psychology* 27(5): 703–22.

Center for Human Resources Research. 1994. *NLS Handbook 1994*. Ohio State University.

Chamberlain, Gary, and Zvi Griliches. 1975. "Unobservables with Variance-Components Structure: Ability, Schooling and the Economic Success of Brothers." *International Economic Review* 16(June): 422–49.

————. 1977. "More on Brothers." In *Kinometrics: The Determinants of Socio-economic Success within and between Families*, edited by Paul Taubman. Amsterdam: North-Holland.

Corcoran, Jill. 1996. *Beyond The Bell Curve and G: Rethinking Ability and its Correlates*. B.A. thesis. Harvard University, Department of Sociology.

Corcoran, Mary, Christopher Jencks, and Michael Olneck. 1976. "The Effects of Family Background on Earnings." *American Economic Review* 66(May): 430–35.

Dickens, William, Thomas J. Kane, and Charles Schultze. Forthcoming. *Does the Bell Curve Ring True? A Reconsideration*. Brookings.

Duncan, Otis D. 1968. "Ability and Achievement." *Eugenics Quarterly* 15(March): 1–11.

Duncan, Otis D., David L. Featherman, and Beverly Duncan. 1972. *Socioeconomic Background and Achievement*. New York: Seminar Press.

Fischer, Claude S., and others. 1996. *Inequality by Design: Cracking The Bell Curve Myth*. Princeton University Press.

Gardner, Howard. 1983. *Frames of Mind: The Theory of Multiple Intelligences*. Basic Books.

Gordon, Robert A. 1976. "Prevalence: The Rate Datum in Delinquency Measurement and Its Implications for a Theory of Delinquency." In *The Juvenile Justice System*, edited by Matthew Klein. Newbury Park, Calif.: Sage Publications, 201–84.

————. 1980. "Labeling Theory, Mental Retardation, and Public Policy: *Larry P.* and Other Developments Since 1974." In *The Labeling of Deviance: Evaluating a Perspective*, edited by Walter R. Grove. Newbury Park, Calif.: Sage Publications, 175–224.

Gottfredson, Linda S. 1986. "Societal Consequences of the *g* Factor in Employment." *Journal of Vocational Behavior* 29(3): 379–410.

Green, Robert Lee, and others. 1964. *The Educational Status of Children in a District without Public Schools*. Co-operative Research Project 2321. U.S. Department of Health, Education, and Welfare, Office of Education.

Griliches, Zvi. 1979. "Sibling Models and Data in Economics: Beginnings of a Survey." *Journal of Political Economy* 87(5, pt. 1): S37–S64.

Hartigan, John A., and Alexandra K. Wigdor, eds. 1989. *Fairness in Employment Testing*. Washington: National Academy Press.

Hauser, Robert M. 1995. "Review of *The Bell Curve*." *Contemporary Sociology* 24(March): 149–53.

Hauser, Robert M., and Thomas N. Daymont. 1977. "Schooling, Ability, and Earnings: Cross-Sectional Findings Eight to Fourteen Years after High School Graduation." *Sociology of Education* 50: 182–206.

Heckman, James J. 1995. "Cracked Bell—*The Bell Curve: Intelligence and Class Structure in American Life* by Richard Herrnstein and Charles Murray." *Reason* 26(10): 49–56.

Herrnstein, Richard J., and Charles Murray. 1994. *The Bell Curve: Intelligence and Class Structure in American Life*. Free Press.

Hunt, Earl. 1997. "The Concept and Utility of Intelligence." In *Intelligence, Genes, and Success: Scientists Respond to The Bell Curve*, edited by Bernie Devlin and others. New York: Springer-Verlag.

Jencks, Christopher, and others. 1972. *Inequality: A Reassessment of the Effects of Family and Schooling in America*. Basic Books.

Jencks, Christopher, and others. 1979. *Who Gets Ahead? The Determinants of Economic Success in America*. Basic Books.

Kaestner, Robert. 1997. "Are Brothers Really Better? Sibling Sex Composition and Educational Achievement Revisited. *Journal of Human Resources*.32(2): 250–84.

Korenman, Sanders D., and Christopher Winship. Forthcoming. "A Reanalysis of *The Bell Curve*: Intelligence, Family Background, and Schooling" In *Meritocracy and Society*, edited by Kenneth Arrow, Samuel Bowles, and Stephen Durlauf. Princeton University Press.

Lillard, Lee A., and M. Rebecca Kilburn. 1997. "Simultaneity of Ability and Education: Family Fixed Effect Estimates." Unpublished paper. Rand Corporation.

Miller, Paul, Charles Mulvey, and Nick Martin. 1995. "What Do Twins Studies Reveal about the Economic Returns to Education? A Comparison of Australian and U.S. Findings." *American Economic Review* 85(3): 586–99.

Sewell, William H., and Robert M. Hauser. 1975. *Education, Occupation and Earnings.* New York. Academic Press.

Sternberg, Robert J. 1985. *Beyond IQ: A Triarchic Theory of Intelligence.* Cambridge University Press.

————. 1990. *Metaphors of the Mind: Conceptions of the Nature of Intelligence.* Cambridge University Press.

Winship, Christopher, and Sanders D. Korenman. 1997. "Does Staying in School Make You Smarter? The Effect of Education and IQ in *The Bell Curve.*" In *Intelligence, Genes, and Success: Scientists Respond to The Bell Curve*, edited by Bernie Devlin and others. New York: Springer-Verlag.

SUSAN E. MAYER
DAVID KNUTSON

4

Does the Timing
of School Affect
How Much Children Learn?

A LL STATES IN THE United States have compulsory school laws that
specify both the age at which children are required to enroll in first
grade and the age at which they are permitted to leave school. Between
1965 and 1990, states increased the number of required years of school.
They did this both by lowering the age at which children were required to
enroll in first grade and raising the age at which children were permitted to
quit school. While most educators and social scientists agree that it is a
good idea for students to stay in school longer, not all agree that they
should start earlier, and there remains considerable variation across states in
the age at which children are required to enroll.

In this chapter we show that children who enroll in first grade at a
young age learn more in school and eventually earn more in the labor market than children who enroll in school at an older age. Early enrollment in
first grade increases eventual wages partly because children who enroll earlier stay in school longer, and partly because children who enroll earlier

We would like to thank the Russell Sage Foundation and the Rockefeller Foundation for financial assistance. We also thank Christopher Jencks, Robert Hauser, and participants in the Harris School
Faculty Workshop at the University of Chicago, the Conference on Meritocracy and Inequality at
Harvard University in September 1996, and the Institute for Research on Poverty's Summer Workshop
in 1997 for helpful suggestions.

learn more even when they have the same amount of schooling as children who enrolled when they were older. Compulsory school laws provide a source of variation in enrollment age that is not associated with characteristics of parents or characteristics of children other than their birthdate. This allows one to compare children who are identical in all ways other than the age at which they started school.

Background

Compulsory school laws are important policy instruments. They have a large effect on when children go to school and how much schooling they get. They are also relatively easy to change. Table 4-1 shows that since 1965, states have increased the number of years of compulsory education and lowered the ages at which children are required to enroll in first grade. In 1965 forty-two states required children to enroll at age seven or older. By 1992, only twenty-five states allowed children to enroll when they were this old. But since the late 1970s, many states have in effect raised the compulsory enrollment age, by moving the date by which children must turn the compulsory age to earlier in the year. For example, until 1985 Virginia law required children who were five by December 1 to enroll in first grade in the previous September. In 1985 the law was changed, so that it eventually required children who were five by September 30 to enroll during that month. That is, prior to the change, children were required to enroll in first grade by the time they were four years and eight months old; once the change was fully implemented, they were not required to enroll until they were four years and eleven months old. Such changes in states' compulsory school laws reflect the ambivalence among policymakers about the appropriate age for school enrollment.

Some cognitive theories suggest that, on average, children are more malleable and receptive to learning when they are young than when they are older, either because of the way the brain develops or because of social influences. This model implies that, on average, children might learn more if they attended school between the ages of, say, five and fifteen than if they attended between the ages of six and sixteen. Other cognitive theories hold that children cannot learn complex material until they are older. [1] Trying to teach these materials too soon is therefore inefficient or even harmful. Thus

1. See Meisels (1992).

Table 4-1. *Number of States with Selected Compulsory School Rules, 1965 and 1992*

	Number of states in	
Rule	1965[a]	1992
Years of school required		
8	3	0
9	34	18
10	7	19
11	3	5
12	2	6
13	0	2
Required enrollment age		
5	0	7
6	7	18
7	38	23
8	4	2
Age permitted to drop out		
16	37	33
17	7	9
18	3	9

Source: Data for 1965 are from U.S. Department of Health, Education, and Welfare (1965); for 1992–93, from Education Commission of the States (1994).

a. In 1965 neither Mississippi nor South Carolina had laws about the ages at which children were required to enroll or permitted to drop out; but in both states the legal minimum age for entering school was six years.

children, on average, might learn more in school, and therefore earn more as adults, if they attend school between the ages of six and sixteen than if they attend between the ages of five and fifteen.

These views are not mutually exclusive: children might learn more if they are exposed to formal schooling at age six than at age seven, but not at age four rather than age five. The data that we use in this paper are most useful for estimating the potential benefit to children from enrolling at the earliest age that is customary in the United States, five years old, rather than at the age that is most common (six) or the most common older age (seven). Our results cannot say much about the effect of beginning school before the age of five. Nor do they address the value of kindergarten or preschool. Kindergarten and preschool are generally not much like first grade: they emphasize different skills, usually last fewer hours per day, and often have fewer requirements for teacher training.

Because schooling is very expensive, changes that make it more efficient or less costly can save a lot of money. Thus if children who begin school at age five learn more than children who get the same amount of schooling but begin at age seven, reducing the compulsory school age might be a good idea. In addition, the opportunity costs of educating young children may be less than the opportunity costs of educating older children. Eighteen-year-olds can enter the labor force; when they are in school, they forgo wages. When five-year-olds are in school, not only do they not forgo wages, but their parents can enter the labor force at a lower cost than if they had to pay for child care.

Understanding whether or not the timing of schooling affects children's life chances is not only important to school policies. It also helps to shed light on questions about the malleability of cognitive skills. If both the timing and the length of schooling influence children's test scores, there is less credibility to the argument that children's cognitive skills are largely the result of genetic or very early childhood influences that cannot be changed.

The age at which children enroll in school can affect their economic outcomes as adults in two ways. First, because compulsory school laws require children to stay in school until a certain age, children who enroll in school at a young age are required to get more schooling than those who enroll when they are older. Some studies use the differences in length of schooling induced by compulsory school laws to estimate the effect of additional schooling on earnings.[2] This research, together with a large body of other research, suggests that additional schooling increases earnings.[3]

Other studies use differences in enrollment age induced by compulsory school laws to estimate the effect of additional schooling on cognitive skills.[4] When researchers give a cognitive test to a group of children who are the same age, those who enrolled in school at a young age will have had more schooling at the time of the test than those who enrolled when they

2. See Angrist and Krueger (1991, 1992); Bound, Jaeger, and Baker (1995); Bound and Jaeger (1996).

3. For summaries of much of this research, see Ceci (1991); Ceci and Williams (1997); Winship and Korenman (1997). See also Jencks and Phillips in chapter 2 and Winship and Korenman in chapter 3 above.

4. See Baltes and Reinert (1969); Cahan and Cohen (1989); Proctor, Black, and Feldhusen (1986).

were older. These studies find that additional schooling increases cognitive test scores. A lot of research shows that higher cognitive skills are associated with higher wages. Therefore studies that show that early enrollment in first grade affects cognitive test scores suggest one important mechanism through which more schooling increases wages.

Children who enter school at a young age are also exposed to formal learning at a young age. If children learn more when they are exposed to learning at an early age, children who enroll in school earlier will get higher test scores than children with the same amount of schooling who enrolled later. We know of no previous research that tries to estimate whether the age at which children are exposed to schooling affects their adult labor market outcomes. If early exposure to learning increases cognitive skills, it could also increase wages. A few studies look at the effect of enrollment age on children who are tested on the same day, rather than at the same age.[5] Put another way, they compare children who entered school at different ages but who have the same amount of schooling at the time of the test. These studies generally find that young enrollees score no lower and they sometimes score higher than older enrollees. This suggests that the age at which children are exposed to schooling affects their test scores. But most of these studies compare children whose parents were allowed to enroll them before the normal enrollment age with children who enrolled at the normal enrollment age. If the characteristics of parents or children that affect enrollment age also affect test scores, these results will be biased.[6]

In this chapter we follow previous research on the length of schooling in using the variation in enrollment age induced by different states' compulsory school laws to estimate the effect of early exposure to schooling on the earnings of adult men.[7] To explain this effect, we then estimate the effect of early exposure to schooling on children's cognitive test scores.

The Effect of Age of Enrollment on Wages

In principle one could estimate the effect of enrollment age on adult wages simply by comparing the wages of people who had enrolled in school at

5. See Proctor, Black, and Feldhusen (1986); Uphoff and Gilmore (1985).

6. See Mayer and Knutson (1998) for a review of the literature on this issue.

7. We confine ourselves to the effect of enrollment age on men's wages. Women's wages are much more strongly influenced by decisions about marriage and fertility than are men's wages, and we wish to estimate the effect of early schooling on economic productivity alone.

different ages. However, parents have some discretion about when they enroll their children in first grade. This is mainly because states set both an age at which children are required to enroll in school and a lower age at which they are permitted to enroll. For example, most states require children to enroll in first grade when they are seven years old, but permit them to enroll when they are six years old. The parental characteristics that cause some parents to enroll their children in school at the permitted age rather than the required age may also affect their child's future wages. Unless one controls all such characteristics, the estimated effect of enrollment age will be biased. For example, parents who place a very high value on schooling may enroll their children at the permitted rather than the required age. These same parents may encourage and help their children with school work. If both early enrollment and parental values affect children's test scores, and one estimates the effect of enrollment age omitting the effect of parental values, some of the benefit that one attributes to earlier schooling will really be due to parental values.

One way to overcome this problem is to take advantage of the fact that state compulsory school laws not only require children to enroll at a particular age, but also specify a cut-off date for enrollment, by which time children must have reached that required age. A child whose birthday falls just before the cut-off date will be nearly a year older when he or she enrolls in school than a child whose birthday falls just after the cut-off date. For example, in a state with a compulsory enrollment age of seven and a cut-off date of September 1, a child whose birthday is in August and who enrolls at the compulsory age will be just seven years old when he enrolls. A child whose birthday is in October, however, will enroll at the age of seven years and eleven months. If some parents decide to enroll their children at the permitted rather the required age, the cut-off date will still provide a source of variation in enrollment age that is unrelated to parental or child characteristics, other than the child's birth date. If birth dates are random, the variation in enrollment age introduced by compulsory school laws allows one to obtain an unbiased estimate of the effect of enrollment age on children's outcomes.

For much of our analysis in this section, we follow the strategy used by Joshua Angrist and Alan Krueger to estimate the wage returns to a year of schooling.[8] The data, variables, and models that we use are described in appendix 4A.

8. Angrist and Krueger (1991, 1992).

Table 4-2. *Estimated Enrollment Ages for Boys Born 1950–52,*
by Enrollment Cut-Off Date
Years

Birth	State cut-off date		
quarter	September	January	All states
January–March	6.63	6.48	6.54
April–June	6.43	6.30	6.36
July–September	6.27	6.10	6.17
October–December	6.35	6.02	6.17

Source: Authors' calculations based on data from the 1960 decennial census, 1 percent sample.

We first use 1960 census data to estimate the age at which boys born in
1950, 1951, and 1952 enrolled in first grade. Table 4-2 shows that different cut-off dates induce different patterns of enrollment ages. In 1960 in
states with a September cut-off date, boys who were born in the third quarter enrolled at the youngest age. In states with a January cut-off, boys born
in the fourth quarter enrolled at the youngest age. Among all boys born in
1950–52, those born in the third and fourth quarters have about the same
average enrollment age, and boys born in the first quarter enrolled 0.37
year earlier than boys born in the fourth quarter.

If enrolling in school at a young age increases earnings, boys born in the
first quarter should have higher earnings when they become adults than
boys born in other quarters. To test this hypothesis, we use 1980 census
data on wages for men aged between twenty-eight and thirty-four; that is,
born between 1946 and 1952.[9] Table 4-3 shows that in 1980 the weekly
earnings for men born in 1946-52 averaged $6.67 less for those born in the
first quarter than for those born in the fourth quarter (in 1994 dollars).
Since boys born in the fourth quarter began school 0.37 year earlier than
boys born in the fourth quarter, this suggests that beginning school a whole
year earlier results in an additional $17.90 per week in earnings. Mean

9. We did not include men born between 1946 and 1949 in the estimates shown in table 4-2
because as children get older, they are more likely to have been held back a grade or promoted early. If
children's probability of being held back varies by birth quarter, this could cause errors in the estimated
differences in enrollment age over birth quarters. As it turns out, grade retention hardly varies by birth
quarter.

Table 4-3. *Effect of Birth Quarter on 1980 Wages of Men Born 1946–52, by Educational Attainment*[a]

Units as indicated

Birth quarter	All men	High school graduate only
January–March	−6.67	−3.77
	(0.708)	(1.49)
April–June	−1.96	−4.78
	(0.709)	(1.49)
July–September	2.80	0.55
	(0.687)	(1.49)
Summary statistic		
Mean wage	669.47	634.93
Number of cases	397,474	142,485

Source: Authors' regressions using ordinary least squares (OLS), based on data from the 1980 decennial census, 5 percent sample.

a. Wages are in 1994 dollars. Standard errors are in parentheses.

weekly earnings were $669.47, so this is a difference of 2.7 percent. For reasons described in appendix 4A, however, these estimates are likely to be somewhat low.

Earnings are higher for men born in the third quarter than for men born in the fourth quarter, even though there is almost no difference in their estimated enrollment age. The difference is small (equivalent to 0.4 percent of earnings) and is not robust to slight variations in the model specification or sample.[10] We therefore conclude that the apparent wage difference between men born in the third and fourth quarters is not likely to reflect a true difference.

These estimates assume that the relationship between earnings and birth quarter is due to compulsory schooling rules that make children born in different quarters differ in age of enrollment, rather than to characteristics

10. For example, our sample here excludes workers with allocated values for any variable, as well as workers with no education. When we include such workers and use their allocated values, wages appear to be the same for workers born in the third and fourth quarters. The difference between workers born in the fourth and first quarters remains large and statistically significant.

of parents or children that affect both when children enroll and their eventual earnings. John Bound, David Jaeger, and Regina Baker argue that the effect of birth quarter on earnings is likely to be biased because birth quarter is correlated with school attendance rates, behavioral difficulties, referral for mental health services, cognitive test scores, schizophrenia, mental retardation, and manic depression.[11] However, many of these outcomes are likely to be the result of age at school entry, not its cause. In addition, the association between birth quarter and these outcomes follows no consistent pattern: for some outcomes being born at the beginning of the year is a benefit, while for others it is a liability.[12] In fact, different studies looking at the same outcome sometimes find different patterns over birth quarters. Although we cannot prove that birth quarter is uncorrelated with parental or child characteristics that affect children's eventual wages, we find no evidence of such a relationship.[13]

Moreover, Bound and Jaeger argue that the variation in earnings over birth quarters holds for cohorts of men born before compulsory school laws were passed, and consequently, that this variation cannot be the result of such laws.[14] But they have no information on the enrollment ages of men born before compulsory school laws were enacted. It is very likely that compulsory school laws in fact encoded preexisting norms about enrollment ages. For example, it is probable that even before compulsory school laws, it was the norm for children who were seven or eight by September to enroll in that year.

If the age at which children are exposed to schooling affects their future earnings, one should be able to specify why this happens. Angrist and

11. Bound, Jaeger, and Baker (1995).

12. Children born in the autumn have more school absences (Carroll, 1992). Children with autism are more likely to be born in March (Gilberg, 1990), but children with dyslexia are more likely to be born in the summer (Livingston, Adam, and Bracha, 1993). Some studies find that children born in the winter are more likely to be diagnosed with schizophrenia as adults (Bradbury and Miller, 1985; Boyd, Pulver, and Stewart, 1986; O'Callaghan and others, 1991). Two studies find that learning disabilities are more frequent among children born in the third quarter of the year (see Whorton and Karnes, 1981), but there is conflicting evidence about the effect of season of birth on measured intelligence (Orme, 1979; Williams and others, 1970).

13. Bound and Jaeger (1996) find that in the 1980 census, family income was lower for very young children born in the first quarter of the year than for other children. However, the crucial question for our analysis is whether parental income varies by quarter for children in the 1960 census. The 1960 census data show that for children born between 1950 and 1952, none of the following factors varies much by child's birth quarter: education, race, or age of household head; household income; marital status of parents; or number of household members (all chi-squared tests are less than 0.10).

14. Bound and Jaeger (1996).

Krueger, among others, argue that the effect of enrollment age can be entirely attributed to the fact that compulsory school laws require children who enroll in school at a young age to stay in high school longer than children who enroll when they are older.[15] Put another way, children who enroll earlier get more schooling, and more schooling increases earnings. If this is true, birth quarter should have no effect on the earnings of adults who have the same amount of schooling. But table 4-3 shows that among men who graduated high school but got no additional schooling (and therefore have the same amount of schooling), those born in the first quarter earn less than those born in the fourth quarter. This suggests that the effect of birth quarter is not entirely explained by length of schooling. One possible explanation is that boys who are exposed to schooling at a young age learn more than boys exposed to schooling at an older age, and as a consequence of this they earn higher wages.

The Effect of Enrollment Age on Cognitive Test Scores

We use data from the National Longitudinal Survey of Youth mother-child files (CNLSY) for 1986 to 1992 to assess the effect of early enrollment on children's cognitive test scores and behavior problems. These data, the variables, and the models that we use in this section are described in appendix 4B.

The CNLSY includes several measures of cognitive skills. Of these, we use the Peabody Individual Achievement Test (PIAT) measures of math achievement (PIAT-math) and reading recognition (PIAT-read), because scores on these tests are available for a large number of children. The PIAT has been extensively validated.[16] We also use the Behavior Problems Index (BPI), which includes ten items reported by mothers. A higher score indicates more behavioral problems. We use raw scores for all assessments.

We focus on children who are approximately between the ages of eight and eleven at the time of interview. We select this age group because eight-year-olds are over the compulsory school enrollment age in all states, and because in the 1992 CNLSY children older than eleven years were born to unusually young mothers and are therefore unrepresentative of their age group. We calculate the age at which each child enrolled in school from information on the child's chronological age and school grade (see appen-

15. Angrist and Krueger (1991).
16. Baker and Mott (1989).

Table 4-4. *Effect of Enrollment Age on Test Scores and Behavioral Problems of Eight- to Eleven-Year-Olds in the CNLSY*

Test	Regression coefficients[a]		Summary statistic	
	No controls	Controls family background[b]	Mean[c]	Number of cases
PIAT-Math	−5.867	−4.840	42.96	2,206
	(0.306)	(0.293)	(9.39)	
PIAT-Read	−7.924	−6.665	46.32	2,201
	(0.382)	(0.370)	(11.83)	
Behavior Problems	0.858	0.438	10.29	2,133
Index	(0.212)	(0.215)	(5.93)	

Source: Authors' calculations based on the National Longitudinal Survey of Youth mother-child files, 1986–92.

a. Unstandardized coefficients estimated from an OLS regression of raw test scores on age. Standard errors are in parentheses.

b. Family background characteristics include family income average over previous five years, family size, mother's highest grade of completed schooling, mother's score on the AFQT, mother's marital status, and mother's race.

c. Standard deviations are in parentheses.

dix 4A). Our calculations will be incorrect for children who are held back a grade and children who skip a grade. Errors in measuring enrollment age are likely to produce downwardly biased estimates of its effect on test scores.

We begin by regressing test scores on enrollment age. Our results are reported in table 4-4. The first column in this table shows that children who begin first grade at an early age have higher test scores and fewer behavioral problems than children who begin at a later age. These effects are large. For example, our results suggest that starting school one year later reduces a child's PIAT-read scores by 7.9 points (0.670 standard deviations).

As noted above, however, the parental characteristics that cause some parents to enroll their children in school at a young age may also affect their children's test scores and behavioral problems. The second column in table 4-4 controls a set of observed family background characteristics likely to be correlated with a child's enrollment age and test scores. These include family income averaged over the previous five years, family size, highest grade of school completed by mother, mother's score on the Armed Forces

Table 4-5. *Estimated Enrollment Ages for Six- to Eight-Year-Olds in the CNLSY, by Birth Quarter*

Birth quarter	Enrollment age
January–March	6.51
April–June	6.33
July–September	6.20
October–December	6.40

Source: Authors' calculations based on the National Longitudinal Survey of Youth mother-child files, 1986–92.

Qualification Test, mother's race, and mother's marital status. Controlling these factors reduces the apparent effect of enrollment age on test scores and behavior problems. Unobserved family background characteristics could account for even more of the effect. To overcome this problem, we follow the same strategy as for men's wages, which is to use birth quarter as a proxy for enrollment age.

Table 4-5 shows enrollment age by birth quarter for children in the CNLSY aged between six and eight years old.[17] As noted above, many states have moved their cut-off dates for first-grade enrollment from the end of the fourth quarter to September 1.[18] That is why in the CNLSY sample children born in the third quarter have the lowest enrollment age, whereas in the 1960 census data children born in the fourth quarter have the lowest enrollment age. Table 4-5 shows that children born in the first quarter started school an average of 0.31 year later than children born in the third quarter.

Table 4-6 shows the effect of birth quarter on test scores. To take account of the fact that children born in the first quarter are older, and therefore possibly more developmentally advanced, than children born in

17. We show enrollment ages for children aged six to eight rather than for the sample of eight- to eleven-year-olds that we use for most of our analyses because older children are more likely to have been held back a grade or skipped a grade. Such grade changes will cause errors in our estimates of the difference in enrollment ages over birth quarters.

18. Between 1965 and 1978, the following states moved their cutoff date from the fourth quarter to September: California, Kentucky, Mississippi, Nevada, New York, Pennsylvania, Tennessee, and Vermont. And the following states moved from a September cutoff to a cutoff in the fourth quarter: Connecticut, Maryland, Michigan, Rhode Island, and South Carolina.

Table 4-6. *Effect of Birth Quarter on Raw Test Scores for Eight- to Eleven-Year-Olds in the CNLSY*[a]

Model and birth quarter	PIAT-read	PIAT-math	Behavior Problems Index[b]
		Test	
No controls			
January–March	–1.758	–1.092	–0.836
	(0.699)	(0.537)	(0.373)
April–June	–1.337	–0.713	0.346
	(0.703)	(0.541)	(0.373)
October–December	–1.020	–0.487	–0.683
	(0.659)	(0.509)	(0.353)
Controlling family background[c]			
January–March	–1.841	–1.113	–0.770
	(0.639)	(0.483)	(0.367)
April–June	–1.023	–0.345	0.285
	(0.663)	(0.458)	(0.347)
October–December	–1.324	–0.623	–0.593
	(0.643)	(0.488)	(0.367)
Summary statistic			
Mean	46.32	42.96	10.29
Standard deviation	11.83	9.39	5.93
Number of cases	2,202	2,207	2,134

Source: Authors' calculations based on the National Longitudinal Survey of Youth mother-child files, 1986–92.

a. The estimation equation is

$$T_i = b_0 + \Sigma b_1 \, Q_j + b_2 \, A_i \, ,$$

where, for child i, T is raw test score, Q is birth quarter, and A is age in months on the test date. Standard errors are in parentheses.

b. Estimates also control child's sex.

c. See table 4-4, note b.

other quarters, we control the age in months at the time when a child took the test. If this measure of children's age does not fully account for the effects of development on test scores, the model will understate any benefit associated with a third-quarter birth.

Children between eight and eleven years old and born in the first quarter score lower on both PIAT assessments than children born in the third quarter who took the tests at the same age. Because children born in the first quarter were an average of 0.31 year older when they enrolled in first grade than children born in the third quarter, these results imply that starting school a year earlier results in an additional 4.75 raw test score points (0.403 standard deviation) on the PIAT reading test and an additional 2.45 points (0.261 standard deviation) on the PIAT math test. Children born in the third quarter also have fewer behavioral problems than those born in the first quarter. Children born in the second and fourth quarters also score lower than children born in the third quarter on these assessments, but none of these coefficients is statistically significant at conventional levels.

Table 4-6 also shows that controlling the observed family background characteristics described above hardly changes the effect of being born in the first rather than the third quarter for any assessment. This increases confidence that birth quarter is an exogenous source of variation in enrollment age. In addition, the effect of enrolling a year earlier estimated using birth quarter is roughly comparable to the estimates in table 4-4 that control family background characteristics. If birth quarter is a random source of variation in enrollment age, this suggests that the measured family background characteristics in table 4-4 account for most of the systematic differences among children who enroll at different ages.[19]

Because older children average higher test scores than younger children, these models control a child's age at the time of the test. When children who are all the same age take a test, those who enrolled earlier will have had more schooling. The effect of enrollment age in table 4-6 could be due to the amount of schooling a child has had or to the age at which the child was first exposed to schooling. Therefore to find out whether early exposure to schooling affects test scores, one needs to control how much schooling a child has had. We estimate a model that controls length of schooling. As we discuss in appendix 4B, this procedure introduces new problems that are likely to yield estimates that are somewhat too low. But since most people seem to assume that the effect of early exposure to learning (as opposed to length of schooling) is zero, even a downwardly biased estimate is useful.

Table 4-7 shows the effect of enrollment age on test scores, controlling the amount of schooling that a child has had at the time of the test. These results suggest that early exposure to schooling raises test scores and reduces

19. See Mayer and Knutson (1998) for a more detailed analysis of the omitted variables problem.

Table 4-7. *Effect of Enrolling One Year Later on Test Scores, Controlling Amount of Schooling, for Eight- to Eleven-Year-Olds in the CNLSY*[a]

Test	No controls	Controls family background[b]
PIAT-math	−1.632	−0.555
	(0.339)	(0.317)
PIAT-read	−3.512	−2.176
	(0.439)	(0.417)
Behavior Problems Index	0.699	0.319
	(0.257)	(0.258)

Source: Authors' calculations based on the National Longitudinal Survey of Youth mother-child files, 1986–92.

a. Estimates are from an equation that regresses raw test scores on length of time spent in school and enrollment age. Standard errors are in parentheses.

b. See table 4-4, note b.

behavioral problems even among children with the same amount of schooling. The second column in the table shows that controlling family background characteristics reduces the benefit of early exposure to schooling on both PIAT assessments and on the Behavioral Problems Index. A comparison of these results with those in table 4-4 suggests that much of the observed effect of early enrollment on test scores is due to the fact that children who enroll at an early age have had more schooling when they are tested than children who enroll at a later age. But the age of first exposure to schooling has an important positive effect on reading scores.

The Persistence of the Early Enrollment Effect

The models that we have estimated so far assume that the effect of early exposure to schooling is constant throughout elementary school. Studies suggest that children who have attended model preschools have higher test scores when they enter elementary school than similar children who have not attended preschool, but that these benefits fade by the time children are in third or fourth grade.[20] The gains from early exposure to elementary school could also fade as children are exposed to similar learning opportunities over time. However, if children who are exposed to schooling at an

20. See Berrueta-Clement and others (1985); Haskins (1989); Currie and Thomas (1995).

early age learn more in the early grades, this could make learning easier in the future. If this were the case, the effect of early exposure to schooling could increase over time.

When we estimate a model of changes in the effect of early exposure to schooling over time, we find that the effect of early enrollment on BPI scores stays about the same through fourth grade. But the effect of early enrollment on PIAT scores declines somewhat over time.[21] After two years of schooling, children who enrolled at age five score 4.185 raw test score points higher on the PIAT-math and 7.7 points higher on the PIAT-read than children who enrolled at age seven. After four years of schooling the difference in PIAT-math scores disappears and the difference on the PIAT-read declines to 4 points. Since four raw test score points represents one-third of a standard deviation, this suggests that early exposure to schooling has a large effect on reading recognition even after four years of schooling.

If the effect of early enrollment on test scores fades completely by the time children reach high school, that would undermine the argument that early exposure to schooling affects wages through cognitive skills. We use the data from the High School and Beyond (HS&B) survey of high school sophomores in 1980 to assess the likely effect of enrollment age on achievement in high school. We estimate the effect of students' ages on their test scores during tenth grade. Once we control the number of times a student reports having been held back a grade, we presume that older tenth graders enrolled in first grade at an later age than younger tenth graders. We find that older tenth graders score lower than younger tenth graders on math, vocabulary, and reading tests.

Unfortunately, the HS&B survey does not include good measures of family background, but when we control student's race, parental income and education as reported by the student, and a measure of parental marital status, older tenth graders still score lower than younger tenth graders. These results suggest that once we control observed family background characteristics and the number of times a child repeated a grade, starting school a year later reduces vocabulary test scores by one-quarter of a standard deviation and reading scores by 0.220 standard deviation. Likewise, our results using CNLSY data suggest that being exposed to schooling a year earlier results in a 0.234 standard deviation increase in PIAT-read scores at the end of elementary school. The HS&B data show that being exposed to school a year earlier increases math scores by 0.280 standard

21. These results are reported in Mayer and Knutson (1998).

deviation, whereas the CNLSY results suggest that the gains on the PIAT-math from early exposure to schooling fade by the fourth grade. This difference may be due to differences in the tests, our inability to control family background adequately, or other factors.

Early exposure to schooling rather than length of schooling could explain some of the effect of enrollment age on wages even if the effect on cognitive skills fades. A consistent finding of research on the effect of preschool on children's outcomes is that while the increase in cognitive test scores from attending preschool fades within a few years, the benefit in terms of social behaviors associated with adult economic success remains. Children who attend preschool are less likely to drop out of high school, less likely to become teenage parents, and less likely to commit crimes than similar children who have not attended preschool.[22]

Wages and Cognitive Skills

Because of compulsory school laws, the age at which children enroll in first grade varies by the calendar quarter in which they were born. Thus we argue that birth quarter is a proxy for age at enrollment in school. Using birth quarters, we show that children who enroll in school at a young age score higher on tests of cognitive skill. We also show that adult wages are higher for men who enrolled in school at a young age than for men who enrolled when they were older.

Our results also show that starting school a year earlier is associated with a 2.7 percent increase in weekly wages for all men and a 1.5 percent increase in wages for men who graduate high school but get no more schooling. Thus about half the effect of starting school at a younger age is accounted for by the fact that children who enroll at younger ages get more schooling. We interpret the other half as the effect of early exposure to learning.

Our results from the HS&B suggest that starting school a year earlier is associated with a gain of about one-fifth of a standard deviation on both reading and math scores for students with the same amount of schooling. The CNLSY results show a similar gain for reading scores but no gain for math scores after children have been in school for several years. If these

22. Berrueta-Clement and others (1985); Consortium for Longitudinal Studies (1983); Haskins (1989).

results are correct, one can conclude that a gain of one-fifth of a standard deviation in reading test scores results in 1.5 percent higher wages in adulthood. Put another way, holding education constant, a one standard deviation increase in test scores is associated with 7.5 percent higher weekly wages. As noted, our estimates are likely to be somewhat low because of our methodology. In chapter 3 above, Winship and Korenman estimate that a one standard deviation increase in test scores is associated with an additional 16.9 percent in wages for men with the same amount of schooling.

The wage benefit from beginning school a year earlier is relatively small: 1.5 percent for high school graduates. But having students start earlier would certainly not cost more than having them start later, and it could cost less, by reducing child care costs without increasing education costs. A policy that provides even a small gain, whether at a small cost or at a saving, is likely to be prudent. And starting school earlier may have additional benefits for children's behavior. While it is possible that starting school earlier could also have some harmful effects, we know of no evidence that suggests this is so.

Appendix 4A
Estimating the Effect of Enrollment Age on Wages

To estimate the effect of enrollment age on wages, we use data from the 1960 decennial census, 1 percent sample, and the 1980 census, 5 percent sample. Our 1980 sample includes native-born men not living in group quarters or currently enrolled in school, and with positive wages, some education, and no allocations on the variables we use.

Hourly wages are calculated by dividing annual earnings by the product of weeks worked last year and usual hours of work. Wages are trimmed by eliminating the top and bottom 1 percent of the distribution.

We calculate the age of child i at enrollment in first grade (a_i) as

(4A-1) $$a_i = (A_i - 2) - [(G_i - 1)*4],$$

where A_i is age measured in quarters of years on census day and G_i is the grade in which a student is currently enrolled. Children born prior to 1953 are above the compulsory age for enrollment in all states. We estimate enrollment age for children born after 1950 because as children progress through school some are held back and others skip a grade, and so equation 4A-1 will produce less accurate enrollment ages for older children than for children just beginning school.

Wages are lower for twenty-eight-year-olds than for thirty-four-year-olds, because older males have more labor market experience and are more likely to have completed their education. Time trends in wages and educational attainment could also affect these comparisons. To avoid confusing the effect of time and age with the effect of birth quarter, we follow Angrist and Krueger in using "detrended" wages. We create a moving average (*MA*), defined as the average wage of men born in the three preceding and three succeeding quarters. The moving average for men born in quarter j of year c is

$$(4A\text{-}2) \qquad MA_{cj} = \frac{(W_{-3} + W_{-2} + W_{-1} + W_{+1} + W_{+2} + W_{+3})}{6},$$

where W_q is the average wage of men in the cohorts born q quarters before or after the cohort cj.

To estimate the effect of quarter of birth on wages for person i in cohort c, we estimate

$$(4A\text{-}3) \qquad (W_{ic} - MA_{cj}) = \alpha + \Sigma\beta_j\, Q_{icj},$$

where MA is the detrended term for the wage variable and Q_{icj} is a variable indicating whether person i was born in quarter j.

The cohort born in 1948–52 is in a steep part of the age-earnings profile in 1980. Their wages will be low relative to their average lifetime wage. Men who only completed high school will have higher wages relative to their lifetime wages. If higher educational attainment results from earlier enrollment in school, the effect of early enrollment on wages will be downwardly biased in these models. In addition, older men have higher average wages than younger men, so men born in the first quarter of a year have higher average wages than men born in the fourth quarter. This, too, could result in downwardly biased estimates of the effect of birth quarter if one does not fully account for the age-wage profile. Finally, the moving average assumes that the relationship between age and wage is linear over eighteen-month periods. We have tested the sensitivity of our estimates to various other controls for the time trend in wages, but find that the results are qualitatively similar.

Angrist and Krueger focus on cohorts born in the 1920s and 1930s because men born in these cohorts were in a flat portion of the age-earnings profile in 1980. We prefer our younger cohort because we have actual census data on their enrollment ages by birth quarter. Angrist and Krueger must assume that the enrollment patterns observed in 1960 mirror the observed enrollment patterns of the 1920s and 1930s.

Bound and Jaeger estimate the effect of birth quarter on log weekly wages for men born in 1940–49, controlling a quadratic of age, and find that the difference in log wages between men born in the third and first quarters is 0.013. They report that they experimented with cubics and quartics but found no discernible effect on the estimated association between quarter of birth and earnings. When we experiment with trend terms, including a quadratic function of age in quarters and linear age in quarters, we find that none of these alternative specifications substantially alters the results reported here.

Appendix 4B
Estimating the Effects of Enrollment Age on Cognitive Skills

Our estimates of the effect of early exposure to schooling on cognitive skills rely on data from the National Longitudinal Survey of Youth mother-child files. The National Longitudinal Survey of Youth is a multistage, stratified, random sample of 12,686 individuals aged between fourteen and twenty-one in 1979. It oversamples black, Hispanic, and low-income youth. Beginning in 1986, women in the original sample who had since become mothers were assessed with the mother-child supplement to the survey, the CNLSY, and their children were given cognitive and other assessments. Interviews were completed in 1986, 1988, 1990, and 1992.

The 1986 data set includes 3,053 originally sampled women with a total of 5,236 children. The mother-child survey oversamples children born to young mothers. With each additional cohort, the children become more representative of all children. We weight the data by the child sampling weight, which is intended to compensate for oversampling. The weights are paired yearly with test scores, so that when we predict test score in 1986, we use the 1986 weight.[23]

Our CNLSY sample includes children tested in 1984 and born in 1973–76, and those tested in 1986 and born in 1975–78. Children are not

---

23. Baker and Mott (1989) provide extensive information on the reliability and validity of test scores. Chase-Lansdale and others (1991) describe many aspects of the NLSY mother-child files, including the 1986 data set.

Table 4B-1. *Summary Statistics for Variables Used in CNLSY Analysis*[a]

Variable	Mean	Standard deviation
PIAT-math	42.947	9.281
PIAT-read	46.316	11.705
Behavior Problems Index	9.822	6.166
Enrollment age	6.610	0.598
Length of schooling	3.432	0.998
Log family income	10.174	0.651
Family size	4.365	1.389
Mother's highest grade	11.836	1.813
Mother's AFQT score	36.323	24.623
Mother married	0.641	. . .
Black	0.221	. . .
Hispanic	0.088	. . .

Source: National Longitudinal Survey of Youth mother-child files, 1986–92.

a. Sample comprises eight- to eleven-year-olds with complete data on family background character-istics and at least one valid test score.

duplicated in the sample if they were tested more than once. Summary statistics for our CNLSY data are presented in table 4B-1.

To calculate the age of child i at enrollment in first grade (a_i), we estimate

(4B-1) $$a_i = (A_i - S) - [(G_i - 1)*12] ,$$

where A_i is age in months on the test date, S is the number of months between the previous September and the test date, and G_i is the grade in which the student is currently enrolled.

To estimate the effect of enrollment age on test scores (T_i), we first estimate[24]

(4B-2) $$T_i = b_0 + b_1 a_i + b_2 A_i + \epsilon_i .$$

We must control children's age (A_i) at the time of the test because older children score higher than younger children. Most research assumes that children's test scores are a function not only of age at the time of the test but also of initial ability and length of schooling (S_i). If age at enrollment

24. See Mayer and Knutson (1998) for a more detailed description of our model.

(a_i) is exogenously determined, we can ignore initial ability, since it will be randomly distributed over enrollment ages. Given $a_i = A_i - S_i$, equation 4B-1 becomes

$$(4B\text{-}3) \qquad\qquad T_i = b_0 + b_2 A_i - b_3 S_i + \epsilon_i .$$

This model ignores the possibility that the timing of schooling affects test scores. If timing is important, the correct model would be

$$(4B\text{-}4) \qquad\qquad T = b_0 + b_1 a_i + b_2 A_i - b_3 S_i + \epsilon_i ,$$

where b_1 indicates the effect of timing. But as this model cannot be estimated directly—because $a_i = A_i - S_i$, and hence the effect of a_i is $b_1 + b_2 - b_3$—most previous research ignores the potential effect of timing. If b_1 is not zero, estimates of b_2 or b_3 in equation 4B-3 will be biased by its omission. Since we do not know whether b_1 is positive or negative, we do not know the direction of this potential bias.

Previous research shows that both b_2 and b_3 are positive. Therefore we estimate the effect of the timing of schooling on test scores from

$$(4B\text{-}5) \qquad\qquad T_i = b_0 + b_1 a_i + b_3 S_i + \epsilon_i .$$

This produces an unbiased estimate of b_3 but a downwardly biased estimate of the effect of timing of schooling, because we omit the effect of A_i:

$$(4B\text{-}6) \qquad\qquad T = b_0 + (b_1 - b_2)a_i + b_3 S_i + \epsilon_i .$$

In addition, we estimate the extent to which early gains in test scores due to early exposure to schooling persist through elementary school by using a model with interactions for S_i and a_i.

We use data from the High School and Beyond Survey to see whether sophomores' scores on that survey's test of math, reading and vocabulary skills vary by birth quarter. We first estimate

$$(4B\text{-}7) \qquad\qquad T = b_0 + b_1 A_i ,$$

where A_i is age in years and months on January 1, 1980. Because the sample is comprised entirely of high school sophomores, A_i is equal to enrollment age, assuming that no one was held back or promoted early. We then reestimate this model, controlling the number of times a child reported being held back and a set of family background characteristics.

References

Angrist, Joshua, and Alan Krueger. 1991. "Does Compulsory School Attendance Affect Schooling and Earnings?" *Quarterly Journal of Economics* 106(4): 979–1014.

——. 1992. "The Effect of Age at School Entry on Educational Attainment: An Application of Instrumental Variables with Moments from Two Samples." *Journal of the American Statistical Association* 87(418): 328–36.

Baker, P. C., and F. L. Mott. 1989. *CNLSY Child Handbook*. Ohio State University, Center for Human Resources Research.

Baltes, Paul, and Guenther Reinert. 1969. "Cohort Effects in Cognitive Development in Children as Revealed by Cross-Sectional Sequences." *Developmental Psychology* 1(2): 169–77.

Berrueta-Clement, John R., and others. 1985. "Changed Lives: The Effect of the Perry Preschool Program on Youths through Age 19." Ypsilanti, Mich.: High/Scope.

Bound, John, and David Jaeger. 1996. "On the Validity of Season of Birth as an Instrument in Wage Equations: A Comment on Angrist and Krueger's 'Does Compulsory School Attendance Affect Schooling and Earnings?'" Unpublished paper. University of Michigan.

Bound, John, David Jaeger, and Regina Baker. 1995. "Problems with Instrumental Variables Estimation when the Correlation between the Instrument and the Endogenous Explanatory Variable Is Weak." *Journal of the American Statistical Association* 90(430): 443–50.

Boyd, J. H., A. E. Pulver, and W. Stewart. 1986. "Season of Birth: Schizophrenia and Bipolar Disorder." *Schizophrenia Bulletin* 12: 173–86.

Bradbury, T. N., and G. A. Miller. 1985. "Season of Birth in Schizophrenia: A Review of Evidence, Methodology and Etiology." *Psychological Bulletin* 98: 569–94.

Cahan, Sorel, and Nora Cohen. 1989. "Age versus Schooling Effects on Intelligence Development." *Child Development* 60: 1239–49.

Carroll, H. C. M. 1992. "Season of Birth and School Attendance." *British Journal of Educational Psychology* 62: 391–96.

Ceci, Stephen J. 1991. "How Much Does Schooling Influence General Intelligence and Its Cognitive Components? A Reassessment of the Evidence." *Developmental Psychology* 27(5): 703–22.

Ceci, Stephen J., and Wendy M. Williams. 1997. "Schooling, Intelligence, and Income." *American Psychologist* 52(10): 1051–58.

Chase-Lansdale, P. Lindsay, and others. 1991. "Children of the National Longitudinal Survey of Youth: A Unique Research Opportunity." *Developmental Psychology* 27(6): 918–31.

Consortium for Longitudinal Studies. 1983. *As the Twig Is Bent: Lasting Effects of Preschool Programs*. Hillsdale, N.J.: Erlbaum.

Currie, Janet, and Duncan Thomas. 1995. "Does Head Start Make a Difference?" *American Economic Review* 85(3): 341–64.

Education Commission of the States. 1994. "Compulsory School Age Requirements." U.S. Department of Education (March).

Gillberg, C. 1990. "Do Children with Autism Have March Birthdays?" *Acta Psychiatrica Scandinavia* 82: 152–56.

Haskins, Ron. 1989. "Beyond Metaphor: The Efficacy of Early Childhood Education." *American Psychologist* 44(2): 274–82.

Livingston, Richard, B. S. Adam, and H. S. Bracha. 1993. "Season of Birth and Neurodevelopmental Disorders: Summer Birth Is Associated with Dyslexia." *Journal of the American Academy of Child and Adolescent Psychiatry* 32(3): 612–16.

Mayer, Susan E., and David Knutson. 1998. "Does Age at Enrollment in First Grade Affect Children's Cognitive Test Scores?" Working paper. Northwestern University-University of Chicago Joint Center for Poverty Research.

Meisels, Samuel J., 1992. "Doing Harm by Doing Good: Iatrogenic Effects of Early Childhood Enrollment and Promotion Policies." *Early Childhood Research Quarterly* 7: 155–74.

O'Callaghan, Eabhard, and others. 1991. "Season of Birth in Schizophrenia: Evidence for Confinement of an Excess of Winter Births to Patients with a Family History of Mental Disorder." *British Journal of Psychiatry* 158: 764–69.

Orme, J. E. 1979. "Ability, Month of Birth and Climatic Temperature." *British Journal of Mental Subnormality* 25: 31–32.

Proctor, Theron, Kathryn Black, and John Feldhusen. 1986. "Early Admission of Selected Children to Elementary School: A Review of the Research Literature." *Journal of Educational Research* 80(2): 70–76.

U.S. Department of Health, Education and Welfare, Office of Education. 1965. "State Law on Compulsory Attendance."

Uphoff, James K., and June Gilmore. 1985. "Pupil Age at School Entrance—How Many Are Ready for Success?" *Educational Leadership* (September): 86–90.

Williams, Phillip, and others. 1970. "Season of Birth and Cognitive Development." *Nature* 228(December): 1033–36.

Winship, Christopher, and Sanders D. Korenman. 1997. "Does Staying in School Make You Smarter? The Effect of Education on IQ in *The Bell Curve*." In *Intelligence and Success: Scientists Respond to The Bell Curve*, edited by Bernie Devlin and others. New York: Springer-Verlag.

Whorton, James, and Frances Karnes. 1981. "Season of Birth and the Intelligence of Samples of Exceptional Children." *Psychological Reports* 49: 649–50.

PART **II**

Improving Schooling

PAUL E. PETERSON

5

School Reforms: How Much Do They Matter?

FOR MORE THAN A century, U.S. elementary and high schools led those of the rest of the world in just about every way that could be counted—enrollment rates, per pupil expenditures, teacher-pupil ratios. But in recent years schools in other parts of the world have caught up and even surpassed those in the United States, despite the country's status as the only remaining superpower. For example, U.S. high school graduation rates have now fallen behind those of Germany, France, Canada, Norway, Ireland, Finland, Poland, South Korea, and the Czech Republic.[1] Instead of advancing along with other sectors of society, U.S. schools are falling further behind.

The problem is not particularly apparent during the initial years of schooling. In fourth grade, at age nine, U.S. children are better skilled in reading and math than they were a couple of decades ago, as indicated by performance on the National Assessment of Educational Progress (NAEP), which provides the best available information on national trends in test scores. Indeed, one hopeful development is that the gains are particularly marked among minorities. At age nine, U.S. students are also doing as well in science and math as their peers in most of Europe and other parts of the world—although Korean and Japanese students outpace them by a wide margin.[2]

1. See Ethan Bronner, "Long a Leader, U.S. Now Lags in High School Graduate Rate," *New York Times*, November 24, 1998, pp. A-1, A-18.

But in the later years of elementary school and in secondary school, the performance of U.S. students slips. By eighth grade, the test scores of U.S. students trail those of students in other major industrial nations.[3] By twelfth grade, their scores lag behind those of their peers in nearly every other country, regardless of level of economic development. Even worse, NAEP data indicate that the United States is trailing its own record. In the 1990s, both black and white students made smaller math gains between fourth and eighth grades than did their peers a generation earlier, despite their greater achievements by fourth grade.[4] To all appearances, the slide is even steeper during high school years.

Some education experts dismiss these facts as unimportant. They argue that the intellectual capacities important to success are not captured by the kinds of test used by NAEP and other surveys of student learning. Says Harvard professor of education Howard Gardner: "The relationship between how you do on tests like these and how you will do in life is very tenuous." Or in the words of Gerald W. Bracey, author of *Setting the Record Straight: Responses to Misconceptions about Public Education in the United States:* "The schools have very little to do with the health of the economy." Echoes Bruce Biddle, author of *The Manufactured Crisis: Myths, Fraud, and the Attack on America's Public Schools:* "The simple-minded notion that there is a direct link between K–12 education and the economy—I don't think has any credence anymore."[5]

If these authors are correct, Americans may be squandering vast resources on an enterprise that has little subsequent economic value. Education is one of the most expensive publicly supported programs in the United States. In 1997 elementary and secondary schools spent nearly $340 billion, or 4.5 percent of GNP. Nearly 51,490,000 students were enrolled in elementary and secondary schools that year, so that public

2. Fourth graders trail students in Japan, Korea, the Netherlands, and the Czech Republic, but do better than students in England, Norway, and New Zealand; see "U.S. 4th Graders Score Well in Math and Science Study," *Education Week,* June 18, 1997, p. 22.

3. Eighth graders clearly outscore their peers in only seven countries—Lithuania, Cyprus, Portugal, Iran, Kuwait, Colombia, and South Africa—none of them a major industrial nation. See "U.S. Students Rank about Average in 41-Nation Math, Science Study," *Education Week,* November 27, 1996, p. 32; Debra Viader, "U.S. Seniors Near Bottom in World Test," *Education Week,* March 4, 1998, pp. 1, 18; U.S. National Research Center (1998).

4. NAEP data are reported in U.S. Department of Health and Human Services (1997, tables EA 2.1, EA 2.2, and EA 2.3) and also Barton and Coley (1998).

5. May Ann Zehr, "Weak Scores, Strong Economy: How Can This Be?" *Education Week,* April 1, 1998, pp. 1, 20.

schools spent an average of about $6,600 per pupil.[6] Fortunately, the chapters in the first part of this volume, which show that the cognitive skills learned in school affect adult well-being, cast serious doubt on any claims that schools have little economic consequence.

The chapters in the second part consider the ways in which the learning experience in school can be made still more productive.[7] Some show that what is learned depends on the quality of the curriculum; others suggest that the teacher-pupil ratio may be important, at least for first-graders. Still others show that student performance can be enhanced through national examinations and by giving parents greater choice. Together, they make the case for educational reforms that both augment the resources devoted to education and increase the efficiency with which these resources are used.

Class Size

Most people believe that students learn more in smaller classes. In smaller classes teachers can interact more with each student and tailor instruction to a student's particular needs. In addition, students can participate directly in class discussions more often. Because the benefits to teachers are obvious but the costs to taxpayers are high, the debate over class size is intense. On the one side, most educators, as well as the organizations and unions that represent them, favor decreasing class sizes—even if by only one or two students—because this reduces the number of papers to correct and makes teachers' jobs less demanding. On the other side, reductions in class size are among the most expensive school reforms that legislators are asked to implement. As Eric Hanushek points out in chapter 7, personnel costs dominate school budgets. A reduction in the number of pupils per teacher from twenty to nineteen increases teacher costs by 5 percent. A truly meaningful reduction in class size, such as from twenty-five students to twenty, increases teacher costs by 20 percent, an extraordinary increment that would have to be offset by saving elsewhere.

There are three kinds of evidence on this issue: trend data, observational studies of the effects of class size, and randomized experiments. Looking at trends over time, the average pupil-teacher ratio in America's schools has

6. National Center for Education Statistics (1997, tables 2, 31).
7. For a review of the earlier literature, see Ceci (1991).

fallen steadily from 28:1 in 1950 to 19:1 in 1995. Yet as Hanushek reports, the average test performance of seventeen-year-old students in the NAEP has not increased. Proponents of smaller classes reply that the drop in actual class sizes has not been as great as the reduction in the pupil-teacher ratio. Much of the decline in the pupil-teacher ratio is the result of growth in special education and other classes that do not include most students. Their point is well taken; nonetheless, Hanushek shows that growth in special education does not fully account for the reduction in class size.

Those who advocate smaller classes also argue that at the same time that the pupil-teacher ratio was declining other changes may have been acting in the opposite direction. For example, the percentage of children living in poverty and in single-parent families increased over the period 1950–95. Both characteristics of family background are associated with lower student test scores. But Hanushek points to other, offsetting, social trends. Children's parents are better educated than in the past, and parental education has a stronger correlation with test score performance than any other family background characteristic. Also, children have fewer siblings and they receive better health care—both factors that should increase test scores. Some evidence suggests that taken together, the improvements in children's background characteristics outweigh the declines, implying that children today should arrive in school better prepared to score higher than in the past.[8]

In this context, the facts noted in the opening to this chapter are especially significant. That test scores in fourth grade are higher now than a generation ago suggests that family background characteristics are more favorable to higher educational performance than previously. However, math score gains between fourth and eighth grades have been smaller in the 1990s than they were in the 1970s, a decline more convincingly attributed to changes within schools than to changes within families.

Because trend data are always open to a variety of interpretations, it is important also to consider more specific studies of class size. As Hanushek points out, few of these studies find much evidence to support the claim that children learn more in somewhat smaller classes. Yet most of these studies are less than definitive, because it is not certain that students in classes of different sizes are similar in all other respects. It is possible, for example, that schools put those children they consider troublemakers in smaller classes. If so, selection effects would lead one to underestimate the effects of class size. Many of these studies do control initial test scores,

8. See Grissmer and others (1994).

however, which addresses one source of selection bias. Hanushek argues that such studies show that a reduction in class size within a realistic range, say, from twenty-five to twenty, does not affect student performance. He interprets these results by observing that within such a range, pedagogical strategies and student participation rates do not vary enough to produce different effects.

Still, the best way of avoiding the selection problem is by means of a randomized experiment. Experiments of this sort randomly assign children to either a treatment group or a control group. Ideally, baseline information is collected prior to the experiment, and changes in the characteristics of all members of the test and control groups are observed throughout the experiment. Average differences (if statistically significant) between the characteristics of the test and control groups can be attributed to the experiment, because it is reasonable to assume that the average characteristics of the two randomly assigned groups are otherwise similar.

One such experiment is Tennessee's Project STAR, summarized by Frederick Mosteller in chapter 6. In the face of intense debate among competing interests, Tennessee legislators authorized the first large-scale randomized experiment to test the proposition that elementary school students learn more in smaller classes. Students entering kindergarten and first grade were assigned to larger or smaller classes at random, as were their teachers. Mosteller reports that the students in the smaller classes learned more in their first year in the program than the students in the larger classes, and that these gains were maintained (in standardized metric), though not increased, as these children continued in smaller classes in subsequent years.

Mosteller concludes that a decrease in class size, when introduced in the initial year of instruction, leads to increases in educational performance of about one quarter of a standard deviation. The results from Project STAR are similar to those reported from earlier, smaller, randomized experiments. Such findings have led many people to think that smaller classes are necessary in all subsequent grades to maintain the gains of smaller class size in the first grade. Mosteller argues that studies of educational innovations repeatedly show that the downstream effectiveness of an experiment wanes if it is not continued, and that one can expect initial test score gains to be maintained only if students are in smaller classes for several years.

When Hanushek looks at the same results in chapter 7, however, he argues that smaller classes improve test scores in the first year of an experiment (kindergarten or first grade), but that no further gain is realized from maintaining small classes in subsequent years. Hanushek's interpretation is that children get a one-time gain from smaller classes that is retained even when children return to average-sized classes. Thus he argues that reductions in class size should be limited to kindergarten and first grade, because the evidence does not justify the great expense of reducing classroom size in other grades.

To find out which interpretation of Tennessee's Project STAR is correct would require another randomized experiment in which the test group of students is kept in small classes, while the control group is initially in small classes but subsequently attends larger classes. This seems worth doing, since the stakes are high. If, as Mosteller argues, students must stay in smaller classes to maintain the modest gains in test scores that they get from a smaller first grade class, the costs of this modest gain are very high. But if Hanushek is correct in saying that the gains can be maintained even when children move on to larger classes, the costs are much less.

Curricular Reform

Many proponents of school reform focus on the content of the curriculum. They often argue that the public school curriculum, especially in high school, has been softened. Instead of offering a limited set of academic courses, high schools have increasingly given students a wide choice of subjects, offered at varying levels of difficulty. Sometimes students' choices are guided by counselors or teachers, sometimes not. Reformers blame "shopping mall" high schools for declining test scores and argue that a more challenging academic curriculum could raise scores. Opponents of curricular reform argue that a high school curriculum needs to be responsive to variations in student abilities and tastes, so as to forestall student alienation. If given a choice and properly advised by guidance counselors, students will gravitate to a level of challenge appropriate to their abilities.

Previous research shows (as do Jencks and Phillips in chapter 2 above) that students who have taken more math courses score higher on tests of math achievement. These studies also show that enrollment in advanced mathematics classes has a large effect on math proficiency, whereas enrollment in general math, business math, and pre-algebra classes has at most a modest effect. But there are two problems with this research. First, studies that look at the amount of math a student has studied cannot show whether particular kinds of math course are better than others. Second, students who enroll in advanced mathematics courses are likely to have an aptitude for mathematics. Consequently, it should be no surprise to learn that they do better than other students on tests of math proficiency.

To understand the contribution of math courses, one must take into account students' math achievement before they take the course. But controlling prior math score exacerbates another problem that is often ignored, namely errors in measuring math achievement. Robert Meyer tries to overcome all three of these problems in his study of the high school math curriculum in chapter 8. First, he develops a model that includes the type of math course a student has taken. Second, he uses data from the High School and Beyond survey, so that he can take into account math achievement in the tenth grade and estimate the effect of math courses on gains in test scores between tenth and twelfth grades. Finally, also like Jencks and Phillips, he tries to correct for errors in the measurement of math achievement.

Meyer finds that 27 percent of all the credits of juniors and seniors were in math courses of one kind or another. Vocational courses accounted for 38 percent of the math courses of non-college-bound students and 20 percent of the math courses of college-bound students. Meyer shows that a general math course is substantially less valuable than pre-algebra or an advanced-track math course. This is consistent with the recommendation that schools encourage or even require students to take challenging math courses. But he also finds that there is substantial mathematics learning in many courses other than traditional math courses. For example, college-bound students gain nearly as much math skill in courses such as business math or applied math as in algebra 2. By contrast, vocational courses are less effective for non-college-bound students, presumably the group for which they were originally designed. Mathematically oriented science courses also appear to improve math scores. In this case, the improvement is greater for non-college-bound than for college-bound students.

Jay Girotto and I also look at the effect of curriculum on students' test scores in chapter 9. We find that students who earn higher grades and take academic courses gain more on standardized tests than students who earn lower grades or take fewer academic course. Students who earn one letter grade higher and take two year-long academic courses gain approximately a 0.5 standard deviation in verbal and math skills. Taken together with the Meyer study, the results underline the central importance of an academic curriculum for the acquisition of cognitive skill.

Girotto and I base our study on a survey of high school students in one moderately large Iowa city. Because all the students in the sample are from the same school district, we are able to use fairly precise measures of the curriculum. For example, all students taking algebra 1 were exposed to nearly the same material, because the three high schools in the study are closely supervised by a strong central administration. For these reasons, we believe that grading practices are reasonably similar in these schools, so that a B grade in first-year algebra has much the same meaning in all three.

Our study, like Meyer's, includes information on tests taken at two different points in time, so that we can estimate the gain in cognitive skills between ninth and eleventh grades. To avoid the selection problem, we take advantage of an idiosyncrasy of Iowa law, which allows some students to take drivers' training during the summer months, freeing up the school year for academic courses. Whether students can do so depends on their birth date. Since birth dates are random, so is a student's opportunity to take an extra course. Our results, like Meyer's, indicate that significant learning gains may be obtained by requiring students to take a more rigorous curriculum.

Structural Reform

Many school reformers today believe that increasing schooling, reducing class sizes, or even introducing a tougher curriculum are not sufficient to cure the problems of public education in the United States. Instead, they call for redesigning school governance. Advocates claim that such innovations would change the incentives for teachers, administrators, and students. And with improved incentives, schools will find better ways for their students to achieve high academic standards. Two of the most important structural reform proposals advanced in recent years are national examinations and school choice.

National or Statewide Examinations

John Bishop recommends in chapter 10 that high school students be required to pass substantive examinations. This recommendation is based on a careful study of the effects of provincial exams in Canada, a practice that is also widespread in Europe and Japan but much more unusual in the United States today. To make his point, Bishop constructs a theory of learning that begins not with schools but with students. He assumes that for adolescents, learning is hard work, and its rewards must outweigh its costs in time and effort. Most adolescents would just as soon chat, socialize, party, or watch television. In addition, adolescents are particularly sensitive to what their peers think.

School assignments, tests, and homework interfere with having a good time. Students who get A's, especially those who achieve their grades through hard work, increase the cost of schooling for other students. This is most obvious when schools grade "on the curve," because high-achieving students raise this curve. Other students must then either study harder or accept lower grades, thereby complicating their relations with parents, teachers, and college admission officers. The situation is not unlike that of employees who are expected to keep up with the productivity of their colleagues. If one can keep one's colleagues from raising the standard for productivity, one can reduce the workload. In school, nagging or harassing fellow students who "overperform" is the most readily available solution.

To reduce "nerd harassment," Bishop suggests that students should not be held to their schools' standards—A's and B's in particular courses—but to external standards over which teachers, administrators, and student peer groups have no control, that is, national or statewide examinations. If an external standard provides the measuring rod, students compete not with their immediate peer group but with a statewide or national age cohort, and consequently nerd harassment no longer has the same payoff. It is important that such examinations test particular achievements and that the standards be known ahead of time, so that teachers can provide a relevant curriculum and students can prepare. Such tests would provide greater incentive to students if they had important consequences for employment opportunities or admission to college, as is the case with the national exams in Britain, France, and Germany. The Scholastic Assessment Test, the most widely used external examination at the high school level in the United States, is no substitute because it prides itself on being a test for which students *cannot* prepare, except for familiarizing themselves with question formatting.

Bishop compares test scores in Canadian provinces that require students to take external exams with scores in provinces that do not. Controlling for many school and family background characteristics, he finds that students score higher in the provinces with an external exam. Bishop also finds that students in the State of New York outperform those in other states, which he attributes to the use of the New York Regents' examinations as an admission and scholarship criterion by state colleges.

School Choice

A proposal that has been widely discussed is to combine national or statewide examinations with arrangements that provide parents with a choice of schools. Parents could then rely on results from a national examination when considering the appropriate schools for their children. So far, most of the discussion on this issue has been speculative. Proponents argue that children benefit when parents can choose the school most appropriate for them. At the same time, schools that are forced to compete for applicants will be motivated to offer higher quality education. Opponents of school choice argue that parents who currently can choose their children's schools do so on the basis of racial or social exclusiveness, sports programs, or location, not on the basis of academic excellence. Schools may compete, but the educational program is not the basis of the competition.[9]

Caroline Minter Hoxby contributes to the debate in chapter 11 by exploiting the fact that the amount of school choice varies from one U.S. metropolitan area to another. Where school districts are smaller and the number of districts per citizen is larger, parents can choose among a greater variety of schools. Among the more important considerations for families in choosing where to live are the characteristics of local schools. If a school district does not have a good reputation, families may try to avoid it, adversely affecting local property values, and hence school revenues. Local school officials, seeing revenues falter, then search for ways to improve the educational programs that they offer. In addition, local residents agitate for change because they are concerned about property values. In sum, metropolitan areas with many school districts provide school choice, and this makes school districts more responsive to parent demands.

Elsewhere, Hoxby has examined the effect of the number of school districts in a metropolitan area on a variety of school outcomes.[10] She uses data on student performance from the National Education Longitudinal Study, combined with other information on school districts

---

9. For reviews of this debate and relevant empirical information, see Peterson and Hassel (1998).
10. Hoxby (1994, 1996a, 1996b).

throughout the United States. She controls family background, region, and a variety of other factors. In general, she finds that students living in metropolitan areas with more school districts learn more, at lower cost to the taxpayer, than students living in similar areas with fewer school districts. In chapter 11 below, Hoxby examines the impact of the number of school districts on types of courses that schools offer. She finds that in metropolitan areas with more school districts, where parents presumably have greater choice about where to send their children, schools have more challenging curricula, stricter academic requirements, and more discipline-oriented environments. Parents are also more involved in the schools. In short, Hoxby's data provide support for those who advocate greater school choice.

Hoxby's findings are reinforced by the results from a randomized experiment reported by David Myers, William Howell, Daniel Mayer, and me in chapter 12. In 1997 low-income, inner-city families in New York City with children entering grades one through five were given the opportunity of school choice through a privately funded intervention undertaken by the School Choice Scholarships Foundation (SCSF). In February of that year the foundation announced that it would provide 1,300 scholarships so that eligible children currently attending public schools could transfer to private schools, both religious and secular. The scholarships were worth up to $1,400 annually and could be renewed for at least three years. SCSF received initial application forms from over 20,000 students between February and late April. Scholarship recipients were selected by lottery in May and began school in the fall.

Our evaluation takes advantage of the fact that the SCSF lottery offers a natural randomized experiment in which students were allocated randomly to scholarship and control groups. After one year, parents of scolarship students reported more homework, more communication with schools, better school discipline, and greater satisfaction with schools. Students attending private schools scored higher in reading and math tests: by 3 percentile points in reading and 6 percentile points in math.

The size of the effects on fourth and fifth graders in the school choice experiment do not differ materially from those observed among first graders in the Tennessee STAR program. In both cases, the effects were about 0.2 standard deviations. However, it remains to be seen whether the first year effects of school choice will be maintained and increased in subsequent years.

References

Barton, Paul E., and Richard J. Coley. 1998. "Growth in School: Achievement Gains from the Fourth to the Eighth Grade." Princeton, N.J.: Educational Testing Service, Policy Information Center, Research Division (May).

Ceci, Stephen. 1991. "How Much Does Schooling Influence General Intelligence and Its Cognitive Components? A Reassessment of the Evidence." *Developmental Psychology* 27(5): 703–22.

Grissmer, David W., and others. 1994. *Student Achievement and the Changing American Family.* Santa Monica, Calif.: Rand Corporation.

Hoxby, Caroline Minter. 1994. "Does Competition among Public Schools Benefit Students and Taxpayers?" Working Paper 4979. Cambridge, Mass.: National Bureau of Economic Research.

————. 1996a. "The Effects of Private School Vouchers on Schools and Students." In *Holding Schools Accountable: Performance-Based Reform in Education,* edited by Helen F. Ladd, 177–208. Brookings.

————. 1996b. "How Teachers' Unions Affect Education Production." *Quarterly Journal of Economics* 3(August): 671–718.

National Center for Education Statistics. 1997. *Digest of Education Statistics, 1997.* U.S. Department of Education.

Peterson, Paul E., and Bryan C. Hassel, eds. 1998. *Learning from School Choice.* Brookings.

U.S. Department of Health and Human Services, Office of the Assistant Secretary for Planning and Evaluation. 1997. *Trends in the Well-Being of America's Children and Youth.* Government Printing Office.

U.S. National Research Center. 1998. "TIMMS High School Results Released." Report 8. Michigan State University, College of Education (April).

FREDERICK MOSTELLER

6

How Does Class Size Relate to Achievement in Schools?

M OST INVESTIGATORS FIND that what, at first, seem to be new attacks on a problem have earlier histories, though not necessarily successful ones. An example is the evaluation of the effect of class size on the learning achievement of school children. Although class size was frequently studied during the years 1900–96, the findings were varied. Part of the difficulty is that the variability in performance of small classes (ten to thirty students) is substantial. This variability has several sources, for example, test-retest unreliability; individual differences, including sampling variability from populations (sample size considerations); and differing populations, including different educational treatments, such as style of teaching or class size. This means that a good many comparisons between smaller and larger classes are required to get reliable results. In addition, the need for a systematic search of the literature was not appreciated early in the century.

Partial support for this work was given by the Andrew W. Mellon Foundation through a grant to the American Academy of Arts and Sciences for the Center for Evaluation of its project Initiatives for Children. I have also been helped by comments from John Emerson, Adam Gamoran, and Bill Nave, and assistance in preparing the manuscript from Marjorie Olson and Cleo Youtz.

Earlier Studies

A useful description of the situation is provided by Gene Glass, Barry McGaw, and Mary Lee Smith.[1] In a comprehensive literature search, Glass and Smith find about 300 documents describing class size experiments in the first eighty years of this century. Of these, half have no data to assess comparative achievement, and about seventy of the remainder treat attitudes and interest rather than achievement. They found 77 studies, including 725 comparisons of the performance of paired classrooms. Of these comparisons, 110 are randomized, 235 are matched, 18 are based on "repeated measures," and 362 are uncontrolled. Since the randomized comparisons produce a stronger relation between class size and achievement than do the other studies, Glass and Smith focus on these.[2]

Effect Sizes

Effect sizes are often measured as

$$(6\text{-}1) \qquad \Delta_{S-L} = \frac{\bar{X}_S - \bar{X}_L}{\sigma},$$

where Δ_{S-L} stands for the observed gain in standard deviation units for smaller compared to larger classes; S and L label the smaller and larger sample sizes, respectively; $\bar{X}_S$ and $\bar{X}_L$ are the sample average achievements in the paired classes; and σ is the sample standard deviation, for convenience often assumed to be a common value for the two classes being compared or the standard deviation for the control group, here the larger group. This notation follows Glass, McGaw, and Smith closely.[3] Note that σ is not the standard deviation of a mean, but the standard deviation of individual measurements in the large classes (or sometimes an average of standard deviations for the two populations). Thus equation 6-1 gives the observed gain in standard deviation units of the smaller class over the larger class if the gain for small class size is positive, or the observed loss if the result is negative.

1. Glass, McGaw, and Smith (1981); Glass and Smith (1979).
2. Glass and Smith (1979).
3. Glass, McGaw, and Smith (1981).

It helps considerably in analyzing data to have a formal model to give structure to the data and focus the strength of the data on the quantities of interest. Glass and Smith develop such a model, which is presented in appendix 6A.[4]

Using Glass and Smith's model fitted to their data and comparing results for a class size of forty with results for a class size of fifteen, I find that the improvement in performance (effect size) by the smaller class is estimated to be a quarter of a standard deviation. One interpretation of this finding is that if a typical student at the 50th percentile in a class of forty had the benefit of being taught in a class of fifteen, he or she would move up to the 60th percentile. Later in this chapter I show that these results underestimate actual results from educational investigations in Tennessee.

One complaint that has been leveled against Glass and Smith's work is that it includes comparisons of results with very small classes. Critics felt this was not realistic, and that they ought to have based their comparisons on class sizes that could be afforded in school districts.[5] I now consider some more recent studies.

Indiana's Project Prime Time

In 1981 the Indiana State Department of Education launched a two-year investigation called Prime Time to see the effect of using a class size of fourteen in twenty-four classes from kindergarten through third grade (K–3). After two semesters, the higher reading and math scores in the smaller classes led the Indiana State Department of Education to stop the experiment and to implement the project statewide, reducing class size to an average of eighteen year by year. Small classes were introduced in first grade in 1984–85, in second grade in 1985–86; in third grade in 1986–87; and in kindergarten in 1987–88.

Jennifer McGiverin, David Gilman, and Chris Tillitski wanted to assess the effect of the new program, but since nearly every school had been affected to some extent by the new program, decided to compare results for classes that had been changed in size with the results of those that had not—

4. Glass and Smith (1979).
5. Had they done this, they probably would have been accused of suppressing part of the data. Perhaps they could have presented more analyses. They make their data available in Glass, McGaw, and Smith (1981, p. 179), so that others can make their own analyses.

some classes had not been reduced because they were already at eighteen or fewer.[6] This plan does not give the direct comparison between equated groups that one would like to see, but it is a step toward evaluation.

The investigators found ten studies of math and reading in six randomly chosen schools and school corporations where class sizes had been reduced under the Prime Time program. Parallel to this, they located four similar studies in three randomly selected school corporations that did not experience class-size reductions. Although randomization played a role in the selection of the schools, this is not a randomized controlled study. The randomization is like that used for a sample survey to make sure that a relevant population is represented.

The tests used were form 3 of the Cognitive Abilities Test, forms 7 and 8 of the Iowa Tests of Basic Skills, and the Stanford Achievement Test. In each study, the comparison is between performance in one year and that in the next. To give an idea of the magnitudes involved, 1,940 scores from reduced-size classes were compared with 2,027 scores from unchanged classes. For the classes with unchanged size, 574 students were scored each year.

A summary of the results of the ten studies comparing results for the classes of reduced size with results for classes of the original size shows a gain in effect size of 0.34 standard deviation. The corresponding value for the classes with unchanged size is −0.15 standard deviation (not significantly different from zero).[7]

McGiverin, Gilman, and Tillitski close their article by pointing to the need for longitudinal studies that would show whether the effects are maintained over time, as opposed to being due to the novelty of the program or especially talented teachers or groups of children. Described next, this longitudinal approach was used in a set of studies carried out in Tennessee.

The Tennessee Projects

Educators and legislators in the state of Tennessee found Indiana's Prime Time study instructive and inviting. It was proposed that class sizes be

6. McGiverin, Gilman, and Tillitski (1989).

7. One cannot compare the 0.34 standard deviation effect with the 0.25 standard deviation effect of Glass and Smith (1979) due to the lack of before and after sample sizes for the schools.

reduced in the early grades in Tennessee. But the Tennessee legislature felt that in view of the greater expense involved in smaller classes, in terms of both additional faculty and additional space, an experiment should be conducted to establish the effectiveness of the treatment of reduced class size. The legislators also wanted to know whether the addition of a teacher's aide would be effective and affordable. In the mid-1980s, the legislature appropriated $3 million per year for four years to carry out the experiment on a statewide basis. In its final form, it was designed to assess both the effect of reduced class size and the benefits of having a teacher's aide in a class of regular size.

The Tennessee investigations were carried out in three phases. Phase 1, called Project STAR (for student-teacher achievement ratio), was the four-year experiment. Phase 2, the Lasting Benefits Study, followed up to see whether students who had participated in the smaller classes continued to benefit after they returned to regular classes. Phase 3, called Project Challenge, started after Phase 1 was completed and implemented the smaller classes in the seventeen districts with the lowest per capita income, which also had the largest proportions of children who received free or reduced-price lunches.

Design

When Tennessee decided to carry out an experiment, the investigators had in mind reducing class size in the early grades. Children entering school from many different backgrounds might need to be acclimated to school as a place to work and learn, as opposed to a place to play. Thus smaller class size in the early grades was intended to help the children organize themselves as students. Once this start-up period was over, larger classes were to be resumed. My reading of this literature finds no intent to reduce class sizes throughout the grades, K–12. If this is not properly understood, an assessment of costs could lead to exaggeration.

The treatments were (a) regular-sized class, (b) regular-sized class with a teacher aide, and (c) small class. The regular classes contained twenty-two to twenty-five pupils; the small classes, thirteen to seventeen. Thus the reduction in class size from regular to small was by about a third. The design of the experiment required that each participating school have at least one class employing each treatment. If different schools provided different treatments, the possibility of observed effects being due to different

schools, teachers, parents, or neighborhoods would undermine the usefulness of the studies. Both teachers and students were randomly assigned to
classes. This produces a statistical balance among students and among
teachers in the three treatments.

One hundred schools initially volunteered to participate in the four-
year experiment, but not all could in fact participate; seventy-nine participated in the first year. Each school had to find its own space if extra rooms
were required. The curriculum remained the same as in the previous year.
Each school had to produce at least fifty-seven students who would be allocated among the three treatments. A few more schools dropped out for
miscellaneous reasons as the experiment progressed. In the second year the
experiment included seventy-six schools, with about 330 classes and about
6,600 students. Approximately one-third of the children were from
minorities, almost all of these being African Americans.

Results

The results of the three phases of the Tennessee investigations are as follows.

PROJECT STAR. It turned out that, on average, the children in the small
classes gained in achievement over those in the regular-sized classes, by a
quarter of a standard deviation on standardized tests and also on tests
geared to the curriculum. The regular-sized classes with a teacher's aide
showed about half as much improvement.

LASTING BENEFITS STUDY. At the end of the four-year experiment, the
Lasting Benefits Study shows that students who had been in the small
classes did perform better than the others when they returned to the regular-sized classes. The subsequent benefit varied from year to year, but averaged across six school subjects, it averaged between 0.1 and 0.2 of a standard deviation. Thus the evidence shows that some of the benefit gained
from small classes in the early years continues into the later grades after a
return to regular-sized classes.[8] The Lasting Benefits follow-up continued
for several years and found that the benefit continued with an effect size
about half of that obtained during the original treatment.

8. Achilles and others (1993).

PROJECT CHALLENGE. By the time the four years of Project STAR were completed, the evidence for improvement in the performance of children in small classes was persuasive. Consequently, Tennessee legislators decided to continue to monitor the effects of the original program through the Lasting Benefits Study, and also to implement the program for a targeted group, in Project Challenge. It was decided to introduce small classes for kindergarten through third grade in the seventeen school districts with the lowest per capita incomes in the state. Thus the program was implemented in only about one-eighth of the 138 districts. That is, given that it was implemented in K–3 and in an eighth of the districts, it covered about 4 percent of all classes.

After Project Challenge began, the seventeen school districts gradually raised their end of the year rankings among all school districts. The best rank is 1, the average rank in the state is about 70, and the bottom rank is 138. In the first year of implementation (1989–90), for example, second graders in the seventeen districts had average end of year ranks of 99 in reading and 85 in mathematics. In the fourth year of the program, second graders' average ranks had improved to 78 in reading and 56 in mathematics, a gain of 21 in reading and of 29 in mathematics.[9]

Three different types of evidence from Tennessee's Project STAR encourage belief in the improvement in student achievement associated with smaller class sizes: the comparisons made during the four-year experimental period of Project STAR; the continuing benefits registered in the Lasting Benefits Study after children resumed regular-sized classes; and the improved end of year rankings of the seventeen school districts in Project Challenge.

By implementing Project Challenge in the seventeen poorest districts in the state, Tennessee was able to take advantage of the effectiveness of small classes without incurring the expense of implementing such a program in all schools. One can make use of a valuable intervention very selectively, for example, by applying it to those who need it most. The four-year findings of Project Challenge show that the implementation had a positive effect.[10]

---

9. For more information on Project Challenge, see Achilles, Nye, and Zacharias (1995).

10. The above discussion skips over some changes that occurred in the execution of the program; for these, see Mosteller (1995) and also the discussion in Blatchford and Mortimore (1994). In 1996 Tennessee comprehensively revised plans that are to be implemented by school districts by the year 2000; I do not know what arrangements will be in place over the next few years.

Discussion

As information about the class size experiments in Indiana and Tennessee has spread, educators have taken active steps both in the United States and abroad. The State of California has been introducing smaller class sizes (twenty students) in the early grades, despite lack of teachers and classrooms, at a cost of about $1 billion. Other states, including Florida, Georgia, and Utah, have been considering similar reductions. Overseas, the Republic of Ireland is spending $5 million per year to reduce class sizes in the more economically depressed regions to about fifteen from kindergarten through second grade. This plan is similar to Tennessee's implementation.

In discussing the Tennessee investigations, some have observed that the studies still do not indicate what matters in the small size classes: what process leads to better learning? They feel that there is more to this than having fewer children in the room. It would be well to pause here and notice that the education community does not have much of a history of evaluating the processes and practices of education, and its researchers conduct relatively few randomized, controlled field trials. This sort of study is used in many fields to learn which procedures work well and to test theories about the processes that produce particular outcomes. We do not have a large community of scholars carrying out controlled investigations in the field of education, nor are funds for such work readily available. For the most part the educational community is consumed with carrying out the extensive activities of teaching, which does not leave much time or many funds for research and evaluation.

To decide how process influences learning means being able to test a large number of hypotheses and to discard some, probably most, of them. Each test of a hypothesis means carrying out some sort of comparative investigation. Therefore when one asks about process, one is implicitly asking for many sets of investigations and perhaps for some agreement on which theories are worth testing. Although I usually find the results of randomized field trials more compelling, various ways of analyzing data from observational studies so as to make causal inferences are also available.

Some people feel that gains from an educational investment should continue to grow even after the treatment is discontinued. That is, if a treatment such as small class size is administered, then after the treatment is administered, any gains should continue to increase each year. This inviting idea may come from an analogy with the notion of an investment that pays accumulating interest. Whether that is the reasoning, it is not the idea of gain that I expect from a good teaching practice. If the treatment produces an improvement of some size, such as improving a student's grade from a D to a C, I do not anticipate that a few years after the treatment is discontinued the student will move up from a C to a B. I hope that the original improvement to a C will reduce the student's risk of dropping out of school altogether, and that, if maintained, the new grade level will make high school graduation more likely. This, in turn, may reduce the likelihood of future dependence on welfare and also later criminal behavior (all of which would represent great gains), but I do not expect the immediate improvement in school grades to continue to grow of their own accord. I mention this issue because it may be one basis for disagreements about the benefits of improved classroom practices.

When I presented a version of this paper at a conference, I was asked why the reduction in class size should be effective only in Tennessee. This question arises from a misapprehension. Glass, McGaw, and Smith find beneficial effects in their meta-analysis data, although not as substantial as those found in Tennessee.

Concern was also expressed that different teachers might use very different styles. This could matter. Discussions with educators suggest that most teachers teach either as they were taught to teach or as they were taught by their own teachers. Thus one can only suppose that teachers were using the methods they were used to.

On the issue of teacher's aides, I understand that no special instruction was offered for their use in the Tennessee study. Nor were teachers taught how they might improve their teaching, given smaller classes. To suggest that one could teach about either the better use of aides or how to give better instruction in small classes implies that someone knows how to improve current practice. And it also implies that comparative studies are available to help in this task. If one wants to know how to improve process, one needs evidence that some methods work better than others. And one must recognize that without comparative studies, one is left with guesses or perhaps theories that need verification. I have argued that in the last 100 years education has not made much progress in evaluating processes of education.[11] I am not aware of comparative studies on the issues raised here, in particular, on the improved cognitive performance of children.

---

11. One exception is Slavin's (1995) summary of current knowledge about cooperative learning; but I do not recall his using any longitudinal study of more than two years.

Conclusion

In the field of education, few practices have been evaluated with controlled field studies or longitudinal studies. The concern that controlled field studies usually do not address the process of education seems to ignore the absence of research showing which educational practices are especially effective. More research on process is also needed.

Although the effect of class size on cognitive achievement has been studied since at least 1900, there have been few longitudinal studies. In the late 1980s a longitudinal field trial of substantial size in Tennessee gave strong evidence that smaller class sizes in the early grades improve performance on both standardized and curriculum-based tests. Further, some evidence showed that children taught in smaller classes in the early grades continue to perform better than those taught in larger classes even after all students have resumed larger classes. And the implementation of the program for students in the districts with low economic status yielded a substantial gain in end-of-the-year test scores compared with students in other districts.

Several questions remain. Are four years (kindergarten through third grade) of small classes required to achieve the gain, or would the same result be produced by three or even two years? Are certain class sizes especially effective?

Can teachers be taught to use their smaller classes more effectively? For example, there is nothing in the Tennessee experiment that would prevent one from also using, say, cooperative learning methods. The general point is that smaller class sizes do not constrain one from using additional teaching practices—if these have been shown to be effective—to help improve children's performance. There is no basis in research for how one might improve one's teaching in the context of smaller class sizes.

Appendix 6A
Glass and Smith's Model

In this appendix I return to the model originally proposed by Glass and Smith.[12] One wants to relate the effect size of equation 6-1 to the class sizes being compared.

12. Glass and Smith (1979).

It is desirable to fit a curve that has both simple form and readily interpreted parameters. In choosing such a curve, Glass and Smith were influenced by the notion that the effect of an increase in class size from one student to two students ought reasonably to be larger than the effect of a move from two students to three students, and so on. The logarithmic model of effect size behaves in just this way.

Applying this model, if the achievement for a class of size C is written as

$$(6A\text{-}1) \qquad z = \alpha - \beta \log_e C + \epsilon ,$$

where ϵ is an error term averaging to zero, then if $C = 1$,

$$z = \alpha + \epsilon .$$

Thus α is the average achievement for a class of one student. The minus sign in equation 6A-1 suggests that (assuming $\beta > 0$) the larger is class size C, the more is subtracted on the right-hand side, and thus the greater is the loss due to class size. The choice of the natural logarithm (base e) is arbitrary and convenient; any other base would work as well.

If one compares the results for two class sizes S and L (smaller and larger, respectively) by subtracting the performance of the larger class from that of the smaller, one would write the effect size as

$$
\begin{aligned}
(6A\text{-}2) \qquad \Delta_{S-L} &= \alpha - \beta \log_e S + \epsilon_S - (\alpha - \beta \log_e L + \epsilon_L) \\
&= \beta \, (\log_e L - \log_e S) + \epsilon_S - \epsilon_L \\
&= \beta \, (\log_e(L/S)) + \epsilon_S - \epsilon_L .
\end{aligned}
$$

Again, suppose that $\epsilon_S - \epsilon_L$ averages to zero. The ratio L/S is an attractive feature of the model because it makes the comparison depend directly on the ratio of the class sizes. If one has a collection of comparisons of the performance of pairs of classes, one can plot the resulting effect size Δ against the $\log_e(L/S)$ for each pair. One can then fit a regression line whose slope would be $\hat{\beta}$, an estimate of β. Fitting a regression line of Δ_{S-L} on $\log_e(L/S)$ produces a line forced through the origin. One way to get an estimate of β is to use the least-squares value

$$(6A\text{-}3) \qquad \hat{\beta} = \frac{\Sigma \Delta_{S-L}(\log_e(L/S))}{\Sigma \, (\log_e(L/S))^2} ,$$

where the values of Δ_{S-L} and $\log_e(L/S)$ are based on collections of data.

Glass and Smith have collected and analyzed studies done from 1900 through 1979.[13] Based on comparisons of student performance in which investigators randomly distributed students between two groups, a smaller class and a larger class, their estimate of β is 0.26.

This work represented an early form of meta-analysis; indeed, Glass and his colleagues seem to have invented the term and initiated in several fields of social science the idea of combining information from independent studies. In 1999 this method is still under serious study, but its successes in the social and medical sciences have substantially improved its standing for the evaluation of interventions and treatments.

If $\beta = 0.26$ in the Glass-Smith meta-analysis, then the estimate of Δ_{S-L} from equation 6A-2, disregarding $\epsilon_S - \epsilon_L$, is $0.26 \log_e(L/S)$. In Tennessee's Project STAR, the small class was about two-thirds of the size of the large class. Thus L/S is about 1.5, leading to an estimated effect size of 0.105 (= $0.26 \log_e 1.5$). Consequently, the Glass-Smith model fitted by the data from 1900 to 1979 would have estimated an improvement of about a tenth of a standard deviation, instead of the 0.25 that was actually observed in Tennessee. (It is an accident that the reduction from forty students to fifteen produced an effect size of 0.25 standard deviation with the fitted model.) And so the meta-analysis would have underestimated the effect size actually achieved in Tennessee by a factor of more than 2. It is my understanding that the Glass-Smith work was helpful in designing the Tennessee investigation.

I have reviewed the data given in Glass-McGaw-Smith.[14] I find ten pairs of classes with sizes similar to those used in the Tennessee experiment. Unfortunately, five of these pairs come from one study. In addition to this weakness, when I plot the Δ against $\log_e L/S$, two points seemed to be potential outliers. I then fit the regression line, first, including all ten points, and find $\hat{\beta} = 0.146$; and second, excluding both potential outliers, and find $\hat{\beta} = 0.162$. The estimated effect sizes for the sample reduction used by Tennessee, based on these data, are 0.059 and 0.066, respectively. Using the subset of points apparently more relevant to the Tennessee data underestimates even further the effects actually found.

13. These data also appear in Glass, McGaw, and Smith (1981).
14. Glass, McGaw, and Smith (1981).

References

Achilles, Charles M., Barbara A. Nye, and Jayne B. Zaharias. 1995. "Policy Use of Research Results: Tennessee's Project Challenge." Paper prepared for the Annual Convention of the American Educational Research Association. San Francisco, April.

Achilles, Charles M., and others. 1993. "The Lasting Benefits Study (LBS) in Grades 4 and 5 (1990–1991): A Legacy from Tennessee's Four Year (K–3) Class-Size Study (1985–1989), Project STAR." Paper prepared for the meeting of the North Carolina Association for Research in Education. Greensboro, N.C., January 14.

Blatchford, Peter, and Peter Mortimore. 1994. "The Issue of Class Size for Young Children in Schools: What Can We Learn from Research?" *Oxford Review of Education* 20(4): 411–28.

Glass, Gene V., and Mary Lee Smith. 1979. "Meta-Analysis of Research on the Relationship of Class-Size and Achievement." *Educational Evaluation and Policy Analysis* 1(1): 2–16.

Glass, Gene V., Barry McGaw, and Mary Lee Smith. 1981. *Meta-Analysis in Social Research.* Beverly Hills, Calif.: Sage Publications.

McGiverin, Jennifer, David Gilman, and Chris Tillitski. 1989. "A Meta-Analysis of the Relation between Class Size and Achievement." *Elementary School Journal* 90(1): 47–56.

Mosteller, Frederick. 1995. "The Tennessee Study of Class Size in the Early School Grades." *Future of Children* 5(2): 113–27.

Slavin, Robert E. 1995. *Cooperative Learning: Theory, Research, and Practice.* 2d ed. Boston: Allyn & Bacon.

ERIC A. HANUSHEK

7

The Evidence
on Class Size

N O TOPIC IN EDUCATION has received such public and professional attention as class size. Calls for reductions in class sizes are rallying points for parents, teachers, and administrators across the nation, and politicians have rushed to claim credit for introducing policies aimed at reducing class size. The pupil-teacher ratio in a school district, for example, is frequently used as the fundamental metric for quality, and comparisons across districts become indexes of equity. A prime reason for the attention to class size is that it represents such an extremely convenient policy instrument, one amenable to general political action. A legislature or a court, wishing to alter student outcomes, can easily specify a change in class size, whereas other potential changes are much more difficult to effect.

The rediscovery and promotion of positive findings from experimental evidence has apparently provided sufficient scientific support that legislators can confidently pursue popular initiatives either mandating smaller classes or providing substantial fiscal incentives for reductions.[1] Yet the surprising fact is that the enormous amount of research devoted to studying class size has failed to make a very convincing case that reducing class size

I wish to thank Charles Achilles for comments on a previous version. Financial support was provided by the William H. Donner Foundation and the Smith Richardson Foundation.
1. See, for example, Mosteller (1995) and chapter 6 above; Krueger (1997).

is likely to improve overall student performance. It will increase costs dramatically, but performance is another matter.

Findings of the general ineffectiveness of reducing class size tend to be controversial if for no other reason than that they seem to defy common sense, conventional wisdom, and highly publicized accounts of the available scientific evidence. Unfortunately, in order to support calls for reductions in class size, there has been a tendency to pick and choose among available studies and evidence. Moreover, the close ties between policy and resources available to schools suggest a variety of conflicts of interest. Therefore, it is useful to review the existing evidence and to reconcile the varying conceptions of what might be expected from class size reductions.

I begin this chapter by examining what the aggregate data indicate about the effectiveness of class size policies. Teachers' resources have been used increasingly intensively throughout the twentieth century, so that the current push for smaller classes is more an extension of past policies than something new.[2] Over the period that student achievement data are available (roughly the past quarter century) there have been no discernible improvements in performance, even though there have been large and steady declines in pupil-teacher ratios.

I then review the international data. Across the world, countries run their school systems in surprisingly different ways, including very different pupil-teacher ratios. When combined with data on student performance, however, the wide discrepancies in pupil-teacher ratios show little relationship to achievement.

Next, I summarize the extensive econometric evidence about the effectiveness of reducing class sizes. This evidence, which incorporates almost 300 different estimates of the effect of class size on achievement, gives no indication that general reductions in class size will yield any average improvement in student achievement. By separating out the influences of families and other school factors, these studies effectively eliminate the primary interpretative concerns raised with the aggregate data. The lack of evidence for significant class size effects that results from analysis of achievement differences across individual classrooms is particularly persuasive.

2. As discussed below, the only consistent data across time and across countries track changes in pupil-teacher ratios, not individual classroom aggregations. In the United States, because of contractual arrangements and management practices, including the use of teachers in a variety of activities outside the regular classroom, pupil-teacher ratios tend to be below average class sizes. Nonetheless, trends in class size will tend to track trends in pupil-teacher ratios. See Lewit and Baker (1997).

I then consider the evidence developed in Project STAR, an experiment conducted by the State of Tennessee in the mid-1980s. This work involves direct comparisons of achievement by students randomly assigned to small classes (thirteen to seventeen students) and large classes (twenty-two to twenty-five students) in kindergarten through third grade. While there is some ambiguity, the overall findings suggest that small kindergarten and perhaps first grade classes might improve initial learning, but that additional resources in later grades did not have a significant influence on subsequent growth in student achievement. This work and related follow-up analyses in Tennessee form much of the scientific basis for the current political debates.[3] Unfortunately, most of the policy discussions go considerably beyond the experimental evidence. In doing so, they tend to ignore the concentration of results in the earliest grades, to generalize to class sizes outside the experiment, and to neglect any consideration of costs relative to potential gains.

In conclusion, I offer possible interpretations for the lack of any general support in the evidence for reducing class size, and then relate the evidence to prospective educational policies.

Basic Aggregate Data

It is common to hear it said that it is not surprising that achievement is what it is, given the large classes that teachers must face. In reality, it is the history of additional teachers without any commensurate increases in student achievement that makes a strong prima facie case about the ineffectiveness of class size policies.

There has been a consistent and dramatic decline in pupil-teacher ratios over most of the twentieth century. Figure 7-1 displays the pattern of pupil-teacher ratios in the United States for the period 1950–94. The overall pupil-teacher ratio fell 35 percent. This decline is the result of steady drops in the pupil-teacher ratio at both the elementary and the secondary levels. The obvious conclusion is that if there is a problem of class size today, there must have been a larger problem in the past.

One closely related trend is that spending per student has grown dramatically over this same period. Because the pupil-teacher ratio indicates the intensity with which school and classroom resources are applied to education, the greater intensity represented by lower instructional ratios translates

---

3. See Mosteller (1995) for a summary.

Figure 7-1. *Pupil-Teacher Ratios*

Ratio

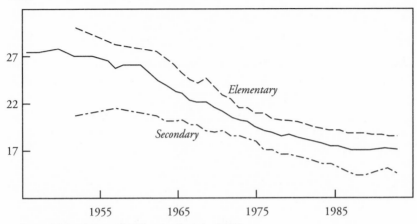

Source: National Center for Education Statistics (1997).

directly into greater spending. Figure 7-2 displays real spending per student over the period 1890–1990. The growth in spending amounts to some 3 1/2 percent per year over the entire period, after adjusting for inflation.

Figure 7-2 breaks down spending per pupil into that related to the salaries of instructional staff and all other spending. Looking at the growth in total instructional staff salaries, one finds that 20 percent of the growth over the century can be attributed to increased intensity of use of instructional staff.[4] This percentage rises in recent periods, reaching 85 percent in 1970–90.[5] In other words, the reductions in pupil-teacher ratios shown in figure 7-1 produce strong effects on spending.

While instructional staff salaries and other spending moved together over the long term, it is also clear from figure 7-2 that nonsalary spending has grown more rapidly in the past two decades. Thus the total growth in spending per pupil is not linked in any simple, mechanical way to pupil-

---

4. Hanushek and Rivkin (1997).

5. The change in spending over the period 1970–90 is complicated by fact that the school-age population actually declined from the mid-1970s through the mid-1980s. During this period, school systems tended to keep the same number of teachers, leading to declines in pupil-teacher ratios. With the recent increase in student population, however, there has been no tendency for the pupil-teacher ratio to increase. For 1980–90 alone, increased intensity of teachers accounted for 34 percent of the growth in total instructional staff spending (Hanushek and Rivkin, 1997).

Figure 7-2. *Instructional Staff and Other Expenditure, 1890-1990*
Spending per pupil (1990 dollars)

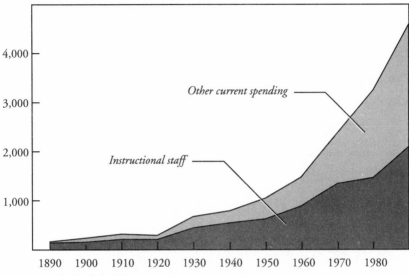

Source: Author's calculations.

teacher ratios, even though increased intensity of use of instructional staff obviously is an important element.[6]

The other component of the basic aggregate picture is patterns of student performance. While representative student achievement data over the century are not available, the National Assessment of Educational Progress (NAEP) does provide data since the 1970s.[7] Figure 7-3-displays

6. While no systematic analysis is available, it seems plausible that the increased intensity of use of instructional personnel is directly related to parallel increases in noninstructional personnel. At least a portion of the increase in other costs is undoubtedly attributable to various legal changes, including mandates for special education (see below) and desegregation efforts.

7. A longer time series can be constructed from the Scholastic Aptitude Test (SAT), although using those data introduces some added interpretive issues. SAT scores fell dramatically from the mid-1960s until the end of the 1970s—suggesting that the achievement decline in the NAEP data neglects an earlier period of decline. The primary interpretive issue, however, revolves around the voluntary nature of the SAT and the increase in the proportion of high school seniors taking the test. The SAT is taken by a selective group of students who wish to enter competitive colleges and universities. As the proportion taking the test rises, so the hypothesis goes, an increasingly lower achieving group will be drawn into the test, leading to lower scores purely because of changes in test taking. While the exact magnitude of any such effects is uncertain, it seems clear that this change in selectivity has caused some, but not all, of the decline in SAT scores; see, for example, Wirtz (1977); Congressional Budget Office (1986).

Figure 7-3. *Achievement on the National Assessment of Educational Progress for Seventeen-Year-Olds, by Race and Ethnicity, 1970–96*

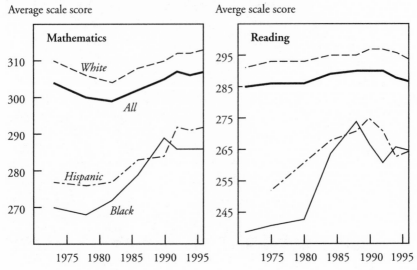

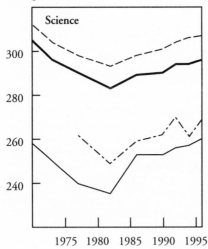

Source: Word and others (1990).

the patterns of NAEP scores for seventeen-year-olds in mathematics, science, and reading. Scores are shown for all students and by racial and ethnic group. Three aspects stand out. First, overall performance is approximately the same in 1970 as in the mid-1990s. While there are some differences in patterns across the subject areas, the composite picture is one of flat scores over the past quarter of a century. Second, there has been some convergence of scores between whites and either blacks or Hispanics. For the period up to 1990, the average black-white gap across subject areas narrowed by 0.4 standard deviation, even though the differences remain substantial.[8] Third, the convergence of scores across racial and ethnic group may have stopped during the 1990s. In fact, since 1990 there has been a noticeable widening of the racial and ethnic achievement gaps that is not captured in the calculations above.

The challenge is to reconcile the data on pupil-teacher ratios and resources with the data on student outcomes. On the surface, they suggest that increases in the intensity of use of teachers and the commensurate increases in spending have had minimal effect on student achievement. But a variety of alternative explanations have also been suggested.

Changes in the Student Population

One simple explanation for why added resources yield no apparent improvement in performance is that students are more poorly prepared or motivated for school than were students twenty-five years ago, so that the additional resources enable performance to stay even. To bolster this view, some point to the growing numbers of children living in single-parent families and the related increases in child poverty rates—both of which are hypothesized to lead to lower student achievement. Table 7-1 displays these major demographic changes. Between 1970 and 1990, the proportion of children living in poverty families rose from 14.9 to 19.9 percent, while the proportion of children living with both parents declined from 85 to 73 percent. But there have been other trends that appear to be positive forces for student achievement. Table 7-1 also shows that family sizes have fallen and levels of parental education have improved. Over the same period, the proportion of adults aged between twenty-five and twenty-nine with a high school diploma or greater level of schooling rose from 74 to 86 percent (up

8. Hauser and Huang (1996); Hedges and Nowell (1998).

Table 7-1. *Selected Family Characteristics, 1970–90*
Percent

Characteristic	1970	1980	1990
Children in poverty	14.9	17.9	19.9
Children living with both parents[a]	85	77	73
Families with 3 or more children	36.3	22.9	20.1
High school graduate or more[b]	73.8	84.5	85.7

Source: U.S. Bureau of the Census, *Statistical Abstract of the United States*, 1992.
a. Children under eighteen years old.
b. Population aged between twenty-five and twenty-nine.

from 61 percent in 1960). Moreover, among all families with children, the share with three or more children fell from 36 to 20 percent.

It is difficult to know how to net out these opposing trends with any accuracy. Extensive research, beginning with the Coleman report and continuing through today, has demonstrated that differences in families are very important for student achievement.[9] Most of these studies do not focus on families per se, however, and thus have not delved very far into the measurement and structure of any family influences, apparently willing to employ any available measure of family structure or socioeconomic status. Susan Mayer suggests that the direct causal impact of family income might be fairly small, and that previous studies have identified associations rather than true causal impacts.[10] That analysis, nonetheless, cannot conclusively indicate whether there have been trends in the underlying causal factors that are correlated in cross-sections with income. In earlier work I have found that family size may have particularly powerful effects on achievement, and indeed may be partly responsible for narrowing the black-white gap in achievement as indicated in figure 7-3, but again it is difficult to compare the influences of the various trends that have been identified.[11]

David Grissmer and coauthors attempt to sort out these factors.[12] They use econometric techniques to estimate how various family characteristics influence children's achievement. They then apply these cross-sectionally estimated regression coefficients as weights to the trended family back-

9. Coleman and others (1966); Hanushek (1997).
10. Mayer (1997).
11. Hanushek (1992).
12. Grissmer and others (1994).

ground factors identified above. Their overall findings are that black students perform better over time than would be expected from the trends in black family factors. They attribute this performance to improvements in schools. By contrast, white students perform worse than would be expected over time, presumably leading to the opposite conclusion, that for the majority of white students schools got worse over time.

Once again, there is reason to be skeptical about these results. First, they do not observe or measure differences in schools, but instead simply attribute unexplained residual differences in the predicted and observed trends to school factors. In reality, any factor that affects achievement, that is unmeasured, and that has changed over their analysis period would be mixed with any school effects. Second, in estimating the cross-sectional models that provide the weights for the trending family factors, no direct measures of school inputs are included. In the standard analysis of misspecified econometric models, this omission will lead to biased estimates of the influence of family factors if school factors are correlated with the included family factors in the cross-sectional data that underlie their estimation. For example, better educated parents might systematically tend to place their children in better schools. In this simple example, a portion of the effects of schools will be incorrectly attributed to the education of parents.[13] Such biased estimates will lead to inappropriate weights for the trended family inputs and will limit the ability to infer anything about the true changes in student inputs over time. Third, one must believe either, contrary to Mayer, that the factors identified are the true causal influences, or that they maintain a constant relationship with the true causal influences.[14]

In sum, a variety of changes in family inputs has occurred over time, making it possible that a portion of the increased school resources has gone to offset adverse family factors. The evidence is nonetheless quite inconclusive about the directions of any trend effects, let alone their magnitudes. At the same time, the only available quantitative estimates indicate that changing family effects are unable to offset the large observed changes in pupil-teacher ratios and school resources. Indeed, for the nation as a whole, these trends are estimated to have worked in the opposite direction, making the performance of schools appear better than it was. Thus the most

13. While it is sometimes possible to ascertain how such statistical misspecification affects the estimated results, in this case the complications—with multiple factors omitted from the modeling of achievement—make that impossible.

14. Mayer (1997).

frequent explanation for the perceived ineffectiveness of historic resource policies does not resolve the puzzle.

Special Education and the Changing Structure of Schools

The discussion until now has focused on pupil-teacher ratios, but these are not the same as class size. Data on pupil-teacher ratios reflect the total number of teachers and students at a given time, but not their utilization. To take a trivial example, consider a district that only has two teachers, one of whom spends all day in class with the students and the other of whom is department head and spends all day evaluating the lesson plans of the classroom teacher. In this case, the pupil-teacher ratio is half that of the class size experienced by the students. More to the point, if teachers are required to meet fewer classes during the day than the number of classes that each student takes, the pupil-teacher ratio will be less than the average class size. Some teachers are also assigned to various duties outside the regular classroom. Thus typical class sizes observed in schools tend to be larger than measured pupil-teacher ratios.

The only data that are consistently available over time reflect pupil-teacher ratios. This is not surprising, because reporting on actual class sizes requires surveying the assignment practices of individual districts. Moreover, class sizes will also be influenced by the range of choices given to students and the number of separate courses that individual students take. Measuring the actual class sizes faced by students requires a variety of decisions about which classes to count and which not to count. For example, should one count physical education and driver's education? Class size is generally best defined in the traditional elementary school grades, where a single teacher is responsible for a self-contained classroom, and the definition gets progressively more problematical as the instructional program becomes more complex.

It remains to be seen, however, how large the influence of any divergence of class size and pupil-teacher ratios might be on the aggregate trends discussed above. In order to influence the trends (as opposed to the observed level during any period), it must be the case that the relationship between pupil-teacher ratios and class sizes is changing over time. For example, Eugene Lewit and Linda Baker show that while class sizes reported in data from the National Education Association are greater than pupil-teacher ratios, they follow a common downward trend.

While the relationship between class size and pupil-teacher ratios could change for a variety of reasons, from altered work days for teachers to expanded curricular offerings, the increased emphasis on special education has received the most attention and deserves examination. The growth in the number of students identified as handicapped, coupled with legal requirements for providing them with educational services, has increased the size of the special education sector since the late 1970s. Since this sector is relatively staff-intensive, its expansion could reduce the overall pupil-teacher ratio without commensurate decreases in regular class sizes. To the extent that mandated programming for handicapped students is driving the fall in the pupil-teacher ratio, regular class sizes may not be declining and, by extension, one might not expect any improvement in measured student performance.[15] This discussion that follows draws on earlier work by Steven Rivkin and me and provides a simple analysis of the potential importance of special education in explaining the decline in pupil-teacher ratios and the commensurate increase in educational expenditure.[16]

Concerns about the education of children with both physical and mental disabilities were translated into federal law with the enactment of the Individuals with Disabilities Education Act in 1976.[17] The act prescribes a series of diagnostics, counseling activities, and services for handicapped students. To implement this and subsequent laws and regulations, school systems expanded staff and programs, in many cases developing entirely new administrative structures. The general thrust of the educational services has been to provide regular classroom instruction where possible ("mainstreaming"), along with specialized instruction to deal with specific needs. The existence of partial categorical funding from outside and of intensive instruction for individual students creates incentives both for school systems to expand the population of identified special education students and for parents to seek admission for their children to special

15. It is frequently asserted that special education students are not generally included in tests and other measures of performance. If so, it would be appropriate to link expenditure on regular-instruction students alone with their test performance. On the performance side, however, if a larger proportion of students is identified as needing special education, and if these are generally students who would perform poorly on tests, the shift to increased special education over time should lead to general increases in test scores, *ceteris paribus*. Direct analysis of special education in Texas indicates that many special education students do take standard achievement tests, although this varies widely by type of disability, due to various state and federal regulations (Hanushek, Kain, and Rivkin, 1998).

16. Hanushek and Rivkin (1997).

17. P.L. 94-142 was originally titled the Education for All Handicapped Children Act.

Table 7-2. *Special Education Student Population and*
Related School Personnel, 1978–90
Units as indicated

Year	Disabled children[a] (thousands)	Percentage of elementary and secondary students	Special education personnel (thousands)		
			Teachers	Other instructional	Non-instructional
1978	3,777	8.7	195	140	32
1979	3,919	9.2	203	178	37
1980	4,036	9.7	221	159	56
1981	4,178	10.2	233	167	40
1982	4,233	10.6	235	168	46
1983	4,298	10.9	241	168	57
1984	4,341	11.1	248	173	53
1985	4,363	11.1	275	172	54
1986	4,370	11.1	292	183	47
1987	4,422	11.1	296	175	48
1988	4,494	11.2	301	192	49
1989	4,587	11.4	303	208	48
1990	4,688	11.6	308	220	53

Source: Data are from various annual reports on the Individuals with Disabilities Education Act of 1976. In particular, student numbers are from U.S. Department of Education (1991, p. 4).

a. Aged up to twenty-one years.

education programs.[18] The result has been growth of children classified as special education students, even as the total student population has been falling.

The aggregate changes in the population identified as disabled between 1978 and 1990 are shown in table 7-2.[19] Despite the fact that overall public school enrollment declined by over 1.5 million students between 1980 and 1990, the number of students classified as disabled increased from 4.0 million to 4.7 million. Therefore the percentage of students classified as dis-

18. See Hartman (1980); Monk (1990).

19. Data on special education come from annual reports required under the Individuals with Disabilities Education Act of 1976. Prior to the act, there were no consistent data on handicapped students or their schooling.

abled increased from 9.7 to 11.6 percent during this period. Almost all of this increase represents students classified as having "learning disabilities," a not very well defined category. Moreover, the number of special education teachers increased much more rapidly than the number of children classified as disabled. Table 7-2 shows that the number of special education teachers and other instructional staff increased by over 50 percent between 1978 and 1990: the number of special education teachers rose from 195,000 to 308,000, while the number of other special education instructional personnel (including teacher's aides) rose from 140,000 to 220,000.[20] The number of noninstructional special education staff grew before 1980, but remained roughly constant during the 1980s.

These numbers suggest that the previously noted decline in pupil-teacher and pupil-staff ratios during the 1980s might simply reflect the growth in the number of students receiving special education services and an increase in the intensity of special education—that is, a decrease in effective pupil-teacher ratios for special education. While it is not possible to calculate directly the intensity of special education, since many of the students classified as disabled attend regular classes for much of the day, the maximum impact of the special education changes on overall pupil-teacher and pupil-staff ratios can be estimated. Specifically, by assuming historic values for special education students, instructional staff, and classroom teachers, one can roughly approximate the impact of the growth in special education on the overall ratios. Results are reported in table 7-3.

As shown in the table, the actual pupil-teacher ratio, counting all students and teachers, falls from 19.1 in 1980 to 17.2 in 1990, a decline of 10 percent. The next column estimates what the overall pupil-teacher ratio would have been in 1990 if the observed special education pupil-teacher ratio had remained at its 1980 level instead of falling. The right-hand column shows what the 1990 pupil-teacher ratio would have been if, additionally, the proportion of students classified as disabled had remained at its 1980 level instead of climbing. The simulations indicate that most of the fall in the pupil-teacher ratio during this period was not caused by the expansion of special education. If the proportion of students classified as disabled and the observed pupil-teacher ratio for special education had remained constant, the aggregate pupil-teacher ratio would have fallen at

20. Precise accounting for special education personnel is frequently difficult, suggesting that these data contain more error than the other aggregate data presented.

Table 7-3. *Estimated Effects of Changes in Special Education on Pupil-Teacher Ratios, 1980 and 1990*

| | | Overall pupil-teacher ratio if the following remained at 1980 levels: | |
| | Actual pupil-teacher ratio | Special education pupil-teacher ratio | Special education pupil-teacher ratio and proportion of disabled students |
Year			
1980	19.1	19.1	19.1
1990	17.2	17.6	17.9

Source: Author's calculations as described in text.

least to 17.9. In other words, just over one-third of the fall in the pupil-teacher ratio could possibly be attributed to increases in special education. This calculation reflects an upper bound on effects. Importantly, the graphs of pupil-teacher ratios and survey information on class size reported by Lewit and Baker do not appear to show divergences in the two trends that could be attributable to the introduction of special education.[21]

The overall conclusion is that special education could have had some significant effect on pupil-teacher and pupil-staff ratios, but that much more has also been going on during recent times. In terms of the basic issue of flat student performance over recent decades, however, there have clearly been reductions in class size and increases in the resources available for regular classrooms.

Black-White Differentials

An alternative interpretation of the basic aggregate trends follows the observation that there has been a narrowing of the racial gap in NAEP performance, particularly during the 1980s. A variety of commentators have taken this as evidence that school resources have an important effect. They point, in particular, to the increase in federal compensatory programs during the 1970s and 1980s, including Title 1 and Head Start. Since these programs are aimed at disadvantaged students, and since blacks and Hispanics are disproportionately disadvantaged, the narrowing of the differential merely reflects the increased resources.

21. Lewit and Baker (1997).

One problem with this argument, however, is the magnitude of specific programs for the disadvantaged. At the federal level, compensatory education spending amounted to just $7 billion in 1995. These programs target poor students of all racial and ethnic groups, not merely minorities. Moreover, the amount is relatively small compared with total spending on elementary and secondary schools, which exceeds $300 billion.[22]

Michael Cook and William Evans analyze the black-white achievement differential using the panel of NAEP data.[23] They attempt to decompose the differences in performance into family, school, and other factors. Their analysis indicates that school resources and specific schoolwide factors cannot account for the narrowing of the gap. In related analysis, Jeffrey Grogger analyzes the effects of specific school resources on black-white differences in earnings.[24] He also concludes that school resources have not had a significant effect on these differences. Furthermore, there is no indication that pupil-teacher ratios have a significant effect on students' subsequent earnings.

Summary

The available evidence and data suggest some uncertainty about the underlying relationships among families, school organization, class size, and achievement. Allowing for changes in family background and in special education, however, it remains difficult to make a case for reduced class size from the aggregate data. Pupil-teacher ratios and, as best one can tell, average class sizes have been falling significantly for a long time. The increases in teacher intensity have been large enough that discernible impacts on average student performance might reasonably be expected. Nonetheless, overall achievement data do not suggest that it has been a productive policy. The aggregate data are, however, quite limited, restricted to a small number of performance observations over time, and it has been difficult to rule out conclusively other fundamental changes that might affect school success. Therefore it is useful to turn to other evidence, including more detailed school-level information.

---

22. The federal government has other relevant programs: Head Start added $3.5 billion and child nutrition was $7.6 billion. Such expenditures, even if included in the totals for elementary and secondary spending, still yield small relative total spending.

23. Cook and Evans (1996).

24. Grogger (1996).

International Evidence

Somewhat surprisingly, similar kinds of results concerning the relationship between pupil-teacher ratios and student performance are found across countries. While it is difficult to develop standardized data that control for the many differences in populations and schools across countries, international comparisons have some appeal. The international variations in class size and pupil-teacher ratios are larger than those found within the United States, offering some hope that the effects of alternative intensities of teacher usage can be better understood. Even given these wide differences, there is no evidence that lower pupil-teacher ratios systematically lead to increased student performance.

The Third International Mathematics and Science Study was conducted during 1995. A series of mathematics and science tests were given to students in voluntarily participating nations. As a simple exercise, the eighth grade math and science scores can be correlated with the primary school pupil-teacher ratio in each country.[25] For the seventeen nations with consistent data, there is a positive relationship between pupil-teacher ratios and test scores, and it is statistically significant at the 10 percent level for both tests. When Korea, the sampled country with the largest pupil-teacher ratio, is left out of the analysis, the statistical significance disappears but the positive result remains. Nonetheless, while this international evidence points to the surprising result that performance is better when there is less intensive use of teachers, there cannot be much confidence that such differences are more than statistical artifacts.

A more systematic attempt to investigate the relationship between student performance and pupil-teacher ratios draws on the six prior international tests in math or science, conducted between 1960 and 1990.[26] Using seventy country-test-specific observations of test performance, this analysis finds a positive but statistically insignificant effect of pupil-teacher ratios on performance, after allowing for differences in parental schooling. Again, while there are very large differences in pupil-teacher ratios, they do not appear significantly to influence student performance.[27]

---

25. Test scores are reported in Beaton and others (1996a, 1996b). Primary pupil-teacher ratios for public and private schools are found in Organization for Economic Cooperation and Development (1996).

26. Hanushek and Kim (1996).

27. At the same time, differences in test performance are extraordinarily important in determining differences in national growth rates (Hanushek and Kim, 1996).

Finally, while uniform data on class size differences are not available, some investigations have shown that class sizes vary more than pupil-teacher ratios across countries. Specifically, Japan and the United States have quite similar pupil-teacher ratios, but because of decisions about how to organize schools and to use teachers, Japanese classes are much larger than U.S. classes.[28] Student performance in Japan is, on average, much better than in the United States. There are many differences in the schooling and societies of the sampled nations, so it would be inappropriate to make too much of these results. They do, however, underscore the fact that common presumptions about the achievement effects of pupil-teacher ratios and class size are not supported by the evidence.

Econometric Evidence

The most extensive information about the effects of class size comes from attempts to estimate input-output relationships, or production functions, for schools. The investigation of the effects of school resources began in earnest in the late 1960s, after the publication of the Coleman report.[29] This congressionally mandated study by the U.S. Office of Education startled many by suggesting that schools do not exert a very powerful influence on student achievement. Subsequent attention was directed at both understanding the analysis of the Coleman report and additional evidence about the effects of resources.[30]

Over the past thirty years, a steady stream of research has built up a consistent picture of the educational process. The following summary concentrates on a set of published results available through 1994.[31] The basic

28. Stevenson and Stigler (1992).

29. Coleman and others (1966).

30. These analyses suggest serious flaws in the statistical methodology and interpretation of the Coleman report, but most of that discussion is not relevant for the present purposes; see Bowles and Levin (1968), Cain and Watts (1970), Hanushek and Kain(1972).

31. See Hanushek (1997) for greater detail. The tabulations do include results in Hanushek, Rivkin, and Taylor (1996), since this updating was conducted as part of that research. Some analyses have been published subsequently—for example, Betts (1995), Ehrenberg and Brewer (1995), Lamdin (1995), Staley and Blair (1995), Ferguson and Ladd (1996), Grogger (1996), and Wenglinsky (1997)—but their results will not affect the overall conclusions here (see Hanushek, 1997). While they have some unique features, these studies are conceptually similar to prior studies and can be considered within the context of prior results. Moreover, given the number of studies sampled, a few additional results could not affect the overall conclusions reported here even if they uniformly pointed in the same direction, which they do not.

studies include all available that meet minimal criteria for analytical design and reporting of results. Specifically, the studies must be published in a book or journal (to ensure a minimal quality standard), must include some measure of family background in addition to at least one measure of resources devoted to schools, and must provide information about statistical reliability of the estimate of the effect of resources on student performance.

The summary relies on all of the separate estimates of the effects of resources on student performance. For tabulation purposes, a "study" is a separate estimate of an educational production function found in the literature. Individual published analyses typically contain more than one set of estimates, distinguished by different measures of student performance, different grade levels, and frequently entirely different sampling designs. If, however, a publication includes estimates of alternative specifications employing the same sample and performance measures, only one of the alternative estimates is included.[32] Thus the ninety individual publications that form the basis for this analysis contain 377 separate estimates of production functions. While several of the studies were produced in more or less immediate reaction to the Coleman report, half of the available studies were published since 1985.

These econometric estimates relate class size or teacher intensity to measures of student performance, while also allowing for the influence of family and other inputs into education. The precise sampling, specification of the relationships, measurement of student performance, and estimation techniques differ across studies, but here I concentrate on the summary of a relationship across studies. To do this, studies are aggregated according to the estimated sign and statistical significance of the relationship.[33]

Table 7-4 summarizes the available results for estimates of the effects of teacher-pupil ratios on student outcomes. Of the total of 377 available

32. Some judgment is required in selecting among the alternative specifications. As a general rule, the tabulated results reflect the estimates that are emphasized by the authors of the underlying papers. In cases where this rule did not lead to a clear choice, the tabulation emphasizes statistically significant results among the alternatives preferred by the original author. An alternative approach is followed by Betts (1996), who aggregates the separate estimates of a common parameter in a given study.

33. More details about the methodology and the available studies can be found in Hanushek (1979, 1997). Some controversy also exists about the best way to summarize the results of different studies, but these issues have little bearing on the present discussions; see Greenwald, Hedges, and Laine (1996) and Hanushek (1996a, 1997). Other issues concerning estimation strategies are raised in Card and Krueger (1996), Heckman, Layne-Farrar, and Todd (1996), and Hanushek (1996b). These latter issues, while relevant, are very technical and in my opinion do not affect the policy conclusions presented below.

Table 7-4. *Distribution of Estimated Influence of Teacher-Pupil Ratios on Student Performance, by Level of Schooling*
Percent, except as indicated

School level	Number of estimates	Statistically significant		Statistically insignificant		
		Positive	Negative	Positive	Negative	Unknown sign
All	277	15	13	27	25	20
Elementary	136	13	20	25	20	23
Secondary	141	17	7	28	31	17

Source: Author's calculations. Sources of underlying data are detailed in Hanushek (1997).

econometric studies of the determinants of student performance, 277 consider teacher-pupil ratios. (Estimates of the effect of class size or pupil-teacher ratios are reversed in sign, so that conventional wisdom would call for a positive effect in all cases.) The first row of the table shows that just 15 percent of all studies find a positive and statistically significant relationship between teacher intensity and student performance. At the same time, 13 percent of all studies find negative and statistically significant relationships with student performance. Ignoring the statistical significance, or the confidence that there is any true relationship, the estimates are almost equally divided between those suggesting that small classes are better and those suggesting that they are worse.[34] This distribution of results is what one would expect if there was no systematic relationship between class size and student performance. Fully 85 percent of the studies suggest either that fewer teachers per student are better (that is, they yield negative estimates) or that there is little confidence of any relationship at all (that is, they are statistically insignificant).

Some people have suggested that the effect of class size may differ at different points in the schooling process (see, for example, the interpretations of Tennessee's Project STAR study discussed below). To consider this possibility, the overall estimates of the effects of teacher-pupil ratios are divided into estimates for the elementary and secondary school levels. Table 7-4 shows that there is little difference between the estimated effects in elementary and in secondary schools, but, if anything, there is less support for increasing teacher-pupil ratios at the elementary level. For elementary

34. Twenty percent of the studies do not report the sign of any estimated relationship. Instead, they simply note that the estimates were statistically insignificant.

schools, more estimated effects are negative, that is, indicate that smaller classes are worse. This is true for all studies and for those with statistically significant estimates. Unfortunately, there are too few studies to permit one to look at individual grades, as opposed to all elementary grades combined.

With these data, it is also possible to address explicitly the distinction between the pupil-teacher ratio and class size. While these two concepts differ, they are highly related, and it remains to be seen whether they provide similar evidence about the effectiveness of smaller classes. The estimates include both studies that measure class size and those that contain aggregate measures of teacher-pupil ratios for a school, district, or state. Studies that investigate performance within individual classrooms invariably measure class size, whereas those at higher levels of aggregation most often measure average teacher-pupil ratios. In particular, studies that are highly aggregated, such as those investigating performance across entire districts or states, are almost always forced to consider only the overall teacher-pupil ratio.

Table 7-5 displays the results of estimates according to the level of aggregation of the teacher-pupil measure. As the table shows, analyses conducted at the state or district levels are more likely to indicate that teacher-pupil ratios have a positive and statistically significant relationship to student performance. Nonetheless, while this pattern coincides with the less precise measure of class size at the classroom level, it is more likely to come from other fundamental analytical problems than from the pure measurement issues. The more aggregated analyses are subject to a series of specification problems (independent of the ones considered here) that are exacerbated by the aggregation of the analysis.[35] In particular, these analyses leave out all consideration of state-by-state differences in school policies, which appears to bias the results toward finding stronger effects of teacher-pupil ratios and school resources in general. At a minimum, one can conclude that the insignificance of the results appears real and is not just an artifact of measuring teacher-pupil ratios instead of actual class size. The best studies, with the most precise measurements of class size and school resources, arrive at the same general conclusions, indicating that the results are not easily explained away by poor data or research methods.

Statistical investigations that employ a value-added specification are generally regarded as conceptually superior and likely to provide the most reliable estimates of education production functions. These studies relate

---

35. See Hanushek, Rivkin, and Taylor (1996).

Table 7-5. *Distribution of Estimated Influence of Teacher-Pupil Ratios on Student Performance, by Aggregation of Resource Measure*
Percent, except as indicated

Aggregation	Number of estimates	Statistically significant		Statistically insignificant		
		Positive	Negative	Positive	Negative	Unknown sign
Total	277	15	13	27	25	20
Classroom	77	12	8	18	26	36
School	128	10	17	26	28	19
District	56	21	16	39	20	4
County	5	0	0	40	40	20
State	11	64	0	27	9	0

Source: Author's calculations. Sources of underlying data are detailed in Hanushek (1997).

an individual's current performance to his or her performance at some prior time and to school and family inputs during the intervening period. The superiority of this approach comes from the use of prior achievement to mitigate any problems arising from missing data about past school and family factors and from differences in the innate abilities of students.[36]

Table 7-6 provides a summary of value-added results, both for all seventy-eight estimates of class-size effects and for the twenty-three estimates that come from samples in a single state. On the one hand, there are many fewer such estimates than in the overall set, and thus any conclusions are subject to more uncertainty. On the other hand, because of the superiority of these analyses, each study deserves more weight than one of the general studies reviewed above. The restriction to samples within single states corrects for differences in school policies to avoid the biases previously discussed. From the results in table 7-6, there is little reason to believe that smaller classes systematically lead to improvements in student achievement. Of the best available studies (single-state, value-added studies of individual classroom achievement), only one out of twenty-three, or 4 percent,

36. For a more thorough discussion of estimation approaches, see Hanushek (1979). Krueger (1997) points out that value-added studies cannot identify any impact of resources prior to the period of study. While he argues from this that one should not use value-added models, the very essence of such models is to provide more precise estimates of the magnitude and timing of any resource effects on student performance. Statistical models of the level of student performance that do not include measures of prior achievement will tend to be biased by all time-varying historical factors, such as prior class size or teacher quality, that are not explicitly measured.

Table 7-6. *Distribution of Other Estimated Influences of Teacher-Pupil Ratios on Student Performance, Based on Value-Added Models*
Percent, except as indicated

School level	Number of estimates	Statistically significant		Statistically insignificant		
		Positive	Negative	Positive	Negative	Unknown sign
All	78	12	8	21	26	35
Within a single state	23	4	13	30	39	13

Source: Author's calculations. Sources of underlying data are detailed in Hanushek (1997).

finds that smaller classes have a statistically significant positive effect on student performance.

As noted by Alan Krueger, if the effects of class size on performance are small, a number of the reported econometric studies may not have adequate data to distinguish between "small effect" and "no effect," possibly leading to the pattern of statistically insignificant results reported.[37] Preliminary analysis of achievement data for several cohorts of students in the State of Texas provides partial support for this hypothesis.[38] From over 300,000 observations of gains in student performance across the schools of Texas, statistically significant positive results are found for smaller classes in fourth and fifth grade mathematics and reading performance.[39] Even with such large samples, however, class size is a statistically insignificant determinant of sixth grade performance in either subject. More important, the estimated magnitudes are very small. A class size reduction of ten students, which cuts average class size approximately in half and represents a 2 1/2 standard deviation movement, is never estimated to yield more than 0.11 standard deviation of improvement in student achievement for the results that are statistically significant. When one separates out the results for students eligible for free or reduced lunches, the performance of these disadvantaged students is found to be more sensitive to class size: a targeted

37. Krueger (1997).
38. Rivkin, Hanushek, and Kain (1998).
39. The analysis of student performance is based on complicated statistical analysis involving regression of achievement growth with individual fixed effects, a design employed to eliminate both unmeasured differences in individual ability and the potential effects of student selection into specific schools. The small results reported here are also consistent across alternative estimation strategies based on simple models of achievement growth.

class size reduction of ten students could yield as much as 0.18 standard deviation of improvement in fourth grade math performance. Estimated class size effects for students ineligible for free or reduced lunch, however, are less than half as big as those for disadvantaged students and are more frequently insignificant.

A final set of questions about the econometric studies of teacher-pupil ratios involves the underlying mechanism for establishing small and large classes. If, for example, a school district uses a subjective method of assigning "weaker" students to small classes and "stronger" students to large classes, the econometric methods might not provide an accurate assessment of the direct, causal influence of class size.[40]

The econometric evidence is clear. There is little reason to believe that smaller class size systematically yields higher student achievement. While some studies point in that direction, an almost equal number point in the opposite direction. Moreover, restricting attention to the best of these studies, including those with the most accurate measurement of individual class size, merely strengthens the overall conclusion.

Project STAR

In the mid-1980s, because of ambiguity about the effects of class size on student performance, the State of Tennessee launched a random assignment experiment on the effects of reducing class size on student achievement called Project STAR.[41] The design was heavily influenced by an early summary of research by Gene Glass and Mary Lee Smith.[42] Glass and

40. Hoxby (1998) employs other information about the source of decisions about class size in order to correct for such problems, but she finds that class size still has no consistent effect on student outcomes. Note, moreover, that this problem arises only when decisions are made on the basis of unmeasured student characteristics. If, for example, students are assigned to classes on the basis of their early test scores, and if these test scores are controlled for in the econometric analysis as in the value-added estimation, these problems do not arise. The statistical analysis in Rivkin, Hanushek, and Kain (1998) provides an alternative approach to the selection problems. In another attempt to correct for possible influences of school decisionmaking, Angrist and Lavy (1999) do find significant class size effects. Their study considers special features of Israeli law that permit alternative statistical approaches to identifying small class effects. The applicability to U.S. schools is unclear. An alternative instrumental variable approach is found in Akerhielm (1995). Taken together, these analyses do not suggest that the prior results are merely statistical artifacts.

41. STAR stands for student-teacher achievement ratio. See Word and others (1990); Finn and others (1990); Finn and Achilles (1990).

42. Glass and Smith (1979).

Smith combined evidence from different experimental studies and suggested that student achievement is roughly constant across class sizes until the pupil-teacher ratio gets down to approximately 15 to 1. Beyond this, reductions in class size appeared to yield significant gains in student performance. Project STAR is a large and complicated program. Beginning in 1985, a group of students from kindergarten through third grade was randomly assigned to either regular classes of twenty-two to twenty-five students or small classes of thirteen to seventeen students. The regular classes were divided into two groups, one with teacher's aides and one without. To be eligible to participate in the experiment, a volunteer school had to be large enough to ensure that there was at least one small and one large class of each type. The experimental design placed students in the same randomly assigned treatment group from kindergarten through third grade—although, as discussed below, attrition, experimental replacement, and change of treatment group were considerable over the course of the experiment. Over 11,000 students in seventy-nine schools eventually participated in the program; 48 percent of the 6,324 original students who started in kindergarten remained in the experiment for the full four-year period.

A variety of natural and design factors, discussed below, introduce uncertainty into the analysis and interpretation of the results of Project STAR. The most obvious issue is that many popular interpretations of the results are not supported by the basic data. Most important, even though the experiment ran through the third grade, any beneficial impact of small classes on achievement is confined to the first year of treatment.

The basic data from Project STAR indicate that, at best, very specific and limited achievement effects might follow from reductions in class size. Figure 7-4 illustrates the basic achievement results of the program. The two panels of the figure plot average reading and math scores from kindergarten through third grade for students randomly assigned to the three different classroom situations.[43] Three facts are immediately obvious from these graphs. First, for both reading and mathematics, students in small classes have significantly greater average achievement at the end of kindergarten. Second, on average, the performance of students in regular classes is virtually the same as that of students in regular classes with aides

---

43. For a more complete description of the experiment, see Word and others (1990). A series of different tests was given. Figure 7-4 reports results from the nationally normed Stanford Achievement Test. Using data from the alternative tests would not change the patterns or conclusions.

Figure 7-4. *Stanford Achievement Test Scores in Project STAR*

Score

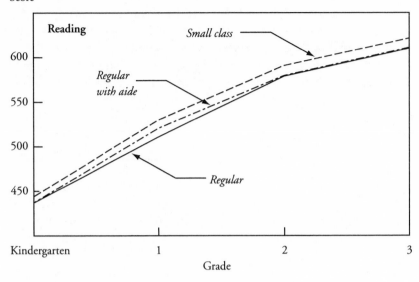

Score

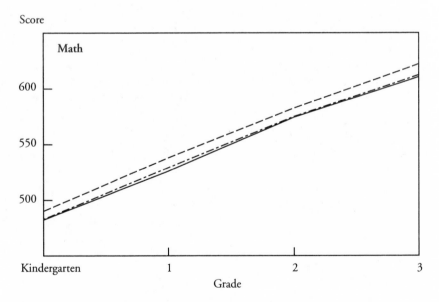

Source: Word and others (1990).

throughout the experiment (and students were rather freely reassigned across these treatments after the first year of the experiment). Third, the kindergarten gap between small and regular classrooms is maintained at essentially the same level through the first, second, and third grades.[44]

The original analyses of the experiment reported the differences in performance between the small and regular classes at each grade, giving the impression that the added classroom resources at each grade level led to significant gains in achievement in each grade. This interpretation is reinforced by the widely cited review of the study's findings by Harvard statistician Frederick Mosteller. He writes, for example, that "after four years, it was clear that smaller classes did produce substantial improvement in early learning and cognitive studies."[45] In reality, the differences appeared in the first year of the experiment and simply reappeared in subsequent years.

For policy purposes, the key to the interpretation of Project STAR involves expectations about student performance over time. Perhaps the most standard interpretation from learning theory begins with the view that education is a cumulative process, building on past achievement. If students learn certain skills in, say, the first grade, they tend to carry them over to later grades, even if with some depreciation, and to build on this base as they progress. According to this view, the basic evidence of Project STAR suggests that while smaller classes may be important at kindergarten, they have no average effect subsequently. Specifically, since the growth in achievement across experimental and control students is the same from first through third grades, the added resources of the smaller classes appear to add nothing to student performance. Early differences remain the same over time. If resources had a continuing impact, one should observe a greater disparity of achievement as more and more resources are applied. The achievement curves in figure 7-4 should fan out if smaller classes have an on-going, cumulative impact. Thus the cumulative effect learning model is rejected.

Alternatively, some have argued that the observed pattern could be consistent with small classes making a difference in all grades if students are

44. There is some ambiguity about the effect of small classes in first grade. The Project STAR results in Word and others (1990) indicate some faster growth in achievement during the first grade for those in small classes, and slower growth from first through third grades for students in small classes. But this finding is complicated by the lack of universal kindergarten in Tennessee and the introduction of new students into the experiment in the first grade. Krueger (1997) demonstrates that the overall results are consistent with small classes having an effect only in the first year of schooling.

45. Mosteller (1995, p. 113).

expected to fall back to a common mean performance each year. This is equivalent to saying that educational performance is not cumulative. Under this set of expectations, maintaining the difference in performance at the end of kindergarten requires the continued infusion of resources. Lowered class size might be effective if it stemmed the "inevitable" reversion of achievement to lower levels when resources were removed. Such interpretations are most common in discussions about the education of disadvantaged students, since they provide (a largely untested) way of explaining achievement reversions from initial gains in Head Start and other early childhood programs for the disadvantaged.[46] In this context, it is important to remember that Project STAR was a program for the broad spectrum of Tennessee children. Therefore interpretation of its results must be consistent with underlying notions of the learning process for all children, not just the disadvantaged.

In the presence of these alternative interpretations, the way to identify the effects of class size would be to assign randomly some of the experimental children to larger classes after they had been in small classes in the earliest grades. Unfortunately, this was not done systematically within the experiment (even though some movement across treatment groups did occur, in violation of the experimental protocol). However, follow-ups of Project STAR students after they had returned to regular class settings provide important information. The Lasting Benefits Study, which has traced students after Project STAR finished, shows that students from the small classes in kindergarten through third grade maintained most of the prior differences through the sixth grade.[47] Experimental comparisons of small versus regular classes yield effect sizes on norm-referenced third grade tests in reading and math of 0.24 standard deviation and 0.21 standard deviation, respectively.[48] In the sixth grade, three years after the end of any differential resources for the two groups, the effect sizes for comparisons of students previously in small versus regular classrooms were 0.21 standard deviation and 0.16 standard deviation for reading and math, respectively.[49] In other words, the differentials in performance found at kindergarten remain essentially unchanged by third grade after class size reductions of

46. See, for example, Barnett (1992).

47. Nye and others (1993). These results should be treated with caution, because the data have never been made available to other researchers; see Hanushek (1999).

48. Word and others (1990). Effect sizes indicate the differences in average performance for the two groups measured in units of standard deviations of the test; see Mosteller (1995).

49. Nye and others (1993).

one-third were continuously applied (see figure 7-4), and they remain largely unchanged by sixth grade, after regular class sizes had been resumed for three years. This latter finding leads to rejection of the fall-back model and indicates that class size reductions after kindergarten have little potential effect on achievement.

A third interpretation is that small classes, particularly early in the schooling process, have a one-time effect on student performance that is not linked to the acquisition of cognitive skills per se. This one-time effect could reflect early training in the "activity of school." Students in small classes learn norms, behavior, and learning patterns that are useful in subsequent years, so that they are able to continue achieving at a higher level. In fact, this last interpretation is the one most consistent with the Project STAR data, ignoring the other possibilities of flaws in the underlying experimental design and data collection.[50] It provides a parsimonious explanation of why there is a one-time but lasting effect of class size reductions in kindergarten. It also has powerful implications for policy.

The most expansive conclusion that can be reached from Project STAR and the Lasting Benefits Study is that they might support an expectation of positive achievement effects from moving to small kindergartens, and maybe small first grades. None of the Project STAR data support a wholesale reduction in class size across grades. Moreover, the achievement results come from large reductions (one-third of the existing regular class size) that make the small classes quite small (fifteen students) compared with most existing classroom situations. The data do not provide evidence about what might happen with lesser changes that take class sizes down to levels above the Tennessee experiment, say, to between eighteen and twenty students. (Recall that the original motivation for Project STAR involved research results suggesting no effects for class sizes greater than fifteen students.) This policy interpretation is quite different from that commonly attributed to analysis of the Project STAR data, which many cite to justify almost any sort of reduction in class size at almost any school grade.

Project STAR and its related programs do support one aspect of the econometric results from Texas noted above: disadvantaged students appear more sensitive to variations in class size than the majority of stu-

---

50. Krueger (1997) reanalyzes the Project STAR data and finds that there is a large first-year effect from reduced class size, but little continuing effect. Krueger incorporates the fact that some students begin small classes in the first grade, rather than in kindergarten. If students were not in small kindergartens, he suggests that they achieve gains from small classes in first grade, that is, in their first year with small classes. See also Hanushek (1999).

dents.[51] Again, however, disadvantaged students, on average, are not currently in larger classes than more advantaged students, and the effects appear small relative to the costs of programs and alternative policy approaches.

Up to this point the discussion has taken the reported results at face value, but some aspects of the experimental design and implementation of Project STAR introduce additional uncertainty into the analysis.[52] The most important concerns are as follows. First, not all students started the experiment at the same time, in part because kindergarten is not mandatory or universal in Tennessee, and in part through the replacement of children who dropped out of the experiment. Second, sizable attrition occurred over the course of the experiment, due to mobility and other factors, and this attrition was likely not random. Third, parents, teachers, and schools knew they were part of an experiment, and parental pressure led to part of the experiment being compromised by the reassignment of students: approximately 10 percent of the students in small classes in grades one through three had been in regular-sized classes the previous year.[53] Fourth, no student took an achievement test prior to entering the experiment, so it is difficult to analyze whether elements of the random assignment process contributed to any observed differences in achievement during the program.[54] Fifth, in any given year, up to 11 percent of students did

51. Mosteller (1995).

52. A full description and preliminary analysis of the effects of these issues is found in Hanushek (1999). See also Prais (1996); Goldstein and Blatchford (1998); Krueger (1997).

53. After the first year, students in the regular classes and the regular classes with aides were randomly reassigned. Preliminary analyses from kindergarten had indicated that these two treatments did not result in significantly different performance, but the reassignment made analysis of aide effects difficult. A much more serious problem is that some students in regular classes were moved to the small class treatment (and a smaller number were moved in the opposite direction). Such transfers were "intended to separate incompatible children and 'to achieve sexual and racial balance'"(Mosteller, 1995, p. 124). Such transfers potentially bias simple comparisons of small and regular classrooms, because treatments are no longer independent of student characteristics.

Virtually no attention has been given to how teachers responded to the experiment. Each teacher clearly knew whether they were part of the small or regular class portion of the experiment. And, teachers in general would prefer smaller to larger classes. Whether these factors influenced work effort or behavior is not known.

54. Considerable controversy exists about how early in schooling reliable achievement testing is possible, but few people suggest that it is either reliable or useful before kindergarten. Nonetheless, approximately half of the students who ever participated began the experiment in the first grade or later—that is, when tests were readily available within the experiment itself. Krueger (1997) demonstrates that there does appear to be random assignment based on key student characteristics, such as race or eligibility for free or reduced-price lunch, providing a prima facie case that kindergarten differences are not just the result of simple biases in treatment assignment.

not take the examinations, although there is little indication that this proportion differs by treatment group. Finally, there was some drift from the target class sizes of thirteen to seventeen and twenty-two to twenty-five students, so that there is actually a distribution of realized class size outcomes over time in both treatment groups. Each of these issues has been raised by the initial researchers and by later interpreters of the results, but the experimental data do not provide information that permits one to ascertain fully the effects of such possible problems.[55] One indication of bias comes from the smaller effects of class size for students in the experiment for the full four years, as compared with each sample taken separately, but this is not conclusive.[56]

It is particularly important to note that Project STAR has never been replicated. The contaminating conditions described above clearly suggest that further experimentation would be useful in reducing uncertainties arising from the original study. Indeed, practical problems of implementation suggest that no single experiment is likely to be entirely free of ambiguities.

Nonetheless, the power of random assignment experimentation should not be ignored. One of Mosteller's strongest messages is the ability of random assignment experiments to circumvent some of the difficulties of relying on statistical analyses of observations from natural outcomes of the schooling process.[57] It has been argued that there has been no replication or extension of the approach taken by Project STAR because experiments are expensive. Project STAR involved appropriations of about $3 million per year.[58] Yet the proper frame of reference is the cost of a full-scale program, such as the 1996 California class size initiative for kindergarten through third grade, which involves annual expenditures of over $1 billion. Proposed national programs go far beyond this. The potential costs of implementing an ineffective policy on that scale dwarf the costs of designing, implementing, and evaluating a series of extensive random assignment studies designed to investigate alternative policy proposals.[59] Further, when class size reductions are implemented for an entire state, they defy subse-

---

55. See, for example, Finn and Achilles (1990); Mosteller (1995); Krueger (1997).

56. See Hanushek (1999). Because the annual samples and the four-year sample have various selection biases, it is difficult to estimate the magnitude of any one type of bias. Nonetheless, if the potential biases have no effects on the treatment estimates, the four-year effects should be as high as or higher than the annual effects.

57. Mosteller (1995). See also Hanushek and others (1994).

58. Word and others (1990).

59. Hanushek and others (1994).

quent analysis of their effectiveness. In other words, it is unlikely that one will ever obtain reliable evaluations of whether the $1 billion spent annually in California is achieving any positive educational results. But if reductions in class size are viewed as policies with political rather than educational objectives, it is perhaps the case that policymakers do not want to know whether performance improves.

Interpretation and Conclusions

The extensive investigation of the effects of class size on student performance has produced a very consistent picture. There appears to be little systematic gain from general reductions in class size. This story comes through at the aggregate level, where pupil-teacher ratios and class sizes have fallen dramatically over the past three decades and student performance has remained virtually unchanged. It also comes through from international data, where one finds extraordinarily large differences in class sizes without commensurate differences in student performance. But since the aggregate analyses could be misleading for a variety of analytical reasons, more weight should be put on school-level analyses and on experimental data. From production function estimates, there is little reason to believe that overall reductions in class size will yield much in the way of positive achievement gains. Across several hundred separate estimates of the effects of reduced class size, positive and negative effects almost balance each other out, underscoring the ineffectiveness of overall class size policies such as those being currently advocated. Finally, the one major random assignment experiment, Tennessee's Project STAR, provides no support for widespread reductions in class size, although it holds out hope for gains from smaller kindergartens.

None of this says that smaller classes never matter. Indeed, the micro-level evidence, which shows instances where differences in teacher-pupil ratios appear to be important, suggests just the opposite. My own interpretation is that there are likely to be situations—defined in terms of specific teachers, specific groups of students, and specific subject matter—where small classes could be very beneficial for student achievement. At the same time, there are many other situations where reduced class size has no important effect on achievement, even though it always has very significant impacts on school costs. Thus, for example, across-the-board policies of class size reductions, such as those enacted in 1996 in California for elementary education through grade three, are unlikely to have a beneficial effect on overall student achievement.[60]

The real difficulty is that we do not know how to describe, a priori, situations where reductions in class size will be beneficial. Thus it is not possible to legislate only good outcomes from the state capital, or to institute only good outcomes from the courtroom. Policies developed in these contexts can only expect average gains, which appear to be very small or nonexistent.

The California policy, which many other states are apparently on the verge of emulating, illustrates another aspect of the relationship between research evidence and policymaking. This program was designed to reduce class sizes close to the regular-sized classes in the Tennessee experiment. No evidence from Project STAR relates to the likely effects of such a policy change, as opposed to moving classes down to the level of fifteen students. Moreover, Glass and Smith's original analysis, on which Project STAR was based, casts serious doubts on the potential for any improvement in student performance from such a policy.[61]

Much of the case for reduced class size rests on common sense. With fewer students, teachers can devote more attention to each child and can tailor the material to an individual child's needs. But consider, for example, a change from classes of twenty-six students to classes of twenty-three. This represents an increase of over 10 percent in teacher costs alone (and most likely would raise other costs as well). It is relevant to ask whether teachers would in fact notice such a change and alter their approach. The observational information from teacher and classroom process effects of the one-third class size reductions in Project STAR suggest no noticeable changes.[62]

The policy issue is not defined exclusively by whether one should expect positive effects from reducing class size. Class size reduction is one of the most expensive propositions for change in the schools. Project STAR involved increasing the number of classroom teachers by one-third, a pol-

---

60. In the short run, it is quite conceivable that the California program could have negative effects. Because it was introduced unexpectedly and with little lead time, many districts found themselves without the necessary classrooms or teachers to permit the desired reductions in class sizes, leading to transitional difficulties with consequences for a number of years. Unfortunately, it will never be possible to analyze the effects of this program because it was available to all school districts. Although some districts did not immediately lower class sizes, these surely were not otherwise comparable to the districts that did.

61. Glass and Smith (1979).

62. Finn and Achilles (1990).

icy with massive expenditure implications if implemented on a widespread basis. The expense of such policies puts natural limits on what is feasible, so that many reductions are ultimately rather marginal. Marginal changes, however, are even less likely to lead to underlying changes in the behavior of teachers.[63]

But could reducing class size hurt? Many argue (correctly) that improving the quality of U.S. schools should be a very high priority for policy at the local, state, and national levels. Moreover, this argument is supplemented by concerns about equity and equality of opportunity that follow from significant disparities in outcomes across economic and racial groups. Faced with these real concerns and given the strong advocacy for reducing class sizes from teachers and parents, many politicians appear to find proposals to reduce class size simply irresistible. After all, some students will undoubtedly benefit from smaller classes even if all do not.

The primary argument against pursuing policies with little chance of success is that bad policy drives out good policy. There are clear limits to the amount of funds and attention available to education. Squandering public and political attention on policies that reinforce existing inefficiencies and promise little hope of success is likely to have long-term consequences, although these will not be apparent until some time in the future.

The available evidence indicates that the ultimate effect of any large-scale program to reduce class size will depend much more importantly on the quality of the new teachers hired than on the effects of smaller classes per se. Variations in teacher quality have been shown to be extraordinarily important for student achievement, and econometric studies indicate that these variations completely dominate any effects of altered class size.[64] Thus

63. The magnitude of achievement effects versus expenditure can be put into perspective from the analysis of Texas schools by Rivkin, Hanushek, and Kain (1998). In that study, an increase in spending of $1,000 per student would yield a reduction in class size by from three to six students, depending on how it was accomplished. Such an expenditure, which represents a 14 percent increase from the 1996 national average of $7,000 per student, is estimated to yield an increase of 0.05 to 0.10 standard deviation of performance for low-income students in the fourth grade and half that amount in fifth grade. For students not eligible for free or reduced-price lunches and for low-income students in later grades, there is no reason to expect any average improvement for such an increase. Reductions of the magnitude considered in Project STAR would cost even more than those considered here.

64. Rivkin, Hanushek, and Kain (1998) demonstrate that class size variation can explain just a very small portion of the variation in student achievement and that variations in teacher quality are much more significant. Hanushek (1992) estimates variations in total teacher differences (measured and unmeasured) and shows that the differences in student achievement with a good versus a bad teacher can represent more than one grade level within a single school year. See other references in Hanushek (1997).

if new hires resulting from a class size reduction policy are above the average quality of existing teachers, average student performance is likely to increase; if below the average teacher quality, average student performance is likely to fall with class size reductions. But from past experience there is little reason to believe that the quality of new teachers will be significantly different from that of existing teachers unless the incentives facing schools also change.[65]

To many in the system, one appeal of simple class size policies is that they maintain the existing structure of schools while simply adding more resources. Yet the existing organization and incentives have proved very ineffective at translating resources into student performance. Moreover, much of the expenditure growth in the past came from pursuing the very policies being proposed today. If such policies failed previously, why should the next round be any different?

The uncertainty about the specific circumstances that lead to desirable student performance through smaller classes and the ineffectiveness of current selection, hiring, and retention policies for teachers are exactly what lie behind calls for improved incentives in the schools.[66] The current school structure provides few incentives for improving student performance. In essence, nobody's job or economic reward depends on student performance. In such a situation, nobody really expends much effort to discover in which situations small classes will succeed. Decisions about class size are discussed in terms of fairness rather than student performance or cost control. Would it be fair to allow one group of students or teachers to have small classes while others must have large classes? Such logic, which totally ignores consideration of effectiveness, has almost certainly contributed to the growth in expenses and use of resources underlying the currently ineffective school operations.

Most discussions of class size reductions begin with the assertion that student performance will increase only if class sizes are reduced, a proposition generally shown to be erroneous. These discussions then move quickly to policies of large-scale reductions in pupil-teacher ratios that offer no direct linkage between specific decisions about class size and student per-

---

65. Under some circumstances, such as the large unexpected hiring in 1996 for the California class size reduction program, one might expect the average quality to fall. In general, however, there is no shortage of trained teachers, and the real issue is selection from the substantial pool not currently employed in the schools. See Ballou and Podgursky (1997); Murnane and others (1991).

66. Hanushek and others (1994).

formance. The situation in the schools and the resulting educational outcomes might change significantly if everyone had stronger incentives to use budgets wisely and to improve student performance.

References

Akerhielm, Karen. "Does Class Size Matter?" 1995. *Economics of Education Review* 14(3): 229–41.

Angrist, Joshua D., and Victor Lavy. 1999. "Using Maimonides' Rule to Estimate the Effect of Class Size on Scholastic Achievement." *Quarterly Journal of Economics* 114(2): 533–75.

Ballou, Dale, and Michael Podgursky. 1997. *Teacher Pay and Teacher Quality.* Kalamazoo, Mich.: Upjohn Institute for Employment Research.

Barnett, W. Steven. 1992. "Benefits of Compensatory Preschool Education." *Journal of Human Resources* 27(2): 279–312.

Beaton, Albert E., and others. 1996a. *Mathematics Achievement in the Middle School Years: IEA's Third International Mathematics and Science Study (TIMSS).* Boston College, Center for the Study of Testing, Evaluation, and Educational Policy.

———. 1996b. *Science Achievement in the Middle School Years: IEA's Third International Mathematics and Science Study (TIMSS).* Boston College, Center for the Study of Testing, Evaluation, and Educational Policy.

Betts, Julian R. 1995. "Does School Quality Matter? Evidence from the National Longitudinal Survey of Youth." *Review of Economics and Statistics* 77(2): 231–47.

———. 1996. "Is There a Link between School Inputs and Earnings? Fresh Scrutiny of an Old Literature." In *Does Money Matter? The Effect of School Resources on Student Achievement and Adult Success*, edited by Gary Burtless, 141–91. Brookings.

Bowles, Samuel, and Henry M. Levin. 1968. "The Determinants of Scholastic Achievement—An Appraisal of Some Recent Evidence." *Journal of Human Resources* 3(1): 3–24.

Cain, Glen G., and Harold W. Watts. 1970. "Problems in Making Policy Inferences from the Coleman Report." *American Sociological Review* 35(2): 328–52.

Card, David, and Alan B. Krueger. 1996. "Labor Market Effects of School Quality: Theory and Evidence." In *Does Money Matter? The Effect of School Resources on Student Achievement and Adult Success*, edited by Gary Burtless, 97–140. Brookings.

Coleman, James S., and others. 1966. *Equality of Educational Opportunity.* Government Printing Office.

Congressional Budget Office. 1986. *Trends in Educational Achievement.*

Cook, Michael D., and William N. Evans. 1996. "Families or Schools? Explaining the Convergence in White and Black Academic Performance." Unpublished paper.

Ehrenberg, Ronald G., and Dominic J. Brewer. 1995. "Did Teachers' Verbal Ability and Race Matter in the 1960s? Coleman Revisited." *Economics of Education Review* 14(1): 1–21.

Ferguson, Ronald F., and Helen F. Ladd. 1996. "How and Why Money Matters: An Analysis of Alabama Schools." In *Holding Schools Accountable: Performance-Based Reform in Education*, edited by Helen F. Ladd, 265–98. Brookings.

Finn, Jeremy D., and Charles M. Achilles. 1990. "Answers and Questions about Class Size: A Statewide Experiment." *American Educational Research Journal* 27(3): 557–77.

Finn, Jeremy D., and others. 1990. "Three Years in a Small Class." *Teaching and Teacher Education* 6(2): 127–36.

Glass, Gene V., and Mary Lee Smith. 1979. "Meta-Analysis of Research on Class Size and Achievement." *Educational Evaluation and Policy Analysis* 1(1): 2–16.

Goldstein, Harvey, and Peter Blatchford. 1998. "Class Size and Educational Achievement: A Review of Methodology with Particular Reference to Study Design." *British Educational Research Journal* 24(3): 255–68.

Greenwald, Rob, Larry V. Hedges, and Richard D. Laine. 1996. "The Effect of School Resources on Student Achievement." *Review of Educational Research* 66(3): 361–96.

Grissmer, David W., and others. 1994. *Student Achievement and the Changing American Family.* Santa Monica, Calif.: Rand Corporation.

Grogger, Jeffrey T. 1996. "Does School Quality Explain the Recent Black/White Wage Trend?" *Journal of Labor Economics* 14(2): 231–53.

Hanushek, Eric A. 1979. "Conceptual and Empirical Issues in the Estimation of Educational Production Functions." *Journal of Human Resources* 14(3): 351–88.

————. 1992. "The Trade-Off between Child Quantity and Quality." *Journal of Political Economy* 100(1): 84–117.

————. 1996a. "A More Complete Picture of School Resource Policies." *Review of Educational Research* 66(3): 397–409.

————. 1996b. "School Resources and Student Performance." In *Does Money Matter? The Effect of School Resources on Student Achievement and Adult Success*, edited by Gary Burtless, 43-73. Brookings.

————. 1997. "Assessing the Effects of School Resources on Student Performance: An Update." *Educational Evaluation and Policy Analysis* 19(2): 141–64.

————. 1999. "Some Findings from an Independent Investigation of the Tennessee STAR Experiment and from Other Investigations of Class Size Effects." *Educational Evaluation and Policy Analysis* 21(2) (forthcoming).

Hanushek, Eric A., and John F. Kain. 1972. "On the Value of 'Equality of Educational Opportunity' as a Guide to Public Policy." In *On Equality of Educational Opportunity*, edited by Frederick Mosteller and Daniel P. Moynihan, 116-45. Random House.

Hanushek, Eric A., John F. Kain, and Steven G. Rivkin. 1998. "Does Special Education Raise Academic Achievement for Students with Disabilities?" Working Paper 6690. Cambridge, Mass.: National Bureau of Economic Research.

Hanushek, Eric A., and Dongwook Kim. 1996. "Schooling, Labor Force Quality, and the Growth of Nations." Unpublished paper. University of Rochester, Department of Economics (December).

Hanushek, Eric A., and Steven G. Rivkin. 1997. "Understanding the Twentieth-Century Growth in U.S. School Spending." *Journal of Human Resources* 32(1): 35–68.

Hanushek, Eric A., Steven G. Rivkin, and Lori L. Taylor. 1996. "Aggregation and the Estimated Effects of School Resources." *Review of Economics and Statistics* 78(4): 611–27.

Hanushek, Eric A., and others. 1994. *Making Schools Work: Improving Performance and Controlling Costs.* Brookings.

Hartman, William T. 1980. "Policy Effects of Special Education Funding Formulas." *Journal of Education Finance* 6(Fall): 135–59.

Hauser, Robert M., and Min-Hsiung Huang. 1996. "Trends in Black-White Test-Score Differentials." Discussion Paper 1110-96. University of Wisconsin, Institute for Research on Poverty (October).

Heckman, James S., Anne Layne-Farrar, and Petra Todd. 1996. "Does Measured School Quality Really Matter? An Examination of the Earnings-Quality Relationship." In *Does Money Matter? The Effect of School Resources on Student Achievement and Adult Success*, edited by Gary Burtless, 192–289. Brookings.

Hedges, Larry V., and Amy Nowell. 1998. "Black-White Test Score Convergence since 1965." In *The Black-White Test Score Gap*, edited by Christopher Jencks and Meredith Phillips, 149–81. Brookings.

Hoxby, Caroline Minter. 1998. "The Effects of Class Size and Composition on Student Achievement: New Evidence from Natural Population Variation." Working Paper 6869. Cambridge, Mass.: National Bureau of Economic Research (December).

Krueger, Alan B. 1997. "Experimental Estimates of Education Production Functions." Working Paper 6051. Cambridge, Mass.: National Bureau of Economic Research (June).

Lamdin, Douglas J. 1995. "Testing for the Effect of School Size on Student Achievement within a School District." *Education Economics* 3(1): 33–42.

Lewit, Eugene M., and Linda Schurmann Baker. 1997. "Class Size." *Future of Children* 7(3): 112–21.

Mayer, Susan E. 1997. *What Money Can't Buy: Family Income and Children's Life Chances*. Harvard University Press.

Monk, David H. 1990. *Educational Finance: An Economic Approach*. McGraw-Hill.

Mosteller, Frederick. 1995. "The Tennessee Study of Class Size in the Early School Grades." *Future of Children* 5(2): 113–27.

Murnane, Richard J., and others. 1991. *Who Will Teach?* Harvard University Press.

National Center for Education Statistics. 1997. *Digest of Education Statistics, 1997*. U.S. Department of Education.

Nye, Barbara A., and others. 1993. "The Lasting Benefits Study: A Continuing Analysis of the Effect of Small Class Size in Kindergarten through Third Grade on Student Achievement Test Scores in Subsequent Grade Levels: Sixth Grade Technical Report." Tennessee State University, Center of Excellence for Research in Basic Skills.

Organization for Economic Cooperation and Development. 1996. *Education at a Glance: OECD Indicators*. Paris.

Prais, S. J. 1996. "Class-Size and Learning: The Tennessee Experiment—What Follows?" *Oxford Review of Education* 22(4): 399–414.

Rivkin, Steven G., Eric A. Hanushek, and John F. Kain. 1998. "Teachers, Schools, and Academic Achievement." Working Paper 6691. Cambridge, Mass.: National Bureau of Economic Research.

Staley, Samuel R., and John P. Blair. 1995. "Institutions, Quality Competition and Public Service Provision: The Case of Public Education." *Constitutional Political Economy* 6: 21–33.

Stevenson, Harold W., and James W. Stigler. 1992. *The Learning Gap: Why Our Schools Are Failing and What We Can Learn from Japanese and Chinese Education*. Summit Books.

U.S. Department of Education. 1991. *To Assure the Free Appropriate Public Education of All Children with Disabilities*. Thirteenth annual report to the Congress on the implementation of the Individuals with Disabilities Education Act.

Wenglinsky, H. 1997. "When Money Matters: How Educational Expenditures Improve Student Performance and When They Don't." Unpublished paper. Princeton, N.J.: Educational Testing Service.

Wirtz, Willard. 1977. *On Further Examination: Report of the Advisory Panel on the Scholastic Aptitude Test Score Decline.* New York: College Entrance Examination Board.

Word, Elizabeth, and others. 1990. *Student/Teacher Achievement Ratio (STAR), Tennessee's K–3 Class Size Study: Final Summary Report, 1985–1990.* Nashville: Tennessee State Department of Education.

ROBERT H. MEYER

8

The Effects of Math and Math-Related Courses in High School

DURING THE 1980S, a renewed interest developed in improving the academic skills of high school students in the United States. It was motivated in large part by widespread concern over the deteriorating performance of high school students on the Scholastic Aptitude Test (SAT) and other national examinations throughout the 1960s and 1970s, the exceedingly poor performance of American high school students in international comparisons of math proficiency, and the reported dissatisfaction among employers with the basic skills of young workers.[1] In mathematics and science, this concern was heightened by the fact that whereas high school students tended to enroll in the full complement of English courses, many students took no mathematics or science coursework beyond the ninth or tenth grades.

As a result, a number of steps have since been taken to improve students' academic performance, particularly with respect to high school mathematics. I briefly mention three. First, there has been a major effort to increase

This chapter grew out of research supported by the National Assessment of Vocational Education, the U.S. Department of Education, and the Institute for Research on Poverty, University of Wisconsin–Madison. I have benefited from discussions with Charles Benson, Robin Horn, John Wirt, and David Wise, and from comments by Joseph Altonji, David Ellwood, Richard Freeman, Art Goldberger, Eric Hanushek, Susan Mayer, Donald Rock, Aaron Pallas, and Paul Peterson.
1. Congressional Budget Office (1986, 1987); McKnight and others (1987).

student enrollments in math and science courses, particularly advanced-track courses such as algebra, geometry, and calculus, as opposed to basic and general math. A number of schools and states now require high school students to take a minimum of three years in math and in science in grades nine through twelve.[2]

Second, in the early 1980s mathematics educators, under the auspices of the National Council of Teachers of Mathematics, embarked on a thorough review of the elementary and secondary math curriculums. In 1989 they released *Curriculum and Evaluation Standards for School Mathematics*, a report that called for a substantially new approach to teaching the subject.[3] A key principle of the new approach is that mathematics skills should be taught in an applied context that gives students the opportunity to use mathematics to solve real-life problems. Efforts are currently underway to develop and implement new applied mathematics courses consistent with the report.

Finally, stimulated in part by the Carl Perkins Vocational Education Act of 1990, vocational educators have begun to integrate mathematics and other academic skills into the vocational curriculum.[4] The idea behind integrating vocational and academic education is that the applied, "hands-on," orientation of vocational education encourages student interest in learning and provides concrete opportunities to learn the abstract principles taught in mathematics and other academic subjects. This is not unlike the philosophy that undergirds the new math standards. Additionally, the move to introduce academic content into vocational education opens the possibility that mathematics instruction need not be the sole province of mathematics educators, but rather could be the shared responsibility of all educators. This idea is not without precedent. "Writing across the curriculum" programs, which require that writing skills be taught in all courses, not just in English, reflect a similar motivation.

The common thread among these three reform strategies is an emphasis on remaking the high school curriculum in order to provide students with substantially better and more extensive training in mathematics. They are based on the belief that cognitive skills are at least partly determined by the investments that students, families, and schools make in the learning process. If heredity or very early environmental influences largely deter-

2. Meyer (1991).
3. National Council of Teachers of Mathematics (1989).
4. Grubb (1995a, 1995b); Grubb and others (1991).

mine student achievement, as some critics have argued, these initiatives may be doomed to failure.[5]

The purpose of this chapter is to develop a statistical model of a curricular production function that can be used to assess the effectiveness, if any, of math and math-related courses of the type discussed above. I estimate such a curricular production function using transcript and achievement test score data from the High School and Beyond (HS&B) study, a data base that contains information on almost 11,000 students from approximately 1,000 high schools. Over the period 1978–82, these students collectively enrolled in approximately 1,000 different courses, including a variety of applied mathematics courses and numerous math-related courses in the sciences and vocational education. These data thus allow one to compare the effectiveness of four alternative sets of courses:

— traditional advanced-track math,

— basic and general math,

— applied math, and

— math-related, or integrated courses.

The empirical analysis is limited somewhat by the fact that the HS&B mathematics test is a traditional multiple choice examination with limited applied context. A test of this type is probably biased in favor of traditional rather than applied mathematics skills.

An important new finding of the study is that participation in advanced-track mathematics courses significantly enhances mathematics proficiency for all students, including non-college-bound students. By contrast, high school courses such as basic and general math contribute little to the development of mathematics skill. This result corroborates the finding of Jay Girotto and Paul Peterson in chapter 9 below that challenging courses and hard work enhance cognitive skills.

A second important finding is that some courses other than traditional mathematics—for example, applied mathematics, chemistry, and physics—produce substantial growth in mathematics achievement. This implies that learning mathematics in an applied context, as suggested above, is a potentially viable alternative or complement to traditional mathematics courses. More generally, the evidence suggests that it is sensible to consider a systemic approach to teaching mathematics—in particular, sharing responsibility for math instruction across vocational education, science, and mathematics.

---

5. See chapter 1 above for a discussion of this view.

On a methodological note, an important finding of the paper is that estimates of the curricular production function are extremely sensitive to model misspecifications. In particular, models that control for prior achievement using proxies, such as family background, rather than actual prior achievement yield severely biased parameter estimates. In addition, models that control directly for prior achievement but do not correct for measurement error in that variable also yield badly biased parameter estimates. The paper offers two alternative statistical models designed to address this problem: an instrumental variables or two-stage least squares (2SLS) model and an errors in variables (EV) model.[6]

The paper is organized as follows. The next section articulates a curricular model of mathematics learning that relates growth in mathematics proficiency from the end of tenth to the end of twelfth grades to courses taken during that two-year period. I begin the section with a brief review of related literature. The following section describes the course enrollment data used in the empirical analysis. Next, I discuss the statistical problems encountered in trying to estimate the consequences of alternative courses, given that students with different levels of prior achievement tend to enroll in different courses. I then present my empirical results. I conclude by examining the implications of the empirical analysis for specific academic reforms.

A Curricular Production Function for High School Mathematics Achievement

Since the publication of the Coleman report just over three decades ago, numerous researchers have examined the links between academic achievement, as measured by student performance on standardized tests, and school quality.[7] At face value, their research findings seem surprising and even contradictory.[8] On the one hand, studies by Eric Hanushek, Richard Murnane, and others find that some teachers and schools contribute substantially to student achievement.[9] On the other hand, many studies find that obvious measures of school and teacher quality and school inputs, such as per pupil expenditures, student-teacher ratios, and teacher experi-

6. Details of these models are presented in Meyer (1992).
7. Coleman and others (1966).
8. See, for example, chapter 6 above by Frederick Mosteller and chapter 7 by Eric Hanushek.
9. See Hanushek (1971); Murnane (1975).

ence, are not strongly related to student performance. Rather, they find that the primary documented influences on student performance are student and family backgrounds—characteristics that cannot easily be changed in the short run, if at all.[10]

Although these results may be due in part to poor measurement of school inputs, an alternative explanation is that student and school performance are determined primarily by factors other than conventionally defined school inputs, for example, curricular content, the organization and process of education, student effort, and the quality of school inputs in the context of specific student and classroom needs. I focus on the first factor, in particular, the curricular production function for high school mathematics achievement.

Researchers who have examined this issue have concluded, almost without exception, that enrollment in advanced mathematics is a powerful determinant of mathematics proficiency.[11] Wayne Welch, Ronald Anderson, and Linda Harris, drawing on data from the seventeen-year-old wave of the 1977–78 National Assessment of Educational Progress (NAEP) in mathematics, estimate a model of math achievement that includes measures of family and community characteristics and total number of semesters of mathematics taken, but no control for achievement before high school.[12] They find, as do previous educational production function studies, that family and community characteristics account for a large share (25 percent) of the variance in mathematics achievement on the NAEP. Total enrollment in advanced mathematics courses—algebra, advanced algebra, geometry, trigonometry, and calculus, as reported by the students—explains an additional 34 percent of the variance, raising the total variance explained to 59 percent. Low- and mid-level math courses—for example, general math, pre-algebra, and business math—on the other hand, contribute essentially nothing to mathematics achievement.

William Schmidt reports similar results in his analysis of the National Longitudinal Study of the High School Class of 1972.[13] He finds that in grades ten through twelve, personal characteristics and hours of instruction in mathematics and other subjects explain 57 percent of the variance in mathematics achievement. These results are too strong to be

10. See Hanushek (1986).

11. One exception is the research in the First International Mathematics Study; see Torsten Husen, "Does More Time in School Make a Difference?" *Saturday Review*, April 29, 1972, pp. 32–35.

12. Welch, Anderson, and Harris (1982).

13. Schmidt (1983).

credible: at face value they imply that mathematics instruction in elementary and middle school contributes very little to mathematics proficiency among high school students. The problem is that the achievement models used in these studies fail to control adequately for math achievement prior to high school. The data sets used simply did not include the necessary variables.

Aaron Pallas and Karl Alexander, however, analyze a data set that includes measures of math achievement at the middle of twelfth grade and the beginning of ninth grade: the Educational Testing Service's Study of Academic Prediction and Growth.[14] They report that personal and family characteristics plus prior achievement account for 57 percent of the variation in math scores in the senior year, with course enrollments explaining an additional 12 percent. The latter percentage is substantially less than is found in either of the two studies described above, thereby confirming the need to control for prior achievement in estimations of the value added by courses or other school inputs.

Pallas and Alexander, in contrast with the other two studies, estimate the contribution of individual courses, rather than total years or semesters of mathematics coursework, to growth in mathematics proficiency. Their course variables are derived from high school transcripts, and thus are likely to be relatively free of error.[15] They include thirteen mathematics courses, as well as three math-related courses: physics, quantitative business, and quantitative industrial arts (that is, drafting and drawing). Their estimates, like those of the other two studies, indicate that growth in mathematics proficiency is spurred exclusively by upper-level courses, such as geometry, trigonometry, calculus, and physics. Algebra 1 and 2 make no contribution to the development of mathematics skills, and the contributions of general math 1, applied math, and quantitative business are actually negative, although generally not statistically significant.

In terms of value added, the negative coefficient estimates are completely implausible, since they indicate that students *lose* mathematics skills by participating in these courses. In fact, the heavy tilt of the estimates—large positive coefficients for upper-level courses, zero coefficients for intermediate courses (algebra 1 and 2), and negative coefficients for low-level

---

14. Pallas and Alexander (1983).

15. Fetters, Stowe, and Owings (1984) report that relative to high school transcripts, student reports tend somewhat to overstate enrollments in mathematics, with a reliability of only 70 percent.

courses—strongly suggests that these coefficients reflect something other than the value added or causal effect of the courses.

The problem, once again, is failure to control *fully* for prior achievement. As I demonstrate below, if prior achievement tests are measured with error they fail to control fully for differences in "true" prior achievement among students. Most achievement tests are subject to measurement error, and it is essential to address this problem when estimating a curricular production function model. In an earlier paper, I have presented two alternative methods of doing so.[16]

Definition of Course Variables

I follow the example of Pallas and Alexander by specifying a model that includes course variables.[17] The distinctive feature of my approach is that the course variables are designed so as to capture the entire high school curriculum, grouped by major courses in mathematics, and by math and non-math-related subjects. Previous studies have generally included only math or advanced math variables, thereby running the risk of obtaining biased effect estimates due to omitted math-related variables. Since most high school students enroll in five to six courses in any given semester, the students included in the analysis could have taken eighteen or more courses (some lasting a single semester) during eleventh and twelfth grades. Quite a few of these could have been math or math-related courses. It is therefore useful to think of the model developed in this paper as having multiple treatments, rather than a single treatment.[18]

My curricular model of mathematics achievement distinguishes nineteen different course-, field-, or subject-level variables, fourteen of which are hypothesized to have large positive effects on mathematics learning.[19]

16. See Meyer (1992).

17. Pallas and Alexander (1983).

18. In most of the models estimated in this study, I include course variables without allowing for possible interactions. In future work, it would be interesting to investigate the degree of substitutability and complementarity among different courses. Unfortunately, the HS&B data used here are simply too weak to support a more elaborate specification. The main problem is the enormous measurement error in the growth in mathematics proficiency, the outcome variable: approximately 70 percent of the variance of the change in math test scores (see Meyer, 1992, table A-1).

19. The course variables are constructed from transcripts that include over 1,000 different course titles from approximately 1,000 high schools. In order to make the analysis more manageable, I aggregate these course titles. See Meyer (1992) for a discussion of the statistical issues involved in aggregating the course variables.

The latter variables include traditional mathematics courses, applied and vocational math courses, and math-related courses drawn from the sciences and vocational education.[20] By design, the course variables included in the analysis span a continuum that ranges from formal abstract mathematics to applied mathematics. In addition, some courses involve the full-time study of mathematics, while others involve part-time, perhaps incidental, study of mathematics.

The formal abstract mathematics courses are (in ascending order of difficulty) basic math, general math, computer math, pre-algebra, algebra 1, geometry, algebra 2, pre-calculus (algebra 3, trigonometry, advanced geometry, and mathematical analysis), and calculus. The related course variables are reasonably well defined and reflect minimal or no aggregation. Enrollments in these and other courses are discussed below.

I include two applied math variables, both with a full-time focus on mathematics instruction: applied math and specific vocational math.[21] The essential difference between them is that specific vocational math courses are structured around a particular vocational subject, such as business, and presumably draw most or all of their examples from that subject. In addition, it may be that specific vocational math courses are often taught by vocational educators rather than math teachers. The HS&B data, however, provide no information on this point.

Vocational education courses are split into two groups: math-related and non-math-related.[22] Courses are assigned to these groups on the basis of their titles and descriptions. Although these designations are subjective, and therefore subject to error, they are influenced by well-defined guidelines (see appendix 8B). Moreover, since the guidelines and course classifications were determined prior to any data analysis, the empirical results are not contaminated by "data mining." To the extent that some vocational courses have been misclassified, the estimated differential between math-related and non-math-related courses is apt to be understated.

Finally, science courses are divided into two groups: chemistry and physics, and biology and survey science. It is hypothesized that the former is more math-related than the latter.

20. Although other subjects may also contain math-related courses, it was not possible to identify these courses in the transcript data.

21. See appendix 8B for details of the construction of these variables.

22. Robin S. Horn, Mark Braddock, and I prepared the classification of math-related and non-math-related vocational courses for the National Assessment of Vocational Education. Becky Hayward and Nancy Adelman provided helpful comments.

Data

The data used in this study are derived from the sophomore cohort of the High School and Beyond study, a nationally representative sample of tenth grade students in 1980. Participants were surveyed and tested during the spring of 1980 and again exactly two years later. All estimates reported in this paper were computed using the HS&B transcript sample weight (*TRWT*). The sample consists of 10,961 students with valid test score data and complete transcript information for all four years of high school. It includes 10,106 high school graduates and 855 students who dropped out after participating in the spring 1980 (base-year) survey.

Courses recorded in the transcript files are coded according to the Classification of Secondary School Courses, which defines and describes well over 1,000 high school courses. They are then grouped into fields and subject areas using the Secondary School Course Taxonomy.[23] Vocational education courses are identified as math-related or non-math-related according to the rules given in appendix 8B. All tables in this chapter report course enrollments in terms of standard Carnegie credits. A course worth one Carnegie credit typically meets five times a week in fifty- to fifty-five-minute periods, throughout the school year. Course enrollments reflect all courses passed and failed. Failed courses, which represent less than 5 percent of all enrollments, are included because the empirical evidence suggests that they make some contribution to growth in math test scores.

The HS&B sample took a battery of six tests: mathematics, reading, vocabulary, writing, science, and civics. Although at face value they measure competency in six distinct areas, a factor analysis conducted by Donald Rock and coauthors indicates that two underlying factors—one mathematical and one verbal—account for essentially all of the legitimate (error-free) variance in scores on these six tests.[24] In addition, the estimated reliability of the civics test is exceptionally low: approximately 50 percent.[25] As a result, I base my empirical analysis on a subset of test results: mathematics scores, composite verbal scores (the sum of reading and vocabulary scores), and science scores. I include the verbal and science tests as additional explanatory variables in the econometric model of mathematics

23. The Secondary School Taxonomy is presented and discussed in National Assessment of Vocational Education (1988). See also Brown and others (1989).
24. Rock and others (1985).
25. Meyer (1992, table A-1).

learning to pick up possible effects of skills other than those measured by the HS&B math test.[26]

Total testing times were twenty-one minutes for the mathematics test and forty-seven minutes for the five others. The math test consisted of thirty-eight items, eighteen involving arithmetic skills, twelve involving algebra skills, and eight involving geometry skills. The inclusion of items related to specific high school mathematics courses—algebra and geometry—raises the possibility that the HS&B math test taps both cognitive mathematics ability and specific skill in algebra and geometry. If so, estimates of the contribution of algebra and geometry to the growth of mathematics skills may be overstated, relative to the contributions of other courses.

In order to allow for the possibility that the math effectiveness of different courses varies in the population, the data are disaggregated into college-bound and non-college-bound students, and into students with low, medium, or high prior mathematics achievement. In the base-year (sophomore) survey, approximately 60 percent of the sample said that they expected to attend college. The remaining 40 percent said either that they had no plans to obtain postsecondary education (25 percent) or that they planned to obtain postsecondary vocational training (15 percent).

Course Enrollments

As reported in table 8-1, students in the HS&B sample take an average of 2.72 credits in vocational education and applied or specific vocational math during their junior and senior years, representing approximately 27 percent of all credits.[27] Course enrollments in this area substantially exceed enrollments in all other subject areas, including English (1.82 credits), social studies (1.79 credits), mathematics (0.86 credits), and science (0.75 credits).

The enrollment patterns of college-bound and non-college-bound students are very different. Vocational education, including applied or specific

---

26. Rock and others (1985) find that the HS&B science test is highly correlated with both their mathematics and verbal factors. In a model that includes the HS&B math, composite verbal, and science tests, it may be reasonable to interpret the science test as a measure of math skills not explicitly measured in the mathematics test, or a measure of mathematics aptitude.

27. This section considers high school enrollments in grades eleven and twelve for college-bound and non-college-bound students and for all students. See table 8A-1 in appendix 8A for high school enrollments in grades nine through twelve for the same groups, and table 8A-2 for high school enrollments in grades eleven and twelve for students sorted into three groups (triptiles) based on tenth grade math achievement.

Table 8-1. *Average Course Enrollments in Eleventh and Twelfth Grades by Graduation Status and Postsecondary Plans in the High School and Beyond Study*[a]

Credits

| | | Graduates | | |
| | | Non-college-bound | College-bound | All |
Course	Dropouts	bound	bound	students
Vocational education				
Math-related	0.157	0.576	0.505	0.509
Non-math-related	1.056	3.143	1.503	2.110
All	1.213	3.719	2.008	2.619
Specific vocational math	0.041	0.053	0.030	0.040
Applied math	0.051	0.088	0.043	0.061
Mathematics				
Basic	0.040	0.032	0.009	0.020
General	0.104	0.108	0.064	0.084
Computer	0.007	0.014	0.036	0.025
Pre-algebra	0.016	0.022	0.027	0.024
Algebra 1	0.035	0.060	0.077	0.067
Geometry	0.048	0.089	0.186	0.139
Algebra 2	0.038	0.094	0.412	0.263
Precalculus	0.013	0.047	0.316	0.191
Calculus	0.000	0.005	0.089	0.050
All[b]	0.301	0.471	1.216	0.863
Science				
Survey	0.108	0.096	0.063	0.079
Biology	0.126	0.163	0.277	0.223
Chemistry	0.020	0.092	0.475	0.296
Physics	0.011	0.035	0.260	0.155
All	0.265	0.386	1.075	0.753
English	0.928	1.805	1.956	1.828
Social studies	0.862	1.808	1.893	1.790
Fine arts	0.256	0.644	0.718	0.658
Foreign languages	0.062	0.130	0.559	0.359
Personal and other	0.595	1.036	1.164	1.076
Summary statistic				
Total credits	4.574	10.140	10.662	10.047
Sample size	855	3,759	6,347	10,961

Source: Author's computations from school transcripts collected by the High School and Beyond study.

a. Course enrollments are measured in Carnegie credits. A course worth one Carnegie credit typically meets five times a week in fifty- to fifty-five-minute periods throughout the school year. A typical one-semester course earns half a credit.

b. Excluding applied and specific vocational math courses.

vocational math, accounts for a larger share of the total credits of non-college-bound graduates (38 percent) than for either college-bound graduates (20 percent) or high school dropouts (29 percent). Nonetheless, vocational education is the predominant area of study for college-bound students. Conversely, college-bound students take relatively more of their credits than non-college-bound students in mathematics (1.22 versus 0.47 credits), science (1.08 versus 0.39 credits), and foreign languages (0.56 versus 0.13 credits). Enrollments in English, social studies, fine arts, and personal and other courses are nearly identical for college-bound and non-college-bound students.

Courses identified as math-related account for only one-fifth of all vocational credits, representing slightly more than a one-semester course worth half a credit, on average. Applied or specific vocational math represents only 4 percent of all vocational courses. The number of courses taken in math-related vocational education is nearly identical for college-bound and non-college-bound students.

These numbers suggest that from the limited perspective of the development of mathematics skills, the effectiveness of vocational education, both math-related and non-math-related, is especially important for non-college-bound students. During their junior and senior years, non-college-bound graduates in the sample take roughly equivalent amounts of mathematics and math-related vocational education (about one semester in each), and five to six times as much non-math-related vocational education (almost six semesters).

Mathematics Test Scores

Table 8-2 summarizes the performance of students on the HS&B mathematics test. The average sophomore score in 1980 is 13.44, with a standard deviation of 9.70. The average gain in test scores from tenth grade to twelfth grade is 1.92 points, approximately one point per year. Although this change is modest relative to the (accumulated) variation in tenth grade achievement, this need not imply that the observed gain in math scores is small and inconsequential, but rather that individual variation in growth in mathematics achievement from preschool through tenth grade was substantial.[28] The table indicates that high school dropouts score poorly on the

---

28. Jencks (1985); Hoffer, Greeley, and Coleman (1985).

Table 8-2. *Average Math Test Scores by Graduation Status and Postsecondary Plans in HS&B*[a]

Score

| Grade level | Dropouts | Graduates | | All students |
		Non-college-bound	College-bound	
Sophomore	5.78	9.46	17.22	13.44
	(6.86)	(8.10)	(9.35)	(9.70)
Senior	6.15	10.54	19.93	15.35
	(7.50)	(8.61)	(10.02)	(10.65)
Senior gain	0.37	1.08	2.71	1.92
	(5.78)	(5.92)	(5.72)	(5.87)
Summary statistic				
Sample size	855	3,759	6,347	10,961

Source: Author's computations from school transcripts collected by the High School and Beyond study.

a. Standard deviations are in parentheses.

sophomore test (5.78) and do not score appreciably better two years later. In contrast, non-college-bound and college-bound graduates have higher sophomore scores and increase their scores by 1.08 points and 2.71 points, respectively, between the tenth and twelfth grades.

Variation in mathematics learning depends critically on the number and type of courses taken by high school students. However, before discussing my best estimates of the contributions of different courses to mathematics development, it is informative to examine table 8-3, which reports the average gain in math scores for students with different levels of total mathematics enrollment in eleventh and twelfth grades. These results cannot be used to infer the contribution of mathematics courses to mathematics learning, because they ignore the influences of other math-related courses and possible variation in the effects of different math courses. Nonetheless, they suggest that mathematics instruction has a powerful effect on the growth of mathematics skills. Students who take no mathematics during their junior or senior years essentially fail to improve their math scores from the tenth to the twelfth grades. In contrast, students who enroll in even a half-credit course significantly improve their mathematics proficiency, and students with the highest math enrollments achieve the greatest gains.

Table 8-3. *Average Sophomore Math Test Scores and Sophomore to Senior Gains by Eleventh and Twelfth Grade Math Credits and Postsecondary Plans in HS&B*

Score

Math credits	Non-college-bound		College-bound		All students	
	Sophomore	*Gain*	*Sophomore*	*Gain*	*Sophomore*	*Gain*
0	8.50	0.13	12.43	0.41	9.75	0.22
1/2	8.37	1.15	12.93	1.64	10.21	1.35
1	9.16	1.58	15.61	2.23	12.99	1.96
1 1/2	9.30	1.58	17.54	2.94	15.45	2.60
2	10.87	3.03	20.68	4.19	18.88	3.98
2 1/2 or more	12.78	3.59	21.91	4.37	20.77	4.28
Summary statistic						
Overall mean	8.94	0.97	17.01	2.67	13.44	1.92
Sample size	4,448		6,513		10,961	

Source: Author's computations from school transcripts collected by the High School and Beyond study.

College-bound students improve their scores somewhat more than non-college-bound students, perhaps due to the fact that they tend to enroll in more advanced courses (see table 8-1).

Statistical Considerations in Estimating Models of Student Achievement

I have argued above that it is essential to control *fully* for prior achievement when estimating a model of student achievement. This section presents a brief nontechnical discussion of why the traditional models of student achievement fail to do this. The consequences of using inappropriate statistical methods are illustrated using data from HS&B.[29]

The goal of the statistical analysis is to estimate the effects of alternative course enrollments in grades eleven and twelve on mathematics achievement measured at the end of high school. To simplify the discussion, I ignore the possibility that schools may differ in their effectiveness in dif-

29. Meyer (1992) provides a more technical discussion of these issues.

ferent courses and subject areas. Given this simplification, the estimates of course effectiveness below should properly be interpreted as average course effects for the nation. The structure of my model of achievement is as follows. Achievement measured at the end of twelfth grade is determined by four sets of factors: prior achievement, measured at the end of tenth grade; student and family characteristics that are associated with student learning; courses taken in eleventh and twelfth grades; and additional, possibly random, factors that are not measured in the data.

This model is given by the following equation:[30]

$$Post\ achievement = \theta\ prior\ achievement + \delta\ student\ characteristics +$$
$$\alpha_1\ course_1 + \alpha_2\ course_2 + \ldots + unknown\ factors,$$

where the parameters θ, δ, α_1, α_2, . . ., represent the effects of each variable on achievement at the end of twelfth grade.[31] If the final and prior achievement tests are measured in the same units (as they are in HS&B), θ captures the degree to which prior achievement passes through to twelfth grade achievement. A parameter value equal to one represents full pass-through of achievement. A parameter value somewhat less than one, say 0.90 to 0.95, represents a modest depreciation in achievement. I would argue that a reasonable model of student achievement should yield an estimate of θ slightly less than one.[32]

The above model estimates the effectiveness of a given course by the average twelfth grade achievement of students enrolled in that course compared with the twelfth grade achievement of students not enrolled in the course but otherwise identical with respect to prior achievement, student characteristics, and other coursework. Thus the effectiveness of a calculus course is based on a comparison of twelfth grade test scores for students enrolled in calculus with the scores of students who had similar tenth grade achievement scores and student characteristics but did not take calculus. It is perhaps intuitively obvious that if the twelfth grade test scores of calculus

30. To simplify the notation, prior achievement and student characteristics are included in the equation as single variables. In practice, the model includes a set of student characteristics and possibly prior achievement variables in more than one subject area.

31. Alternatively, twelfth grade student achievement could be expressed as the outcome of "educational inputs" in eleventh and twelfth grades *and* in all years up to eleventh grade. One apparent advantage of this approach is that it obviates the need to include a measure of prior achievement in the model. However, it does not yield unbiased parameter estimates; see Meyer (1992). Moreover, most data sets (including HS&B) contain little, if any, information on past educational inputs. As a result, most analyses of student achievement use a model of the type used in this chapter.

32. This holds only when post and prior achievement tests are defined in the same units.

students were compared with those of students with low prior achievement, the apparent effectiveness of calculus would be hugely overstated. The bottom line is that it is crucial to control fully for differences in prior achievement and other characteristics across students, particularly if these variables are highly correlated with patterns of course enrollment.[33]

As discussed in the literature review above, previous models of student achievement generally fail to control fully for differences across students in prior achievement. Some, for example, do not include prior achievement at all. This is equivalent to forcing the coefficient on prior achievement to be equal to zero. A model that fails to control for prior achievement is likely to produce upward-biased estimates of the effectiveness of courses taken by students with high prior achievement and downward-biased estimates for courses taken by students with low prior achievement. In effect, in such a model the course variables act as signals of low and high prior achievement.

More subtly, some models of achievement use a prior achievement variable that is fallible; that is, measured with error. Ordinary least squares (OLS)—the method traditionally used to estimate models of student achievement—produces parameter estimates that are potentially quite biased in the presence of measurement error. Moreover, the bias is similar to that produced by a model with no prior achievement variable, in the sense that estimates of the effectiveness of courses taken by students with high prior achievement are upward biased, and vice versa. The magnitude of the bias depends directly on the reliability of the prior achievement variable *and* the degree to which the prior achievement variable is correlated with the other variables in the model. In a model that includes course enrollment variables and student characteristics, the intercorrelation of these variables is likely to be enormous. Thus even if the error in measuring prior achievement is modest, the bias due to measurement error could be substantial.

Fortunately, it is possible to solve the problem of measurement error in prior achievement by using either of two methods: instrumental variables or two-stage least squares and error in variables.[34] Both approaches give

---

33. The need to control for differences in prior achievement and student characteristics arises precisely because these variables are highly correlated with course enrollments. This situation would not arise in an experimental evaluation where students are assigned randomly to different treatments (courses). In the HS&B data, by contrast, students freely selected the courses that interested them. Not surprisingly, students with the highest prior mathematics scores tended to take the most advanced courses, and those with the lowest prior scores took the least advanced courses.

34. Both methods are developed in Meyer (1992).

Table 8-4. *Selected Parameter Estimates for Alternative Statistical Models*[a]

	Parameter				
Model	Sophomore math test[b]	Pre-algebra	Chemistry or physics	Foreign languages	Calculus
Simple difference equation	1.000	2.285	0.680	0.048	1.197
Two-stage least squares	0.947 (0.029)	2.164 (0.626)	0.828 (0.281)	0.112 (0.239)	1.647 (1.332)
Errors in variables	0.913	2.055	0.926	0.154	1.939
Ordinary least squares, uncorrected measurement error	0.678	1.548	1.583	0.434	3.939
Including proxies for prior achievement[c]	0.430[d]	0.897	2.465	0.315	6.039
Omitting prior achievement	0.000	−0.007	3.488	1.248	9.718

Source: Author's regressions based on data from the High School and Beyond study, 1980 and 1982.

a. Sample comprises non-college-bound students only. Estimated standard errors are in parentheses. Since standard errors vary very little across estimators, they are reported only for the 2SLS model. The estimates shown in this table are drawn from the complete model estimates in Meyer (1992).

b. Value of the sophomore math test coefficient is fixed at 1.00 in the simple difference equation model, and at 0.0 in the model with limited proxies for prior achievement.

c. Proxies for prior achievement include all ninth and tenth grade course enrollment variables, grade point averages in all subject areas in ninth grade, and plans (as of tenth grade) for postsecondary vocational education.

d. This estimate is intended to illustrate the implicit level of bias caused by replacing the prior test with proxy variables. For details of the procedure used to construct the estimate, see Meyer (1992, note 46).

remarkably similar results in the present context; this paper focuses on the results from the former.

The simplest way to assess the practical importance of the statistical issues addressed in this section is to examine the estimates produced by various statistical models. Table 8-4 presents parameter estimates of the sophomore test coefficient and several course effects for the sample of non-college-bound students, using six different models. The models are ordered in terms of their respective estimates of θ, the coefficient on prior math achievement. Hence the first row gives results for the simple difference equation ($\theta = 1$) and the last row gives results for the model with no prior achievement variable ($\theta = 0$).[35]

The principal conclusion to be drawn from table 8-4 is that the models that have dominated previous studies of educational outcomes—the OLS model with no correction for measurement error, the model with proxies for prior achievement, and the model without a variable for prior achievement—perform atrociously within the context of a curricular model of mathematics achievement. With respect to the coefficient on prior achievement, these estimators deviate radically from the preferred 2SLS estimate of 0.95. As expected, they also yield severely distorted estimates of curricular effectiveness. The coefficients on calculus and foreign language coursework, in particular, are extremely sensitive to incomplete control for prior achievement. In the model with no prior achievement variable, for example, the calculus coefficient is inflated by a factor of 590 percent, and the foreign language coefficient by a factor of 1,114 percent, over the corresponding 2SLS coefficients. In the prior achievement proxy model, the comparable figures are 239 percent and 388 percent, respectively.

The good news is that the two models that address the problem of measurement error in prior achievement—two-stage least squares and errors in variables models—yield remarkably similar estimates. In other contexts the results of the two approaches could differ. On the basis of this study, however, it would generally be better to use either model to correct for measurement error than to ignore the problem altogether.

This section demonstrates the importance of controlling adequately for prior mathematics achievement when estimating the value-added contribution of high school coursework to mathematics proficiency. Apparently slight imperfections in measured prior achievement can significantly affect estimates of curricular effectiveness. The above analysis suggests that empirical studies of curricular effectiveness must be based on longitudinal outcome data. The models that are based solely on senior mathematics achievement generate quite unsatisfactory results. This means that large and expensive databases, such as the NAEP, are not very useful for exploring the determinants of growth in achievement. Given the vital importance of this type of research, it seems obvious that greater national atten-

---

35. Table 8-4 includes two models not discussed in the text: a simple difference equation model in which θ is forced to equal one and a model that includes proxies for prior achievement. The proxies for prior achievement include all ninth and tenth grade course enrollment variables, grade point averages in all subject areas in ninth grade, and plans for postsecondary vocational education.

tion should be given to developing longitudinal databases that, like the High School and Beyond study, include extensive data on achievement, students, and schools.

Estimates of the Effects of High School Coursework on Growth in Mathematics Skill

Table 8-5 reports estimates of the determinants of math achievement for college-bound students, non-college-bound students, and all students.[36] Estimates for students with low, medium, and high prior mathematics achievement are reported in table 8A-3 in appendix 8A.[37] In order to interpret these estimates properly, the following points should be kept in mind.

First, estimates of course effectiveness are quite imprecise for courses taken by only a small number of students. In general, the standard errors are high (greater than 0.30) for courses taken by less than 5 percent of the sample or subgroup subsample. These coefficients should not be given undue emphasis, particularly if they are unusually high or low—unless a consistent pattern exists across several such courses.

Second, differences in estimates of course effectiveness across subgroups could have either of two very different explanations. One is that there could be actual differences in the effectiveness of courses for different groups. For example, courses with low- to mid-level mathematics content might be beneficial for students with weak mathematics proficiency but quite unproductive for students with high proficiency. Conversely, courses with high-level content might be most beneficial to students with high mathematics proficiency. But the other explanations is that students who enrolled in courses with the same title might actually have been presented with substantially different academic content.

Third, as mentioned above, the HS&B math test includes items specifically related to some high school mathematics courses (algebra and

---

36. All of the estimates discussed in this section are based on the two-stage least squares model discussed in Meyer (1992). This model includes a single measure of prior achievement: tenth grade mathematics achievement. Virtually identical results are obtained using a 2SLS model with multiple measures of prior achievement (math, verbal, and science achievement) and EV models with single and multiple measures of prior achievement; see Meyer (1992) for further details.

37. Students are classified into math triptiles on the basis of their predicted rather than their actual sophomore math scores, in order not to use a fallible variable. For the equation used to predict tenth grade achievement, see Meyer (1992, table A-5).

Table 8-5. *Estimates of the Determinants of Math Achievement in HS&B*[a]

Right-hand-side variable	Non-college-bound		College-bound		All students	
	Coefficient	Standard error	Coefficient	Standard error	Coefficient	Standard error
Sophomore math test[b]	0.947	0.029	1.024	0.026	0.997	0.018
Credits in grades 11 or 12						
Basic math	-0.569	0.495	1.644	0.780	0.044	0.406
General math	0.301	0.270	1.044	0.276	0.743	0.190
Computer math	-1.705	0.856	-1.293	0.423	-1.291	0.386
Pre-algebra	2.164	0.626	1.507	0.431	1.790	0.358
Algebra 1	2.503	0.387	2.271	0.277	2.406	0.225
Geometry	2.031	0.326	1.236	0.186	1.427	0.161
Algebra 2	1.893	0.337	1.671	0.156	1.728	0.142
Precalculus	1.512	0.426	0.969	0.188	1.115	0.169
Calculus	1.647	1.332	0.441	0.283	0.726	0.269
Specific vocational math	0.026	0.400	1.605	0.441	0.679	0.293
Applied math	0.645	0.305	1.403	0.378	0.953	0.233
Chemistry or physics	0.828	0.281	0.473	0.123	0.613	0.112
Biology or survey science	0.015	0.186	-0.164	0.133	-0.084	0.108
Math-related vocational education	0.205	0.101	-0.085	0.099	0.069	0.070
Non-math-related vocational education	-0.117	0.048	-0.145	0.058	-0.136	0.036

English or social studies	0.083	0.069	−0.144	0.062	−0.029	0.045
Foreign languages	0.112	0.239	0.063	0.102	0.153	0.094
Fine arts	−0.146	0.098	−0.089	0.071	−0.075	0.057
Personal and other	−0.143	0.092	−0.151	0.073	−0.142	0.057
Graduation indicator	0.701	0.332	0.669	0.503	0.757	0.265
Female	−0.901	0.174	−0.420	0.148	−0.639	0.111
Black	−0.194	0.355	−0.155	0.293	−0.161	0.216
Asian	−0.543	0.268	−0.845	0.561	−0.716	0.508
Hispanic	−1.985	1.088	−0.351	0.294	−0.381	0.196
Urban	−0.039	0.192	0.266	0.212	0.097	0.161
Suburban	0.008	0.251	0.151	0.164	0.081	0.124
Northeast	−0.584	0.248	0.611	0.207	0.079	0.158
West	0.353	0.288	0.118	0.225	0.219	0.177
South	−0.117	0.220	−0.262	0.191	−0.172	0.144
Constant	0.934	0.398	0.809	0.626	0.634	0.310

Summary statistic

R^2 $(T_2 - T_1)$[b]	0.061	0.080	0.085
Sample size	4,448	6,472	10,960

Source: Author's regressions based on data from the High School and Beyond study, 1980 and 1982.

a. Estimates are based on the 2SLS model. See Meyer (1992) for the variables included in each first stage.

b. Dependent variable is mathematics achievement in twelfth grade. However, table reports R^2 statistic for the essentially equivalent model of growth in mathematics achievement, since this is more informative.

geometry) but not others. In particular, there are no items that relate specifically to advanced-track and applied courses. This implies that estimates of the contributions of algebra and geometry to the growth of mathematics skills could be overstated relative to the contributions of other courses.

Finally, it is possible that estimates of course effectiveness could be attenuated for courses that are taken by students with very high test scores, in particular, precalculus, calculus, chemistry, and physics. These are likely to have a disproportionate number of students at or near the ceiling (maximum score) of the HS&B math test. One straightforward solution to this problem—the strategy that I employ—is to exclude from the sample those students who are most likely to be near the test ceiling. Table 8-6 reports estimates for students with predicted prior math scores between the 50th and 90th percentiles.[38]

The first important finding of this study is that advanced-track math courses—algebra 1 through calculus—tend to be substantially more effective in raising mathematics achievement than most other high school courses (see table 8-5). Consider, for example, the estimated effectiveness of algebra 2, the math course most often taken during the eleventh and twelfth grades by both non-college-bound and college-bound students who graduate: on average, 0.094 credit and 0.412 credit for these groups, respectively (see table 8-1). A full year of algebra is associated with an increase in math achievement of 1.9 units (test items) for non-college-bound students and 1.7 units for college-bound students. This is a reasonably large effect in light of the fact that the mean and standard deviation of the sophomore math tests are 13.4 and 9.7, respectively (see table 8-2).

The most effective course for both college-bound and non-college-bound students is algebra 1, with an effect estimate of 2.4 for all students. The least effective courses among the advanced-track group appear to be precalculus and calculus. These effect estimates are particularly low for college-bound students. As mentioned above, this result could be due to a ceiling effect in the HS&B. Indeed, when I use the sample that excludes the

---

38. I do not resolve the ceiling effect problem by eliminating from the sample students with the maximum score on the twelfth grade test: it is well known that censoring or truncating a dependent variable produces biased parameter estimates (see, for example, Maddala, 1983). Note also that I select the sample using a predicted measure of prior achievement rather than actual prior achievement, because the prior achievement variable is endogenous in the model (due to measurement error). This approach works extremely well in the present context, because twelfth grade achievement is highly correlated with variables used in the prediction model.

Table 8-6. *Estimates of the Determinants of Math Achievement for Students with Prior Math Scores in 50th to 90th Percentiles in HS&B*[a]

Right-hand-side variable	Coefficient	Standard error
Sophomore math test[b]	0.976	0.036
Credits in grades 11 and 12		
Basic math	3.427	1.371
General math	1.589	0.386
Computer math	−1.405	0.552
Pre-algebra	3.171	0.629
Algebra 1	2.487	0.374
Geometry	1.482	0.211
Algebra 2	2.008	0.172
Precalculus	1.579	0.216
Calculus	1.601	0.558
Specific vocational math	0.962	0.569
Applied math	1.219	0.547
Chemistry or physics	0.930	0.140
Biology or survey science	−0.223	0.161
Math-related vocational education	0.066	0.100
Non-math-related vocational education	−0.056	0.064
English or social studies	−0.051	0.076
Foreign languages	0.108	0.122
Fine arts	−0.066	0.079
Personal and other	−0.254	0.087
Summary statistic		
R^2 $(T_2 - T_1)$[b]	0.111	
Sample size	4,381	

Source: Author's regressions based on data from the High School and Beyond study, 1980 and 1982.

a. Estimates are based on the 2SLS model. See Meyer (1992) for the variables included in each first stage. Model also includes the other variables listed in table 8-5.

b. Dependent variable is mathematics achievement in twelfth grade. However, table reports R^2 statistic for the essentially equivalent model of growth in mathematics achievement, since this is more informative.

students most likely to be at the test ceiling, the calculus coefficient more than doubles, from 0.73 to 1.60 (see table 8-6). Thus advanced-track math courses appear to have a consistently large effect on growth in mathematics skill for all students, whether or not they are college-bound and whatever their level of prior mathematics skill. These results reinforce findings based on entirely different data reported by Girotto and Peterson in chapter 9 below.

Second, general math tends to be substantially less effective than pre-algebra or most advanced-track courses, particularly for students with low prior achievement and those who are not college-bound: the coefficient for non-college-bound students is only 0.3. The basic math coefficient for non-college-bound students is also low—in fact, it is negative at –0.6— although imprecisely estimated. This suggests that the push begun in the 1980s to encourage students to enroll in upper level mathematics courses was a very good idea. Unfortunately, many students still take no mathematics beyond tenth grade. Approximately 28 percent of high school graduates from the class of 1987 earned two credits or less of mathematics.[39]

The third important finding is that substantial mathematics learning takes place in many courses other than traditional mathematics. For college-bound students, for example, participation in a specific vocational math course, such as business math, or an applied math course increases mathematics achievement by 1.4 to 1.6 points, which is comparable to the effectiveness of algebra 2 for this group. For students in the upper third of the distribution of prior math, the effects are even larger: 1.8 to 2.4 points. This result is striking in light of the fact that the HS&B mathematics test has minimal applied content. However, these courses appear to be substantially less effective for non-college-bound students and students with low prior achievement. The effect estimates range from zero to only 0.6 point. My interpretation of this result is that the applied and specific vocational math courses taken by these students were probably pitched at too elementary a level. In practice, they may have been quite similar to—and as ineffective as—general math courses. This evidence reinforces the conclusion that *all* students benefit from courses with challenging academic content and are poorly served by courses with low-level content.

Math-related science courses (chemistry and physics) make surprisingly large contributions to math achievement for both non-college-bound and college-bound students: on the order of half the effects of geometry, of algebra 2, or of precalculus. The effect appears to be somewhat smaller for college-bound students and students at the top of the prior math distribution, but once again this is due to a ceiling effect (see table 8-6). These

---

39. Meyer (1991).

results provide the strongest evidence that mathematics can be learned through application.

The results for math-related vocational education also provide support for learning through application. In this case, though, effectiveness is limited to non-college-bound students and students with low prior achievement, perhaps because these courses typically feature fairly low-level mathematics skills. In addition, the effects are small: 0.21 for non-college-bound students and 0.37 for students in the lower third of the prior math distribution. Note, however, that these estimates reflect the effectiveness of a single one-credit course. The cumulative effect of enrollments in multiple courses could be substantial. If, for example, a student from the lower third of the prior math distribution took two credits of math-related vocational education in eleventh grade and three credits in twelfth grade—a typical enrollment pattern for a vocational concentration—the gains in these courses alone would amount to 1.35 points.[40] This is somewhat less than the effect of a single traditional math course or a pair of math-related science courses. Nonetheless, it would more than double the average two-year increase in math scores for non-college-bound students.

Conclusion

Is mathematics achievement largely predetermined or can it be increased by schools? This study provides strong evidence that growth in mathematics achievement in high school is determined by students' decisions about course enrollment. Participation in advanced-track courses such as algebra, geometry, and calculus significantly enhances mathematics proficiency for all students, both college-bound and non-college-bound. In contrast, high school courses such as basic and general math contribute little to the development of mathematics skill. This finding corroborates the results of Girotto and Peterson in chapter 9 below that hard courses and hard work enhance cognitive skills.

I also demonstrate that there is substantial development of mathematics skills in certain kinds of vocational and technical courses, quantitatively oriented science courses such as chemistry and physics, and applied math

40. This prediction is based on a model that allows for, and finds, diminishing returns in the effectiveness of math-related vocational education.

courses such as business and consumer mathematics. In other words, learning mathematics in an applied context appears to be a viable alternative or complement to taking traditional mathematics courses. These results would presumably be even stronger if they were based on a mathematics test that emphasized the application of mathematics skills.[41] My analysis therefore provides support for the reform strategies discussed at the beginning of the chapter: the development of new courses in applied and problem-solving mathematics, as recommended by the National Council of Mathematics Teachers, and the integration of academic and vocational education. These courses could potentially attract students who shy away from traditional math courses. Given that it is still the case that an enormous number of students take only limited amounts of mathematics in high school, this is a promising development. In addition, the new types of course could provide much more useful training in mathematics, at least for some students.

New math-related curriculum options, especially in the vocational curriculum, could be particularly advantageous for non-college-bound and academically disadvantaged students, who tend to take the minimum amount of mathematics required but substantial amounts of vocational education; in fact, they take eight times as much vocational education as mathematics. The new options could also be important for college-bound students, who as a group take more vocational education than mathematics in high school (see table 8-1). The estimates presented above suggest, however, that the mathematical rigor of the math-related vocational courses and specific vocational math courses taken by non-college-bound students needs to be greatly increased. For these courses to be viable alternatives to other math courses, they must utilize mathematics at a fairly high level, for example, that used in high school chemistry and physics courses.

My findings suggest that policies that encourage or require students to enroll in challenging high school math or math-related courses are likely to yield substantial improvements in mathematics skills. Requiring students to take a challenging math course and a challenging math-related science course in both the eleventh and twelfth grades, for example, would increase math achievement by 5 to 6 points, three times the actual average gain.

---

41. The testing community is currently devoting tremendous resources to developing the types of applied, performance-based tests that would be appropriate for such an analysis.

Christopher Jencks and Meredith Phillips demonstrate in chapter 2 above that an increase of this magnitude in achievement would significantly enhance adult earnings.[42]

The results of this study also imply that it may be sensible to consider a systemic, schoolwide approach to teaching mathematics and other cognitive skills—specifically, shared responsibility for mathematics instruction across mathematics, science, vocational education, and other subject areas. This idea is not without precedent. Writing across the curriculum programs, which require that writing skills be taught in all courses, not just in English, reflect a similar motivation. The recent national emphasis on student and school performance in core academic skills may provide the impetus for schools to adopt such an approach.

Finally, this study shows that estimates of the curricular production function are extremely sensitive to model misspecifications. It is particularly important to control adequately for prior achievement, a variable that is inevitably measured with error. I obtain reasonable and consistent results with two alternative methods for addressing the problem of measurement error: a two-stage least squares model and an errors in variables model. Other researchers interested in estimating educational production functions should consider using these methods to address the problem of measurement error in tests.[43]

Appendix 8A
Supplementary Results

Tables 8A-1 to 8A-3 report results that support the main analysis in the text.

---

42. Jencks and Phillips show that the payoff to growth in student achievement between tenth and twelfth grades is comparable to the effect of tenth grade achievement on earnings. They conclude that the labor market values the types of cognitive skill that are taught in high school.

43. In chapter 2 above Jencks and Phillips correct for measurement in achievement by using a LISREL-based approach that is very similar to the errors in variables approach used here.

Table 8A-1. *Average Course Enrollments in Ninth through Twelfth Grades by Graduation Status and Postsecondary Plans in HS&B*[a]

| | | Graduates | | |
| | | Non-college- | College- | All |
Course	Dropouts	bound	bound	students
Vocational education				
Math-related	0.432	0.909	0.700	0.763
Non-math-related	2.644	4.783	2.489	3.390
All	3.076	5.692	3.189	4.153
Specific vocational math	0.112	0.128	0.051	0.085
Applied math	0.130	0.156	0.066	0.105
Mathematics				
Basic	0.238	0.136	0.051	0.097
General	0.789	0.633	0.279	0.451
Computer	0.012	0.018	0.041	0.030
Pre-algebra	0.163	0.234	0.230	0.227
Algebra 1	0.305	0.515	0.742	0.624
Geometry	0.115	0.255	0.709	0.493
Algebra 2	0.074	0.167	0.591	0.391
Precalculus	0.023	0.062	0.359	0.221
Calculus	0.000	0.006	0.093	0.053
All[b]	1.719	2.026	3.095	2.587
Science				
Survey	0.786	0.833	0.695	0.755
Biology	0.648	0.819	1.123	0.973
Chemistry	0.038	0.117	0.571	0.359
Physics	0.022	0.045	0.274	0.168
All	1.494	1.814	2.663	2.255
English	3.018	3.924	4.075	3.945
Social studies	2.240	3.250	3.338	3.230
Fine arts	0.936	1.381	1.513	1.423
Foreign languages	0.285	0.459	1.579	1.057
Personal and other	2.396	2.836	3.004	2.898
Summary statistic				
Total credits	15.406	21.666	22.573	21.738
Sample size	855	3,759	6,347	10,961

Source: Author's computations from school transcripts collected by the High School and Beyond study.

a. Course enrollments are measured in Carnegie credits; see table 8-1, note a.

b. Excluding applied and specific vocational math courses.

Table 8A-2. *Average Course Enrollments in Eleventh and Twelfth Grades by Predicted Sophomore Math Test Triptiles in HS&B*[a]

Credits

Course	Predicted sophomore math achievement			All students
	Lower third	Middle third	Upper third	
Vocational education				
Math-related	0.341	0.617	0.561	0.509
Non-math-related	2.893	2.433	0.995	2.110
All	3.234	3.050	1.556	2.619
Specific vocational math	0.060	0.046	0.012	0.040
Applied math	0.108	0.058	0.017	0.061
Mathematics				
Basic	0.053	0.007	0.002	0.020
General	0.143	0.070	0.041	0.084
Computer	0.003	0.015	0.060	0.025
Pre-algebra	0.030	0.031	0.012	0.024
Algebra 1	0.090	0.072	0.041	0.067
Geometry	0.048	0.208	0.160	0.139
Algebra 2	0.042	0.194	0.555	0.263
Precalculus	0.011	0.050	0.519	0.191
Calculus	0.000	0.003	0.150	0.050
All[b]	0.419	0.648	1.534	0.863
Science				
Survey	0.117	0.076	0.044	0.079
Biology	0.181	0.209	0.279	0.223
Chemistry	0.031	0.186	0.673	0.296
Physics	0.012	0.044	0.414	0.155
All	0.341	0.515	1.410	0.753
English	1.732	1.803	1.949	1.828
Social studies	1.610	1.859	1.897	1.790
Fine arts	0.500	0.741	0.728	0.658
Foreign languages	0.110	0.285	0.681	0.359
Personal and other	0.959	1.123	1.143	1.076
Summary statistic				
Total credits	9.074	10.130	10.933	10.047
Sample size	3,648	3,647	3,666	10,961

Source: Author's computations from school transcripts collected by the High School and Beyond study.

a. Course enrollments are measured in Carnegie credits; see table 8-1, note a.

b. Excluding applied and specific vocational math courses.

Table 8A-3. *Estimates of the Determinants of Math Achievement by Sophomore Math Test Triptile in HS&B*[a]

| | Sophomore math achievement | | | | | |
| | Lower third | | Middle third | | Upper third | |
Right-hand-side variable	Coefficient	Standard error	Coefficient	Standard error	Coefficient	Standard error
Sophomore math test[b]	0.991	0.071	0.909	0.047	0.913	0.035
Credits in grades 11 and 12						
Basic math	-0.453	0.473	3.125	1.307	2.985	2.302
General math	0.436	0.288	0.782	0.346	1.429	0.408
Computer math	-2.626	2.251	-1.461	0.902	-1.163	0.380
Pre-algebra	1.749	0.584	1.570	0.570	2.342	0.734
Algebra 1	2.276	0.358	2.617	0.391	2.014	0.425
Geometry	1.406	0.509	1.027	0.238	1.839	0.252
Algebra 2	1.992	0.548	2.080	0.265	1.592	0.170
Precalculus	-0.427	1.005	1.797	0.445	1.284	0.177
Calculus	1.865	7.036	3.974	1.869	1.055	0.271
Specific vocational math	-0.045	0.417	1.110	0.495	2.379	0.781
Applied math	0.632	0.305	1.187	0.442	1.816	0.712

Chemistry or physics	0.165	0.488	0.944	0.233	0.576	0.122
Biology or survey science	0.111	0.200	−0.179	0.200	−0.144	0.157
Math-related vocational education	0.369	0.146	0.016	0.111	−0.136	0.107
Non-math-related vocational education	−0.158	0.053	−0.179	0.061	0.042	0.086
English or social studies	0.057	0.076	−0.079	0.080	−0.108	0.084
Foreign languages	0.144	0.307	−0.037	0.179	0.239	0.108
Fine arts	−0.059	0.123	−0.126	0.096	−0.038	0.082
Personal and other	−0.147	0.106	−0.165	0.099	−0.177	0.087

Summary statistic

R^2 $(T_2 - T_1)$[b]	0.044		0.073		0.076	
Sample size	3,647		3,646		3,665	

Source: Author's regressions based on data from the High School and Beyond study, 1980 and 1982.

a. Estimates are based on the 2SLS model. See Meyer (1992) for the variables included in each first stage. Model also includes the other variables listed in table 8-5.

b. Dependent variable is mathematics achievement in twelfth grade. However, table reports R^2 statistic for the essentially equivalent model of growth in mathematics achievement, since this is more informative.

Appendix 8B
Definitions of Selected Course Variables

I construct two applied math course variables, each with a full-time focus on mathematics instruction: applied math and specific vocational math. Titles of the courses included in these variables are as follows, with Classification of Secondary School Course codes in parentheses.

Applied math: consumer mathematics (27.0114), mathematics as a liberal art (27.0109), mathematics for employment (27.0110); science mathematics (27.0108), technical mathematics (27.0111), vocational mathematics (27.0110), other applied mathematics (27.0300).

Specific vocational math: agricultural mathematics (01.0151), business mathematics 1 (07.0171), business mathematics 2 (07.0172), nurse's mathematics (17.0651).

The essential difference between the two variables is that specific vocational math courses are structured around a particular vocational subject, such as business, and presumably draw most or all of their examples from this subject. It may also be that specific vocational math courses tend to be taught by vocational educators rather than math teachers. The HS&B data, however, provide no information on this point.

A vocational course is considered math-related if it satisfies any one of the following conditions:

—it is one of several vocational science specialties, such as agricultural science;

—it includes any of the following: architecture or drafting, accounting or bookkeeping, computer programming, data processing, economics or finance (including investment and taxation), electricity, electronics, insurance, or real estate;

—it relies on geometric or spatial skills.

The courses were classified prior to any data analysis. Thus the empirical results reported above are not contaminated by data mining. To the extent that some vocational courses have been misclassified, the estimated differential between math-related and non-math-related courses will be understated.

The math-related vocational courses grouped according to the Secondary School Course Taxonomy are as follows, with Classification of Secondary School Course codes in parentheses.

Consumer and homemaking: home management 1 (20.0191); clothing 3 or sewing 3 (20.0135); clothing 4, alterations, sports wear (20.0136); tailoring (20.0137); consumer education 2 (20.0142); home management 2 (20.0192); business or home economics, other (19.0200); family or consumer resource management, other (19.0400); food sciences and human nutrition, other (19.0500).

General labor market preparation: electricity and electronics, introduction (21.0119); business economics (06.0511).

Agriculture and renewable resources: agricultural business (01.0111); agricultural business and management, other (01.0100); agricultural business operation (01.0121); farm and ranch management (01.0131); agricultural microprocessing (01.0161); electricity and electronics, agricultural (01.0251); surveying, agricultural (01.0271).

Business and business management: business, introduction (06.0111); financial careers (06.0311); accounting, other (06.0200); banking and finance, other (06.0300); business economics, other (06.0500); international business management, other (06.0900); investments and securities, other (06.1000); investment and taxation (06.1011); management science, other (06.1300); taxation, other (06.1900).

Business support: bookkeeping (107.0111); accounting 1 (07.0121); bookkeeping and accounting 1 (07.0141); business computer concepts (07.0311); business data processing 1 (07.0321); business computer programming 1 or business computer applications (07.0331); bookkeeping 2 (07.0112); accounting 2 (07.0122); bookkeeping and accounting 2 (07.0142); business data processing 2 (07.0322); business computer programming 2 (07.0332); accounting, bookkeeping, and related programs, other (07.0100); accounting, college (07.0131); banking and related financial programs, other (07.0200); bank teller (07.0211); financial mathematics (07.0221); bank proof operator (07.0231); business data processing and related programs, other (07.0300).

Marketing and distribution: insurance careers (06.0811); insurance and risk management, other (06.0800); marketing management and research, other (06.1400); marketing management and decisionmaking (06.1411); real estate, other (06.1700); real estate marketing (06.1711); entrepreneurship, other (08.0300); starting your own business (08.0311); financial services marketing, other (08.0400); insurance marketing, other (08.1000).

Health: chemistry for health science (17.0581); epidemiology, other (18.0600); pharmacy, other (18.1400); prepharmacy, other (18.1900); public health laboratory science, other (18.2200); toxicology (clinical), other (18.2300); health sciences, other (18.9900); personal services occupations (12.0431).

Occupational home economics: baking (20.0431); chef (20.0441); home furnishing, equipment management, production (20.0500); home decorating (20.0531); custom drapery and window treatment design (20.0551); custom slipcovering and upholstering (20.0561).

Trades and industry (T&I): Construction trades: electricity 1 (21.0113); carpentry 1 (46.0211); building construction 1 (46.0411); electrical trades, advanced or 2 (21.0114); carpentry 2 (46.0212); carpentry 3 (46.0213); building construction 2 (46.0412); carpentry, other (46.0200).

T&I: Mechanics and repairer: radio and TV repair 1 (47.0121); radio and TV repair 2 (47.0122); radio and TV repair 3 (47.0123); electrical and electronic equipment repair, other (47.0100); business machine repair (47.0151); industrial electricity (47.0161); industrial electronics (47.0171); hydraulics and pneumatics (47.0521).

T&I: Precision production: electronics, basic or 1 (21.0115); mechanical drawing or drafting 1 (48.0111); architectural drawing or drafting 1 (48.0121); engineering drawing or drafting 1 (48.0131); cabinet-making 1 or millwork (48.0731); electronics 2 or electronics digital (21.0116); electronics 3 (21.0117); electronics 4 (21.0118); electricity and electronics, advanced (21.0120); architectural drawing or drafting 2 (48.0122); architectural drawing or drafting 3 (48.0123); architectural drawing 4 or architectural model building (48.0124); engineering graphics 2 (48.0132); drafting 1, cooperative (48.0151); drafting 2, cooperative (48.0152); cabinet-making (48.0732); architecture and environmental design, other general (04.0100); architecture, other (04.0200); architectural theory (04.0221); city, community, and regional planning, other (04.0300); environmental design, other (04.0400); landscape architecture, other (04.0600); urban design, other (04.0700); architecture and environmental design, other (04.9900); drafting, other (48.0100); sketching and blueprint reading (48.0141).

Technical and communications: aeronautics 2 (49.0112); marine engine and boat repair 2 (49.0312); navigation (49.0331); computer programming 1 (11.0211); data processing, introduction (11.0311); electronic technology 1 (15.0331); chemical technology 1 (17.0321); computer programming 2 (11.0212); data processing 2 (11.0312); data processing, advanced (11.0313); electronic technology 2 (15.0332); chemical technology 2 (17.0322); communication technologies, other (10.0100); communications media production (10.0121); radio production (10.0161); cable television (10.0181); computer and information sciences, other general (11.0100); computer applications (11.0131); computer applications, independent study (11.0132); computer science, advanced placement (11.0141); computer programming, other (11.0200); FORTRAN, introduction (11.0221); PASCAL, introduction (11.0231); BASIC, introduction (11.0241); COBOL, introduction (11.0251); data processing, other (11.0300); architectural technologies, other (15.0100); surveying (15.0211); electrical and electronic technologies, other (15.0300); audio electronics (15.0311); electrical technology (15.0321); electromechanical instrumentation and maintenance technologies (15.0400); electromechanical technology (15.0411); instrumentation technology (15.0421); environmental control technologies, other (15.0500); environmental control technologies (15.0511); industrial production technologies, other (15.0600); industrial production technology (15.0611); chemical manufacturing technology (15.0621); optics technology (15.0631); quality control and safety technologies, other (15.0700); quality control technology (15.0711); mechanical and related technologies, other (15.0800); mining and petroleum technologies, other (15.0900); mining technology (15.0911); petroleum technology (15.0921); engineering and engineering-related technologies, other (15.9900); biological technologies, other (41.0100); nuclear technologies, other (41.0200); physical science technologies, other (41.0300); science technologies, other (41.9900).

References

Brown, Cynthia, and others. 1989. "The Secondary Schools Taxonomy." Discussion paper for the National Assessment of Vocational Education. U.S. Department of Education (February).

Coleman, James S., and others. 1966. *Equality of Educational Opportunity.* Government Printing Office.

Congressional Budget Office. 1986. *Trends in Educational Achievement.*

————. 1987. *Educational Achievement: Explanations and Implications of Recent Trends.*

Fetters, William B., Peter S. Stowe, and Jeffrey A. Owings. 1984. *High School and Beyond, A National Longitudinal Study for the 1980s: Quality of Responses of High School Students to Questionnaire Items.* Washington: National Center for Education Statistics.

Grubb, W. Norton. 1995a. *Education through Occupations in American High Schools.* Vol. 1, *Approaches to Integrating Academic and Vocational Education.* New York: Teachers College Press.

————. 1995b. *Education through Occupations in American High Schools.* Vol. 1, *The Challenges of Implementing Curriculum Integration.* New York: Teachers College Press.

Grubb, W. Norton, and others. 1991. "The Cunning Hand, the Cultured Minds: Models for Integrating Vocational and Academic Education." Berkeley, Calif.: National Center for Research in Vocational Education.

Hanushek, Eric A. 1971. "Teacher Characteristics and Gains in Student Achievement: Estimation Using Micro Data." *American Economic Review, Papers and Proceedings* 61(2): 280–88.

————. 1986. "The Economics of Schooling." *Journal of Economic Literature* 24(September): 1141–177.

Hoffer, Thomas, Andrew M. Greeley, and James S. Coleman. 1985. "Achievement Growth in Public and Catholic Schools." *Sociology of Education* 58(2): 74–97.

Jencks, Christopher. 1985. "How Much Do High School Students Learn?" *Sociology of Education* 58(2): 128–35.

McKnight, Curtis, and others. 1987. *The Underachieving Curriculum: A National Report on the Second International Mathematics Study.* Champaign, Ill.: Stipes.

Maddala, G. S. 1983. *Limited-Dependent and Qualitative Variables in Econometrics.* Cambridge University Press.

Meyer, Robert H. 1991. "Beyond Academic Reform: The Case for Integrated Vocational and Academic Education." Unpublished paper. University of Wisconsin–Madison.

————. 1992. "Applied versus Traditional Mathematics: New Econometric Models of the Contribution of High School Courses to Mathematics Proficiency." Discussion Paper 966-92. University of Wisconsin–Madison, Institute for Research on Poverty.

Murnane, Richard J. 1975. *The Impact of School Resources on the Learning of Inner City Children.* Cambridge, Mass.: Ballinger.

National Assessment of Vocational Education. 1988. *First Interim Report of the National Assessment of Vocational Education.* U.S. Department of Education.

National Council of Teachers of Mathematics. 1989. *Curriculum and Evaluation Standards for School Mathematics.* Reston, Va.

Pallas, Aaron M., and Karl L. Alexander. 1983. "Sex Differences in Qualitative SAT Performance: New Evidence on the Differential Coursework Hypothesis." *American Educational Research Journal* 20(2): 165–82.

Rock, Donald A., and others. 1985. "Psychometric Analysis of the NLS and High School and Beyond Test Batteries." U.S. Department of Education, National Center for Education Statistics (September).

Schmidt, William H. 1983. "High School Course-Taking: Its Relationship to Achievement." *Journal of Curriculum Studies* 15(3): 311–32.

Welch, Wayne W., Ronald E. Anderson, and Linda J. Harris. 1982. "The Effects of Schooling on Mathematics Achievement." *American Educational Research Journal* 19(1): 145–53.

JAY R. GIROTTO
PAUL E. PETERSON

9

Do Hard Courses and Good Grades Enhance Cognitive Skills?

NUMEROUS STUDIES HAVE SHOWN that additional years of schooling improve a student's likelihood of earning a higher income. These results are usually interpreted as indicating that additional years of schooling improve the cognitive skills that employers value. Researchers have had more difficulty showing how schooling enhances cognitive skills. In particular, research examining the importance of curriculum and student effort has been bedeviled by methodological problems, including inadequate baseline information, selection bias, and crude measures of student achievement. These methodological issues have made it difficult to confirm the hypothesis that curriculum and student effort are important to the development of cognitive skills. Yet it would seem intuitively obvious that students achieve greater gains in cognitive skills if they spend more time on

Financial support for this project has been received from the Ford Foundation, the Rockefeller Foundation, the Russell Sage Foundation, and the James Dusenbury Grant administered by the Harvard Department of Economics. We are grateful to the superintendent of secondary education in River City, Iowa, without whose unstinting support the data could not have been collected. River City area education administrators helped to extract the electronically formatted data from the River City records. High school principals and teachers assisted in the distribution of the social survey. David Abrams designed and coded a searching program that facilitated the analysis of the electronic data. Catherine James helped to complete the seven-month process of constructing the data set. Caroline Minter Hoxby gave valuable advice at every stage of the research process, kept the econometric analysis on track, and played a particularly large role in designing the selection equation.

challenging courses in math, English, and science rather than on less demanding courses in life studies and personal development.

Despite this intuition, more research on this question is needed because many public schools in the United States are organized in ways that discourage students from taking a challenging academic curriculum. Instead, schools resemble shopping malls designed to attract as many students as possible.[1] Students are treated as customers with different tastes and objectives. They are allowed to choose from a broad range of classes and activities. They may attend academic classes, which prepare them for college and higher skilled occupations. They may take skill courses, such as driver education and homemaking, which can assist them in nonacademic pursuits. They can enjoy extracurricular activities, such as fine arts and sports, which may enlarge their range of interests and provide social opportunities. The choice among this potpourri is often left in the hands of the student, although guidance counselors are available to help with scheduling conflicts. The overall goal of the shopping mall school, it seems, is to retain as high a percentage of customers as possible until graduation day. If schools are revenue-maximizers, this policy may make sense. After all, the amount of money the school receives from the state typically depends on the number of days its customers are in attendance.

The shopping mall high school has been criticized for its limited capacity to enhance student cognitive skills. Two studies comparing public and private schools find that students learn more in private schools, in part because these schools concentrate student efforts on academic pursuits.[2] Yet the curriculum is only one of many differences that could account for the superior performance of private school graduates. And few, if any, studies that focus exclusively on public schools have shown convincingly that the curriculum has much effect on student cognitive skills.

A Review of Prior Research

The few studies that have found positive effects of coursework on cognitive skill have serious methodological difficulties. Three studies that find positive effects do not control for the level of cognitive skill before the student

---

1. Powell, Farrar, and Cohen (1985, pp. 1–3).
2. Chubb and Moe (1990, p. 3); Bryk, Lee, and Holland (1993, p. 13).

took the course.[3] Even a more sophisticated study by Karl Alexander and Aaron Pallas seems contaminated by selection bias.[4] Although the study estimates the effects of courses after controlling for both family background and a prior measure of cognitive skill, it is entirely possible that students who decided to take more academic courses may have had unmeasured attributes that could account for gains in skill that are attributed to coursework.

The failure to find a connection between coursework and cognitive skill has led some to argue that it does not exist. For example, Richard Herrnstein and Charles Murray argue that cognitive skill is either innate or decisively determined in the very first months or years of life. Their assessment of Head Start reflects this belief: "Next to nothing can be learned about how to raise IQ by more evaluations of Head Start. . . . It is tough to alter the environment for the development of general intellectual ability by anything short of adoption at birth."[5] Education is just one of those things more talented people do. Herrnstein and Murray contend that the observed correlation between the number of years of schooling and cognitive skill is largely due to the fact that the more able tend to obtain more schooling.

This line of argument has been forcefully challenged by a number of creative studies that have figured out ways to distinguish genuine educational effects from spurious ones. Orley Ashenfelter and Alan Krueger compare genetically identical twins with different levels of schooling.[6] An alternative approach has been to construct instrumental variables that enable the investigator to control for the propensity of the more talented to pursue more education.[7] All in all, it is pretty much accepted that those who remain in school longer learn more, achieve higher earnings, and enjoy a better life.

Still, it is one thing to say that the number of years of education make a difference, another to say that the curriculum and student effort are critical. After all, the shopping mall high school has been constructed on what might be called an incarceration theory of education: it is more important

---

3. Schmidt (1983, p. 332); Laing, Enger, and Maxey (1990, pp. 335–39); Sebring (1987, pp. 258–62).

4. Alexander and Pallas (1984, pp. 391–400).

5. Herrnstein and Murray (1994, p. 413).

6. Ashenfelter and Krueger (1994).

7. See Angrist and Krueger (1991).

to keep students inside the school's four walls than that they take quality courses. Very little in the educational research literature effectively challenges this proposition. For example, findings from Joseph Altonji's recent study of the effect of the high school curriculum on labor market outcomes are quite consistent with incarceration theory. Drawing on data collected from a national sample of 1972 high school graduates, he finds that the courses students took in high school had little effect on their wages some years later.[8] Even when one does not control for family background, the estimates indicate that one more year of academic science, math, and English classes leads to a wage increase of only 0.3 percent.

Although Altonji's analysis is as careful as any that can be conducted on a national data set, his results may still be contaminated by serious measurement error. All studies that depend on data from a national cross-section of American schools must make the heroic assumption that similarly labeled courses have essentially the same contents. But a high school English course in Evanston, Illinois, is likely to cover a quite different set of materials than a course of the same name offered in Washington, D.C. A student who receives an A in geometry in Concord, Massachusetts, is likely to have had a different educational experience from a student receiving the same grade in the "same" course in Natchez, Mississippi.

Incarceration theory places no more emphasis on the student's commitment and effort than it does on the curriculum. As long as the student is retained in school, it is assumed that learning takes place. The idea that students are active producers, not passive recipients, of knowledge has yet to be fully incorporated into econometric models.

A perfectly good, if dreadfully old-fashioned, measure of student effort has long been available: grades for coursework. But once again, those seductive national samples create the problem. Although their external validity is nearly beyond question, their internal reliability on such matters as student grades has dissuaded most investigators from thinking—or at least publishing—about the question. Since work that would fail to pass muster in one school receives an A in another, there is little point in asking whether good grades make a difference. To learn more about these questions requires a step back from national surveys. We have chosen instead to take a close look at student learning in a single school system.

8. Altonji (1995, p. 410).

Overview of the Data

To estimate the effects of curriculum and student effort on cognitive skills, we use information from the school system of River City, Iowa, about the cognitive skills of all 869 members in the class of 1995 and the 816 members in the class of 1996.[9] Cognitive skills were measured in the freshman and junior years by the Iowa Test of Educational Development (ITED). Data were also collected on the courses taken and the grades received. Using a shortened version of the 1979 National Longitudinal Survey of Labor Force Behavior (NLSLF), family background characteristics were obtained for randomly selected groups of 364 students from the class of 1995 and 366 students from the class of 1996.[10] We also obtained the college or employment choice of these students. Appendix 9A presents the definitions of the variables used in our regression analyses.

The River City schools are in no way average or typical. River City is a bustling town of approximately 200,000 residents. Many are engaged in blue-collar work in agricultural processing firms, while others are white-collar, high-technology professionals. The city's largest employer designs and manufactures electronics equipment ranging from circuit boards to radios. The third largest employer employs low-skilled workers in traditional manufacturing. A nearby university also helps to shape the economy and the demography of the city.

River City is proud of its school system. Many schools, programs, and staff members have received state and national recognition. The average ITED scores in ninth and eleventh grades are approximately 15 percentile points higher than the national norm. For most of the ITED tests, the standard deviation is approximately 25 percentile points. Nearly 90 percent of students plan to go on to advanced schooling, and 80 percent expect to obtain a degree beyond a high school diploma. Of the seniors who graduated in the class of 1995, 58 percent enrolled in a four-year bachelor's degree program.

The socioeconomic background of River City students is also above average. Their mothers' education is higher than the national average. The number of two-parent households stands at 77 percent, compared with a

9. A more extended presentation of the evidence, methodology, sources, and supporting documentation can be found in Girotto (1996).

10. National Opinion Research Center (1979).

national average of 59 percent. The full-time labor force participation rate for mothers is over 70 percent. Sixty percent of households earn over $40,000 a year. Ethnically, the River City school system is 90 percent European American, 3 percent African American, 2 percent Asian American, with a scattering of other nationalities. Eighty-four percent of the students surveyed report having a term-time or summer job.

The River City school system is administered with a substantial amount of central direction, and as a result the curriculum in the three high schools is nearly identical. Some minor differences occur in foreign-language offerings and studio art. However, if a student at Johnson High School wants to take Japanese and this is offered only at Adams High School, the school system will arrange for the student to travel across town. While each teacher has his or her own style and modifies the lesson materials, each high school uses the same textbooks, supplementary books, and prescribed lesson structure. Decisions about changes in the textbooks and basic curriculum are made at the district level, with the participation of the department heads of each high school. When we include dummy variables for each of the three schools in estimating equations that control for family background characteristics, we can find no statistically significant differences among the three high schools.

The ITED was administered in October of the students' ninth grade year and again in April of the students' eleventh grade year. The ITED is designed to measure skills that play an important role in adult life. Tests include giving the meaning of a wide variety of words, identifying the moods and implicit intent of literary materials, recognizing the essential characteristics of effective writing, solving quantitative problems, analyzing discussions of social issues, selecting sound methods of scientific inquiry, and using a variety of sources of information. The tests are designed to be appropriate for all high school students, regardless of the courses they have taken.[11] ITED tests are also designed to be reliable from one test setting to the next, and they are graduated so as to yield similar average test scores at different stages of educational growth.[12] We use these test reliability scores to correct for test score measurement error in all relevant equations.[13]

---

11. Personal communication from Robert Forsyth, principal author of the ITED, Iowa City, Iowa, November 7, 1995.

12. *Technical Summary of ITED* (1995, p. 75).

13. The reliability scores are incorporated into the analysis using errors-in-variables regression models. Standard regression models would underestimate the effect of the ITED score, and the other coefficients would be biased to the extent that they were correlated with the ITED score. When ITED

Estimating the Effect of Curriculum on Cognitive Skills

We initially estimate the effect of the curriculum on cognitive skills according to three models. Model 1 estimates the effect of academic credits on eleventh grade cognitive skills score, controlling for initial skills in ninth grade and grade point average. Model 2 and 3 estimate the same relationship, with the addition of controls for family background. The models can be summarized as follows (the underlying equations, 9A-1 to 9A-3, are given in appendix 9A, as are descriptions of all variables):
—Model 1: No controls for family background.
—Model 2: All possible family background characteristics.
—Model 3: Key family background characteristics, including number of parents in the household (*pliving*), number of natural parents in the household (*tliving*), mother's educational attainment (*emother*), father's educational attainment (*efather*), labor force participation of the parents (*mwork, fwork*), family income (*income*), and ethnic background (*white*).

Each model has certain advantages. The advantage of model 1 is that it allows one to estimate effects with the maximum number of observations. The advantage of model 2 is that it allows one to control for the combined effects of all social characteristics. Model 3's advantage is that it maintains a reasonable sample size while controlling for key family background characteristics.

Table 9-1 reports the results of the three models. Consistent with Alexander and Pallas, our results indicate that the number of courses a student takes and the grades that student receives in these courses affect the student's cognitive skills in the junior year.[14] Inclusion of the social background characteristics does not materially affect the size of the course and grade coefficients. In comparison with the large impact of courses taken and grades received, the effects of the social background variables are modest. It should be kept in mind that the results reported in table 9-1 control for student's cognitive skills in the freshman year. By that time, most of the impact of family background on student capabilities may have already had its effect. This equation captures only the additional effect of family background on the growth in skill level between the freshman and junior years.

---

scores are used as independent variables, the appropriate reliability score is inserted into the regression equation to correct for measurement error.
    14. Alexander and Pallas (1984).

Table 9-1. *Initial Estimates of the Effects of School and Social Background Characteristics on Cognitive Skills*[a]

Independent variables	No social variables (1)		All social variables (2)		Key social variables (3)	
	Coefficient	Standard error	Coefficient	Standard error	Coefficient	Standard error
acad crd	0.12**	0.02	0.14***	0.03	0.11***	0.03
GPA	5.91***	0.89	6.97***	1.80	6.63***	1.41
comp9	0.63***	0.02	0.59***	0.05	0.60***	1.41
female	−0.45	0.77	−1.16	1.44	0.15	1.12
income			0.01	0.27		
class			−0.47	0.71	−0.72	0.54
birth			−1.50	5.06		
sibling educ			0.35	0.70		
sibling age			−2.17**	0.87		
fsibling			0.11	1.92		
msibling			−0.19	1.91		
# sibling			0.81	0.60		
pliving			2.94*	1.76	0.82	1.31
tliving			−3.62*	1.96	−2.15	1.39
emother			1.50	1.90	2.70**	1.31
efather			−1.45	1.87	−2.11	1.34
mwork			0.05	1.97	−0.83	1.22
mhours			0.75	1.91		
fwork			6.85***	2.61	0.60	1.72
fhours			−1.15	2.34		
absent	−0.07***	0.02	0.11*	0.05	−0.03	0.04
mtype			0.02	0.11		
ftype			0.01	0.12		
white			0.52	3.13		
constant	3.00	1.91	0.24	6.61	1.42	2.06

Summary statistic			
N	1,470	309	615
R^2	0.7098	0.7543	0.6920

Source: Authors' calculations as described in text.

a. See appendix 9A for descriptions of all variables. Statistical significance at the 0.1 level is denoted by *; at the 0.05 level, by **; and at the 0.01 level, by ***.

These results suggest that the courses students select and the effort they put into their courses affect their cognitive skills. But they are contaminated by a potential selection bias that has bedeviled earlier research in this area. One cannot know whether taking the course was the critical factor in raising a student's cognitive skill level or some other characteristic of students influenced both their willingness to take academic courses and their growth in cognitive capacity. The policies and practices of the River City school system allow for the construction of two types of instrumental variable that enable one to control for possible selection bias, one based on driver education and the other based on scheduling conflicts. Of these, the driver education instrumental variable is intuitively the most satisfying.

The Driver Education Instrumental Variable

It is the policy of the River City school system that students may not enroll in driver education until the semester of their sixteenth birthday. Yet almost every student wants to take driver education as early as possible. Only on the completion of the course can a student obtain a license to drive a car, which in a city lacking public transportation seems to all teenagers virtually a necessity. For the lucky ones whose birthdays fall during the summer, the sixteenth birthday rule creates no academic problems. Inasmuch as academic courses are not offered during the summer, these students can take driver education without any adverse affect on their curricular choices. But for those unlucky enough to have their birthday during the school year, the rule may create a curricular conflict.

In table 9-2 we show the impact of a student's birthday on the number of academic courses taken. As can be seen from the table, the term in which driver education is taken correlates with the number of academic classes a student takes. Those students whose birthdays occur during the summer and therefore take driver education in the summer are more likely to take a greater number of academic courses. This is both true in general and specifically for English, mathematics, and science.

To create an appropriate instrumental variable for driver education, we sort students into two groups. Students whose birthdays fall in the summer are put into the "nonconflict" group because their participation in driver education will not conflict with academic classes. Students whose birthdays fall during the school year are put into the "conflict" group because they may have to choose between an academic course and the extremely attractive course in driver education.

Table 9-2. *Number of Academic Credits by Student Birthdate*[a]

Sixteenth birthday	Number of academic credits				
	Total	English	Math	Science	Social studies
Third semester, freshman year (N = 27)	60.93	14.07	14.07	27.41	36.67
Summer, after freshman year (N = 90)	80.83	19.61	19.33	34.89	42.22
First semester, sophomore year (N = 364)	67.02	14.22	15.89	27.57	39.09
Second semester, sophomore year (N = 358)	70.56	15.49	16.69	29.01	40.24
Third semester, sophomore year (N = 410)	67.12	14.90	16.32	27.79	38.84
Summer, after sophomore year (N = 58)	76.21	16.29	21.55	33.53	41.72
First semester, junior year (N = 219)	65.41	13.08	16.64	27.35	38.68
Second semester, junior year (N = 34)	54.26	10.29	11.32	22.21	37.65
Total summer (N = 148)	79.02	18.31	20.20	34.36	42.02
Total during school year (N = 1,412)	67.27	14.47	11.82	27.83	39.16

Source: Authors' calculations as described in text.
a. See appendix 9A for descriptions of all variables.

The Scheduling Conflict Instrumental Variables

The second instrument used to predict taking academic courses is a collection of variables measuring conflicts between academic classes and certain extracurricular activities. After examining class schedules for each high school in detail, it became apparent that students who took certain extracurricular classes were unable to take academic classes. The "conflict classes," such as band, journalism, and drawing, interfered with a student's ability to take academic classes such as advanced English or trigonometry.[15] A student taking a conflict course will take fewer academic courses because of direct scheduling conflict. Therefore these course conflict variables satisfy the first condition for an instrumental variable: they are correlated with the theoretically significant independent variable, academic course selection.

But is the selection of extracurricular courses independent of cognitive skill? It is reasonable to assume that the decision to take driver education as determined by a student's birthdate is uncorrelated with cognitive skill, because almost all young people in this city are eager to acquire the mobility that a driver's license facilitates. With respect to extracurricular course selection, however, there is less confidence. It may be that some students pursue extracurricular activities simply because they do not have academic talents or interests. But one can also readily imagine an academically talented student with a burning desire to participate in band, chorus, drawing, or sports. Put more generally, the desire to socialize with peers in nonacademic settings may be assumed to be randomly distributed among teenagers. If this is so, conflicts between extracurricular courses and academic courses are correlated with course selection but are not independently correlated with cognitive skill.

We identify course conflict variables for the first semester of each year, because most of the academic classes run for an entire year and missing the first semester bumps a student from an academic sequence for the entire year. Careful examination of class schedules reveals that a substantial minority of students experience scheduling conflicts during the first semester of the year in each of the principal subject areas. The data indicate that about 10 percent of the student population experience class conflicts in their sophomore and senior years and nearly 25 percent face such problems in their junior year. Simple correlations between each scheduling conflict

15. See Girotto (1996, p. 107).

variable and the academic class ratios indicate minor levels of correlation between the variables.[16]

The Selection Equation and the Regression Results

The effectiveness of the instrumental variables for predicting course selection is tested by running selection equation regressions (see equation 9A-4 in appendix 9A). We found statistically significant negative coefficients for at least one instrumental variable in all but one subject area. The birthdate and math sophomore-year conflict variables have the most robust performance in the selection equations, especially when estimating both the overall number of academic classes taken and the number of academic English and science classes taken. Using the F statistic as a guide, the instrumental variables equation as a whole appears to be a solid predictor of the overall number of academic courses, as well as of the number of English, science, and social studies courses. However, the instrumental variables equation is not an effective predictor of the number of math courses taken.[17] We therefore estimate the effect of taking math courses on math skills only by means of an ordinary least squares (OLS) equation.

The Effect of Students' Choices on Cognitive Skills

We use our instrumental variables to construct two additional models that correct for selection bias when estimating the effects of taking academic courses on cognitive skills. Model 4 includes the instrumental variables but excludes social background characteristics. It doubles the number of observations from which the estimate can be calculated. Model 5 includes both the key social background variables and the instrumental variables. With this model, we finally have an unbiased estimate of the effects of taking academic courses on cognitive skills. Model 5 is estimated from equations 9A-5 (see appendix 9A); model 4 is estimated from the same equation without the social variables.

Table 9-3 compares the results from models 4 and 5 with the results from models 1 and 3, which do not include instrumental variables. The results using the instrumental variables are generally consistent with those

16. Girotto (1996, p. 107).
17. See Girotto (1996, pp. 111–12).

Table 9-3. *Estimated Effects of Academic Credits on Cognitive Skills*[a]

Independent variable	Ordinary least squares		Two-stage least squares	
	Without social variables (1)	With social variables (3)	Without social variables (4)	With social variables (5)
Total academic credits	0.12***	0.11***	0.10	0.17
	(0.02)	(0.03)	(0.19)	(0.25)
Academic English credits	0.21***	0.30***	0.28	0.72**
	(0.05)	(0.07)	(0.31)	(0.33)
Academic math credits[b]	0.28***	0.09	...	...
	(0.05)	(0.09)	...	...
Academic science credits	0.19***	0.13**	0.55	0.80**
	(0.04)	(0.06)	(0.44)	(0.39)
Academic social studies credits	0.07	–0.02	0.34	0.92
	(0.06)	(0.12)	(0.39)	(0.60)
Summary statistic				
N	1,470	615	1,470	615

Source: Authors' calculations as described in the text.

a. Each column represents the set of regressions for a different model, as indicated. Each row represents the effect of a different measure of academic credits on the corresponding category of cognitive skill. For example, the first row uses a measure of total academic credits earned to determine the effect on composite cognitive skill. The only variables to change across rows are the measure of academic credits (independent variable) and the measure of cognitive skill (dependent variable). The independent-dependent variable pairs are as follows: *acad crd-comp11, Eng crd-verb11, math crd-math11, sci crd-sci11, soc crd-soc11.* See appendix 9A for descriptions of models and all variables. Statistical significance at the 0.05 level is denoted by **; and at the 0.01 level, by ***. Standard errors are in parentheses.

b. Models 4 and 5 are not reported because no effective instrumental variables are available.

from the earlier models. The signs for all coefficients are positive. The size of the coefficients remains large whether or not social variables are included and whether the estimate is by ordinary least squares or two-stage least squares (2SLS). However, the inclusion of instrumental variables increases the standard error, making some of the estimates that are statistically significant in models 1 and 3 no longer so in models 4 and 5.

The most stable estimates are obtained for the overall effects of academic classes on overall cognitive skill level, as measured by the composite student ITED score. The effects remain essentially the same, whether academic courses are measured as a percentage of all courses taken or as a percentage of required courses taken. Remarkably, the regression coefficients do not vary in any consistent fashion across the four models.

When one looks at the specific effects of taking courses in particular subjects on performance on the respective ITED tests, the results are actually larger than those from the model estimating the combined effects of all courses. Larger coefficients in these more specific equations are probably due to the fact that we are estimating the effect of specific types of courses on the same, specific cognitive skills, that is, the effects of English courses on language skills, of science courses on science knowledge, and of social studies courses on social studies knowledge. The effects of the English and science courses are both large and statistically significant. The especially large effects in specific subject domains provide further evidence that the model is in fact estimating curricular effects on cognitive skills.

Table 9-4 translates the coefficients given in table 9-3 into substantively meaningful categories. Table 9-4 indicates the percentile point gain in cognitive skills that occurs for an increase of one or two year-long academic courses. For example, taking two additional year-long academic courses results in a 5.1 percentile point increase in composite cognitive skills. The standard deviation of the composite cognitive skills measure is approximately 25 percentile points. Therefore taking two additional year-long academic courses can move a student one-fifth of a standard deviation upward in cognitive skills. Even larger substantive effects are obtained when using subject-specific measures of academic courses and cognitive skills. Taking just one additional year-long academic English course results in a 10.8 percentile point increase in verbal skills. Taking one additional year-long academic science course results in a 12.0 percentile point increase in science skills. Taking one additional year-long social studies course results in a 13.8 percentile point increase in social studies skills.

These shifts constitute approximately one-half of a standard deviation, which is generally thought to be a large educational effect. The results complement Robert Meyer's findings in chapter 8 above. Meyer focuses solely on the effect of additional and more difficult math classes on mathematics achievement and finds almost as large an effect as ours of the combined consequence of taking first-year algebra and one additional math course. Taken together, the two studies emphasize the critical role of an academic curriculum in the acquisition of cognitive skills.

Table 9-4. *Estimated Substantive Effects on Cognitive Skills from Taking Academic Courses*[a]

Percent

| | Effect of an increase of one or two year-long academic courses | | | |
| | Ordinary least squares | | Two-stage least squares | |
Independent variable	Without social variables (1)	With social variables (3)	Without social variables (4)	With social variables (5)
Total academic credits, two year-long academic courses	3.6***	3.3***	3.0	5.1
Academic English credits, one year-long English course	3.2***	4.5***	4.2	10.8**
Academic math credits, one year-long math course	4.5***	1.4	. . .	. . .
Academic science credits, one year-long science course	2.9***	2.0**	8.3	12.0**
Academic social studies credits, one year-long social studies course	1.1	−0.3	5.1	13.8
Summary statistic				
N	1,470	615	1,470	615

Source: Authors' calculations as described in text.

a. See appendix 9A for descriptions of models and all variables. Statistical significance at the 0.05 level is denoted by **; and at the 0.01 level, by ***.

The Effect of Student Effort on Cognitive Skills

Our data also allow us to use a student's grade point average (GPA) to measure the effects of student effort on cognitive skills.[18] For this variable we are unable to identify an appropriate instrument that would allow us to solve the selection problem. We think that in an equation that controls for

18. Student grade point average includes grades on all classes taken between the ninth grade ITED test and the eleventh grade ITED test. The GPA is calculated on a scale from 0.0 to 4.0, with straight C's being equivalent to 2.0, straight B's equivalent to 3.0, and straight A's equivalent to 4.0. Advanced placement grades are not enhanced, as they are in conventional GPA calculations in most school systems.

Table 9-5. *Estimated Effects of Student Effort on Cognitive Skills*[a]

	Ordinary least squares		Two-stage least squares	
Independent variable	Without social variables (1)	With social variables (3)	Without social variables (4)	With social variables (5)
Coefficient on GPA				
Regression using total	5.9***	6.6***	6.9*	6.2
academic credits	(0.9)	(0.0)	(4.2)	(4.9)
Regression using	8.9***	9.4***	10.1***	9.0***
English credits	(0.9)	(1.5)	(1.7)	(2.0)
Regression using	4.6***	5.5***	...	...
math credits	(1.6)	(1.6)	...	...
Regression using	7.1***	9.1***	6.1	4.3
science credits	(1.0)	(1.6)	(5.4)	(4.6)
Regression using	7.0***	3.2	10.6***	7.3***
social studies credits	(1.2)	(2.6)	(1.2)	(2.4)
Summary statistic				
N	1,470	615	1,470	615

Source: Authors' calculations as described in text.

a. See appendix 9A for descriptions of models and all variables. Statistical significance at the 0.1 level is denoted by *; and at the 0.01 level, by ***. Standard errors are in parentheses.

ninth grade cognitive skills, grade point average is primarily a measure of student effort. As can be seen in table 9-5, the overall measure of student effort, cumulative GPA for all courses, performs well in all five models (model 2 not shown). The coefficients are large, stable, and statistically significant in both the OLS and 2SLS equations. Results by subject area are also relatively stable, though once again the effect of GPA is greatest for performance on the verbal ability test.

Table 9-5 reports the percentile point gain in cognitive skills that occurs for every letter grade increase in a student's grade point average. In our opinion, model 5 provides the best estimate of the effect of student effort. It indicates that a one-grade increase in a student's GPA results in a 9.0 percentile point increase in verbal skills, a 4.3 percentile point increase in science skills, and a 7.3 percentile point increase in social studies skills. This one-grade increase moves a typical student upward nearly one-fourth of a standard deviation in a subject-specific measure of cognitive skill.

The combined effects of course selection and student effort are considerable. For example, students who take two additional year-long academic courses and raise their GPA by one letter grade can expect to see an 11.3 percentile point increase in cognitive skills from the ninth through eleventh grades.[19] Since the eleventh grade cognitive skill score has a standard deviation of approximately 25 percentile points, course selection and student effort combined can boost a student's cognitive skill level by nearly one-half of a standard deviation.

The Effect of Students' Choices on College Entrance

It is becoming increasingly well established that the cognitive skills of high school students can affect their future life outcomes, including educational opportunities, success in the labor market, and success in sustaining family relationships.[20] But there is still not much evidence that any enhancement of cognitive skills as a result of course selection and student effort in high school has long-term benefits. Indeed, Altonji's finding that high school coursework has no long-term wage benefits suggests the opposite.[21]

The River City data provide some useful insights on this matter. Information on the colleges that the students decided to attend the following September was collected in May of their senior year. College choice is divided into six categories: none, community college, in-state public college or university, out-of-state public college or university, in-state private school; and out-of-state private school.[22]

The college one attends the first year after high school is not a perfect indicator of one's permanent income, to say nothing of one's success in finding happiness in life. But these data do allow one to see whether ITED performance correlates with real world events in the lives of high school graduates. To ascertain whether high school learning yields long-term benefits, we employ an ordered probit regression (equation 9A-6 in appendix 9A) to estimate the power to predict college choices using a variable representing the change in cognitive skills between the ninth and eleventh grades (*dcomp*)

19. Using the estimates in tables 9-4 and 9-5: 5.1 percent + 6.2 percent = 11.3 percentile points.
20. See Winship and Korenman in chapter 3 above.
21. Altonji (1995).
22. An improved measure would rank order colleges according to their selectivity or according to the earnings of their graduates.

and controlling for social background variables. The probit regression results indicate that gains in cognitive skill during high school have a statistically significant effect on college choice.[23]

Another method of examining the correlation between academic performance and real world events is to look at the direct effects of coursework and student effort on college choice. We employ an ordered probit regression to estimate the ability to predict college choices using the various measures of academic coursework and the GPA measure of student effort (see equation 9A-7 in appendix 9A). The student's ninth grade ITED score is included, along with socioeconomic status variables to control for academic performance prior to ninth grade. The ordered probit regression produces a student's predicted college choice on a scale from 0 to 5.

The probit results are presented in table 9-6. The table demonstrates that academic courses and student effort have a substantive and statistically significant impact on college choice. It is intriguing to note that student effort has a significantly larger effect on college choice than academic courses. A one-grade increase in GPA improves predicted college choice by 0.69 point. But taking two additional year-long academic courses only improves a student's predicted college choice by 0.06 point. These results support the unfortunate conclusion that colleges take a cursory look at the courses a student takes and focus on the grades a student receives.

Conclusions and Policy Implications

The findings from the River City data show that both the selection of academic courses and the level of student effort play crucial roles in determining cognitive skill. Combining the impact of course selection and student effort, a one-grade increase in GPA and taking two additional year-long academic courses results in an 11.3 percentile point increase in composite cognitive skill. This change in cognitive skill represents an upward shift of one-half of a standard deviation. On a standard IQ test, one-half of a standard deviation amounts to an 8 point shift. This is not trivial. Herrnstein and Murray argue that to achieve such a change in a student's cognitive skill the child must be adopted by a family from another

---

23. See Girotto (1996, pp. 122–23). The regression results confirm those of Jencks and Phillips in chapter 2 above, who find that later cognitive skill scores are better predictors of life outcomes than early scores.

Table 9-6. *Predicting the Effect of Academic Courses and Student Effort in High School on College Choices*[a]

Independent variable	Effect of an increase of one or two year-long academic courses	Effect of an increase in one grade of GPA
Total academic credits		
Two year-long academic courses	0.0630***	
Coefficient on GPA		0.6917***
Academic English credits		
One year-long English course	0.0864**	
Coefficient on GPA		0.7942***
Academic math credits		
One year-long math course	. . .	
Coefficient on GPA		. . .
Academic science credits		
One year-long science course	0.0675***	
Coefficient on GPA		0.6674***
Academic social studies credits		
One year-long social studies course	–0.0423	
Coefficient on GPA		0.8778***
Summary statistic		
N	589	589

Source: Authors' calculations as described in text.

a. Estimates are from an ordered probit model with key social variables. See appendix 9A for descriptions of model and all variables. Statistical significance at the 0.05 level is denoted by **; and at the 0.01 level denoted by ***.

social class.[24] Moreover, the changes in cognitive skill that take place during high school appear to have significant downstream consequences. For example, they predict the first college that the student attends. This conclusion is supported by the finding of Christopher Jencks and Meredith Phillips (in chapter 2 above) that what children learn between the tenth and twelfth grades affects their future educational attainment and wages.

24. Herrnstein and Murray (1994).

These findings are intuitively satisfying. If students take harder courses and put more effort into their studies, they learn more. And what they learn can make a difference later on. Indeed, our nonacademic friends regard these findings as banal. And so they would be, were it not for the fact that both academic scholarship and educational policy seem at odds with common sense. The difficulty of obtaining unbiased estimates of the effects of coursework on ability has persuaded too many social scientists to conclude that not much relationship exists. Problems of measurement have been confused with questions of existence.

Were this only an idle error of a self-contained scholarly community, it would be of little concern. But such errors have provided the foundation for the incarceration theory of education, which seems to say that it is only the quantity, not the quality, of the educational experience that counts. From this conclusion it is only a short step to the construction of the shopping mall high school, designed to attract as many customers as possible.

Though incarceration theory is an affront to common sense, its validity is promoted by those who have a vested interest in sustaining the myth. Almost everyone in the education industry receives money on the basis of the quantity rather than the quality of the educational experience. Most state aid is distributed to local school districts on the basis of the number of students in average daily attendance. Federal compensatory education dollars are distributed according to a similar quantity-based formula. Many state colleges and universities receive money based on the number of full-time equivalent students they admit and retain. Even elite private universities charge students for the number, not the quality, of the courses they take. If quantity is all that counts, these policies are easily justified.

We are not yet prepared to recommend a return to the medieval practice in which students tip professors according to the quality of their lectures and seminars. But we have two reasons for endorsing John Bishop's suggestion that college admissions be determined by substantive external examinations for which students can prepare by taking academic courses. First, it would provide a more objective standard by which to assess students for admission to college than the current emphasis on grades. Second, Bishop finds that Canadian students who attend high school in a province that requires satisfactory performance on an external examination acquire more cognitive skill.[25] His interpretation of these results is that when confronted by an external examination, students have a greater incentive to take more aca-

25. Bishop (1995, p. 1).

demic courses and to study more assiduously. Our results are entirely consistent with both his findings and his interpretation.

Our findings come from one moderate-sized midwestern city. Since the education provided by River City schools seems to be considerably above the average, one cannot conclude from these results that students in all parts of the United States can enhance cognitive skill simply by taking the more academic courses offered in their high schools. Yet our findings should not for that reason be discounted. The significance of the study is that it tells one what is possible and has indeed happened within a public high school system that serves a fairly diverse social population. If selection of academic courses can enhance cognitive skill in River City, cognitive skill is not beyond school influence. The findings challenge all those who say that not much can be done. They challenge all those who say that learning is genetically determined or is decisively shaped by the student's family life. They challenge those who think the most that can be done for American education is to construct a shopping mall.

Appendix 9A
Data

In this appendix, we describe the equations and the variables used in the models discussed in the text.

Equations

Model 1

$$(\text{9A-1}) \quad comp11 = \beta_0 + \beta_1 acad\ crd + \beta_2 GPA + \beta_3 comp9 + \beta_4 female + \beta_5 absent + \epsilon_1$$

Model 2

$$(\text{9A-2}) \quad comp11 = \delta_0 + \delta_1 acad\ crd + \delta_2 GPA + \delta_3 comp9 + \delta_4 female + \delta_5 income + \delta_6 class + \delta_7 birth\ loc + \delta_8 sibling\ educ + \delta_9 sibling\ age + \delta_{10} fsibling + \delta_{11} msibling + \delta_{12}\#\ sibling + \delta_{13} pliving + \delta_{14} tliving + \delta_{15} emother + \delta_{16} efather + \delta_{17} mwork + \delta_{18} mhours + \delta_{19} fwork + \delta_{20} fhours + \delta_{21} absent + \delta_{22} mtype + \delta_{23} ftype + \delta_{24} white + \epsilon_2$$

Model 3

(9A-3) $comp11$ = $\alpha_0 + \alpha_1 acad\ crd + \alpha_2 GPA + \alpha_3 comp9 + \alpha_4 female +$
$\alpha_5 class + \alpha_6 pliving + \alpha_7 tliving + \alpha_8 emother +$
$\alpha_9 efather + \alpha_{10} mwork + \alpha_{11} fwork + \alpha_{12} absent + \epsilon_3$

The selection equation

(9A-4) $acad\ crd$ = $\gamma_0 + \gamma_1 comp9 + \gamma_2 GPA + \gamma_3 female + \gamma_4 absent +$
$\gamma_5 class + \gamma_6 emother + \gamma_7 efather + \gamma_8 mwork +$
$\gamma_9 fwork + \gamma_{10} tliving + \gamma_{11} pliving + \gamma_{12} white +$
$\gamma_{13} birthdate + \gamma_{14} econfjun + \gamma_{15} mconfsop +$
$\gamma_{16} sconfsop + \gamma_{17} sconfsen + \gamma_{18} cconfjun + \epsilon_4$

The two-stage least squares regression:
first stage

(9A-5) $acad\ crd$ = $\theta_0 + \theta_1 comp9 + \theta_2 GPA + \theta_3 female + \theta_4 absent +$
$\theta_5 class + \theta_6 emother + \theta_7 efather + \theta_8 mwork +$
$\theta_9 fwork + \theta_{10} tliving + \theta_{11} pliving + \theta_{12} white +$
$\theta_{13} drivconf + \theta_{14} econfjun + \theta_{15} mconfsop +$
$\theta_{16} sconfsop + \theta_{17} sconfsen + \theta_{18} cconfjun + \epsilon_5$

second stage

(9A-5) $comp11$ = $\mu_0 + \mu_1 comp9 + \mu_2 GPA + \mu_3 acad\ crd_{pred} +$
$\mu_4 female + \mu_5 absent + \mu_6 class + \mu_7 emother +$
$\mu_8 efather + \mu_9 mwork + \mu_{10} fwork + \mu_{11} tliving +$
$\mu_{12} pliving + \mu_{13} white + \epsilon_6$

Ordered probit regression—direct effects

(9A-6) $college$ = $\sigma_0 + \sigma_1 comp9 + \sigma_2 acad\ crd_{pred} + \sigma_3 GPA +$
$\sigma_4 female + \sigma_5 class + \sigma_6 pliving + \sigma_7 tliving +$
$\sigma_8 emother + \sigma_9 efather + \sigma_{10} mwork + \sigma_{11} fwork +$
$\sigma_{12} white + \sigma_{13} absent + \epsilon_8$

Ordered probit regression—cognitive skill change

(9A-7) $college$ = $\sigma_0 + \sigma_1 comp9 + \sigma_2 dcomp + \sigma_3 female + \sigma_4 income +$
$\sigma_5 class + \sigma_6 sibling\ educ + \sigma_7 sibling\ age +$
$\sigma_8 fsibling + \sigma_9 msibling + \sigma_{10} \#\ sibling +$
$\sigma_{11} pliving + \sigma_{12} tliving + \sigma_{13} emother + \sigma_{14} efather +$
$\sigma_{15} mwork + \sigma_{16} mhours + \sigma_{17} fwork + \sigma_{18} fhours +$
$\sigma_{19} mtype + \sigma_{20} ftype + \sigma_{21} white + \sigma_{23} absent + \epsilon_7$

Dependent Variables

comp11, comp9	National ITED composite score, ninth and eleventh grades
verb11, verb9	National ITED reading score, ninth and eleventh grades
math11, math9	National ITED math score, ninth and eleventh grades
science11, science9	National ITED science score, ninth and eleventh grades
college	Ordered college choice, two-year public to four-year private
acad crd	College prep and academic class credits (5 credits = 1 class)

Independent Variables

GPA	Overall GPA between ninth and eleventh grades (scale to 4.0)
acad crd	College prep and academic class credits (5 credits = 1 class)
eng crd	College prep and academic English credits
math crd	College prep and academic math credits
sci crd	College prep and academic science credits
soc crd	College prep and academic social studies credits
female	Sex (0 male, 1 female)
income	Household income (1 under $10K through 9 over $80K)
class	Self-identified social class (1 lower class through 5 upper class)
birth loc	Country of birth (0 America, 1 other)
sibling educ	Highest grade achieved by oldest sibling (1 high school through 6 doctorate)
sibling age	Age of oldest sibling (1 elementary through 5 post-college)
fsibling	Female sibling (0 no, 1 yes)
msibling	Male sibling (0 no, 1 yes)
# siblings	Number of siblings
pliving	Number of parents in household (0 one, 1 two)

tliving	Type of parents in household (0 step-parent, 1 natural)
emother	Mother's education (0 associate or less, 1 bachelor's or more)
efather	Father's education (0 associate or less, 1 bachelor's or more)
mwork	Mother's work (0 part time, 1 full time)
fwork	Father's work (0 part time, 1 full time)
mhours	Mother's work hours (0 ≤ 35 per week, 1 > 35 per week)
fhours	Father's work hours (0 ≤ 35 per week, 1 > 35 per week)
mtype	Mother's type of work (occupational prestige: 1 janitor through 29 doctor)
ftype	Father's type of work (occupational prestige: 1 janitor through 29 doctor)
absent	Number of absences from ninth through eleventh grades
white	Origin or descent (0 African American or Hispanic, 1 Caucasian)
college	College choice (0 none through 5 out of state private school)

Instrumental Variables

birthdate	First opportunity to take driver education based on birthday (0 conflict semester during the school year, 1 nonconflict semester during the summer)
econfjun	Class conflicts with academic English classes, junior year (0 none, 1 one, etc.)
econfsen	Class conflicts with academic English classes, senior year
mconfsop	Class conflicts with academic math classes, sophomore year
sconfsop	Class conflicts with academic social studies classes, sophomore year
sconfjun	Class conflicts with academic social studies classes, junior year

sconfsen	Class conflicts with academic social studies classes, senior year
cconffun	Class conflicts with academic science classes, junior year
cgrdrt	Class conflicts with any academic class, any year

References

Alexander, Karl L., and Aaron M. Pallas. 1984. "Curriculum Reform and School Performance: An Evaluation of the 'New Basics.'" *American Journal of Education* 92(4): 391–420.

Altonji, Joseph. 1995. "The Effect of High School Curriculum on Education and Labor Market Outcomes." *Journal of Human Resources* 30(3): 409–38.

Angrist, Joshua D., and Alan B. Krueger. 1991. "Does Compulsory School Attendance Affect Schooling and Earnings?" *Quarterly Journal of Economics* 106(4): 979–1014.

Ashenfelter, Orley, and Alan B. Krueger. 1994. "Estimates of the Economic Return to Schooling from a New Sample of Twins." *American Economic Review* 84(5): 1157–73.

Bishop, John H. 1995. "The Impact of Curriculum-Based External Examinations on School Priorities and Student Learning, 1995." Working Paper 95-30. Cornell University, Center for Advanced Human Resource Studies.

Bryk, Anthony S., Valerie E. Lee, and Peter B. Holland. 1993. *Catholic Schools and the Common Good.* Harvard University Press.

Chubb, John E., and Terry M. Moe. 1990. *Politics, Markets, and America's Schools.* Brookings.

Girotto, Jay R. 1996. "How School Policies Can Affect Cognitive Skills: An Econometric Analysis of the Effects of Student Choices." Senior thesis. Harvard College of the Arts and Sciences.

Herrnstein, Richard J., and Charles Murray. 1994. *The Bell Curve: Intelligence and Class Structure in American Life.* Free Press.

Laing, Joan, John Enger, and James Maxey. 1990. "Coursework Patterns, ACT Assessment Scores, and Related Data." *College and University* 65(4): 335–44.

National Opinion Research Center. 1979. *National Longitudinal Survey of Labor Force Behavior Youth Survey.* NORC-4270 1/79, OMB 44 R-1671. Chicago.

Powell, Arthur G., Eleanor Farrar, and David K. Cohen. 1985. *The Shopping Mall High School: Winners and Losers in the Education Marketplace.* Boston: Houghton Mifflin.

Schmidt, W. H. 1983. "High School Course-Taking: Its Relationship to Achievement." *Journal of Curriculum Studies* 15(3): 332–47.

Sebring, Penny A. 1987. "Consequences of Differential Amounts of High School Coursework: Will the New Graduation Requirements Help?" *Educational Evaluation and Policy Analysis* 9(3): 258–73.

Technical Summary of ITED I: Riverside 2000. 1995. Chicago: Riverside Publishing Company.

JOHN H. BISHOP $\quad$ 10

Nerd Harassment, Incentives, School Priorities, and Learning

A TALL, AWKWARD, studious eighth grade boy (call him Bill) was playing with devil sticks during lunch period. A girl called him over to a group of her friends and, in a voice intended to be overheard, said: "Using devil sticks doesn't make you cool.

You're a dork!

You've always been a dork!

You will always be a dork!

There is nothing you can do about it!"

Bill did not respond. Ten feet away, Bill's friend (call him Alan) did not respond. Bill turned, returned the devil sticks to Alan, and then left the lunch room. Alan thought: "Why doesn't Bill insult her back? Not retaliating simply invites others to pick on you. This is embarrassing. If I'm seen hanging out with Bill much longer, other students may think I'm a nerd too."

This paper was initially prepared for the Conference on Meritocracy and Inequality at the Kennedy School of Government, Harvard University, September 2–27, 1996. The research was supported by the Center for Advanced Human Resource Studies, New York State School of Industrial and Labor Relations, Cornell University, and the Consortium for Policy Research in Education, funded by the U.S. Department of Education's Office of Educational Research and Improvement. The findings and opinions expressed below do not reflect the position or policies of the Office of Educational Research and Improvement or the U.S. Department of Education. This chapter has not undergone formal review or approval of the faculty of the New York State School of Industrial and Labor Relations.

Bill had just lost another round in the middle school "dominance by insult game." Bill did what teachers and parents had told him to do, he walked away from the confrontation. He had prevented escalation and kept the peace, but he lost "rep" (reputation) and slid down a notch or two in the school's dominance or status hierarchy. Does Bill have a winning response available to him? If not, why not? How could he have avoided getting into this situation? This is an example of a repeated game where credible threats of future action can influence how players act.[1] I begin this paper with a case study of Bill's situation and of the dominance by insult game. Descriptions of peer interaction come from confidential interviews with eight male middle school students at two middle schools in Ithaca, a small city in New York that is home to two large universities. The game theoretic analysis of the dominance by insult game explains a number of the characteristic features of middle school male peer culture: highly fragmented cliquishness, high prestige accorded to sports ability, and negative value attributed to being studious.

It is hypothesized that studiousness is denigrated in U.S middle schools, in part because it shifts up the grading curve and forces others to work harder to get good grades. This has led some education reformers to hope that peer support for learning and studying can be improved by standards-based reform, in particular, by conditioning high school graduation on rigorous curriculum-based external exit examinations. Advocates of standards-based reform argue that curriculum-based external exit examinations also induce teachers to set higher standards and school administrators to focus their attention and resources on improving teaching. These arguments have led a number of blue ribbon panels to propose that American states establish curriculum-based external exit examination systems (CBEEES). The second section of the chapter looks at the rationale for these proposals and describes what a CBEEES is and is not.

The third section examines the likely impact of CBEEES on student effort, school priorities, and learning, and specifies eleven testable hypotheses about these effects. The final section of the paper uses data on 1,460 Canadian middle schools to test these hypotheses by comparing student achievement in provinces with curriculum-based external exams with student achievement in provinces without such exams.

---

1. Gibbons (1992).

The Dominance by Insult Game

To return to the extract at the start of the chapter, Bill faces the following choices:

SHARE THE HURT. Telling his parents probably would gain him sympathy, but his humiliation would be multiplied. Victims of nerd harassment hardly ever tell their parents, their siblings, or their friends. Most accept the proposition that being nerdy or acting like a dork is bad and worry that complaining to friends or parents will just add to the number of people who consider them a dork.[2] A second reason why parents are rarely told about harassment is that many of the insults are comments about one's mother. Examples include "Mother F_____"; "Your mom's like a hardware store: 5 cents a screw"; "Your mom's like a soccer ball: everyone takes a kick"; and "Your mom is so fat, when she put on a green dress, people mistook her for a football field."

TATTLETALE. Complaining to a teacher is self-defeating. Squealing on classmates only exacerbates one's dork status and often provokes the harasser to retaliate. In grade school, teachers significantly influence the culture of their classroom and are generally successful at suppressing the dominance by insult game. Middle school teachers are with a particular class for only fifty minutes a day and so are powerless to stop the game. They must allocate the limited disciplinary sanctions available to the task of maintaining classroom discipline and their own authority. Ninety-five percent of nerd harassment and other types of verbal harassment occurs outside the earshot of adults.

GO TO THE TOP. Complaining to school administrators is also ineffective. Parents who complain about nerd harassment get a sympathetic hearing but no effective action. The school district responds decisively to fights and to racial or ethnic insults. There is a campaign underway to reduce sexual harassment and homophobia. The school disciplinary handbook defines actionable "harassment" as follows:

---

2. In Ithaca, "dork" and "nerd" mean the same thing. Dork is used among middle school students.

Ithaca City School District believes that students should be free to gain an education, study and enjoy the educational and social environment at school without being subject to sexual harassment or harassment on the basis of race, color, religion, gender, national origin, age or disability. . . . Harassment is verbal or physical conduct that denigrates or shows hostility or aversion toward an individual because of his race, color, religion, gender, national origin, age or disability, or that of his/her relatives or friends, and that (1) has the purpose or effect of creating an intimidating, hostile or offensive educational or social environment; (2) affects the individual's education; or (3) otherwise affects an individual's educational opportunities. Students who feel they have been harassed should see the Principal or School Nurse to discuss their situation. School reports will be turned over to the Director of Affirmative Action—Intercultural Relations Services for appropriate action, if any. The Board of Education will be informed about the disposition of these cases on a monthly basis.[3]

Note that this definition of harassment does not include what happened to Bill. The humiliations daily visited on the school's nerds and dorks are not actionable under this policy.

WANNA FIGHT? Threatening a fight is not an option in this case because the harasser is a girl. If the harasser were a boy (as it usually is), it would be an option if Bill was strong and big enough to make a fight reasonably even. The school's punishment for fighting is a one- to three-day suspension of both individuals, regardless of who starts the fight. Consequently, by starting a fight at school, the victim of verbal harassment can impose costs on the harasser and hopefully deter others from picking on him in the future. Punishment by the school is not the only risk Bill would take by threatening to fight. Harassers often have friends with them when they initiate a confrontation with insults, so Bill takes the risk of having to fight a couple of guys. There is no strong norm that these confrontations are one-on-one affairs. Winning a confrontation does not necessarily end the situation. Harassers who lose such confrontations may recruit friends to help them with retaliation. Thus threatening a fight is generally not a very good

3. Ithaca City School District (1994, p. 31).

option. Nevertheless, the risk that an insult will provoke a fight affects who is harassed and when harassment occurs. Generally, victims of harassment are smaller and physically weaker than the harasser or have a reputation of not standing up for themselves in such confrontations.[4] Usually, they are picked on when they are alone, outnumbered, or with kids who are small or of a pacifist persuasion.

TIT FOR TAT. The most common active response to a verbal insult is the counterinsult. A counterinsult generally induces the initiator to respond in kind, so that often many rounds of insults are traded. The winner of these tit for tats is the student who comes up with the most cutting or creative insult or by persistence forces his opponent to break off the engagement. Insults that are completely fanciful are easy to blow off, so the winning strategy is to find something that will embarrass your opponent, such as incompetence in sports, unstylish clothes, height, weight, or saying something stupid in class. When the insult game is played in front of an audience, getting one's friends to laugh at one's insults is another way to dominate the interaction. Comedy makes one's insults more effective. Rather than call someone fat, one calls them "horizontally gifted" or says, "You're so fat, when you sit on a dollar bill, 10 dimes pop out." Insult jokes such as these can be overused. Stale insult jokes leave one open to counterinsults such as: "That is so old. You're pathetic. Can't you come up with something better than that?" Harassers can generally forestall the counterinsult by victimizing students who sit adjacent to them in a class. The insult is whispered when the teacher's attention is elsewhere. Since the victims are generally students who do not want to get in trouble for talking in class, the harasser is generally able to avoid retaliation.

LET'S TAKE A VOTE. When there is an audience for the confrontation, an alternative response is to ask whether they support the harasser or the victim. The victim might do this if he anticipates that the audience will take his side. If the audience is a random sample of students, the most popular student will win the vote. On one occasion a popular kid (call him Peter)

---

4. There is one exception to this generalization. Male harassers gain additional dominance credit with their peers by harassing someone who is of equal or greater size. Picking on someone who is bigger than oneself is a way of exhibiting courage. This makes tall students like Bill targets once they gain a reputation for backing down from such confrontations.

asked the crowd waiting by the door to a class, "Who thinks Edward is a
dork?" Everyone put up his hand. Edward asked the crowd, "Who thinks
Peter is an idiot?" Only he raised his hand, and everybody laughed. Edward
clearly lost this round. Understandably, potential victims tend to hang out
with friends who will support them and to avoid individuals and groups
who have harassed them in the past or have a reputation for bullying.
Harassers respond by setting up traps to lure a victim over to their clique
and then greet him with a series of insults.

WALK AWAY. To carry off the "ignore the harasser and walk away" tactic,
one must act as if the insult has not hurt. If one visibly flinches at an insult
and then walks away, one increases the risk of being thought a coward, and
one's "rep" is further damaged.

The Consequences of the Dominance by Insult Game

Many of the characteristic features of the peer culture of Ithaca's middle
schools can be viewed as defensive adaptations to or evolutionary consequences of the dominance by insult game.

Foul language has become a pervasive mode of communication among
middle school students when adults are not nearby. "Your mom" jokes and
many other insults are so overused that they have lost their shock value.
Behavior that used to be considered deviant is now normal, accepted, and
considered funny. This evolution of the definition of deviance and what is
shocking resulted from the overuse of insults generated by tit-for-tat confrontations and having to pretend that one was not really hurt by the insult
when one walked away. Eventually, participants started believing their own
fiction.

Cliques and friendship circles forestall and deter harassers, and therefore
are pervasive and remarkably stable. They are formed in the first month of
sixth grade and typically last for three years. Each clique has its special table
in the lunch room. Some cliques are on friendly terms with other cliques,
so there are generally a few other tables where a student would feel
accepted. However, 80 percent of the tables are off limits. When asked
what would happen if an unpopular group of kids tried to sit down at a
table, a student said, "I don't know. That's never happened. Nobody has
ever tried. . . . There is no point. Everybody has their special place where
most of the times they sit."

Some students believe they can gain prestige in the eyes of their peers by harassing and humiliating weaker, less popular students. As one student put it: "Maybe they like to prove to their friends that they're cool, that they can put someone else down" without being put down themselves. While other qualities—achievement in sports, outgoingness, and attractiveness—are more important avenues to high status, playing and winning the dominance game is for some a primary way to gain respect and prestige. The school's bullies do more than their share of the harassing, but persuading them to stop would not solve the problem; most students are perpetrators at one time or another.

Being part of the popular crowd reduces one's vulnerability to harassment. This is one of the reasons why everyone aspires to be in a popular clique. The primary indicator of popularity is whom one hangs out with. "If you're friends with popular people, you are considered more popular." Thus popularity carries the power to admit new students to the popular crowd and to blackball others. "*Really* popular people can do anything without being criticized." By contrast, "if a nerd goes over and sits next to a jock or somebody who's really popular—it doesn't happen very often—they would probably tell him to leave." Being a nerd is like having a communicable disease: "If you hang out with people who are unpopular, most of the time you are unpopular."

To most middle schoolers, gaining the respect of one's peers is the single most important goal of school life. They feel they are on exhibit every minute they are in school or on the bus. Their "rep" determines their quality of life during the seven to ten hours of the day that they spend with their peers. Compared with one's peers, parents are clueless about what is happening at school and consequently have little influence on behavior. A reputation as a nerd or dork is very costly. It means more than knowing that one is not welcome at certain lunch tables or parties. In the dominance by insult game, one is also a special target for verbal and physical harassment that is intended "to wear down your self-esteem." Some friends from primary school will probably desert you. In middle school, the outcast students are disunited and unable to articulate and advocate alternative norms that would allow them to feel better about themselves, such as that math is fun or learning is important. As one student said of middle school peer culture: "I don't make the world, I just live in it." Most internalize the norms of the peer culture and come to believe that the personal qualities that their age mates denigrate, such as studiousness, are indeed undesirable.

How Does One Become Popular?

Despite the fact that children of university professionals account for a significant share of Ithaca's students, academic achievement is not valued by the
middle school male peer culture.[5] For boys, popularity depends first and fore-
most on being good in sports. A swagger and baggy pants worn low on the
hips also help. In addition, it is essential not to be a "suck up."[6] To avoid
being characterized as a suck up one must avoid eye contact with teachers; not
hand in homework early for extra credit; not raise one's hand in class too frequently; and talk and pass notes to friends during class, demonstrating that
one values relationships with friends more than one's "rep" with the teacher.

Being smart is OK, but being studious is not. Indeed in the seventh grade,
the boys in the most popular crowd in Boynton middle school get poor
grades, frequently fail to hand in homework, and proudly reject the norm
that learning is important. This is not a new finding. In 1960 Abraham
Tannenbaum asked students at a predominantly Jewish high school in New
York City to react to written descriptions of eight fictitious students.[7] The
ratings, from most positive to most negative, were as follows:

—Athlete: brilliant, nonstudious;
—Athlete: average, nonstudious;
—Athlete: average, studious;
—Athlete: brilliant, studious;
—Nonathlete: brilliant, nonstudious;
—Nonathlete: average, nonstudious;
—Nonathlete: average, studious; and
—Nonathlete: brilliant, studious.

Note how being smart is all right, if it is not combined with studiousness. It is not getting good grades that gets one into trouble with one's
peers, but trying to get good grades.[8] Worse still is to be openly competitive about academics and grades. In fact, studiousness does not inevitably

---

5. In this town, 90 percent of high school graduates attend college. About 30 percent of eighth
graders are in an accelerated math sequence that ends with calculus in twelfth grade.

6. In Ithaca, this norm does not apply to girls. If this is generally true, it may explain why among
students with the same scores on external exams, secondary school girls get significantly better teacher
grades than boys.

7. Tannenbaum (1960).

8 The insults used by middle schoolers provide further support for Tannenbaum's finding. In
Ithaca, students who fail to hand in their homework are not accused of being slackers or "goof offs."
But not having the ability to do school work is perceived as a weakness, and therefore a good target for
insults. "Stupid" (referring to an action or to the person) is a popular insult. Due to overuse, it is los-

place one at the bottom of the popularity ranking. Other positive traits, such as athletic ability, cool clothes, attractiveness, and outgoingness can counter the negative effects of studiousness.

James Coleman's study of the peer culture of ten high schools yielded similar findings.[9] The value attributed to academic achievement was not associated with the wealth or general educational level of the community. Executive Heights, a school serving a rich and highly educated community, had one of the most anti-intellectual peer cultures.

More recently, a study of nine high schools in California and Wisconsin finds that "less than 5 percent of all students are members of a high-achieving crowd that defines itself mainly on the basis of academic excellence. . . . Of all the crowds the 'brains' were the least happy with who they are—nearly half wished they were in a different crowd."[10]

How the Structure of External Rewards for Student Achievement Influences Peer Culture

Why is cooperating with teachers—being a suck up—denigrated by middle school boys in Ithaca? From the perspective of my seventh grade respondents, who are not part of the leading crowd, the anti suck-up norm is imposed by a group of about twenty popular boys who are doing poorly in school and have therefore established a schoolwide norm that it is uncool to exhibit interest in school subjects. This observation, however, does not get to the root of the matter. One needs to explain why for boys in so many schools, having a don't cooperate with teachers attitude is strongly correlated with being popular and is perceived to contribute to becoming popular.[11]

---

ing its bite, and it tends to be used by "goodie two shoes," students who have qualms about using four-letter words in the insult game.

9. Coleman (1961).

10. Steinberg (1966, pp. 145–46).

11. Coleman (1961) found that different graduating classes from the same school often had different norms. The norms that prevailed appeared to reflect the values of the natural leaders—for example, the best athletes—in the class. My interviews in Ithaca have uncovered the same phenomenon. The dominant norms of the middle school class that graduated in 1994 were different from those of the class graduating in 1998, the seventh grade described above. The star athletes of the 1994 graduating class came from a primary school serving an upper middle class neighborhood where many college faculty lived. The "most popular" crowd that formed around these star athletes were all in top track accelerated mathematics classes and tended to set the tone for the whole school.

Why is athletic achievement valued by most middle school students and academic achievement denigrated? Some have argued that adolescent values simply reflect the sports-mad character of adult society. However parents say that they place academic achievement well above athletic achievement. In Coleman's study, the peer culture priorities of public schools serving upper class communities were not substantially different from those in middle and working class communities. And as anyone who has attended a soccer match in Europe or Asia will attest, these societies are no less sports mad than ours. Yet their adolescents honor academic achievement in their peers more than do American adolescents.

Coleman provided the beginning of the explanation of this phenomenon thirty-five years ago: "The athlete gains so much status in these schools [because] he is doing something for the school and the community in leading his team to victory, for it is a school victory. . . . The outstanding student, by contrast, has few ways—if any—to bring glory to the school. His victories are purely personal ones, often at the expense of his classmates, who are forced to work harder to keep up with him. Small wonder that his accomplishments gain little reward, and are often met by such ridicule as 'curve raiser' or 'grind,' terms of disapprobation having no analogues in athletics."[12] In many European countries, youth sports are organized by towns and cities rather than by schools, so that sports ability is less important to a young person's status at school.

To Coleman's explanation I would propose a second: American society's almost exclusive reliance on signals of academic achievement that assess performance relative to other students in a class—grades and class rank—rather than relative to a fixed external standard, such as results on a national or provincial examination. This gives students a personal interest in persuading each other not to study. As one student said, "It was my friends who did better than I on this test. But it was my friends, and still, I was mad at them."[13] The studious are called nerds, dorks, and suck-ups in part because they are making it more difficult for others to get good grades or to be ranked near the top of the class. Devoting time to studying for an exam is costly, and when exams are graded on a curve, the welfare of the entire class is maximized if no one studies for them. The cooperative solution is that no one studies more than the minimum. Participants are generally able to tell who has broken the code and to reward those who con-

12. Coleman (1961, p. 309).
13. Wexler (1992, p. 58).

form and punish those who do not. Side payments and punishments are made in a currency of friendship, respect, ridicule, and harassment that is not in limited supply. For most students, the benefits that might result from studying for the exam are less important than the very certain costs of being considered a "brain geek", a "grade grubber," or as "acting white."

One student, Tim, described his experience in 1986:

> Being a brain really did have a stigma attached to it. Sometimes during a free period I would sit and listen to all the brains talk about how much they hated school work and how they never studied and I had to bite my lip to keep from laughing out loud. I *knew* they were lying, and they knew they were lying too. I think that a lot of brains hung around together only because their fear of social isolation was greater than their petty rivalries. I think that my two friends who were brains liked me because I was almost on their level but I was not competitive.[14]

Note how those who broke the minimize studying norm tried to hide that fact from classmates. They did not espouse an alternative norm that learning is fun and important.

The costs and benefits of studying vary across students because of differences in interest in the subject, ability, proximity to the college application process, and parental pressure and rewards. This heterogeneity means that some students break the minimize studying norm. When they are a small minority, they cannot avoid feeling denigrated by classmates. In the top track and at schools where many students aspire to attend competitive colleges, they are numerous enough to create a subculture of their own, with norms denigrating those who do poorly on tests or who disrupt classroom activities. This is the structural basis of the "brains" and "preppie" cliques found in most American middle and high schools.[15] However, most secondary school students are in crowds that do not respect studiousness. At a few especially troubled schools, awards ceremonies held during school time are marred by "some in the crowd jeer[ing] 'Nerd!'" as students are called to receive an award.[16]

14. Personal communication with the author.

15. The denigration of studiousness is less of a problem in Ithaca's high school. The change appears to be due to the approach of college, the greater tolerance that comes with maturity, the existence of many distinct peer cultures in the larger school, and the support network that honors and advanced placement classes offer the studious.

16. Ron Suskind, "Put Down, Kicked Around, Honor Students Struggle On," *Wall Street Journal*, May 26, 1994, p. 1.

Peer pressure against studying does not derive from laziness. In jobs after school and at basketball practice, American adolescents work very hard. In these environments they are part of a team where individual effort is visible and appreciated by teammates. Competition and rivalry are not absent, but they are offset by shared goals, shared successes, and external measures of achievement, that is, satisfying customers or winning the game. On the sports field, there is no greater sin than giving up, even when the score is hopelessly one-sided. On the job, tasks not done by one worker will generally have to be completed by another.

When learning is assessed relative to an external standard and exam results influence access to college and jobs, students no longer have a personal interest in getting the teacher off track or persuading each other not to study. I taught for two years in a Nigerian secondary school that was preparing students for the external exams at the end of eleventh grade. In contrast to Coleman and Tannenbaum's findings regarding American high schools, the smarter and more studious Nigerian students were highly respected by their peers. Over the last seven years, I have interviewed approximately 180 students and teachers from a variety of countries about peer pressure and study habits. Respondents from countries without curriculum-based external exit exams—Mexico, Spain, Sweden, and the United States—report considerably more anti-intellectual peer pressure than respondents in countries with these exams, such as Britain, Canada, Denmark, Finland, France, Hong Kong, India, Ireland, Korea, Japan, Malaysia, the Netherlands, and Taiwan. In residential secondary schools in Taiwan, for example, students sneak into the bathroom after lights out, not to smoke, but to get a few extra hours of studying. When the first group finishes their stint, they wake the next group, and so on throughout the night.

Proposals for Curriculum-Based External Exit Exams in the United States

Two presidents, the National Governors Association, and numerous blue ribbon panels have called for the development of state or national content standards for core subjects and curriculum-based examinations that assess the achievement of these standards. The American Federation of Teachers also advocates a system in which "students are periodically tested on whether they're reaching the standards, and if they are not, the system responds with appropriate assistance and intervention. Until they meet the standards, they won't be able to graduate from high school or enter college."[17]

While the implementation of such exams would probably reduce nerd harassment, the primary motive behind these proposals lies elsewhere. The Education Subcouncil of the Competitiveness Policy Council, a nonpartisan group appointed by the president and congressional leaders, gives the following rationale for its advocacy of curriculum-based external exit exams:

> Working hard and achieving in school must count for them [students], too. And presently, high school students who plan to go on to college do not need to work hard and get good grades in order to achieve their goal. Except for the tiny percentage of kids who want to go to selective colleges, students know that, no matter how poor their grades, they will be able to find a college that will accept them. . . . The vast majority of employers give exactly the same message to students going directly from high school to work: What you did in high school does not count. . . . Hard working kids do not . . . have an edge since few employers ever inquire about what courses a young applicant took or ask to see a transcript.[18]

National or provincial curriculum-based external exit examination systems improve the signals of achievement available to colleges and employers, and thus are likely to induce them to give academic achievement greater weight when they make admission and hiring decisions.

Rewards for study and learning should be increased and made more visible. Rewards are necessary because learning is not a passive act; it requires the time and active engagement of the learner. Students have many other uses for their time and attention, so learning is costly for them. The intensity of their investment in learning depends on a comparison of benefits—intrinsic and extrinsic rewards for learning—to costs. When the benefits of learning increase, student effort will increase, and learning will increase as well.

Parents, school administrators, and teachers are also influenced by comparisons of the benefits of learning to the costs of focusing school resources and policies on academic achievement. With a CBEEES, exam

---

17. American Federation of Teachers (1995, pp. 1–2).
18. Competitiveness Policy Council (1993, p. 30).

results displace social class as the primary determinant of school reputations, and this in turn should induce school staff to give higher priority to enhanced learning. Teachers will upgrade curriculums and assign more homework, and parents will demand better science labs and more rigorous teaching. School administrators will be pressured to increase the time devoted to examination subjects and to hire more qualified teachers. This hypothesis is elaborated in the next section.[19]

A further benefit of a CBEEES is the professional development that teachers receive when they are brought to centralized locations to grade the extended answer portions of the examinations. In May 1996 I interviewed a number of activists in the Alberta Teachers Union about the examination system in Alberta, Canada. Even though the union opposes the exams, these teachers reported that serving on grading committees was "a wonderful professional development activity." In having to agree on what constituted excellent, good, poor, and failing responses to essay questions or open-ended math problems, the teachers shared perspectives and teaching tips.

Skeptics point out that American students already take lots of standardized tests. They ask why the proposed curriculum-based external exit examination system should significantly improve incentives. Advocates respond that curriculum-based external exit exam systems have uniquely powerful incentive effects because of the following characteristics:

—1. They produce signals of accomplishment that have real consequences for the student.

—2. They define achievement relative to an external standard rather than to other students in the classroom or the school. Thus they allow fair comparisons of achievement across schools and across students at different schools. Robert Costrell's formal analysis of the optimal setting of educational standards concludes that more centralized standard setting (that is, through state or national achievement exams) results in higher standards, higher achievement, and higher social welfare than decentralized standard setting (for example, through grading by teachers or school graduation requirements) when cross-district heterogeneity is not high.[20]

—3. They are organized by discipline and keyed to the content of specific course sequences. This focuses responsibility for preparing the student for particular exams on a small group of teachers.

---

19. For a fuller presentation, including the underlying mathematical details, see Bishop (1996).
20. Costrell (1994a, 1994b).

—4. They signal multiple levels of achievement in the subject. If an exam generates only a pass-fail signal, the standard will have to be set low enough to allow almost everyone to pass, and thus will not stimulate the majority of students to greater effort.[21]

—5. They cover almost all secondary school students. Exams for a set of elite schools, advanced courses, or college applicants will influence standards in the top track but will probably have limited effects on the rest of the students. The school system as a whole must be made to accept responsibility for how students do on the exams. It is not essential to have a single exam that is taken by all students. Many nations allow students to choose on which subjects they will be examined and offer high and intermediate level exams in the same subject.

—6. They assess a major portion of what students are expected to know or be able to do in a particular subject. However, it is not essential that the external exam assess every instructional objective. Teachers can be given responsibility for evaluating dimensions of performance that cannot be reliably assessed by external means.

Commercially prepared achievement tests such as the California Achievement Tests, the Iowa Tests of Basic Skills, and the Iowa Test of Educational Development are not curriculum-based external exit exams because they do not fulfill characteristic 1 in the list above. Students have no stake in doing well on these tests. Where there are incentives associated with student performance, it is teachers and school administrators who experience the consequences, not individual students.

The minimum competency exams that many American states require students to pass in order to graduate from secondary school do not fulfill characteristics 3, 4, or 5. While minimum competency exams have apparently reduced the number of students with very low basic skills levels, the threshold is quite low.[22] These tests are typically first taken in the ninth or tenth grades, and most students pass on the first sitting. In most states, high school transcripts indicate only whether the student eventually passes the test, not whether achievement is above the minimum level. Thus for the great majority of students who pass them on the first try, the tests no longer stimulate study. Incentive effects are focused on the small minority who fail on the first try and must repeat the test. Minimum competency

21. Kang (1985); Costrell (1994b).
22. Lerner (1990).

exams can be a useful part of a CBEEES, but it is necessary also to have other, more demanding curriculum-based exams signaling higher levels of performance.

Characteristic 4, that a curriculum-based external exit exam signals various levels of achievement, rather than merely whether the student has achieved a minimum level, is critical because it has major effects on the incentive effects of exams. By age thirteen, students differ greatly in levels of achievement. On the National Assessment of Educational Progress (NAEP), 7 to 9 percent of eighth graders are four or more grade-level equivalents behind their classmates, and 15 to 17 percent are four or more grade-level equivalents ahead of their classmates. When achievement differentials among students are as large as this, incentives for effort are stronger for most students if the full range of achievement is signaled, as opposed to whether the individual has passed some absolute standard.[23] When only a pass-fail signal is generated by a test, many students pass without exertion, and thus are not stimulated to greater effort by the reward for passing. Some of the least well-prepared students will judge the effort required to achieve the standard to be too great and the benefits too small to warrant the effort. They give up on meeting the standard. On the question of making scores on external examinations available, rather than just indicating whether an individual passed or failed, Costrell argues: "The case for perfect information would appear to be strong, if not airtight: for most plausible degrees of heterogeneity, egalitarianism, and pooling under decentralization, perfect information not only raises GDP, but also social welfare."[24]

The Scholastic Assessment Test (SAT)-I reasoning tests are not curriculum-based external exit exams because they do not fulfill characteristics 3, 5, and 6. They are not organized around school subjects and fail to assess most of the material that high school students are expected to learn. The SAT was initially designed to minimize backwash effects on teaching and student study habits. Indeed, Richard Gummere, admissions director for Harvard College when the machine-scored multiple-choice SAT replaced the curriculum-based essay-style College Board Examinations, was very candid about just what adopting the SAT meant: "Learning in itself has ceased to be the main factor [in college admissions]. The aptitude of the pupil is now the leading consideration."[25]

---

23. Kang (1985).
24. Costrell (1994b, p. 970).
25. Gunmere (1943, p. 5).

The subject-specific SAT-II achievement tests meet some of the requirements of a curriculum-based external exit exam. However, since colleges admit on the basis of the SAT-I, students have little incentive to take the SAT-II and few do so. In 1982–83 only 6 percent of those who took the SAT-I also took a science SAT-II, and only 3 to 4 percent took an SAT-II in history or a foreign language. Schools do not assume responsibility for preparing students for SAT-II tests.

Advanced placement (AP) examinations are the one exception to the general observation that the United States lacks national curriculum-based external exit examinations. Although it is growing rapidly, AP is still a very small program. In 1995 only 3.2 percent of juniors and seniors took AP English or AP history exams, and only 2 percent took AP calculus or science exams.[26] Low participation means that AP exams fail characteristic 5. They can, however, serve as a component of a larger CBEEES.

Hypotheses about the Impacts of Curriculum-Based External Exit Exams

The theory sketched above generates several hypotheses about the effects of curriculum-based external exit exams on various aspects of the educational system.

STUDENTS. Hypothesis 1 states that curriculum-based external exit examinations will result in higher achievement, even when student characteristics, school resources, curriculums, teacher qualifications, and teaching techniques are held constant. The effects should be strongest in the eleventh and twelfth grades, but they should reach down to middle school, though probably not to the early years of primary school.

Hypothesis 2 states that external exams will result in students spending less time watching television. It is expected that students will try harder at school work, partly because CBEEES increase the rewards for achievement, and partly because CBEEES are hypothesized to decrease peer denigration of studiousness.

PARENTS. Curriculum-based external exams also change the incentives faced by parents. The theory predicts that parents will talk with their

26. National Education Goals Panel (1995).

children about school more frequently and make greater efforts to induce their children to study regularly. Thus hypothesis 3 states that external exams will induce parents to spend more time talking with their children about school and result in students' perceiving their parents to be more interested in their performance in examination subjects.

Opponents of external exams argue that focusing students' attention on extrinsic rewards for learning will weaken their intrinsic motivation to learn. George Madeus argues that "test scores come to be regarded by parents and students as the main, if not the sole, objective of education," leading to "undue attention to material that is covered in the examinations, thereby excluding from teaching and learning many worthwhile educational objectives and experiences."[27] If these critics are right, students in school systems with external exams should be less likely to read for pleasure or to watch science programs like "NOVA" and "Nature." Therefore hypothesis 4 states that students will spend less time watching science documentaries on television and less time reading for fun.

SCHOOL ADMINISTRATORS. In the United States and Canada, locally elected school boards and the administrators they hire make the thousands of decisions that determine academic expectations and program quality. Academic achievement is not the only goal of American and Canadian schools. They are also expected to foster self-esteem and to provide counseling, supervised extracurricular activities, musical training, health services, community entertainment (for example, interscholastic sports), driver education—and to do all this in a racially integrated setting. These goals require additional and different kinds of staff. They may not be served by hiring teachers with strong backgrounds in calculus or chemistry.

When there is no external assessment of academic achievement, students and their parents benefit little from administrative decisions that favor higher standards, more qualified teachers, or a heavier student work load. The immediate consequences of such decisions are all negative: higher taxes, more homework, having to repeat courses, lower grade point averages (GPAs), complaining parents, greater risk of being denied a diploma.

By contrast, the positive effects of choosing academic rigor are negligible and delayed. If college admission decisions are based on rank in class,

27. Madeus (1991, p. 7).

GPA, and aptitude test scores rather than on externally assessed achievement in secondary school courses, upgraded standards will not improve the college admission prospects of next year's graduates. Graduates will probably do better in difficult college courses and will be more likely to get a degree, but that benefit is uncertain and far in the future. Over time the school's reputation, and with it the admissions prospects of its graduates, may improve because current graduates are more successful in local colleges. That possibility, however, is even more uncertain and delayed. Published data on proportions of students meeting targets on standardized tests probably speed the process by which real improvements in a school's performance influence its local reputation. However, other indicators, such as SAT scores, the proportion of students going to various types of colleges, and students' socioeconomic backgrounds tend to get more attention. Schools' reputations are determined largely by things over which teachers and administrators have little control.

Few American employers pay attention to a student's achievement in high school or the school's reputation in their hiring decisions.[28] Those that do pay attention to achievement use indicators of relative performance, such as GPA and rank in class, as their criteria. Consequently, higher standards do not benefit students as a group.

External exams in secondary school subjects transform the signaling environment. Hiring better teachers and improving the school's science laboratories now yields a visible payoff: more students pass the external exams and are admitted to top colleges. Schools' reputations will now tend to reflect student academic performance rather than family backgrounds or the success of football and basketball teams.

Hypothesis 5a states that external exams will cause priorities to shift in favor of achievement in examination subjects and away from interscholastic sports, band, and other activities intended to make school fun and entertain the public. Administrators and school boards will be induced (a) to improve the school's science laboratories, if science is an examination subject; (b) to offer additional courses in examination subjects and scale back offerings outside the core academic program; (c) to increase the share of the school week devoted to examination subjects; (d) to lengthen the school day and the school year; (e) to use specialists to teach examination subjects; (f) to hire teachers with thorough backgrounds in their fields;

---

28. Bishop (1989, 1992); Hollenbeck and Smith (1984).

(g) to offer accelerated or enriched math and science tracks; (h) to reduce class sizes in examination subjects; (i) to give teachers additional preparation time; (j) to pay teachers higher salaries; and (k) to spend more per pupil.

Hypothesis 5b states that external exams will make administrators less tolerant of absenteeism and more likely to view absenteeism as a problem. It is not clear, however, how actual rates of absenteeism would be affected. Absenteeism and discipline problems might increase because teachers focus more on teaching rather than entertaining students or lose authority because they are no longer the sole judges of students' work. Alternatively, students might attend more regularly because they are afraid of missing something they might need for the exam.

Where students and parents choose secondary schools and state subsidies follow the student, the incentive effects of a CBEEES are greatly magnified. In countries that have both school choice and a CBEEES, newspapers typically publish league tables reporting examination results by school. These results have major effects on enrollment applications the following year. Marginal instructional costs are typically below the level of state aid per student, so the schools at the top of the league table often expand, forcing those with poor results to shrink and lay off staff.

Hypothesis 6 states that external exams will induce larger shifts in the priority given to academics when parents are able to choose which schools their children attend and dollars follow students.

TEACHERS. Thirty percent of American teachers say that they "feel pressure to give higher grades than students' work deserves" and "feel pressure to reduce the difficulty and amount of work [they] assign."[29] Under a system of external exams, teachers and local school administrators lose the option of lowering standards in order to lower failure rates and raise self-esteem. Instead, they strive to prepare their students for the external exam.

Hypothesis 7 states that external exams will induce teachers (a) to set higher standards; (b) to assign more homework; (c) to increase the number of experiments that students do in science classes; (d) to have students solve mathematics problems alone rather than in groups; (e) to give more quizzes and tests; (f) to increase their use of other teaching strategies that they believe improve exam performance; (g) to spend less time trying to enter-

---

29. Hart Research Associates (1995).

tain students; and (h) to pay less attention to nonacademic goals, such as self-esteem, good discipline, and low absenteeism.

Some educators contend that external exams can have negative effects on teaching. It is argued, for example, that "preparation for high stakes tests often emphasizes rote memorization and cramming of students and drill and practice teaching methods," and that "some kinds of teaching to the test permit students to do well in examinations without recourse to higher levels of cognitive activity."[30]

The assumption of such opponents appears to be that the tests developed by individual teachers for use in their classes are better than examinations developed by the committees of teachers at the state or national levels. To the contrary, the tests that teachers presently develop for themselves are generally of very low quality. M. Fleming and B. Chambers have studied tests developed by high school teachers, using Benjamin Bloom's taxonomy of instructional objectives, and find that "over all grades, 80 percent of the items on teachers' tests were constructed to tap the lowest of the taxonomic categories, knowledge (of terms, facts or principles)."[31] William Rowher and John Thomas find that fully 99 percent of items on college-level instructor-developed tests in American history require the integration of ideas, compared with only 18 percent of junior high school and 14 percent of senior high school test items.[32] Secondary school teachers test low-level competencies because that is what they teach. Students do not take state-mandated tests in history, so poor history teaching cannot be blamed on standardized tests. More evidence is needed on this issue. Hypothesis 8 states that external exams will cause teachers to focus on teaching facts and definitions, not the scientific process. Students will conduct fewer experiments in science classes and computation will be stressed in mathematics.

SCHOOL CHOICE AND NONPUBLIC SCHOOLS. In their influential 1990 book, John Chubb and Terry Moe argue that bureaucracy and democratic government inevitably result in public schools being less effective than nonpublic schools that must compete for students, and thus are required to survive a market test. Consequently, hypothesis 9 states that nonpublic schools should give academics greater priority and have higher levels of student achievement even when the social status of students is held constant.

---

30. Madeus (1991, pp. 7–8).
31. Fleming and Chambers (1983), reported in Thomas (1991, p. 14).
32. Rowher and Thomas (1987).

Elsewhere, I have argued to the contrary that

if American parents and students were allowed to choose their high school, however, the Gresham's law of course selection [that easy courses displace rigorous courses because rigor is not well signaled to colleges] might become a Gresham's law of school selection. . . . In order for school choice to generate an environment that induces schools to focus on upgrading instruction and improving learning, (1) the skills and competencies of individual graduates must be assessed relative to an external standard that is comparable across schools and (2) individual rewards—e.g., access to preferred university programs and better jobs—must be attached to these results. Only then are students and parents encouraged to select schools on the basis of their expected value added, rather than on the basis of reputations that school staff are unable to change by doing a better job of teaching.[33]

Two hypotheses flow from this perspective. Hypothesis 10 states that in the absence of curriculum-based exams, there is no reason to expect students at nonpublic schools to learn more math and science than students at public schools. In fact, the priority given to discipline and religious education at nonpublic schools may result in lower priority for math and science teaching.

Hypothesis 11 states that because they are more sensitive to market pressures, nonpublic schools will respond more radically to an external exam system than will public schools. Consequently, there will be a positive interaction between curriculum-based exams and nonpublic schools. The hypotheses 4 through 8, relating to school and teacher behavior, will be stronger for private schools than for public schools. In addition, following hypothesis 1, the student achievement effects of exam systems will be greater at nonpublic schools.

Mathematics and Science Achievement in Canada

Probably the best place to test hypotheses about the impact of curriculum-based external examinations is Canada. Some Canadian provinces have

33. Bishop (1996b).

curriculum-based exams, others do not. In 1990–91, when the International Assessment of Educational Progress (IAEP) data used in this study were collected, Alberta, British Columbia, Newfoundland, Quebec, and Francophone New Brunswick had curriculum-based provincial examinations in English, French, mathematics, biology, chemistry, and physics. These exams accounted for 50 percent of the final grade in Alberta, Newfoundland, and Quebec and 40 percent in British Columbia. Alberta's examination system was reestablished in 1984, so it was seven years old when the IAEP data were collected.

Of the other Canadian provinces in 1990–91, Ontario had eliminated curriculum-based provincial examinations in 1967, Manitoba in 1970, and Nova Scotia in 1972. Nova Scotia substituted multiple-choice norm-referenced achievement tests in reading, language usage, proofreading, mathematics, science and social studies, which do not influence student grades. Anglophone New Brunswick had provincial exams in language arts and mathematics, but these grades were not reported on transcripts or counted toward final course grades. They had little credibility and many students refused to take them. In Ontario, a few local school districts have district level exams for core subjects. But in any case, one would not expect local district subject exams to have as powerful incentive effects as provincial or national exams.

Figure 10-1 plots provincial means for mathematics achievement of sixteen-year-olds from the 1993 School Achievement Indicators Program against the mean literacy level of parents in each province. The provinces with a CBEEES are shown in boldface. Most of these provinces had higher scores on the assessments than the provinces without CBEEES with the same level of parental literacy but without a curriculum-based external exit exam system.[34]

Three of the provinces that lacked a CBEEES in 1991 have since introduced them.[35] Manitoba introduced a twelfth grade examination in the winter of 1991, about the time the IAEP exam was being administered to eighth grade students in the province. This system rotates the subjects under assessment on a five- or six-year cycle. Manitoba has assessed math and language arts every year since 1996 and requires the exams to count for 30 percent of the student's final grade.

34. Canada, Council of Ministers of Education (1993); Jones (1993). Stan Jones also kindly provided me with unpublished data on literacy levels by age.
35. White (1993).

Figure 10-1. *Mathematics Achievement of Canadian Sixteen-Year-Olds and Parental Literacy, by Province*[a]

SAIP math score[b]

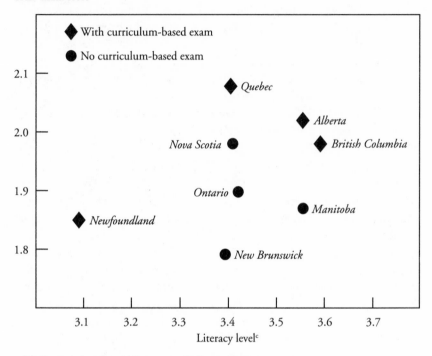

Source: Canada, Council of Ministers of Education (1993); Jones (1993).

a. Achievement is defined by average scores on the 1993 School Achievement Indicators Program (SAIP) problem-solving test.

b. SAIP math results are reported by level, on a scale from 1 to 5.

c. The literacy indicator reported in the figure is a weighted average of the mean level (from 1 to 4) for three different age groups: those between thirty-five and forty-four years old had a weight of 0.5, those between forty-five and fifty-four had a weight of 0.3, and those between twenty-five and thirty-four had a weight of 0.2.

Starting in 1995, Anglophone New Brunswick required that math and English exam results account for 30 percent of course grades. Exam results are also included on transcripts and in published school-level results.

In terms of governance and finance, the Canadian system of elementary and secondary education is quite similar to that in the United States. Comprehensive schools predominate. As in the United States, education is a provincial or state responsibility. Localities administer schools and use property taxes to raise their share of the funding. In 1980, localities accounted for 43 percent of school funding in the United States and 28.5 percent in Canada. Funding levels vary less within Canadian provinces than within American states: the average within-province coefficient of variation is 0.09 for Canada and 0.17 for the United States.[36] In some provinces, negotiations over teacher salaries occur at the provincial level.

The analysis in this section proceeds as follows. I first describe the data. I then discuss the impact of provincial exam systems on the behavior of parents, students, teachers, and school administrators. Finally, I analyze the determinants of math and science test scores.

The IAEP Data

I test the hypotheses outlined in the previous section using data on the mathematics and science competence of about 40,000 Canadian thirteen-year-olds from 1,338 schools. When invited by the Educational Testing Service to participate in the 1991 International Assessment of Educational Progress, Canada decided to collect sufficient data to allow valid comparisons between provinces and between the Anglophone and Francophone school systems of the five provinces with dual systems. The Yukon, the Northwest Territories, and Prince Edward Island did not participate. Stratified random samples of between 105 and 128 secondary schools were selected from the French-speaking school systems of Ontario and Quebec and the English-speaking school systems of Alberta, British Columbia, Manitoba, Saskatchewan, Ontario, Quebec, New Brunswick, Nova Scotia, and Newfoundland.[37] A school's likelihood of selection was roughly proportional to its estimated number of thirteen-year-old students. All French-speaking schools in New Brunswick, Saskatchewan, and Manitoba were invited to participate. About 23 percent of the schools were religiously controlled and 2 percent were nondenominational.

Random samples of between thirty and thirty-four thirteen-year-olds were selected from each school. Half were assigned to the mathematics

---

36. McDonald (1993); National Center for Education Statistics (1992).

37. In Canada the highest refusal rates for participation were for English-speaking schools in Quebec (15 percent) and Saskatchewan (12 percent) and French-speaking schools in New Brunswick (12 percent). In the rest of the provinces, refusal rates were below 7 percent, and in many provinces all invited schools participated. In the United States, the refusal rate was 21 percent. When sampled schools declined to participate, an alternate school was selected from the same stratum. (International Assessment of Educational Progress, 1992a.)

assessment and half to the science assessment. Students also completed a brief questionnaire that asked about books in the home, number of siblings, language usually spoken at home, hours spent watching television, hours spent doing homework, reading for pleasure, watching science programs on television, home availability of mathematics and science resources, attitudes towards math and science, and teaching methods. The principals of the participating schools completed questionnaires describing school policies, school resources, and the qualifications of eighth grade mathematics and science teachers.

The student questionnaires provide data on the behavior and attitudes of students, parents, and teachers. School means on each variable were calculated for the schools with at least nine students in the school sample, and provided the dependent variables for the analysis.[38]

Estimating the Impact of External Exam Systems

The backwash effects of curriculum-based provincial exams on the behavior of thirteen-year-olds, their parents, teachers, and school administrators were examined by estimating models predicting these behaviors, using schools as observations.

The specification was the same for all dependent variables. Twelve variables were used: logarithm of the mean number of books in the home, mean number of siblings, proportion of a school's students whose home language was different from the language of instruction, school size (operationalized as the logarithm of the average number of students in a grade), a dummy for schools that include elementary grades, a dummy for schools that include all kindergarten through eleventh grade in one building, a dummy for French-speaking school, a dummy for being a province with an exam system, and a dummy equal to one when a nonpublic school is in a province with an exam system. There are also dummies for three types of

---

38. Some of the schools selected to participate in the IAEP had considerably fewer than thirty age-eligible students. In developing the IAEP sampling frame, schools predicted to have only a few age-eligible students were combined into "superschools" for purposes of drawing the sample. When one of these schools was selected, the target sample of thirty to thirty-four students was distributed among the schools forming the relevant superschool. (International Assessment of Educational Progess, 1992a.) Principal questionnaires were completed in each school, but in come cases there were too few student interviews to obtain reliable estimates of school means. If the very small schools had been included, the estimated impacts of the *EXAM* variable would have been slightly larger than shown in tables 10-1, 10-2, and 10-3 below.

nonpublic school: schools run by school boards elected by people of a particular faith (generally Catholic), independent denominational schools, and independent nonsectarian schools.

The results are presented in tables 10-1, 10-2, and 10-3. Each row represents a separate regression on data from 1,230 to 1,338 schools. The far right-hand column summarizes the hypotheses presented in the previous section. To the left of the slash is the expected sign, based on a priori reasoning and the literature, of the impact of having an external exam system on this measure of home or school behavior. A question mark indicates that no hypothesis was generated for this variable. The signs to the right of the slash mark summarize my findings on the effect of test scores at age thirteen from analysis of the IAEP data.[39]

EFFECTS ON HOME BEHAVIOR. The hypotheses about the behavior of parents are strongly supported by the results in table 10-1. As predicted in hypotheses 2 and 3, public school students in provinces with exams watch fifty-three minutes (0.87 hour) less television a week, and are 7.6 percentage points more likely to report that their parents want them to do well in mathematics, as well as more likely to report that their parents have talked to them about what they are learning in school. They are significantly more likely to have a calculator.

Hypothesis 4 reflects the fact that opponents of externally set curriculum-based examinations predict that they will cause students to cut back on learning activities that do not have a direct relationship to the exams. This hypothesis is operationalized by testing whether exam systems are associated with less reading for pleasure and less time spent watching science programs like "NOVA" and "Nature." Neither of these hypotheses is supported; indeed, for private school students the effects are statistically significant in the opposite direction.

EFFECTS ON ATTITUDES. Examination systems appear to have increased positive attitudes toward science. Students in provinces with exam systems are more likely to believe that science is important in everyday life. They are more likely to report that their parents are "interested in science."

Examination systems are not associated with a higher proportion of students thinking that mathematics or science is important for getting a job.

---

39. See table 10-5 below; also Bishop (1996b).

Table 10-1. *Estimated Effects of Canadian Provincial Diploma Exams and School Governance on Attitudes and Behavior of Students and Parents*[a]

Student and parent variables	School variables					Summary statistic			
	Exam province	Nonpublic, with exam	Religious school board	Independent religious	Independent nonsectarian	Mean	Standard deviation	Adjusted R^2	Hypothesis[b]
Hours of TV per week (school average)	-0.873 (5.09)	0.878 (2.47)	0.399 (1.62)	-0.402 (8.09)	-3.590 (6.43)	14.7	2.85	0.289 2.32	-/-
Read for fun (index)	0.013 (0.68)	0.145 (3.64)	-0.071 (2.58)	-0.053 (0.96)	-0.080 (1.28)	1.85	0.28	0.141 0.261	-/0
Watch "NOVA," "Nature"	0.023 (0.86)	0.172 (3.11)	0.005 (0.14)	-0.203 (2.62)	-0.045 (0.52)	0.97	0.38	0.132 0.361	-/0
Have calculator	0.043 (4.69)	-0.047 (2.44)	0.074 (5.63)	0.019 (0.69)	0.041 (1.38)	0.88	0.13	0.087 0.125	?/+
Parents talk about math class	0.043 (3.47)	0.005 (0.20)	0.032 (1.83)	0.027 (0.75)	0.063 (1.57)	0.62	0.17	0.041 0.166	+/?
Parents talk about science class	0.055 (4.37)	0.026 (1.00)	0.001 (0.07)	-0.027 (0.76)	0.063 (1.54)	0.47	0.17	0.056 0.169	+/?

Parents want me to do well in math	0.076 (4.94)	−0.087 (2.72)	0.139 (6.31)	0.122 (2.72)	0.238 (4.76)	2.53	0.22	0.105 0.208	+/+
Parents interested in science	0.072 (2.98)	−0.055 (1.10)	0.127 (3.68)	0.039 (0.56)	0.124 (1.57)	1.67	0.34	0.059 0.328	+/+
Think math useful for solving everyday problems	0.034 (1.54)	−0.044 (0.97)	0.132 (4.18)	0.032 (0.50)	0.085 (1.19)	2.04	0.35	0.085 0.298	+/+
Think science useful in everyday life	0.078 (2.93)	−0.072 (1.30)	0.203 (5.29)	0.025 (0.33)	0.160 (1.84)	1.93	0.33	0.117 0.362	+/+
Think math important to get a job	0.025 (1.67)	−0.094 (2.97)	0.143 (6.55)	0.052 (1.18)	0.153 (3.07)	2.56	0.21	0.075 0.207	+/+
Think science important to get a job	−0.028 (1.23)	−0.033 (0.68)	0.214 (6.48)	−0.030 (0.45)	0.034 (0.46)	1.93	0.33	0.141 0.312	+/+

Source: Author's calculations based on data from the International Assessment of Educational Progress (IAEP).

a. Regressions are based on data from 1,230 to 1,338 schools; t statistics are shown in parentheses. Control variables not shown include logarithm of the mean number of books in the home, mean number of siblings, proportion of a school's students whose home language is different from the language of instruction, logarithm of the number of students per grade, and dummies for schools that include elementary grades, for schools that include kindergarten through eleventh grade in one building, and for French-speaking schools.

b. To the left of the slash mark is the expected sign, based on a priori reasoning and on the literature, of the effect of having an exam system on the given measure of behavior. Sign to the right of the slash mark summarizes the analysis of the IAEP data. A significant positive effect on test scores at age thirteen is indicated by +; a significant negative effect, by −; no significant relationship, by 0; and no hypothesis, by ?

These student attitudes apparently reflect reality. Canadian employers apparently seldom use exam grades in hiring. Job applications were obtained from seven large companies located in Quebec, a province with a long tradition of exit exams. Each company requested information about degrees and certificates of skills, but none requested information on grades in secondary school. A few asked for school transcripts, but employers reported that this was to confirm graduation, not to screen on grades in school. These practices are not a consequence of legal prohibitions on requesting and using such information. A government-approved Canadian Manpower form obtained from the University of Montreal's College Placement office requests such information. Apparently, the availability of more reliable information on student performance in secondary school has not caused Canadian employers in Quebec (or, presumably, other provinces with examination systems) to ask applicants to provide such information.

Thus provincial exams in Canada appear to increase rewards for studying by signaling performance to students, parents, colleges, and universities and making graduation dependent in part on externally assessed achievement—but not by directly signaling achievement to employers.

EFFECTS ON SCHOOL RESOURCES AND POLICIES. Estimates of the effect of exam systems on school resources and priorities is presented in table 10-2. The schools in provinces with exam systems are, on average, twice as large as schools in provinces without exams and are less likely to have primary grades in the building. Since these characteristics influence school policies and resource allocation, it is important to control for them.

Under hypothesis 5a, items (a) through (g) about administrator behavior are supported. A striking effect of a CBEEES is the increased tendency to hire specialists who have majored in their subject in college. In provinces with exam systems compared with those without, the proportion of public school teachers who have taken courses in their specific subject at university is 12 percentage points higher in math and 15.6 percentage points higher in science. The percentage of specialist teachers is 16.6 points higher in mathematics and 13 points higher in science. The quality of science labs index is a quarter of a standard deviation higher. In addition, tracking is more common particularly in math.

The hypothesis that public schools in exam provinces will try to hire more experienced teachers in all subjects, not just in math and science, receives little support. In fact, the reverse was observed. Also rejected are the predictions that exam systems will stimulate reductions in public school class sizes and increases in teacher preparation time.

As suggested by hypothesis 11, private schools are more responsive to the incentive effects of external exam systems than are public schools. Their propensity to hire highly qualified specialist teachers rises dramatically when there are external exams. Science labs are also substantially better. Exam systems also induce private schools to increase classroom instruction hours by one-third in math and by one-fifth in science. Total hours in the school year do not rise, so the increase in time devoted to math and science comes at the expense of other activities. Private schools also appear to employ more experienced teachers and give them more time for preparation when they are located in province with exam systems; public schools do not.

EFFECTS ON TEACHER BEHAVIOR. Estimates of the effect of exam systems on teaching are presented in table 10-3. Under hypothesis 7, all of the items concerning teacher behavior tested in these data receive strong support. Provincial exams are associated with students doing 0.82 additional hours of homework per week, including 0.19 additional hours of math homework and 0.15 additional hours of science homework. Public school students report taking more quizzes and tests in class, but private school students do not.

Hypothesis 8, which is derived from the writings of opponents of external examinations, generates opposite predictions to hypothesis 7. Contrary to hypothesis 8 but consistent with hypothesis 7, in provinces with exams emphasis on computation using whole numbers—a skill that should be learned by the end of fifth grade—declines significantly. In addition, students do more, not fewer, experiments in science class, and teachers do more experiments in front of the class. Apparently, teachers subject to the pressure of a provincial exam four years in the future adopt strategies that are conventionally viewed as "best practice," not those designed to maximize scores on multiple choice tests. Private school teachers also schedule more class time for students to work on problems by themselves.

Estimating the Impacts of Curriculum-Based Examinations on Math and Science Achievement

I now turn to the impact of exam systems on student learning. In this analysis, the dependent variable is the school mean percent correct answers

Table 10-2. Estimated Effects of Canadian Provincial Diploma Exams and School Governance on School Policies[a]

Student and parent variables	School variables					Summary statistic			
	Exam province	Nonpublic, with exam	Religious school board	Independent religious	Independent nonsectarian	Mean	Standard deviation	Adjusted R^2	Hypothesis[b]
Math specialist teacher	0.166 (5.53)	0.072 (1.17)	−0.228 (5.39)	0.028 (0.33)	0.013 (0.13)	0.45	0.50	0.280 0.422	+/+
Science specialist teacher	0.129 (4.29)	0.089 (1.23)	−0.143 (3.38)	−0.061 (0.72)	−0.066 (0.67)	0.46	0.50	0.280 0.423	+/+
Math teachers were math majors	0.119 (4.46)	0.209 (3.79)	−0.214 (5.70)	−0.191 (2.55)	−0.135 (1.55)	0.66	0.39	0.136 0.362	+/0
Science teachers were science majors	0.156 (6.16)	0.160 (3.05)	−0.244 (6.83)	−0.131 (1.81)	−0.084 (1.02)	0.69	0.38	0.204 0.345	+/0
Hours of math instruction	0.057 (0.94)	1.244 (9.80)	−0.492 (5.75)	−0.875 (5.14)	−1.204 (6.06)	3.98	0.89	0.187 0.821	+/0
Hours of science instruction	0.029 (0.56)	0.611 (5.59)	−0.634 (8.62)	−0.463 (3.16)	−1.069 (6.24)	2.92	0.82	0.152 0.707	+/+

Variable									
Science lab quality	0.179 (3.15)	0.453 (3.84)	-3.04 (3.78)	-0.209 (1.30)	-0.019 (0.10)	1.95	0.95	0.281 0.802	+/+
Track 8th grade math	0.135 (5.95)	-0.128 (2.71)	0.004 (0.12)	0.185 (2.88)	0.119 (1.57)	0.13	0.32	0.056 0.320	+/0
Track 8th grade science	0.030 1.84	-0.003 (0.10)	-0.023 (0.99)	0.094 (2.03)	0.035 (0.65)	0.06	0.23	0.039 0.231	+/0
Proportion new teachers	0.032 (2.93)	-0.088 (3.93)	0.048 (3.00)	0.085 (2.80)	0.055 (1.57)	0.16	0.15	0.082 0.147	-/0
Proportion experienced teachers	-0.043 (2.45)	0.077 (2.17)	-0.048 (1.92)	-0.106 (2.22)	-0.063 (1.13)	0.59	0.24	0.093 0.232	+/0
Teacher preparation time	-0.011 (1.02)	0.055 (2.48)	-0.014 (0.91)	0.032 (1.07)	0.049 (1.41)	0.31	0.17	0.225 0.145	+/-
Class size	-0.244 (0.68)	0.397 (0.53)	2.891 (5.68)	2.207 (2.17)	6.13 (5.16)	24.8	6.2	0.369 0.492	-/+

Source: Author's calculations based on data from the International Assessment of Educational Progress.

a. Regressions are based on data from 1,230 to 1,338 schools; *t* statistics are shown in parentheses. See table 10-1, note a, for control variables not shown.

b. See table 10-1, note b.

Table 10-3. *Estimated Effects of Canadian Provincial Diploma Exams and School Governance on Teaching*[a]

Teacher variables	School variables					Summary statistic			Hypothesis[b]
	Exam province	Nonpublic, with exam	Religious school board	Independent religious	Independent nonsectarian	Mean	Standard deviation	Adjusted R^2	
Total homework time	0.818 (7.61)	−0.794 (3.56)	1.036 (6.71)	2.331 (7.47)	3.135 (8.95)	4.41	1.62	0.171 1.46	+/+
Math homework time	0.185 (3.95)	0.071 (0.73)	0.124 (1.84)	0.125 (0.92)	0.190 (1.25)	1.66	0.64	0.051 0.634	+/+
Science homework time	0.149 (4.36)	0.082 (1.17)	0.113 (2.32)	0.087 (0.88)	−0.048 (0.43)	1.04	0.47	0.063 0.461	+/+
Emphasize whole number operations	−0.061 (0.17)	−0.123 (1.70)	0.041 (0.84)	−0.035 (0.36)	−0.035 (0.31)	1.68	0.49	0.036 0.475	−/?
Math quiz (index)	0.160 (5.45)	−0.282 (4.62)	0.039 (0.93)	0.303 (3.55)	0.556 (5.81)	1.62	0.52	0.422 0.398	+/?

Science quiz (index)	0.115 (4.97)	−0.099 (2.06)	−0.050 (1.50)	0.143 (2.13)	0.098 (1.30)	0.89	0.38	0.242 0.313	+/?
Do math problems alone in class	0.006 (0.22)	0.122 (2.24)	0.052 (1.38)	0.007 (0.09)	1.07 (1.25)	3.22	0.37	0.067 0.358	+/+
Math problems solved in groups	−0.047 (1.12)	0.022 (0.25)	0.079 (1.29)	−0.223 (1.81)	−0.202 (1.46)	. . .	. . .	0.143 0.575	−/0
Do science experiments	0.302 (7.02)	−0.096 (1.08)	0.191 (3.10)	−0.115 (0.92)	0.090 (0.64)	1.52	0.63	0.155 0.583	+/+
Watch science experiments	0.129 (4.00)	0.088 (1.32)	0.067 (1.44)	−0.112 (1.19)	−0.143 (1.36)	2.42	0.47	0.119 0.438	+/+

Source: Author's calculations based on data from the International Assessment of Educational Progress.

a. Regressions are based on data from 1,230 to 1,338 schools; t statistics are shown in parentheses. See table 10-1, note a, for control variables not shown.

b. See table 10-1, note b.

on the IAEP at age thirteen, with adjustments for guessing.[40] Adjusted for guessing, the students in provinces with exam systems got an average of 47.2 percent in math and 57.3 percent in science. The standard deviation across individuals for these variables is 24 points for math and 20.2 points for science.

Table 10-4 presents estimates of the impact of curriculum-based exams taken in the twelfth grade on eighth grade test scores. In the panels for math and science, the first row presents simple regressions containing no controls for school characteristics. These results show that students in provinces with exam systems score 7.0 points higher in math and 3.6 points higher in science. Adding controls for school size and type (including elementary grades, kindergarten through eleventh grade, Francophone) in row 2 lowers the effect of having an exam system effect on public school students to 5.2 points for math and 2.5 points for science. Adding additional controls for three types of school governorship in rows 3 and 4 lowers the effect of having an exam system to 4.5 points for math and 3.0 points for science.

Row 5 adds controls for the demographic background of the school's student body: school means for books at home, number of siblings, and proportion of students whose home language is different from the language of instruction. In this model, exam systems raise scores of public school students by 4.3 points in math and 3.0 points in science.

The sixth row of each panel includes two additional control variables: availability of calculators and computer use. Having a calculator at home and using computers for school work are associated with higher math achievement but not with higher science achievement. Including these variables in the model lowers the estimated effect of having an exam system on math achievement but does not affect its impact on science achievement. Both of these variables are hypothesized to be influenced by the existence of external exams.

Consequently, row 5 presents the best estimate of the total impact (including indirect effects) on IAEP test scores at age thirteen of having a provincial exam in the subject at the end of secondary school. Provincial exams have large effects on public school students: 18 percent of a U.S. standard deviation (about two-thirds of a U.S. grade-level equivalent) in mathematics and 15 percent of a standard deviation (about half a grade-

---

40. It is defined as [number of correct answers – (0.25 × number of answers)]/(0.75 × number of test items).

level equivalent) in science. In a standard deviation metric, the impact of provincial exams on math scores is close to the 22.6 percent of a standard deviation decline in SAT math scores in the United States between 1969 and 1980, and three times the magnitude of the increase in SAT math scores since 1980. For mathematics, exam effects are significantly bigger in nonpublic schools.

The gains in mean achievement generated by exam systems do not come at the price of greater inequality. Exam provinces have less variability of achievement across schools. The variance of school mean science achievement is smaller in Alberta, British Columbia, and Quebec than in other provinces. For math achievement, the variance is lowest in New Brunswick, British Columbia, Saskatchewan, Quebec, and Alberta. The bottom panel of table 10-4 presents regressions predicting the standard deviation of achievement among students at a school. For public schools, within-school standard deviations for science achievement are smaller in exam provinces. For mathematics, within-school standard deviations are unrelated to being an exam province for public schools and are significantly smaller for nonpublic schools in exam provinces.

IS THE EFFECT CAUSAL? One possible skeptical response to these findings is to point out that the correlation between having an external exam system and other outcomes may not be causal. Maybe the people of Alberta, British Columbia, Newfoundland, Quebec, and Francophone New Brunswick—the provinces with exam systems—place higher priority on education than the people of Manitoba, Saskatchewan, Ontario, Nova Scotia and Anglophone New Brunswick.[41] Maybe this trait also results in greater political support for examination systems. If so, one would expect that schools in the provinces with exam systems were better than schools in other provinces along all dimensions, not just by academic criteria. For example, schools in exam provinces should have fewer problems with discipline and absenteeism.

41. This will seem like a strange idea to people who know Canada. With the exception of Alberta and British Columbia, these provinces have little in common. Historically, they do not seem to have valued education more than the rest of Canada. Adult literacy is lower, on average, in these four provinces than in the rest of Canada. Newfoundland is quite poor and has significantly lower levels of adult literacy than other provinces. A study of adult literacy places Quebec in the middle of the pack, along with Ontario, Nova Scotia, and New Brunswick. Two of the top four provinces with respect to adult literacy have exam systems and two do not. Saskatchewan is number one when it comes to adult literacy, yet thirteen-year-olds in this province lag substantially behind students from Alberta and British Columbia in mathematics and science.

Table 10-4. *Estimated Effects of Canadian Provincial Diploma Exams and School Governance on Student Achievement*[a]

	Diploma exam	Nonpublic, with exam	Religious school board	Independent religious school	Independent nonsectarian	Log books in home[b]	Elementary K–11, size, French	Adjusted R²
Math achievement								
1	0.070*** (9.53)							0.0666
2	0.052*** (6.87)						X	0.1012
3	0.045*** (5.22)		-0.054*** (6.00)	0.157*** (7.05)	0.089*** (3.82)		X	0.1717
4	0.045*** (5.22)	0.003 (0.13)	-0.056*** (4.56)	0.155*** (6.20)	0.086*** (3.13)		X	0.1710
5	0.043*** (5.29)	0.028 (1.63)	-0.054*** (4.65)	0.094*** (3.98)	0.042 (1.57)		X	0.3126
6	0.034*** (4.32)	0.044*** (2.63)	-0.075*** (6.45)	0.081*** (3.51)	0.027 (1.03)	0.141*** (14.12) SchDemog, Calc, Comp	X	0.3533
Science achievement								
1	0.036*** (6.68)							0.0335
2	0.025*** (4.52)						X	0.0586
3	0.031*** (5.78)		-0.052*** (8.02)	0.017 (1.07)	0.042** (2.49)		X	0.1664

	(1)	(2)	(3)	(4)	(5)	(6)	Controls		R^2
4	0.033*** (5.37)	-0.010 (0.76)	-0.048*** (5.42)	0.023 (1.30)	0.050** (2.51)			X	0.1661
5	0.030*** (5.24)	-0.004 (0.31)	-0.039*** (4.75)	-0.020 (1.22)	0.014 (0.80)	0.116*** (16.65)		X	0.3461
6	0.030*** (5.17)	0.000 (0.02)	-0.042*** (5.06)	-0.025 (1.53)	0.011 (0.59)		*SchDemog, Calc, Comp*	X	0.3486
Principal reports of problems[c]									
Absenteeism	0.109** (2.15)	0.137 (1.30)	-0.062 (0.86)	-0.507*** (3.54)	-0.465*** (2.76)	-0.406*** (7.14)		X	0.1317
Discipline	-0.072 (1.49)	0.244*** (2.40)	-0.243*** (3.51)	-0.490*** (3.58)	-0.365** (2.24)	-0.277*** (5.03)		X	0.0828
Within-school standard deviation[d]									
Math	0.0047 (1.21)	-0.0165** (2.08)	0.005 (0.96)	-0.007 (0.68)	-0.020 (1.54)		*SchDemog, StdBk*	X	0.0576
Science	-0.007** (2.10)	0.0024 (0.37)	-0.0018 (0.41)	0.0061 (0.69)	-0.0171* (1.67)		*SchDemog, StdBk*	X	0.0322

Source: Author's calculations based on data from the International Assessment of Educational Progress.

a. t statistics are shown in parentheses. Significance at the 10 percent level (two-tailed test) is denoted by *; at the 5 percent level (two-tailed test), by **; and at the 1 percent level (two-tailed test), by ***.

b. *SchDemog* comprises books in the home (*bk*), average number of siblings (*sib*), and the share of students whose language at home is different from the school's language of instruction (*lang*). *Comp* indicates student uses computers at home or at school. *Calc* indicates student owns a calculator. *StdBk* is the standard deviation of books in the home.

c. Measured on an index from 0 (no problem) to 3 (serious). For discipline, the mean is 0.78 and the standard deviation is 0.72. For absenteeism, the mean is 0.82 and the standard deviation is 0.77.

d. For math, the mean is 0.22 and the standard deviation is 0.50. For science, the mean is 0.17 and the standard deviation is 0.040.

The theory outlined above (hypotheses 5b and 7), by contrast, predicts that exam systems may induce students and schools to redirect resources and attention toward learning and teaching exam subjects and away from other goals such as low absenteeism and good discipline. These competing hypotheses are evaluated in the third panel of table 10-4. Consistent with the theory and contrary to the "provincial taste for education" hypothesis, public school principals in provinces with exams do not report significantly fewer discipline problems and are significantly more likely to report problems with absenteeism. Private school principals in exam provinces also report bigger problems of discipline and absenteeism.

Another way of dealing with possible selection bias in the Canadian data set is to test these hypotheses in other data sets. Elsewhere, I provide a number of additional tests.[42] When GDP per capita is controlled, students from countries with a CBEEES do better on international exams than students from countries that lack such a system. Their teachers are paid more. When social background is controlled, New York State students outscore students in other states on the SAT and the NAEP mathematics test in eighth grade. New York teachers are also very well paid.[43]

Still another approach is to look at the effects of eliminating or reestablishing examination systems. Unfortunately, only a few countries have started or eliminated an exam system in the last few decades and before-after data on achievement are available only for Sweden. After Sweden eliminated its exams, the proportion of students taking college preparatory courses in mathematics and science declined substantially.[44]

MODELS THAT INCLUDE ENDOGENOUS VARIABLES AS CONTROLS. The impacts of family behavior and school policies and priorities on achievement are described in table 10-5. Watching television has large and significant negative effects on math and science achievement. An increase of five hours per week in television watching by all students at a school lowers school mean percent correct by 3.9 to 5 points. School means of reading for fun and watching science documentaries do not significantly influence achievement.

42. Bishop (1996a, 1997, 1998).
43. Bishop, Mane, and Moriarty (1998).
44. Bishop (1996a).

The school characteristics with significant impacts on both math and science achievement are average hours of homework in the subject and quality of science laboratories, an indicator of the priority given to science teaching. Math achievement is also significantly affected by the use of specialist teachers and the use of computers at school. Science achievement is significantly greater when more classroom hours are scheduled and when science teachers have studied the subject in college. Student tracking and the experience profile of the teaching staff have no significant effects on achievement in either subject. Class size has a significant positive relationship with math achievement and a negative relationship with teacher preparation time.

Adding the endogenous indicators of family behavior and school priorities changes the estimated impact of being in a diploma exam province. Relative to the preferred specification (model 5 in table 10-4) containing controls for only school type, size, governance, and demography, coefficients on the diploma exam variable fall by 40 percent for mathematics and 63 percent for science. This suggests that induced changes in television watching, home resources for math and science, school policies, and teacher behavior are responsible for an important part of the higher achievement in provinces with curriculum-based exams. The CBEEES coefficients remain significantly positive, however, indicating that diploma exams change the effort and achievement of students, not just the behavior of parents, teachers, and school administrators. Exactly how a CBEEES induces students to work harder cannot be determined in these data. Possible key factors include increases in rewards for achievement or reductions in peer denigration of studiousness.

The Effectiveness of Nonpublic Schools

As in the United States, most nonpublic schools in Canada were started by religious denominations. Canadian governments are not constitutionally prohibited from subsidizing religious schools, however, so these institutions receive considerable public funding. Indeed four provinces—Alberta, Newfoundland, Ontario, and Saskatchewan—have Catholic school systems that are overseen by school boards elected by members of the religious faith (and Newfoundland also has a similar Protestant school system). The schools run by these religious school boards account for 20.6 percent of the Canadian schools in the sample and four-fifths of all nonpublic schools.

Table 10-5. Determinants of Math and Science Achievement at Age Thirteen[a]

	Math percent correct		Science percent correct		Summary statistic	
Variable	Coefficient	t statistic	Coefficient	t statistic	School mean	Standard deviation
School demography						
Log average books in home	0.100***	9.56	0.094***	12.00	2.23	0.43
Average number of siblings	−0.027***	3.50	−0.032***	5.70	1.60	0.47
Speak different language in home	−0.012	0.68	−0.092***	7.01	0.14	0.22
School system characteristics						
Francophone	0.071***	6.42	0.014*	1.72	0.25	0.43
Elementary grades	−0.008	0.92	0.008	0.80	0.40	0.49
K–11	0.010	0.84			0.09	0.29
Curriculum-based exam	0.030***	3.78	0.015**	2.26	0.41	0.49
Nonpublic with exam	0.051***	3.16	−0.009	0.74	0.11	0.31
Religious school board	−0.072***	6.06	−0.021**	2.41	0.20	0.40
Independent denominational school	0.035	1.61	−0.041***	2.78	0.026	0.16
Independent nonsectarian school	−0.028	1.14			0.021	0.14
Log size of 8th grade	−0.003*	0.60	−0.0057*	1.75	4.15	1.03

Parent and student behavior

Read for pleasure (index)	0.011	1.59	−0.004	0.45	1.85	0.31
Use computer for schoolwork	0.055***	3.96	0.001	0.09	0.40	0.25
Have a calculator	0.076***	2.91	0.008	0.38	0.88	0.15
Watch science programs on TV	−0.006	0.71	0.004	0.60	0.98	0.43
Hours of TV per week (school average)	−0.0077***	5.88	−0.0093***	9.87	14.7	3.04

School policies and characteristics

Class hours in subject	−0.002	0.57	0.0095***	2.86	3.97/3.00	0.89/0.82
Average homework per week in subject	0.015***	3.16	0.0132***	2.78	1.66/1.04	0.64/0.47
Specialist teachers in subject	0.013*	1.88	−0.004	0.82	0.48/0.49	0.50/0.50
Teachers majored in subject	0.004	0.42	0.0176**	2.57	0.66/0.69	0.38/0.38
Specialized science lab	0.004	1.06	0.0059**	1.97	1.95	0.95
Tracking in 8th grade in subject	0.002	0.22	0.002	0.15	0.16/0.08	0.37/0.27
Proportion experienced teachers	0.014	0.77	−0.014	0.96	0.59	0.22
Proportion new teachers	−0.015	0.53	0.001	0.04	0.16	0.15
Class size	0.0023	3.13	0.000	0.06	24.8	6.1
Teacher preparation time	−0.049	2.02	−0.006	0.31	0.31	0.16

Summary statistic

Adjusted R^2	0.4176		0.4042
Mean square error	0.0923		0.0729
Number of observations	1056		1043
Mean value of dependent variable	0.477		0.547

Source: Author's calculations based on data from the International Assessment of Educational Progress.

a. Significance at the 10 percent level (two-tailed test) is denoted by *; at the 5 percent level (two-tailed test), by **; and at the 1 percent level (two-tailed test), by ***.

They have a religious character but are elements of quasi-public bureau-cracies, and are therefore likely to be constrained by the political process, an important disadvantage in Chubb and Moe's view.[45]

The parents of students attending schools run by religious school boards are more economically advantaged, more concerned about school, more interested in science, and more likely to buy their child a calculator than are parents in public schools (see table 10-1). Students are more likely to think that math and science are useful and are necessary to get a good job. Home-work assignments are greater and discipline is better. However, these schools do not appear to make math and science instruction top priorities. They are less likely to have teachers who studied math and science in college or to have specialists teaching math and science. They schedule less time for teaching science and have lower-quality science labs (see table 10-2). When background characteristics of the students are controlled, students in schools run by religious school boards in provinces without external exams score 5.4 to 3.9 points lower on IAEP math and science tests than public school students in these provinces. However, their principals are signifi-cantly less likely to report discipline problems. Apparently the religious denominations that control these schools and the parents who send their children to them primarily seek better discipline and ethical and moral cli-mates consistent with their beliefs, not better math and science teaching. Fewer resources are devoted to math and science teaching and lower achievement results.

The other 20 percent of nonpublic schools are divided pretty evenly between nonsectarian independent schools and sectarian schools controlled by religious denominations. These schools look a lot like American private schools. Parents are more advantaged and are more likely to talk to their children about math classes and to be characterized as urging their children to do well in math than parents of public school children. These private school students are assigned two to three hours more homework per week than public school students. Students in the nonsectarian private schools watch two to three hours less of television per week than public school stu-dents. However, where there are no provincial diploma exams, these schools are less likely to hire math and science teachers who majored in the subject in college, and they schedule 0.88 to 1.2 fewer hours of math instruction per week and 0.46 to 1.07 fewer hours of science instruction

45. Chubb and Moe (1990).

than comparable public schools. Their teachers are less experienced and class sizes are larger than public schools in the province. Absent controls for the family background of students, achievement levels are substantially higher. When the family background of students is controlled, students at independent schools outperform public school students in mathematics but not in science.

Comparisons with public schools are more favorable to independent private schools when they are located in provinces with diploma examinations. These private schools have better science laboratories, are more likely to hire teachers who majored in the subject in college, schedule at least as much time for math and science instruction as public schools in the province, and give their teachers more time to prepare lessons. Their teachers tend to be more experienced than teachers at private schools in provinces without diploma exams.

Therefore it may be necessary to amend Chubb and Moe's theory that because they operate in a competitive environment, private schools are more effective at producing academic achievement than public schools.[46] Competition does tend to force institutions to be more effective, but the salient criterion for effectiveness may not be student achievement in mathematics and science, or in any other subject. In provinces without diploma exams, parents may not have the information that would allow them to pick schools on the basis of academic achievement. Lacking reliable comparative information on student achievement, parents will judge schools by other criteria that are easier to measure, such as discipline, the availability of special instruction programs, and specific cultural and religious values. Thus the character, behavior, and effectiveness of private schools in a given community will depend on how well student achievement is signaled and how the larger society honors and rewards different types of student achievement.

Summary and Conclusions

At this writing, the incident described at the opening of the chapter is more than three years old. Bill and Alan shared many of their ninth grade classes, but they did not walk from class to class or eat lunch together. In seventh

---

46. Chubb and Moe (1990).

and eighth grades Bill more than pulled his own weight when partnered with Alan in science labs. This ended in ninth grade. Although he is still in honors classes, Bill now seems to have cut back on class participation. In Alan's view, Bill has either become lazy or is trying to cast off his nerd reputation by not showing enthusiasm for school work. He has not succeeded. He has a few friends, but they too are viewed as nerds. Once, in gym class, Alan overheard Bill talking to himself about being lonely. He walks quickly from class to class, avoiding opportunities to socialize. The dominance by insult game is uncool in high school, so he is not singled out for harassment. Most classmates ignore him; a few pity him.

In the first three sections of this chapter, I proposed a series of reasons why a curriculum-based external exit exam system should be expected to induce students, teachers, and school administrators to devote more time and attention to academics. The arguments relating to increased student rewards and teacher and school accountability (hypotheses 5 through 8) have been made before. When grades and class rank are the primary signals, there is little incentive to hire challenging specialists in a subject or to avoid scheduling pep rallies during the school day. If, however, achievement is signaled by student performance on external examinations, there are strong incentives to attract talented teachers and focus the school on academic pursuits.

The argument that curriculum-based external exit exams influence peer support and the denigration of studiousness is, to my knowledge, new. It starts from the observation that the peer culture of American middle schools rewards and respects sports ability, social skills, physical attractiveness, and conformity to group norms, rather than studiousness. Studiousness is associated with nerdiness, and nerds often become the object of harassment intended to wear down self-esteem. The studious are denigrated in part because studying hard is counter to the interests of their classmates. They are raising the curve and making it more difficult for others to get into the college of their choice. Peer pressure against learning, it is hypothesized, is an almost inevitable consequence of the relativistic way American schools assess achievement and then signal it to colleges and employers. If academic achievement was defined in terms of a fixed external standard, students might be less inclined to pressure each other not to study.

I tested the hypothesis that curriculum-based external exit exams induce students, parents, teachers and school administrators to refocus their energies on academic achievement by comparing schools in

Canadian provinces with such examination systems to school in provinces without them. I find that students from provinces with exams watch less television and are more likely to have calculators. Their parents are more frequently reported to care more about science and math and more likely to talk to them about what they are learning at school. In the provinces with external exams, schools are more likely to employ specialist teachers of mathematics and science, hire math and science teachers who have studied the subject in college, have high-quality science laboratories; schedule extra hours of math and science instruction; assign more home-work (in math, science and other subjects), have students do or watch experiments in science classes, and schedule frequent tests in math and science classes.

Public school students in provinces with exam systems are 18 percent of a standard deviation better prepared in mathematics and 15 percent of a standard deviation better prepared in science than comparable students from provinces lacking such exams. Among private school students, those in diploma exam provinces score 30 percent of a standard deviation better in math and 14 percent of a standard deviation better in science than those from provinces without such exams.

There is no evidence that external exams cause any of the undesirable effects that their opponents predict. Students in the Canadian provinces with exit exams do not watch fewer science programs on television and they read more for fun. Contrary to the predictions of critics, mathematics teachers place less emphasis on low-level skills like computation, and science teachers arrange for students to do more, not fewer, experiments.

I also compare achievement levels in public schools with those in various types of nonpublic school. Twenty percent of the schools in the sample are run by school boards elected by members of a religious denomination. They tend to serve a more advantaged clientele, but are clearly less effective at teaching math and science than public schools.

Independent sectarian and nonsectarian schools account for about 5 percent of the schools in the sample. Some, but not all, receive modest subsidies from the government. All charge tuition. Among children from families of comparable socioeconomic status, students at independent schools do not outperform public school students in science. In mathematics, however, they do outperform public school students. The achievement advantage of private independent schools is greatest in provinces with diploma exams.

These findings suggest that it is the independence of private schools, not their sectarian character, that makes them more effective than public schools. Moreover, this advantage is greatest when student achievement is signaled by curriculum-based external exit examinations.

References

American Federation of Teachers. 1995. *Setting Strong Standards: AFT's Criteria for Judging the Quality and Usefulness of Student Achievement Standards.* Washington.

Bishop, John H. 1989. "Why the Apathy in American High Schools?" *Educational Researcher* 18(1): 6–10.

———. 1992. "The Impact of Academic Competencies on Wages, Unemployment and Job Performance." *Carnegie-Rochester Conference Series on Public Policy* 37: 127–95.

———. 1996a. "The Impact of Curriculum-Based External Examinations on School Priorities and Student Learning." *International Journal of Education Research* 23(8).

———. 1996b. "Incentives to Study and the Organization of Secondary Instruction." In *Assessing Educational Practice: The Contribution of Economics*, edited by William Becker and William Baumol. MIT Press.

———. 1997. "The Effect of National Standards and Curriculum-Based External Exams on Student Achievement." *American Economic Review* 97(2): 260–64.

———. 1998. "The Effect of Curriculum-Based External Exit Exams on Student Achievement." *Journal of Economic Education* 29(2): 171–82.

Bishop, John H., Ferran Mane, and Joan Moriarty. 1998. "Diplomas for Learning, Not Seat Time: The Effects of New York State's Regents Examinations." In *Educational Finance to Support High Learning Standards*, 56–77. The University of the State of New York and New York State Education Department.

Canada. Council of Ministers of Education. 1993. *Report on the Mathematics Assessment.* Toronto.

Chubb, John, and Terry Moe. 1990. *Politics, Markets and America's Schools.* Brookings.

Coleman, James S. 1961. *The Adolescent Society.* Free Press.

Competitiveness Policy Council. 1993. *Reports of the Subcouncils.* Washington (March).

Costrell, Robert M. 1994a. "Centralized vs. Decentralized Educational Standards under Pooling." University of Massachusetts, Amherst, Department of Economics (July).

———. 1994b. "A Simple Model of Educational Standards." *American Economic Review* 84(4): 956–71.

Fleming, M., and B. Chambers. 1983. *Teacher-Made Tests: Windows on the Classroom.* San Francisco: Jossey-Bass.

Gibbons, Robert. 1992. *Game Theory for Applied Economists.* Princeton University Press.

Gummere, Richard. 1943. "The Independent School and the Post-War World." *Independent School Bulletin* 4(April).

Hart Research Associates. 1995. "Valuable Views: A Public Opinion Research Report on the Views of AFT Teachers on Professional Issues." Washington: American Federation of Teachers.

Hollenbeck, K., and B. Smith. 1984. *The Influence of Applicants' Education and Skills on Employability Assessments by Employers*. Ohio State University, National Center for Research in Vocational Education.

International Assessment of Educational Progress. 1992a. *IAEP Technical Report*, vol. 1. Princeton, N.J.: Educational Testing Service.

Ithaca City School District. 1994. "School Conduct and Student Discipline: A Handbook of Student Rights and Responsibilities" (July).

Jones, Stan. 1993. *Reading but not Reading Well*. Ottawa: National Literacy Secretariat.

Kang, Suk. 1984. "A Formal Model of School Reward Systems." In *Incentives, Learning and Employability*, edited by John H. Bishop. Ohio State University, National Center for Research in Vocational Education.

Lerner, Barbara. 1990. "Good News about American Education." *Commentary* 91(3): 19–25.

McDonald, Judith. 1993. "The Canadian Educational System." In *The Economic Consequences of American Education*, edited by Robert J. Thornton and Anthony P. O'Brien, 167–88. Greenwich, Conn.: JAI Press.

Madeus, George. 1991. "The Effects of Important Tests on Students: Implications for a National Examination or System of Examinations." Paper prepared for the American Educational Research Association Invitational Conference on Accountability as a State Reform Instrument. Washington, June 1–19.

National Center for Educational Statistics. 1992. *The Condition of Education: 1993*, vol. 1. U.S. Department of Education.

National Education Goals Panel. 1995. *Data for the National Education Goals Report: 1995*, vol. 1. Government Printing Office.

Powell, Arthur, Eleanor Farrar, and David Cohen. 1985. *The Shopping Mall High School*. Houghton Mifflin.

Rohwer, William D., and John W. Thomas. 1987. "Domain-Specific Knowledge, Cognitive Strategies, and Impediments to Educational Reform." In *Cognitive Strategy Research*, edited by M. Pressley. New York: Springer-Verlag.

Steinberg, Laurence. 1996. *Beyond the Classroom*. Simon and Schuster.

Tannenbaum, Abraham J. 1960. "Adolescents' Attitudes toward Academic Brilliance." Ph.D. dissertation. New York University.

Thomas, John W. 1991. "Expectations and Effort: Course Demands, Students' Study Practices and Academic Achievement." Paper prepared for the Conference on Student Motivation sponsored by the Office of Educational Research and Improvement.

Wexler, Philip. 1992. *Becoming Somebody: Toward a Social Psychology of School*. Washington: Falmer Press.

White, Kathleen D. 1993. *Educational Testing: The Canadian Experience with Standards, Examinations and Assessments*. GAO/PEMD-93-11. U.S. General Accounting Office (April).

CAROLINE M. HOXBY

11

The Effects of School Choice on Curriculum and Atmosphere

M ANY CURRENTLY PROPOSED school reforms, such as vouchers and charter schools, depend on the idea that if parents are given more ability to choose among schools, schools will be forced to be more responsive to parents, because parents' choices will determine enrollments and budgets. Thus the wisdom of choice-based reforms depends to a large extent on the wisdom of parents' ideas about schools and their ability to perceive what schools do. For instance, if parents place a high priority on academic quality, can correctly perceive academic quality, and choose schools based on academic quality, one would expect that schools with strong academic programs would do well under school choice reforms. If parents want their children to learn disciplined work habits, schools that teach such habits would thrive under school choice. If parents choose schools based on sports programs, schools with good coaches and sports facilities would succeed under school choice. In fact, parents look for schools that offer a balance of academic, disciplinary, and other training. The question "If parents were given greater choice, how and what kind of schools would they choose?" is central to the debate over school choice. It is contentious because little is known about how parents actually choose among schools. In this chapter I attempt to provide an empirical answer.

How parents choose is not the only important question that needs to be answered in order to assess school choice reforms. Other questions concern the effects of school choice on school efficiency, school finance, student peer groups, and the achievement of students at choice and nonchoice schools. I have addressed these issues in other studies.[1] Still other questions concern whether choice schools, such as voucher schools and charter schools, provide high-quality education, as measured by achievement tests, college attendance, and other indicators. These issues have also been addressed elsewhere.[2] All of these studies leave a black box, however. School choice may generate higher student achievement or greater school efficiency, but how? Choice allows parents to exert more pressure on schools, but it remains to be shown how schools change in response to their pressure. Do schools become more or less academically oriented? Do they assign more or less homework to students? Answers to such questions help to reveal the mechanism by which greater school choice translates into different outcomes for students.

One might consider surveying parents about how they would choose a school if they could—that is, what characteristics they would seek. Such survey evidence exists, and proponents and opponents of choice-based school reforms sometimes support their views by citing it.[3] Both proponents and opponents also support their views by citing the characteristics of schools that must be chosen, such as private schools, voucher schools, charter schools, public schools of choice, and magnet schools. Both survey evidence and evidence based on schools of choice is problematic, unfortunately. The first reason is the selection problem: schools of choice and the parents who choose them are not necessarily representative of the population. Thus they may provide misleading evidence for predicting the effects of a general school choice policy. For instance, parents who send their children to a science magnet school probably have different preferences from the average parent. The second problem affects surveys not only of parents

1. See Hoxby (1994, 1996, 1998, forthcoming).

2. See Greene, Peterson, and Du (1996) for a study of the Milwaukee voucher schools. See Greene, Howell, and Peterson (1997) for a study of the Cleveland voucher schools. Studies of the New York City voucher schools and of charter schools in several states are ongoing.

3. For examples of survey evidence, see Parent-Teacher Association of the United States (1991, 1993); Grolier (1983); Williams (1983); U.S. Department of Education (1991). A number of studies of private schools or school choice discuss parents' preferences, though not necessarily in the context of school choice reform; see Fuller, Elmore, and Orfield (1996), Kirkpatrick (1990), Murnane (1984), Allen (1992), Chubb and Moe (1990), Clune and Witte (1990), Coleman and Hoffer (1987), Moe (1995), and Tucker (1995).

whose children attend choice schools but even of randomly chosen parents. Surveys about preferences are notorious for the difficulty of eliciting the truth, because it is hard to set up realistic choices. For instance, if one asks parents who currently have little ability to choose among schools whether they would prefer a more demanding academic environment for their children, they may say yes, as though every other school characteristic could be held equal. However, were their children to be placed in such an environment, they might object to some of its consequences, such as homework crowding out extracurricular activities.

In fact, an empirical answer to the question of how parents would choose schools faces four major obstacles. The first is the selection problem described above. The second is that one requires objective evidence, such as behavior that reveals parents' preferences, in addition to subjective statements about preferences. The third obstacle is that observed choice programs are likely to be simultaneously determined with other policies. For instance, a school district whose students are apathetic might simultaneously introduce intradistrict choice and a wider array of extracurricular activities. In this case, the intradistrict choice program would not have caused the increase in extracurricular activities. The final obstacle is that one must distinguish between the effects of greater student segregation and the effects of giving parents' preferences more influence.

My empirical strategy in response to these obstacles is, briefly, as follows. I use topographic differences among metropolitan areas to identify differences in the number of school districts (and thus choice among school districts) that each metropolitan area offers. Topography serves as an exogenous source of variation in the degree of choice that parents experience, and this remedies the problems of selection and endogeneity.[4] I have used this strategy successfully elsewhere to identify exogenous differences in the degree of school choice among public school districts.[5] I employ rich data on schools and students, primarily from the National Education Longitudinal Study (NELS), so that I have objective measures of behavior to confirm subjective descriptions of each school's characteristics. I also use demographic data from the Public School Universe and the special school

4. This strategy remedies the selection and endogeneity problems because variation in the degree of school choice in a metropolitan area that stems from topography is very unlikely to be endogenous to the actions of any particular school. Since topography predates schools, literal endogeneity is impossible. This strategy also makes the possibility of omitted variables remote. A school's characteristics would have to have been influenced by some omitted variable that is correlated with the variation in school district concentration that is generated purely by topography.

5. Hoxby (forthcoming).

district tabulation of the 1990 census to distinguish the effects of segregation from the effects of school choice.

Five Issues about Parents' Choice Behavior

Proponents and opponents of school choice disagree about how parents' decisions would affect schools. The disagreement hinges on five issues. The first is how parents would make choices: would they become involved in school decisionmaking, gaining information through discussions with teachers and administrators, bringing their own knowledge about their children and how schools work, militating for improvements? Proponents of choice argue that parents who have more choice over their children's schools are more likely to immerse themselves in school decisionmaking. In other words, "exit" and "voice"—in Albert Hirshman's classic language—are compliments.[6] Opponents argue that exit and voice are substitutes: if parents are able to choose another school, they are less willing to invest time and effort in their children's current school.

The other four issues concern what parents want. Proponents of choice assert that average parents want their children to face challenging academic curriculums, meaning that secondary schools should end with advanced courses close to entry-level courses at college. Opponents assert that average parents prefer easy curriculums. Proponents claim that typical parents like relatively strict academic environments—schools that assign homework and have graduation requirements, for instance. Opponents claim that typical parents prefer a lax academic environment that does not interfere with their children's extracurricular activities. Proponents contend that average parents like schools that enforce firm disciplinary standards. In contrast, opponents argue that although parents say in the abstract that they like firm disciplinary standards (thinking about other people's children being disciplined), they actually undermine school discipline because they so dislike it being applied to their own children. The final point concerns sports and other extracurricular activities. Opponents of choice argue that parents give excessive weight to extracurricular activities when choosing a school, causing schools to sacrifice academic programs to athletic and other extracurricular programs. Proponents of choice argue that parents' first priority is academic preparation.

6. Hirschman (1971).

The Interaction of Parents' Preferences and School Choice

To understand how parents' preferences translate into school characteristics, it is useful to think of schools being governed by two groups of
people: parents and staff.[7] Within each of these groups, there is variation in
preferences. For instance, teachers vary in the degree to which they like a
conventionally strict disciplinary atmosphere. Parents vary in the weight
they put on extracurricular activities.

There are also differences in average preferences between the two
groups, because the two groups do not have identical training or incentives.
Teachers are usually graduates of programs that specialize in education.
They develop preferences for teaching methods that are sometimes unpopular with parents, whose preferences about methods and curriculum are
typically conservative.[8] For instance, there is an average difference between
teachers' and parents' preferences over the teaching of reading, with the
average teacher liking whole language methods more than the average parents. Also, parents naturally tend to prefer teaching and disciplinary methods that are costly in terms of teacher effort, and teachers tend to prefer
methods that are costly in terms of parent effort. Consider alternative
methods of improving students' academic achievement. Afterschool tutor-
ing requires additional teacher effort, but monitoring children's homework
requires additional parent effort. Similarly, students' behavior may improve
if the school enforces stricter disciplinary standards, which requires staff
effort, or if students learn more self-discipline at home, which requires
parental effort.

Thus school choice affects how parents' preferences translate into school
characteristics in two ways. It affects how the variation in preferences
within each group (parents, staff) and the average differences in preferences between groups will play out. School choice will naturally allow more
variation in preferences to be manifested. Some schools may end up with
parents and staff who jointly prefer core academic courses, whereas other
schools may end up with parents and staff who jointly prefer unorthodox
material. However, the predicted increase in the variation of school characteristics is not of interest here, both for data reasons (as discussed below)

---

7. For the purpose of this paper, "staff" comprises teachers, administrators, and bureaucrats from
higher levels of government, such as state superintendents.

8. See Hess (1998) for a discussion of the conservatism of parents' views of teaching methods, relative to the views of school staff and others involved in school policymaking.

and because it is not crucial to the debate over school choice. Most people are willing to see school choice introduce more variety in schools, so long as state guidelines prevent schools from adopting extreme curriculums.[9]

The effect that is of interest in this chapter is the average effect of school choice on curriculums and atmosphere in schools. Choice puts pressure on schools to move away from policies that are, on average, favored more by staff than by parents and toward policies that are favored more by parents than by staff. If average parents desire weaker academic standards than do the staff, greater choice would cause academic standards to fall. If average parents like to use schools that set high academic standards more than staff like to provide such schools, greater choice would raise academic standards.

Data

For an empirical study of the school characteristics that parents choose when they have choice, a serious challenge is the need for rich information on curricular and extracurricular policies. For instance, to measure strictness of grading, one needs information both on the grades a school gives to a student and on the same student's performance on national standardized tests. One also needs rich information on the characteristics of the student bodies and communities of schools, so that one can separate the effects of choice from alternative explanations of a school's characteristics, such as demography. One cannot separate out the effects of choice on disciplinary atmosphere if one does not know whether a school is likely to need a strong disciplinary policy. Some students come from poor urban neighborhoods that are likely to infiltrate schools (through gangs, weapons, and drugs) unless actively excluded. Schools in high-income suburban neighborhoods require fewer overt disciplinary actions to exclude bad elements. Note that the information required to separate the effects of choice from the effects of demographics are not merely the average characteristics of a school's stu-

---

9. States can constrain curriculums and atmosphere at choice schools by two methods. They can regulate what courses a school must offer, for instance, by refusing to accredit a school that offers no mathematics. Alternatively, they can insist that a school must be able to attract a certain number or diversity of students. For instance, a state can implicitly ban curriculums that are highly ethnocentric by refusing to accredit schools that cannot attract a student body that is reasonably diverse, given the available population of students.

dent body and community. One also needs measures of the heterogeneity of the students and the community. This is because some school policies, such as unorthodox courses and strict discipline, are determined by the need to cope with a heterogeneous student population.[10]

Thus I need data that richly characterize the decisions of individual schools and precisely describe the student and community environments in which each school operates. Since no one data source satisfies these requirements, I use data from the restricted-use version of the National Education Longitudinal Study matched to the Public School Universe and the special school district tabulation of the 1990 Census of Population and Housing, which, respectively, describe the student body and the community of each school district in the United States.

The Public School Universe contains administrative data on the students in each school and school district, for example, their racial composition. The school district tabulation contains the demographic and housing variables from the long form of the census, aggregated for the population residing within the boundaries of each school district. Relevant variables are educational attainments, household incomes, ages, and house values. I describe and explain my choice of specific variables below.

The NELS is a longitudinal study of 27,805 students who attended eighth grade in 2,451 schools in 1988. Students are tracked on a biennial basis, in eighth grade, tenth grade (1990) and twelfth grade (1992), the last year used in this paper. The NELS contains student, school, and transcript components which provide both objective information and administrators' subjective assessments on each of the five issues about parent choice behavior discussed above. The sole disadvantage of using the NELS is that, like all the longitudinal surveys with similarly rich information, it covers only a fraction of U.S. school districts. My analysis employs data on 769 of the 4,555 school districts located in metropolitan areas. On average, each metropolitan area is represented by three school districts. The consequence of not having rich information on all school districts in each metropolitan

10. In addition, it is important to choose measures of school policy that are equally relevant for schools with different demographics. That is, a decrease in a measured policy should always indicate a decrease in the school's tendency to enforce that policy. Consider grading standards. A school with less grade inflation is always a school with less tolerance for inflated grades. In contrast, consider weapons checks. A school with fewer weapons checks may have a low underlying tolerance for weapons but no weapons problem, because of its demographics; or it may have a high underlying tolerance for weapons and also have a weapons problem.

area is that while one can reasonably estimate the effects of greater choice on the average characteristics of schools, one cannot plausibly estimate the effects of choice on the dispersion of characteristics among school districts within a metropolitan area.

Most of the variables describing curricular and extracurricular characteristics of schools are drawn from the school component of the NELS, which consists of school-level and district-level aggregates provided by school administrators. An example is the percentage of students who take advanced placement (AP) courses. It is necessary to create a few school-level variables by averaging students' answers to the student component of the survey. Because the sample from each school is small but random, these sample-based variables measure characteristics of the student body consistently, but with error. One would expect results based on these sample-based variables to be unbiased but imprecise.[11]

Five variables measure parental involvement. Four objective measures are the percentages of parents who discuss high school curricular choices with their children, who visit the school, who attend meetings of the parent-teacher association (PTA), and who attend regularly scheduled parent-teacher conferences (as opposed to conferences for the purpose of discussing a particular incident). The fifth, subjective, measure is the administrator's assessment of how much parents are involved in decisions about school policy.

To measure whether a school encourages students to take a challenging curriculum, I use the percentages of students in the tenth and twelfth grades taking AP courses. Advanced placement courses culminate in national, standardized tests, which tend to enforce a certain degree of difficulty in curriculums. To indicate whether a school has challenging math courses, I use an indicator variable equal to one if the school's regular (nonremedial, nonadvanced) mathematics offerings for the ninth through twelfth grades culminate in a twelfth grade course that contains some calculus.

To measure the strictness of the academic environment, I use four objective measures and two subjective ones. The objective measures are an index of grade inflation in mathematics, an index of grade inflation in English,

---

11. These variables, which exhibit classical measurement error, are used as dependent variables in regressions. One would expect estimates based on them to be consistent, but liable to have large standard errors.

number of hours of homework assigned each week, and number of standardized credits required for graduation. The subjective measures are the administrator's assessments of the degree to which students place a priority on learning and are expected to do their homework.

The grade inflation indexes require additional explanation. The index of grade inflation in mathematics is computed as follows. I subtract percentile score on a standardized mathematics test from grade point average in mathematics to obtain a "difference" for each student. Grade point averages are measured on the familiar four-point scale: 1 = D, 2 = C, 3 = B, 4 = A. The percentile scores on the standardized test are divided by 25 before subtracting, so that they are also on a four-point scale: 1 = 25th percentile, 2 = 50th percentile, 3 = 75th percentile, 4 = 100th percentile. I then create an index for each school by averaging students' "differences" within the school. This index is easy to interpret. Suppose that every school had equally tough grading standards and allotted students evenly along the four-point grading scale. Students who scored at the 25th, 50th, 75th, and 100th percentiles would have grade point averages of, respectively, 1.0, 2.0, 3.0, and 4.0. Thus one letter grade's worth of grade inflation is indicated by a increase of 1 in the school's index. For example, if a school typically assigns a grade of 4.0 to a student at the 100th percentile, its grade inflation index equals 0. If a school typically assigns the same grade to a student at the 75th percentile, its grade inflation index equals 1.

The index of grade inflation in English is computed in the same way, except that the standardized test is a reading test. The standardized tests used were administered by the Educational Testing Service to every student in the NELS.

I assess whether a school has a structured, disciplined environment with two objective measures: the number of minutes a student spends in class each day and the action taken by the school against a student who creates a classroom disturbance (first offense). I also use four subjective measures: the administrator's assessment of the degree to which the school has structured classrooms, has a structured school day, does not tolerate deviation from school rules, and provides a flexible environment.

The best indicator of how much weight a school puts on sports programs relative to academic programs is a subjective one: the administrator's assessment of the degree to which the school "emphasizes sports." For an objective measure of emphasis on sports, I use the ratio of physical education faculty to faculty in core subjects, such as English, mathematics, history, and science.[12] I also examine the percentages of students who participate in varsity sports, intramural sports, and band, choir, or orchestra.

Table 11-1 contains descriptive statistics of all the variables just described. Many of these are interesting, a few of which I note here. There is a great deal of variance in parent involvement. About 8 percent of parents visit the school and attend regular parent-teacher conferences, but the standard deviation of these measures is 20 percent. On average, fewer than 8 percent of students take AP classes in the tenth grade and about 20 percent take them in the twelfth grade. However, the percentage of students who take AP courses varies widely: the standard deviation in the twelfth grade is 17 percent. About 50 percent of schools have a regular mathematics track that is challenging, but this statistic also varies widely: the standard deviation is 47 percent. The average amount of homework is 5.37 hours per week, or a little more than an hour per school day. The standard deviation in homework per week is 1.57 hours.

Empirical Strategy

The clearest way to explain the empirical strategy of this paper is to proceed from wrong to right. I start by describing a common but naive empirical strategy and explain why it produces biased estimates. An apparently natural way to determine the effect of choice on school policies would be to compare choice and nonchoice schools with students who are similar in terms of their measured aptitude and demographics (race, parental income, gender, age). It is common to carry out such a comparison by means of a linear regression of a school policy measure, such as hours of homework, on variables that indicate students' aptitude and demographics and on a variable that indicates whether the school is a choice school—that is, a school that students must actively choose in order to attend.[13] Examples of

---

12. Faculty are measured in full-time equivalents.

13. The typical study that tries to estimate the effect of school choice on curricular and extracurricular policies uses an equation of the general form

$$P_{ijk} = C_{ijk}\alpha + X_{ijk}\beta + \epsilon_{ijk},$$

where the subscripts are for school i in district j in metropolitan area k. P is a policy such as hours of homework or a structured school day. C is an indicator for whether school ijk is a choice school. X is a vector of variables that characterize the student body, parents, and community attached to school ijk. ϵ is a residual comprising all the unmeasured determinants of the policy P.

Table 11-1. *Summary of Curricular and Extracurricular Policies of Schools in Metropolitan Areas from the National Education Longitudinal Study*

Variable	Mean	Standard deviation
Number of times parents have discussed curriculum with student	1.98	0.35
Number of times parents have visited school in a year	1.39	0.36
Percent of parents who attend PTA meetings	8.32	21.18
Percent of parents who attend regularly scheduled parent-teacher conferences	8.45	20.25
Parents' involvement in school policy decisions[a]	2.44	0.91
Percent of tenth grade students who take AP courses	7.65	10.01
Percent of twelfth grade students who take AP courses	19.06	16.59
Regular mathematics sequence culminates in twelfth grade course with some calculus	0.50	0.47
Minutes in class per school day	342	38
Action taken against student who causes classroom disturbance[b]	1.13	0.40
Structured classroom environment[c]	4.13	0.77
Structured school day[c]	4.51	0.82
Deviation from school rules not tolerated[c]	4.26	0.81
School environment is flexible[c]	3.48	0.99
School emphasizes sports[c]	3.15	1.07
Ratio of physical education teachers to core subject teachers	0.19	0.12
Number of extracurricular activities sponsored by school	17.34	3.39
Percent of students who participate in varsity sports	44.86	17.73
Percent of students who participate in intramural sports	57.40	15.92
Percent of students who participate in band, choir, or orchestra	24.30	14.03
Ratio of English grades to standardized reading test score[d]	0.99	0.16
Ratio of math grades to standardized math test score[d]	0.96	0.16
Hours spent on homework per week	5.37	1.57
Students place priority on learning[c]	3.63	0.81
Students do homework[c]	4.40	0.80

Source: Author's calculations.
a. Measured on a scale from 0 (not at all) to 4 (very much).
b. First offense.
c. Measured on a scale from 1 (not at all accurate) to 5 (very accurate).
d. Multiplied by 20.

choice schools are charter schools, pilot schools, magnet schools, voucher schools, or within-district choice schools.

A serious selection problem, however, plagues such comparisons. Parents and children who select choice schools differ from those who do not, not just on observable traits (for which one might hope to control) but also on unobservable traits, such as motivation. Only a small percentage of students opt to attend choice schools, and they are probably unusual even among students who appear similar based on observable traits like gender, race, parental income, and previous academic performance. The comparison between choice and nonchoice schools does not allow one to disentangle the effects of being a choice school from the effects of unobservable differences in the people served by the choice school. Put another way, parents and children who would select choice schools might act differently from others even if they used regular schools, so that policy in choice schools will reflect both different policy decisions and different types of student.[14]

Some researchers have sought to address the selection problem by measuring choice at the district level rather than at the school level. That is, a district is specified to be a choice district if it contains at least one school that students must actively choose to attend. The other schools in the district may enroll students purely on the basis of residential location or some or all of them may be choice schools (intradistrict choice). The comparison of choice and nonchoice districts can illustrate how policy is affected when schools are subjected to more parental pressure because of choice—even if they are schools that merely lose students to choice schools. It is common to carry out this type of comparison by means of a linear regression of a school policy measure, such as hours of homework, on variables that describe the demography of the school and on a variable that indicates whether the district is a choice district.[15]

---

14. Formally,

$$Prob(C_{ijk} = 1) = f(X_{ijk}, \epsilon_{ijk}) \Rightarrow cov(C_{ijk}, \epsilon_{ijk}) \neq 0 ,$$

so that estimates of α are likely to be biased, reflecting the type of student likely to attend a choice school.

15. That is, one estimates an equation of the form

$$P_{ijk} = C_{jk}\delta + X_{ijk}\gamma + \eta_{jk} + \eta_{ijk} ,$$

where C_{jk} is an indicator variable for district jk being a choice district, and η_{jk} and η_{ijk} are, respectively, district-level and school-level residuals.

This empirical strategy remedies the selection problem discussed above because schools in a choice district must, on average, deal with all the parents and students in the district, not just those who actively choose. But the strategy leaves the problem that choice programs are likely to be responses to underlying circumstances in the district. For instance, large urban districts with heterogeneous populations or floundering schools sometimes respond by instituting intradistrict choice programs. In some cases, intradistrict choice programs are a method of complying with a court order to desegregate. A district that gets an innovative superintendent may also be more likely to implement an intradistrict choice program. Put another way, comparisons of choice and nonchoice districts do not allow one to distinguish the effects of having a choice program from the effects of the circumstances that generated the program.[16]

For unbiased estimates of the effect of choice on school policy, one must have variation in the degree of choice that is independent of (exogenous to) the circumstances of individual schools and districts. If there were a statewide choice program that had been in effect long enough to have affected school policies by the late 1980s, one might argue that the degree of choice in that state had changed in a manner exogenous to the circumstances of individual districts. However, the earliest, reasonably comprehensive program of this type is that of Minnesota, which was only instituted in 1986. When the NELS began, in 1988, sufficient time had not elapsed for Minnesota's interdistrict choice program to have affected the policies of its schools. Statewide programs may be a subject for future research.[17]

Even so, focusing on statewide programs would neglect a far more important source of variation in the degree of school choice available in the United States: variation due to differences in school districting. In some metropolitan areas, parents face a wide array of school districts in which to reside and school their children. Other metropolitan areas contain only

---

16. That is, there is potential bias from policy endogeneity. Formally,

$$Prob(C_{jk} = 1) = g(\eta_{jk}) \Rightarrow cov(C_{jk}, \eta_{jk}) \neq 0 ,$$

so that estimates of δ are likely to be biased, reflecting the types of district likely to introduce choice programs.

17. One might worry that state choice programs are endogenous to state circumstances. It appears, however, that endogeneity is not a problem in the case of Minnesota, since its circumstances were quite similar to those of neighboring states.

one or a few school districts. The residential choices that households make among school districts ("Tiebout choice") are currently the most powerful form of choice affecting schools.[18] In fact, relative to the amount of household sorting among districts caused by the Tiebout process of residential choice, the amount of student reallocation caused by even the most comprehensive school choice programs has so far been very small. By pointing this out, I do not deny the importance of interdistrict school choice programs. Indeed, contestable markets theory indicates that one need not see any students switch districts to conclude that schools are affected by interdistrict choice. The *potential* to lose or gain students may force schools to behave differently. What I do mean to point out is how unwise it would be to examine only programs with the word "choice" in their titles while ignoring the largest and most widespread source of variation in current school choice.[19]

Formally, Tiebout choice affects school policy because an administrator who institutes policies that deviate from those preferred by parents tends to deter homebuyers, and thus depresses house prices in the district. By means of the property tax, lower house prices result in a smaller budget for schools, which discourages the administrator from pursuing the disfavored policies. Because residential decisions are based more heavily on school conduct when parents have greater opportunity for Tiebout choice, greater opportunity for Tiebout choice intensifies the response of house prices and school budgets to parents' preferences.

The large amount of variation in Tiebout choice among metropolitan areas allows one to derive estimates of the effect of choice on school policy by comparing metropolitan areas. In the next section, I discuss how to construct a measure of school choice based on potential Tiebout choice. Here it is only important to recognize that the results of this chapter are free from biases due to selection and endogenous programs so long as people do not choose to live in a metropolitan area based on its potential for Tiebout choice.

18. Tiebout (1956) initiated a large body of research on local public goods. Tiebout choice is the process whereby households explicitly choose their place of residence based on the availability and costs of local public goods and other amenities.

19. Moreover, it would be wrong to look at the partial effect of school choice programs without considering an area's potential for Tiebout choice. The potential choice provided by interdistrict choice programs depends on the underlying Tiebout process.

Implementing the Empirical Strategy

I use a number of linear regressions to carry out this empirical strategy. In each, a measure of school policy, such as hours of homework, is regressed on variables that describe the demography of a school and on a measure of Tiebout choice in the metropolitan area. A few issues arise in estimating these regressions.[20]

The first issue is how to measure the amount of Tiebout choice in a metropolitan area. One needs a measure that reflects the costs to a household of choosing among school districts within the area. But I am not primarily concerned with the costs of changing residences—such costs do not differ much among metropolitan areas and are incurred infrequently. Rather, I focus on the chronic losses of well-being associated with choosing a residence that would not be preferred other than for its association with a particular school.

Examples will clarify this idea. Suppose that a metropolitan area has one very large school district that covers most of the housing available in the area. Then a family might have to choose a residence with an undesirably long work commute for the parents in order to exercise Tiebout choice. Similarly, suppose that a metropolitan area contains only a few school districts and that they are stratified, so that one has the best houses. Then a middle-income family may only be able to choose from one or two districts that contain residences that match its housing desires. If the middle-income family prefers a school with a very challenging curriculum, and if this is an unusual preference for families of its income, it may not be able to satisfy its schooling desires unless it chooses to reside in a school district where it must overconsume housing (buy a better house than it desires) and sacrifice other types of consumption. By contrast, if the metropolitan area has twenty school districts that include houses for middle-income

---

20. The regression equations are of the type

$$P_{ijk} = C_k\lambda + X_{ijk}\mu + \omega_k + \omega_{ijk}.$$

Here, C_k is a measure of the potential for Tiebout choice in metropolitan area k, ω_k is a metropolitan-area wide residual, and ω_{ijk} is a school-specific residual. The formal identifying assumption is $\text{cov}(C_k,\omega_k) = 0$. This equation must be estimated with a metropolitan area–specific random effect, as well as a school-specific random effect. In practice, this requires an adjustment to the standard errors as described by Moulton (1986). It is not necessary to allow both a school-specific random effect and a district-specific random effect, because I observe only one school within each district.

families, middle-income parents who prefer very challenging curriculums can sort themselves into one of the twenty districts and satisfy their preferences without being forced to overconsume housing and underconsume other goods.

In other work I have demonstrated that a good measure of the number and variety of school districts in a metropolitan area is a Herfindahl index of enrollment concentration.[21] Herfindahl indexes are a widely accepted means of measuring market concentration because they take account of both the number of choices and the availability of each choice. I construct a Herfindahl index for each metropolitan area in the following manner. First, I compute each school district's share of total enrollment in the metropolitan area. I square these shares, sum the squared shares within each metropolitan area, and then multiply by -1.[22] The resulting measure is easy to interpret. The Herfindahl index is equal to -1 if there is no choice at all—that is, if one school district contains all the enrollment. The index moves toward zero as the number of school districts increases and as enrollment is spread more evenly across these districts. For instance, metropolitan areas with two, five, twenty, and fifty equal-sized school districts have indexes equal to, respectively, -0.5, -0.2, -0.05, and -0.02. The key points to remember are, first, that the lower the index, the less choice among districts there is in a metropolitan area; and second, that the difference between a metropolitan area with no choice and one with a lot of choice is approximately a one-unit change in the index.

The average metropolitan area in the United States has an index of Tiebout choice equal to -0.17. There is, however, a great deal of variation:

---

21. Hoxby (forthcoming).

22. Formally, the index for metropolitan area k is equal to

$$-\sum_{j=1}^{j} s_{jk}^2 ,$$

where s_{jk} is school district j's share of the total enrollment in metropolitan area k. The index is multiplied by -1 so that it increases when choice increases. I base the index on enrollment because this provides the most informative summary of the relevant choice and availability of school districts—for instance, whether the housing stock and neighborhood are appropriate for school-aged children. In Hoxby (forthcoming), however, I demonstrate that the results are not sensitive to basing the index on alternative variables, such as the land area of a school district or the number of housing units that it contains. Borland and Howsen (1992) were the first to use a Herfindahl index in this type of context.

the standard deviation in the index is 0.18. Large metropolitan areas do not necessarily have a lot of districts. For example, Miami is a large metropolitan area but has only one school district. At the other extreme, Boston has seventy school districts within a thirty-minute commute of its downtown and 130 districts within the boundaries of its metropolitan area. If one controls for the size of the metropolitan area—by controlling for population, the square of population, land area, and the square of land area—the standard deviation is only slightly smaller at 0.16.

The second issue that arises in estimating the effect of Tiebout choice is due to the fact that successful school districts tend to attract enrollment. That is, parents with school-aged children are likely to concentrate in school districts that are good in unobservable ways—for instance, districts with unusually dedicated teachers. Such parental behavior biases results toward finding that metropolitan areas with highly concentrated enrollment (that is, little choice among districts) have desirable schools. Put another way, reverse causality can generate bias. A central city district that offers good schools keeps residents in the city who would otherwise live in suburban districts, thus concentrating enrollment in one district. In this case, because there are good schools, one observes little choice. One does not observe good schools because there is little choice.

In order to reduce such bias due to reverse causality, one must focus on a metropolitan area's *potential* for Tiebout choice. That is, one wants to know if the metropolitan area is inherently likely to be divided into many districts, and to ignore enrollment concentration resulting from parents choosing more successful districts. To achieve this, I estimate the regressions by instrumental variables (IV), where the instrumental variables are natural boundaries in a metropolitan area. Intuitively, the procedure works as follows. When metropolitan areas were initially divided into districts, boundaries often followed natural boundaries, such as streams, because these affected the time it took students to travel to school. As modes of travel changed and natural boundaries were bridged, the importance of such considerations waned, but the residual influence of natural boundaries can still be seen in school district boundaries today. Because natural boundaries affected district boundaries long before modern school conduct, instrumental variables estimation isolates variation in school districting that is independent of responses to school conduct. As a measure of natural boundaries, I use the number of features classified by the U.S. Geological Survey as streams (rivers, brooks, streams, all other linear natural water features) in the metropolitan area.[23] I show both ordinary least squares (OLS) and instrumental variables estimates.

The final issue that arises in estimating the regressions is how to differentiate between the effects of choice and the effects of a homogeneous student body.[24] This issue is somewhat subtle. Schools do not base their policies only on the average characteristics of students and the force of parents' preferences, but also take into account the homogeneity of their students. For instance, an administrator with heterogeneous students may choose a highly structured school environment, in order to minimize opportunities for conflict among students. If the administrator had, on average, similar students who were more homogeneous, he might choose a less structured environment. The fact that homogeneity may affect policy is problematic because greater Tiebout choice generally results in more homogeneous student bodies. The effects of choice should be distinguished from the effects of homogeneity not only for intellectual reasons, but also because many proposed choice reforms, in contrast to Tiebout choice, explicitly constrain the degree to which students can sort themselves into homogeneous schools.

To address the issue, I control for measures of population homogeneity within districts in the regressions. The inclusion of homogeneity measures

23. I used 1:24,000 U.S. Geological Survey quadrangle maps and the Geographic Names Information System to gather topographical data. I divide streams into two types: large and small. The idea behind this division is the following. Some metropolitan areas are not generally "watery" but do have a few large streams. These are more formidable natural barriers, more likely to form county boundaries, and are rarely crossed by school districts, even when districts are consolidated. Other metropolitan areas are watery and have a large number of small streams. In many cases, these metropolitan areas were initially divided into smaller school districts, but it is more likely that the districts were consolidated across the small streams over time. Hoxby (forthcoming) contains details of the data and results of overidentification tests for the exogeneity of the number of streams as an instrumental variable.

The relevant identifying assumption is that there is nothing about the number of streams that induces the population of a metropolitan area to display characteristics that have independent effects on school curriculums. It is worth pointing out that the number of streams in a metropolitan area is not correlated with industrial composition. This is because the majority of classified streams at the 1:24,000 level are large enough to provide a natural barrier but not large enough to motivate industrial location.

The results of the first-stage regression are as follows. The estimated coefficient on the number of large streams (divided by 10) is 0.2143, with a standard error of 0.0470. The estimated coefficient on the number of small streams (divided by 100) is 0.1056, with a standard error of 0.0356. The standard errors are adjusted for the grouped structure of the data (grouped by schools and metropolitan areas) as described in Moulton (1986). The number of metropolitan areas in the regression is 290, though the first-stage regression for the instrumental variables estimates uses 769 school-level observations and includes all the covariates, except the choice index, listed in table 11A-1 of appendix 11A. Thus the coefficient estimate on the choice index is identified by the two stream variables only.

24. This issue also applies to the common naive methods of estimating the effects of choice.

is the reason why it is essential to use data from the Public School Universe and school district tabulation of the census. These data allow one to calculate measures of within-district homogeneity in family income, educational attainment, race, ethnicity, age, family composition, and house prices.

Results

The estimates of the effect of choice on school policy are presented in tables 11-2 to 11-6. Both OLS and IV estimates are shown, but the IV results are to be preferred for their lack of bias. In any case, the OLS and IV results always have the same signs, though not the same magnitudes. Only the estimated coefficients on the variables of interest are shown, but table 11A-1 shows an example of the full regression results. The small effective sample size does not always allow for precise estimates, so it is useful to check whether the estimated effects on similar dependent variables—for instance, the various measures of parental involvement—have the same sign.[25]

The Effect of Choice on Parental Involvement

Proponents of school choice suggest that parents who have more choice will become more involved in school decisionmaking, while opponents suggest the opposite. Table 11-2 shows the effects of greater Tiebout choice on parental involvement. Both the OLS and IV estimates suggest that choice increases parental involvement. For instance, a one-unit increase in the choice index would lead parents to discuss curriculum with their children 0.6 more times and visit the school once more each year. The same increase in choice would lead the administrator to raise his assessment of parental involvement in policymaking by almost 2 points on a scale ranging from 0 to 4. This is an increase of 2 standard deviations in assessed involvement. This subjective evidence is especially useful because it comes from the policymaker, who is in a position to know how much parents are involved in his decisions. The OLS estimates also suggest that greater

25. I show results from linear estimates because there is no established method of generating efficient standard errors for grouped data in instrumental variables probit and ordered probit estimations. The coefficient estimates from linear estimation are similar to those from IV probit and ordered probit estimation. Angrist (1991) shows that under quite general conditions, linear instrumental variables estimates are consistent for categorical dependent variables.

Table 11-2. *Effect of Choice among Public Schools on Parental Involvement*[a]

	Coefficient on choice index	
Dependent variable	*OLS*	*IV*
Number of times parents have discussed	0.4285	0.6186
curriculum with student	(0.0803)	(0.2762)
	[5.3396]	[2.2401]
Number of times parents visit school in a year	0.0090	0.9630
	(0.0782)	(0.2888)
	[0.1152]	[3.3351]
Percent of parents who attend PTA meetings	10.6285	12.3206
	(5.7153)	(19.3124)
	[1.8596]	[0.6380]
Percent of parents who attend regularly	7.7152	8.0830
scheduled parent-teacher conferences	(5.2737)	(18.1998)
	[1.4630]	[0.4441]
Parent involvement in school policy decisions[b]	0.6741	1.9813
	(0.2291)	(0.7743)
	[2.9430]	[2.5588]
Summary statistic		
Number of observations	769	76

Source: Author's calculations as described in text.

a. Measure of choice is a Herfindahl index based on the enrollment of school districts (see text for further details). It is multiplied by −1, so that an increase in the index indicates an increase in choice, rather than in concentration. Standard errors, adjusted as described in Moulton (1986), are in parentheses. *t* statistics for test of H_0: $\alpha = 0$ are in brackets. The vector **X** includes all the covariates listed in table 11A-1 of appendix 11A.

b. Measured on a scale from 0 (not at all) to 4 (very much).

choice causes a greater percentage of parents to attend PTA meetings and regularly scheduled parent-teacher conferences.

These results suggest that parents think that they get more return from involvement when they have more choice—perhaps because administrators are more willing to set policy in accord with parental preferences when the threat of parent exit is more viable. Such an outcome would be consistent with bargaining theory, which suggests that when a party has better outside options, negotiations result in an agreement closer to the party's preferred position, and thus the party is more likely to engage in negotiation. In other words, the existence of greater exit opportunities does not necessarily mean that the option is exercised more often. Instead, exit opportunities can create greater inside response to voice. It appears that, at least for parents and schools, exit and voice are complementary tools.

The Effect of Choice on the Curriculum

Table 11-3 shows results for three measures of how challenging a school's curriculum is. The three measures all indicate how difficult the courses taken by the school's typical student are, relative to nationally uniform standards. A one-unit increase in the choice index raises the percentage of tenth and twelfth grade students who take AP courses by, respectively, 35 percentage points and 20 percentage points. The same increase in choice would generate a 23 percent increase in the probability that the school's regular mathematics sequence culminates in a twelfth grade class that includes some calculus.

In other words, schools that are under more pressure from parental choice apparently subject their students to more intellectually challenging study. These results are interesting because they confirm survey evidence, in which the majority of parents claim that they want their children to experience more challenging curriculums. The results imply that if left to their own devices, schools would allow students to pursue easier curriculums than parents desire. Perhaps this is not surprising. Even if teachers and administrators wish, in the abstract, that students could pursue difficult material, they bear much of the work of propelling students forward. They must motivate less industrious students, deal with students who are disgruntled about a difficult task, and grade complex and lengthy assignments.

This evidence is also consistent with evidence from one of my previous studies, which shows that students score better on achievement tests and are more likely to attend college if they attend schools that face more competition from other public schools.[26] Jay Girotto and Paul Peterson, in chapter 9 above, demonstrate that student achievement improves when students take more challenging courses. It is reasonable to infer that this is one mechanism in the black box of how school choice translates into student outcomes: schools that face more choice are induced to deliver more

26. See Hoxby (forthcoming).

Table 11-3. *Effect of Choice among Public Schools on the Curriculum*[a]

	Coefficient on choice index	
Dependent variable	OLS	IV
Percent of tenth grade students who take	5.2587	35.5730
AP courses	(2.8795)	(10.5459)
	[1.8263]	[3.3732]
Percent of twelfth grade students who take	11.8423	20.3250
AP courses	(3.9959)	(14.6169)
	[−2.9636]	[1.3905]
Regular math sequence culminates in	26.0900	23.0345
twelfth grade course with some calculus	(12.3550)	(26.4867)
	[2.1117]	[0.8697]
Summary statistic		
Number of observations	769	769

Source: Author's calculations as described in text.

a. Measure of choice is a Herfindahl index based on the enrollment of school districts (see text for further details). It is multiplied by −1, so that an increase in the index indicates an increase in choice, rather than in concentration. Standard errors, adjusted as described in Moulton (1986), are in parentheses. *t* statistics for test of H_0: $\alpha = 0$ are in brackets. The vector X includes all the covariates listed in table 11A-1.

strenuous curriculums to their students, who have higher achievement as a result.

The Effect of Choice on the Academic Environment

In surveys and interviews the majority of parents say that they favor stricter academic standards in schools—that is, schools should set standards and stick to them. Such statements relate to the consistency with which academic standards are applied and to the work habits of students, rather than to the intellectual content of the material. Table 11-4 shows the effects of choice on several variables that encompass possible interpretations of such statements. For instance, one might think of strict standards as a ban on grade inflation, which is measured by the first two dependent variables in the table. The results indicate that schools operating in an environment where parents have more choice allow not less grade inflation but more. For instance, a one-unit increase in the choice index causes English grades

Table 11-4. *Effect of Choice among Public Schools on the Academic Environment*[a]

	Coefficient on choice index	
Dependent variable	OLS	IV
Grade inflation index for English[b]	0.5129	1.4880
	(0.1440)	(0.5020)
	[3.5556]	[2.9760]
Grade inflation index for math[b]	0.8400	1.1321
	(0.1442)	(0.4879)
	[4.3333]	[2.2787]
Hours spent on homework per week	0.6642	1.8083
	(0.3272)	(1.1182)
	[2.0303]	[1.6172]
Number of standardized credits required for high school diploma	0.4136	5.3072
	(0.5450)	(0.9474)
	[0.7589]	[2.7253]
Students place priority on learning[c]	0.6984	0.3160
	(0.1853)	(0.4252)
	[3.7690]	[0.7432]
Students do homework[c]	0.2316	0.4293
	(0.1765)	(0.4071)
	[1.1326]	[1.0544]
Summary statistic		
Number of observations	769	769

Source: Author's calculations as described in text.

a. Measure of choice is a Herfindahl index based on the enrollment of school districts (see text for further details). It is multiplied by −1, so that an increase in the index indicates an increase in choice, rather than in concentration. Standard errors, adjusted as described in Moulton (1986), are in parentheses. t statistics for test of H_0: $\alpha = 0$ are in brackets. The vector X includes all the covariates listed in table 11A-1.

b. The grade inflation index rises by one unit for every letter grade of grade inflation (see text for further details).

c. Measured on a scale from 1 (not at all accurate) to 5 (very accurate).

to inflate by about one and a half letter grades, and math grades by about one letter grade.

This inflation suggests that parents respond to the incentives given by college admissions, assuming that admissions officers have difficulty adjusting fully for grade inflation, since they look at transcripts from so many schools. Alternatively, employers or parents themselves may be misled by inflated grades. For instance, parents may not adjust fully for grade inflation when they examine their children's report cards to determine how well they are matched to their schools. Any or all of these scenarios would explain why more parental pressure would generate grade inflation. Note, however, that the grade inflation goes hand in hand with higher actual achievement. As discussed above, schools that face more choice subject students to more challenging curriculums and induce better performance on standardized tests. Apparently, grade inflation does not mute incentives to perform.[27]

Other dependent variables in table 11-4 measure whether a school induces its students to develop good habits of work and learning. The results indicate that schools are more likely to do so when they are subject to greater choice. A one-unit increase in the choice index causes students to report doing 1.8 more hours of homework each week. It also causes administrators to raise their assessments of students' priority on learning and homework completion rate (the latter estimate is not significantly different from zero at conventional levels of statistical significance.)

Thus real phenomena, such as homework, suggest that parents are reporting honestly when they claim to want strict academic environments. However, strict real standards can apparently be combined with lenient nominal standards, that is, grade inflation. Somewhere there is sufficient "grade illusion"—among parents, college admissions officers, or employers—that the pressures of choice create grade inflation. Fortunately, the inflation does not adversely affect the average student's real achievement.

Overall, this evidence suggests that John Bishop is partly right but too extreme in his analysis of the importance of external examinations in chapter 10 above. Parents are capable of assessing some school policies, such as homework requirements and difficulty of the curriculum, and choosing schools that offer policies closer to their preferences. But the fact that parental choice does not constrain grade inflation suggests that someone is fooled by inflated grades and, in equilibrium, would offer stronger perfor-

27. Costrell (1994) shows that raising standards strengthens performance incentives for some students, while weakening performance incentives for others. Thus the average effect of raising standards depends on how students are distributed relative to the standard. Betts (1997) also investigates this issue. However, these papers assume that standards are absolute and correctly perceived by college admissions officers, employers, and other external authorities. If external authorities are mistaken, grade inflation presents a somewhat different incentive situation: performance incentives will depend on whether the external reward for moving from a B to an A, say, is greater than that for moving from a C to a B.

mance incentives to students if they were able to observe absolute scores accurately.

There is reason to think that the key people fooled by grade inflation are college admissions officers and employers. Admissions officers and employers must compare students from a wide array of secondary schools, they have almost no direct or inside knowledge of what the students experience at different schools, and they have to attempt to control for demographics across students who come from diverse backgrounds. By contrast, parents who are able to choose among school districts face a much simpler inference problem. Generally, they canvass other parents who are similar in terms of demographics and income and ask about their children's actual experiences. They do not want to "control" for demographics, they do not have to correctly assess schools that serve parents with very different incomes, they need not rely exclusively on external indicators of student experience.

The Effect of Choice on a School's Emphasis on Structure and Discipline

Since schools are mainly academic institutions, it is not surprising that parents think of academics first when they think of schools. But after academics, the factor that parents most often cite when they try to explain their choice of schools is discipline. In fact, insistence that discipline should be a priority is one of the most consistent patterns to emerge from parent surveys. It is striking that discipline should consistently rank higher than sports, extracurricular activities, or career and college guidance. However, teachers and administrators often argue that parents do not truly want schools to emphasize discipline. They claim that parents want other people's children to behave well but do not want their own children to be disciplined. It may be that teachers and administrators are focusing on the subset of parents whose children frequently face disciplinary measures. It is likely that such parents' attitudes toward discipline are not representative of the population of parents.

Table 11-5 shows the effects of choice on several variables that measure a school's disciplinary atmosphere. A one-unit increase in the choice index raises the severity of the action taken against a student who causes a classroom disturbance by 0.8 on a scale that ranges from 0 to 3.[28] This

---

28. I focus on classroom disturbances because nearly every school deals with classroom disturbances frequently enough to have a standard response. In contrast, some administrators may only be able to conjecture how they would respond to one student threatening another with a gun.

Table 11-5. *Effect of Choice among Public Schools on the Emphasis on Structure and Discipline*[a]

	Coefficient on choice index	
Dependent variable	OLS	IV
Minutes of class time in school day	21.9715	48.6056
	(10.2871)	(37.1735)
	[2.1358]	[1.3075]
Action taken against student who causes classroom disturbance[b]	0.2661	0.8133
	(0.0993)	(0.3459)
	[2.6811]	[2.3513]
Structured classroom environment[c]	0.4127	1.2115
	(0.1935)	(0.6702)
	[2.1328]	[1.8077]
Structured school day[c]	0.3557	2.3334
	(0.2048)	(0.7345)
	[1.7372]	[3.1769]
Deviation from school rules not tolerated[c]	0.2450	0.8801
	(0.1985)	(0.6924)
	[1.2343]	[1.2711]
School environment is flexible[c]	0.1305	1.5436
	(0.2517)	(0.8894)
	[0.5186]	[1.7356]
Summary statistic		
Number of observations	769	769

Source: Author's calculations as described in text.

a. Measure of choice is a Herfindahl index based on the enrollment of school districts (see text for further details). It is multiplied by −1, so that an increase in the index indicates an increase in choice, rather than in concentration. Standard errors, adjusted as described in Moulton (1986), are in parentheses. *t* statistics for test of H_0: $\alpha = 0$ are in brackets. The vector X includes all the covariates listed in table 11A-1.

b. For first offense, measured on a scale from 0 (warning) to 3 (expulsion).

c. Measured on a scale from 1 (not at all accurate) to 5 (very accurate).

point difference is the difference between "a warning" and "a minor action against the student" or between "a minor action against the student" and "suspension." The table also shows that administrators who face more choice state that their schools and classrooms are more structured. Similarly, schools that face more choice are less likely to be described as having a flexible environment.

It appears that Tiebout choice pressures schools to emphasize discipline and provide more structure. Thus there appears to be some truth in parents' claims that they prefer schools that deliver discipline and structure. The results imply that if allowed to set policy on their own, teachers and administrators would choose less structure and discipline than would parents. One need not infer that teachers and administrators actually like disciplined students less than do parents. It may be that school staff bear more of the costs associated with maintaining school discipline. Bishop points out that staff who confront students and mete out consistent discipline end up with hostile working conditions.[29]

The Effect of Choice on the Priority of Sports and Extracurricular Activities

If parents place more weight on athletics or other extracurricular programs than do school staff, greater parental choice would cause schools to shift emphasis from academics to extracurricular programs. This concern is often voiced by opponents of school choice, even though in representative surveys the average parents rank sports and extracurricular activities low among their reasons for choosing a school. Nevertheless, it is a possibility.

Table 11-6 reports results relating sports and other extracurricular activities to choice. They do not confirm the fear that more choice for parents would expand the priority given to athletics and extracurricular activities. None of the first three measures—a subjective assessment of whether the school emphasizes sports, the ratio of physical education faculty to faculty teaching core subjects, and the number of extracurricular activities sponsored by the school—has a statistically significant relationship with the choice index. The next three measures are the percentages of students who participate in, respectively, varsity sports, intramural sports, and band, choir, or orchestra. The estimated coefficients on these measures indicate that a one-unit increase in the choice index lowers the percentage of students who participate in varsity sports by 6.4 percentage points and the percentage who participate in band, choir, or orchestra by 8.6 percentage points.

Overall, the evidence in table 11-6 is too inconsistent to warrant the conclusion that choice actually suppresses sports and other extracurricular programs. However, it does not support the hypothesis that choice would sacrifice academic programs to extracurricular activities.

29. See chapter 9 above and Bishop (1996).

Table 11-6. *Effect of Choice among Public Schools on the Priority*
of Sports and Extracurricular Activities[a]

	Coefficient on choice index	
Dependent variable	OLS	IV
School emphasizes sports	−0.1300	−0.6858
	(0.2562)	(0.9008)
	[−0.5075]	[0.7614]
Ratio of physical education teachers to	−0.0701	0.0280
core subject teachers	(0.0848)	(0.0247)
	[−0.8271]	[1.1336]
Number of extracurricular activities sponsored	1.2512	0.7849
by school	(2.5781)	(0.8191)
	[0.4853]	[0.9582]
Percent of students who participate in	−0.1988	−0.0638
varsity sports	(0.1185)	(0.0346)
	[−1.6783]	[−1.8439]
Percent of students who participate in	0.1068	−0.0265
intramural sports	(0.1297)	(0.0379)
	[0.8238]	[−0.6992]
Percent of students who participate in band,	−0.1240	−0.0864
choir, or orchestra	(0.1064)	(0.0313)
	[−1.1654]	[−2.7648]
Summary statistic		
Number of observations	769	769

Source: Author's calculations as described in text.

a. Measure of choice is a Herfindahl index based on the enrollment of school districts (see text for further details). It is multiplied by −1, so that an increase in the index indicates an increase in choice, rather than in concentration. Standard errors, adjusted as described in Moulton (1986), are in parentheses. *t* statistics for test of H$_0$: α = 0 are in brackets. The vector X includes all the covariates listed in table 11A-1.

b. Measured on a scale from 1 (not at all accurate) to 5 (very accurate).

The Importance of Accounting for Selection and Endogenous Programs

In introducing my empirical strategy, I emphasized the importance of accounting for selection and endogenous programs. In this section I briefly discuss results from naive strategies to demonstrate that selection and endogenous programs do generate results that are biased, and thus difficult to interpret in any useful way. These results are reported in table 11-7.

First, I compare choice and nonchoice schools. To form an indicator variable for whether an individual school is a choice school, I use two questions on the NELS: whether the school is a magnet school and whether the school is a choice school. I call these schools choice schools to indicate that they only enroll students who choose to attend them, but a choice school can exist in a district where students are not generally allowed to choose their school. For instance, typically only some students qualify to choose whether to attend a magnet school. Sixteen percent of the schools in the NELS are described by their administrators as either magnet or choice schools.

Estimates based on comparing choice and nonchoice schools will suffer from selection bias if the parents and students who choose their schools differ in unobservable ways from the general population. The results will be difficult to interpret if they suffer from bias. One cannot confidently predict the sign of the bias, because choice schools draw from both ends of the student spectrum. Some magnet schools enroll only high-aptitude students, but others enroll only students who are likely to drop out.

As expected, the results in table 11-7 present an inconsistent picture. For instance, choice schools tend to have parents who discuss curriculums with their children less often, but also tend to have higher assessed levels of parental involvement in decisionmaking. Choice schools have slightly greater percentages of tenth graders taking AP courses, but are less likely to have regular mathematics sequences that culminate in a twelfth grade course than contains some calculus. They have less grade inflation, but no evidence of more homework. They have a higher ratio of physical education teachers to core subject teachers, but administrators' assessments suggest that their emphasis on sports is no greater. The only pattern that stands out clearly is that choice schools provide a less structured environment and more lenient discipline than other schools. This finding is reassuring, because choice schools, regardless of whether they are targeted to high-ability students or likely dropouts, often try to free students from conventional constraints on the pace and content of learning.

Next, I compare choice and nonchoice districts. I form the indicator for choice districts using information on intradistrict choice programs from state departments of education. To be classified as a choice district, a district must routinely and generally allow students to choose their school

Table 11-7. *Effect of Other Measures of School Choice on Curricular and Extracurricular Policies*[a]

	Measure of choice	
Dependent variable	Choice school	Choice district
Number of times parents have discussed curriculum with student	−0.0425 (0.0227) [−1.8764]	0.0002 (0.0166) [0.0120]
Parent involvement in school policy decisions[b]	0.2518 (0.0702) [3.5895]	0.0251 (0.0508) [0.4946]
Percent of tenth grade students who take AP courses	1.2666 (0.8310) [1.5242]	0.5514 (0.5968) [0.9239]
Regular mathematics sequence culminates in twelfth grade course with some calculus	−0.1153 (0.0387) [−2.9793]	−0.0624 (0.0276) [−2.2650]
Action taken against student who causes a classroom disturbance[c]	−0.0550 (0.0280) [−1.9643]	−0.0348 (0.0205) [−1.7017]
Structured classroom environment[c]	−0.1762 (0.0543) [−3.2479]	−0.1048 (0.0398) [−2.6365]
School emphasizes sports[d]	−0.0384 (0.0740) [−0.5189]	0.1625 (0.0541) [3.0065]
Ratio of physical education teachers to core subject teachers	0.0222 (0.0079) [2.8101]	−0.0034 (0.0058) [−0.5862]
Ratio of math grades to standardized math test score[e]	−0.0008 (0.0005) [−1.7778]	0.0002 (0.0004) [0.5714]
Hours spent on homework per week	0.0326 (0.1020) [0.3196]	−0.0592 (0.0744) [−0.7957]
Years of required English in grades 9–12	−0.0061 (0.0232) [−0.2635]	−0.0687 (0.0166) [−4.1511]

Source: Author's calculations as described in text.

a. Measures of choice are indicator variables for a school being a choice school or a district being a choice district (see text for further details). Standard errors, adjusted as described in Moulton (1986), are in parentheses. t statistics for test of H_0: $\alpha = 0$ are in brackets. The vector X includes all the covariates listed in table 11A-1.

b. Measured on a scale from 0 (not at all) to 4 (very much).

c. For first offense, measured on a scale from 0 (warning) to 3 (expulsion).

d. Measured on a scale from 1 (not at all accurate) to 5 (very accurate).

e. Multiplied by 20.

instead of assigning students to schools based on their area of residence.[30] Eight percent of the districts in the NELS are choice districts. Estimates based on comparing choice and nonchoice districts will suffer from bias if intradistrict choice programs are endogenous responses to district circumstances. Once again, if they suffer from bias, the results will be difficult to interpret, but one cannot confidently predict the sign of the bias. For instance, the intradistrict choice program in Cambridge, Massachusetts, is the brainchild of well-funded administrators who pride themselves on being at the cutting edge of educational policy. In contrast, the program in Richmond, Virginia, is part of a court-mandated desegregation plan.

Apart from reduced emphasis on structure and discipline, similar to that shown for choice schools, the results based on choice districts in table 11-7 do not show a consistent pattern. Comparison of choice and nonchoice districts does not reveal a relationship with parental involvement. Choice districts are less likely to end their regular mathematics sequences with calculus, but lack of emphasis on challenging courses is not confirmed by the percentage of students who take AP classes. Administrators in choice districts are more likely to say that the school emphasizes sports, but emphasis on sports is not confirmed by the ratio of physical education teachers to core subject teachers.

In summary, the results for choice schools and choice districts appear mainly to reflect the types of student and types of district likely to use such programs. One cannot confidently interpret any of the results in table 11-7 as the effects of giving more sway to parental preferences through choice. Naive comparisons produce results are that difficult to interpret and are unreliable indicators of what the average parent seeks in a school.

Conclusions

Using data on the policies of 769 school districts matched to detailed data on demographics, I find consistent confirmation that what parents say they want out of schools is what they choose when they have the opportunity to do so. I find that schools operating in metropolitan areas where parents can

---

30. Districts are not classified as choice districts if they allow intradistrict migration only for peculiar circumstances or particular students, such as those who are gifted, likely to drop out, or disabled. In choice districts, students' selections are often constrained by rules about schools' enrollment, racial composition, and gender composition.

choose more easily among school districts exhibit more challenging curriculums, stricter academic requirements, and more structured and discipline-oriented environments. I do not find that such schools place a greater emphasis on sports or extracurricular activities. These results confirm survey evidence that the average parents consider athletic and extracurricular programs a low priority compared with academics, discipline, and school atmosphere. Furthermore, I find that parents are more involved in school policymaking and visit schools more often when they have more choice. Choice appears to make parents more, not less, interested in what their local schools do.

An intriguing result is that greater parental choice appears to cause grade inflation. This suggests that someone is fooled by nominal grades, whether college admissions officers, employers, or parents. Fortunately, the grade inflation does not appear to have real effects: students in schools that are subjected to more choice achieve higher scores on standardized tests. That is, the pressure of choice causes schools to raise real standards but lower nominal standards.

In general, the results suggest that choice, which would give parents' preferences more weight relative to those of teachers and administrators, would not undermine academic and disciplinary standards in U.S. schools. On average, parents appear to choose higher academic standards and stricter environments than do school staff. This is not the same as saying the teachers and administrators, as individuals or parents themselves, do not value good academic work or good behavior. The difference in attitude between parents and staff may be due to the fact that it is the staff who have to enforce higher standards in schools, and so they give more weight to the effort that enforcement activities require.

The messages to take away from this study are that parents actually want what they say they want, and that they have relatively traditional goals for schools: students who have learned academic skills, good work habits, and self-discipline. The results imply that school reforms, such as vouchers and charter schools, that allow parents to put more pressure on school policy are likely to trigger somewhat higher academic standards on average, not a collapse of standards.

Appendix 11A
Example of Full Regression Results

Table 11A-1 presents an example of the full regression results. The estimated equation is for the first dependent variable listed in table 11-2: number of times parents have discussed curriculum with a student.

Table 11A-1. *Full Regression Results*[a]

Variable	Coefficient
Choice index	0.4285 (0.0802)
Coefficient of variation for household income in district[b]	−0.0128 (0.0098)
Coefficient of variation for educational attainment in district	0.0178 (0.3281)
Coefficient of variation for monthly housing costs in district[c]	0.0460 (0.0971)
Coefficient of variation for percentage of income spent on housing costs in district	−0.0826 (0.0993)
Coefficient of variation for age in district	−0.0497 (0.0183)
Herfindahl index of racial homogeneity in district[d]	−0.0213 (0.0969)
Median household income in district[b]	0.0037 (0.0038)
Average education attainment in district	0.0458 (0.0213)
Average monthly housing costs in district[c]	0.1034 (0.0463)
Average percentage of income spent on housing in district	−0.0039 (0.0189)
Average age in district	0.0126 (0.0162)
Percent of households receiving AFDC in district	−0.0163 (0.0047)
Percent of households with school-aged children in district	0.0044 (0.0043)
Percent of households below poverty level in district	−0.0027 (0.0049)
Percent of labor force unemployed in district	−0.0133 (0.0096)

(Continued)

Table 11A-1. *Full Regression Results (Continued)*[a]

Variable	Coefficient
Percent of adult population 4-year college graduates in district	0.0039
	(0.0022)
Percent of population 65 or older in district	0.0035
	(0.0117)
Percent of black students in school	−0.0025
	(0.0012)
Percent of Hispanic students in school	−0.0007
	(0.0014)
Percent of Asian students in school	−0.0138
	(0.0059)
Percent of students eligible for free lunch in school	−0.0007
	(0.0009)
Population density in district[e]	0.0131
	(0.0067)
School's enrollment in a single grade[c]	−0.0220
	(0.0082)
Population in district[f]	0.0705
	(0.0875)
Population squared in district[g]	0.0081
	(0.0191)
Land area in district[h]	0.1903
	(0.0643)
Land area squared in district[i]	−0.0248
	(0.0107)
Constant and 8 indicator variables for census divisions	yes
Summary statistic	
R^2	0.35
Number of observations	769

Source: Author's calculations as described in text.

a. Dependent variable is number of times parents have discussed curriculum with student. Estimates are by OLS. All covariates are included. Standard errors, adjusted as described in Moulton (1986), are in parentheses.

b. Divided by 1,000.

c. Divided by 100.

d. Based on racial and ethnic group.

e. Population per square mile, divided by 1,000.

f. Divided by 1,000,000.

g. Divided by $1,000,000^2$.

h. In square miles, divided by 1,000.

i. Divided by $1,000^2$.

References

Allen, Jeanne. 1992. *School Choice Programs: What's Happening in the States.* Washington: Heritage Foundation Press.

Angrist, Joshua. 1991. "Instrumental Variables Estimation of Average Treatment Effects in Econometrics and Epidemiology." Working Paper 115. Cambridge, Mass.: National Bureau of Economic Research.

Betts, Julian. 1997. "Do Grading Standards Affect the Incentive to Learn?" Discussion Paper 97-22. University of California, San Diego.

Bishop, John H. 1996. "The Impact of Curriculum-Based External Examinations on School Priorities and Student Learning." *International Journal of Education Research* 23(8).

Borland, Melvin V., and Roy M. Howsen. 1992. "Student Academic Achievement and the Degree of Market Concentration in Education." *Economics of Education Review* 2(1): 31–39.

Chubb, John E., and Terry M. Moe. 1990. *Politics, Markets, and America's Schools.* Brookings.

Clune, William, and John Witte, eds. 1990. *Choice and Control in American Education.* Vol. 2, *The Practice of Choice, Decentralization, and School Restructuring.* London: Falmer Press.

Coleman, James S., and Thomas Hoffer. 1987. *Public and Private High Schools.* Basic Books.

Costrell, Robert M. "A Simple Model of Educational Standards." *American Economic Review* 84(4): 956–71.

Fuller, Bruce, Richard Elmore, and Gary Orfield. 1996. *Who Chooses? Who Loses? Culture, Institutions, and the Unequal Effects of School Choice.* New York: Teachers College Press.

Greene, Jay P., Paul E. Peterson, and Jiangtao Du. 1996. "The Effectiveness of School Choice in Milwaukee: A Secondary Analysis of Data from the Program's Evaluation." Occasional Paper 96-3. Harvard University Program in Education Policy and Governance.

Greene, Jay P., William G. Howell, and Paul E. Peterson. 1997. "Lessons from the Cleveland Scholarship Program." Occasional Paper. Harvard University Program in Education Policy and Governance.

Grolier, Inc. 1983. "The Grolier Survey: What Parents Believe about Education." Danbury, Conn.

Hess, Frederic. 1998. "Initiation without Implementation: Policy Churn and the Plight of Urban School Reform." In *Rethinking School Governance,* edited by Bryan Hassel and Paul E. Peterson. Brookings.

Hirschman, Albert O. 1971. *Exit, Voice, and Loyalty.* Harvard University Press.

Hoxby, Caroline M. 1994. "Do Private Schools Provide Competition for Public Schools?" Working Paper 4978. Cambridge, Mass.: National Bureau of Economic Research.

———. 1996. "Evidence on Private School Vouchers: Effects on Schools and Students. In *Performance-Based Approaches to School Reform,* edited by Helen F. Ladd. Brookings.

———. "What Do America's Traditional Forms of School Choice Teach Us about Reform?" In *Rethinking School Governance,* edited by Bryan Hassel and Paul E. Peterson. Brookings.

————. Forthcoming. "Does Competition among Public Schools Benefit Students and Taxpayers?" *American Economic Review*.

Kirkpatrick, David W. 1990. *Choice in Schooling*. Loyola University Press.

Moe, Terry. 1995. *Private Vouchers*. Stanford, Calif.: Hoover Institution Press.

Moulton, Brent R. 1986. "Random Group Effects and the Precision of Regression Estimates." *Journal of Econometrics* 32(3): 385–97.

Murnane, Richard J. 1984. "A Review Essay—Comparisons of Public and Private Schools: Lessons from the Uproar." *Journal of Human Resources* 19(2): 263–77.

Parent-Teacher Association of the United States. 1991. "The Second PTA/Chrysler National Parent Survey: A Study of Parental Involvement in Children's Education." Los Angeles: Newsweek, Inc.

————. 1993. "The Third PTA National Education Survey: A Study of Attitudes and Behavior Regarding Children's Education." Los Angeles: Newsweek, Inc.

Tiebout, Charles. 1956. "A Pure Theory of Local Public Expenditures." *Journal of Political Economy* 64(2): 416–24.

Tucker, Allyson, and William Lauber. 1995. *School Choice Programs: What's Happening in the States*. Washington: Heritage Foundation.

U.S. Department of Education, Office of Educational Research and Improvement. 1991. *Private Schools in the United States: A Statistical Profile, with Comparison to Public Schools*. Government Printing Office.

Williams, Mary Frase. 1983. "Parents and School Choice: A Household Survey." U.S. Department of Education, Office of Educational Research and Improvement. Government Printing Office.

PAUL E. PETERSON
DAVID E. MYERS
WILLIAM G. HOWELL
DANIEL P. MAYER

12

The Effects of School Choice in New York City

OVER THE PAST FEW YEARS, the Congress and many state legislatures have put forward proposals that would offer families vouchers or scholarships so that they may choose among a wide range of public and private schools. In 1990 the Wisconsin legislature enacted a pilot program giving public school students access to secular private schools in the City of Milwaukee; in 1996 the legislature expanded this program to include religious schools. After surviving a constitutional challenge in state courts, the program went into effect in the fall of 1998. A similar program for Cleveland, enacted by the Ohio legislature, began its third year of operation

We wish to thank the School Choice Scholarships Foundation (SCSF) for cooperating fully with this evaluation. This research has been supported by grants from the following: the Achelis Foundation, the Bodman Foundation, the Lynde and Harry Bradley Foundation, the Donner Foundation, the Milton and Rose D. Friedman Foundation, the John M. Olin Foundation, the David and Lucile Packard Foundation, the Smith Richardson Foundation, and the Spencer Foundation. We are grateful to Kristin Kearns Jordan and other members of the SCSF staff for their cooperation and assistance with data collection. We received helpful advice from Paul Hill, Christopher Jencks, Donald Rock, and Donald Rubin. Julia Kim was instrumental in preparing the survey and test score data and in implementing many of the analyses reported in the paper. Additional research assistance was provided by David Campbell, Rachel Deyette, and Jennifer Hill; staff assistance was provided by Shelley Weiner. The methodology, analyses of data, reported findings, and interpretations are the sole responsibility of the authors and are not subject to the approval of the SCSF or of any foundation providing support for this research.

317

in the fall of 1998. Florida has established a program scheduled to go into effect in fall 1999. At the federal level, a pilot program for the District of Columbia received congressional approval in 1998, but was vetoed by President Bill Clinton.

Many interest groups, political leaders, and policy analysts have debated the desirability of continuing and expanding these and other ongoing school choice programs. Supporters of school choice assert the following:

—low-income inner city children learn more in private schools;

—the more orderly educational climate in private schools enhances learning opportunities;

—private schools use their limited resources more efficiently;

—families develop closer communications with schools that they have chosen themselves;

—school choice reduces the amount of mobility from school to school, both within the school year and from one year to the next; and

—choice fosters racial and ethnic integration.[1]

Critics challenge these claims by arguing as follows:

—any perceived learning gains in private schools are due to the more selected nature of private-school families;

—private schools select out the "best and the brightest," leaving behind the disadvantaged;

—low-income families choose schools more on the basis of location, religious affiliation, and sports programs than educational quality;

—public schools have a broader range of programs to serve needy populations;

—when choices are available mismatches often occur, and private schools expel problem students, adding to the instability of the education of children from low-income inner city families;

—private school rules, such as uniforms and dress codes, interfere with a child's creativity;

—private schools balkanize the population into racially and ethnically homogeneous educational environments.[2]

---

1. Recent works that make a case for school choice include Brandl (1998); Coulson (1999); Cobb (1992); Bonsteel and Bonilla (1997). For a collection of essays that report mainly positive effects of school choice, see Peterson and Hassel (1998).

2. See Ascher, Fruchter, and Berne (1996); Carnegie Foundation for the Advancement of Teaching (1992); Gutmann (1987); Levin (1998); Fuller, Elmore, and Orfield (1996); Rasell and Rothstein (1993); Cookson (1994).

Much of the debate over school choice is particularly intense, in part because high-quality information about school choice programs is limited. Although many studies comparing public and private schools have been published, they have been criticized for comparing dissimilar populations. Even when statistical adjustments are made, it remains unclear whether findings describe actual differences between public and private schools or simply differences in the kinds of students and families that attend them.[3]

The best way to make sure that two populations are similar is to assign individuals randomly to treatment and control groups. This procedure is standard in medical research. Recently, it has also been used in a number of educational studies, such as Tennessee's Project STAR, which finds that first grade students learn more if classes are smaller.[4] Until now, though, this type of research design has not been used carefully to study the question of school choice.

In this paper we report outcomes from a randomized experiment in New York City made possible by the privately funded School Choice Scholarships Foundation (SCSF). Under the pilot program, a lottery allocates scholarships randomly to applicants, the lottery is administered by an independent evaluation team that can guarantee its integrity, and baseline data on student test performance and family background characteristics are collected from students and their families prior to the lottery. The first year follow-up has a response rate of approximately 83 percent. Inasmuch as data of this quality have not previously been available, the program provides the best opportunity to estimate the effects of a school choice program on student test performance and parental perceptions of school life.

The School Choice Scholarships Foundation Program

In February 1997, the SCSF announced that it would provide 1,300 scholarships worth up to $1,400 annually for four years to children from low-income families who were then attending public schools. The scholarships could be applied toward the cost of attending a private school, either religious or secular. SCSF received initial application forms from over 20,000

---

3. Major studies that find positive educational benefits from attending private schools include Coleman, Hoffer, and Kilgore (1982); Chubb and Moe (1990); Neal (1996). Critiques of these studies are found in Goldberger and Cain (1982); Wilms (1985).

4. See Mosteller (1995). Also, see chapter 6 by Frederick Mosteller and chapter 7 by Eric Hanushek in this volume.

students between February and late April 1997. In order to become eligible for a scholarship, children had to be entering grades one through five in fall 1997, live in New York City, attend a public school at the time of application, and come from families with incomes low enough to qualify for the federal free school lunch program. To ascertain eligibility, students and an adult member of their family were asked to attend meetings to verify their family income and public school attendance. Only families who attended these sessions and documented their eligibility were considered for a scholarship.

Since many more families applied than scholarships were available, a lottery was held to ensure that every family had a fair chance of being offered a scholarship. This evaluation compares two statistically equivalent groups: 1,000 scholarship families and 960 "control" families, randomly chosen from those who had applied.[5] After the lottery, the SCSF assisted scholarship families in finding private school placements. In mid-September 1997, the foundation reported that places had been found at 225 private schools for approximately 75 percent of all those offered scholarships.

Data Collection

During the verification sessions, students were asked to take the Iowa Tests of Basic Skills in reading and mathematics. Students in kindergarten applying for a scholarship for first grade were exempted from this requirement. Parents were asked to provide information on their satisfaction with the school their children were then attending, their involvement in their children's education, and their demographic characteristics.[6] These sessions took place during March, April, and early May 1997.

The response rate on the baseline surveys and tests was 100 percent, because completion of the instruments was a prerequisite to participating in the program. Since scholarships were allocated by a lottery, there were few differences between scholarship recipients and the control group. However, the baseline test scores of nonrecipients were somewhat higher.[7]

5. The procedures for constructing the analysis sample with 1,000 scholarship families and 960 control families are described in Hill, Rubin, and Thomas (1998).

6. Questionnaires are available from Mathematica Policy Research on request.

7. These findings are reported in Peterson and others (1997) and also at (http://data.fas. harvard.edu/pepgl [June 1999]).

The first-year follow-up data were collected in April, May, and June of 1998. The families were invited to attend sessions during which students took the Iowa Test in Basic Skills in mathematics and reading and adult family members completed surveys that asked a wide range of questions about the educational experiences of their oldest child within the age range eligible for a scholarship. Students in grades three, four, and five were also asked to complete short questionnaires.

Eighty-three percent of those selected for participation attended the testing and questionnaire sessions. This high response rate was achieved in part because the SCSF conditioned the renewal of scholarships on partici-pation in the evaluation. Nonrecipients who were selected for the control group were compensated for their expenses and told that they would auto-matically be eligible to apply for a new lottery if they participated in these follow-up sessions.[8]

Data Analysis and Reporting Procedures

The analysis of the data from the first year of the SCSF program takes advantage of the fact that the scholarships were awarded by lottery. As a result, it is possible to compare two groups of students who were similar, on average, in almost all respects except that the members of the control group were not offered scholarships. Two questions frame the analysis reported here. First, what was the effect of the offer of a scholarship on a group of low-income applicants, as measured by test scores and as perceived by the applicants themselves? And second, what was the effect of attending a pri-vate school?

For some analysts, the crucial policy question is as follows: what hap-pens when a school choice program is put into effect? What are the impacts on the population of low-income families who apply for a school choice scholarship? This is similar to a question often asked in medical research: what will happen if a particular pill is marketed? How will the health of potential users be altered, whether or not all patients use the pill as prescribed?

---

8. For a comparison of the characteristics of respondents and nonrespondents, see Peterson and others (1998); also at (http://data.fas.harvard.edu/pepgl [June 1999]).

But other analysts also want an answer to a second question: what is the impact of attending a private school? Specifically, they want to know what difference it makes whether children from low-income inner-city families attend public or private schools. The parallel question in medical research is: what are the consequences of actually taking a pill, as prescribed? The answer to this second question requires comparison between private school students and similar individuals remaining in public school.[9]

Thus in addressing these two questions below, we present four types of information: the responses of all those offered a scholarship, the estimated impact of being offered a scholarship, the responses of all those who attended private school, and the estimated impact of attending private school.

The analytical techniques needed to address these two questions differ in important ways. The first question can be answered straightforwardly, by comparing the responses of those who were offered a scholarship with the responses of the control group. Because scholarships were awarded at random, the two groups may be assumed to be, on average, statistically equivalent, save for the offer of a scholarship. Any differences in outcomes between the two groups can be attributed to the offer.[10]

To compute the effects of a scholarship offer on children's test scores, we estimate statistical models that take into account whether a student was offered a scholarship, as well as baseline reading and math test scores and variables that define the randomization process. Baseline test scores were included to adjust for chance differences between the scores of treatment and control groups on the achievement tests, and to increase the precision of the estimated impacts. We use a similar approach to compute the effects of the program on the parent and student survey responses. However, we

9. To compute the program's impact on those who attended private school, we used an instrumental variables estimator; see Angrist, Imbens, and Rubin (1996). By comparing those in private school with members of the control group remaining in public school, we can estimate the impact of attending a private school.

10. As discussed in the appendix to Peterson and others (1998), differential response rates for test and control groups could account for some differences between the two groups. The observed results most likely to be affected by differential response rates have to do with likelihood of remaining in school throughout the school year and of returning to the same school the next year. Since nonrespondents are likely to be more mobile, differences between test and control group may be underestimated. The response rate for the treatment group was 84 percent; for the control group, 80 percent.

do not include baseline data in equations predicting parent and student responses.[11]

A Context for Interpreting Program Effects

When considering the effects that we report in this chapter, two contextual issues must be taken into account: first, the possibility of response bias from both the treatment group and the control group, and second, the population to which one can generalize the findings.

RESPONSE BIAS. It is well known that people tend to overestimate their good behaviors and underestimate their less attractive ones. Students and parents are no different. They are likely to overestimate the time spent on homework and volunteering for school, as well as their educational expectations for their children. Parents may also view the school their children attend through rose-tinted glasses; few responsible parents are likely to admit to themselves or to others that they are sending their children to terrible schools.

The interpretation of data from the parental and student surveys in the SCSF program must take into account this very human tendency. No special weight should be placed on the frequency with which a particular type of event is said to take place. For example, one should not take too seriously the claim of third through fifth grade students that they spend, on average, approximately one hour and twenty minutes a day doing homework. But if absolute levels may not be estimated accurately, there is no reason to believe that the two groups of parents differ in the accuracy

11. Since all eligible children within a family could receive a scholarship, some families had two or more children in the evaluation. The presence of several children from the same family produces clustering effects. When clustering is present and analyses are conducted under the assumption of simple random sampling—that is, that all observations are independent—researchers may underestimate the standard error of the estimated impact, overestimate test statistics, and conclude inappropriately that a difference between the treatment group and the control group is statistically significant. To better approximate the true standard error, in the test score analyses we supplement conventional estimates with estimates using the "bootstrap" method; see Stine (1990); Effron (1982). This method provides a direct estimate of the variability in the effect of a treatment without having to make an assumption about the independence of the observations in the sample.

Prior research has generally found that the effects of attendance at private schools on test scores are either positive or insignificant, and therefore the one-tailed test of significance is preferred in the test score analysis. However, in the analysis of responses from parents and children the two-tailed test is preferred, because there exist few prior studies on which to base expectations.

of their reports, since individuals were assigned randomly to the two groups. Therefore we emphasize differences between groups, rather than absolute values obtained for any one group.

GENERALIZATION. Only a tiny fraction of low-income students in the New York public schools were offered scholarships, and these constituted only a small proportion of the students attending New York private schools. A much larger program could conceivably have quite different outcomes. Also, generalizations must be made cautiously whenever applicants differ from the eligible population, as we discuss below.

Characteristics of Applicants

Critics of school choice argue that vouchers do not give low-income families a viable choice of schools. In the words of education sociologist Amy Wells, "white and higher-SES [socioeconomic status] families will no doubt be in a position to take greater advantage of the educational market."[12] Defenders of private schools reply that private schools have an ethnically and economically diverse population. For example, it has been pointed out that the social composition of the Catholic school student population does not differ substantially from that of public schools in New York City.[13]

To be eligible to apply for an SCSF scholarship, a family had to qualify for the federal free lunch program, have a child currently in a public school, and live in New York City. To have one's name entered into the lottery, applicants had to participate in eligibility verification sessions. It is possible that the application process attracted a population substantially different from a cross-section of all those eligible.

To estimate the extent to which the applicant population differed from a cross-section of the eligible population, Rachel Deyette of the Kennedy School of Government has obtained demographic information on those who would have been eligible had scholarships been offered in 1990, the last year in which a national census was taken.[14] Her estimate is based on

12. Wells (1996, p. 47).
13. Blue Ribbon Panel on Catholic Schools (1993).
14. Deyette (1999). Information is drawn from the Integrated Public Use Microdata Series data set of the census, created at the University of Minnesota.

data collected when economic and social conditions in New York differed from those when parents were surveyed. For example, 1990 was a recession year whereas 1997, the year of application, was in the midst of a boom period. Also, education levels of the adult population rose over this period. Nonetheless, her estimates provide a preliminary basis for comparison.

Deyette finds no significant difference between the median income of applicants and that of the eligible population, once income is adjusted for inflation between 1990 and 1997. Her findings for employment rates for fathers are similar. The residential mobility of the applicant population and the eligible population is about the same, and applicant mothers are only slightly more likely to be foreign born than mothers in the eligible population.

The applicants do differ from the eligible population in other respects, however. Applicants are more likely to be dependent on government assistance for income. Also, the applicant population is less likely to be non-Hispanic white and more likely to be African American. But if these findings suggest that the applicant population is particularly disadvantaged, other findings point in the opposite direction. In the applicant population, mothers and fathers are considerably more likely to have some college education, English is more likely to be the primary language of the household, and mothers are more likely to be employed either full or part time.

Program Effects

In tables 12-1 to 12-6, we report program effects in two ways. The first two columns show the impact of being offered a scholarship, and the third and fourth columns show the impact of actually attending a private school. Specifically, the first column provides the responses of those offered a scholarship; the second column gives the difference between the responses of those offered a scholarship and the control group. Subtracting the second column from the first generates the responses of the control group. Similarly, the third column provides the responses of those with children in private school, and the fourth column gives the estimated difference between the responses of those in private school and those members of the control group who remained in public school. For the control group, the percentages reported in the text can be obtained by subtracting the fourth

column from the third column.[15] To facilitate clear discussion of these findings, we comment only on the differences between those in private schools
and the appropriate control group.

Experiences in School

Table 12-1 shows that attendance at a private school had a substantial impact on the daily life of students at school, according to parental reports.
Private school parents were less likely to report the following as serious
problems at school: students destroying property, being late for school,
missing classes, fighting, cheating, and racial conflict. For example, 39 percent of the private school parents thought fighting was a serious problem
at their school, compared with over two-thirds of parents in the control
group. For tardiness, 38 percent of the private school parents versus 60 percent of the control group perceived this as a serious problem. Nearly
30 percent of private school parents but 47 percent of the control group
said destruction of property was a serious problem.

Although student reports of the climate in schools and classrooms are
not as sharply differentiated, they are consistent with parental assessments.
Scholarship students, for example, were more likely to report that students
got along with teachers and were proud to go to their school.

It appears that public and private schools use somewhat different mech-
anisms to maintain discipline. Private schools seem to emphasize dress and
orderliness; public schools use rules and regulations. No less than 97 percent of the private school parents reported that their schools required uniforms, as compared with 26 percent of parents in the control group.
Similarly, 94 percent of the private school parents reported that certain
kinds of clothing were forbidden, whereas less than half of the control
group did so. By contrast, sign-in sheets and hall passes are more frequently
employed by public schools. More than 95 percent of the control group
reported that parents had to sign in when they came to school, compared
with only about 80 percent of the private school parents. To leave their
classes, 87 percent of students in the control group had to obtain hall
passes, according to their parents, whereas only about 71 percent of the private school parents said that this was a requirement.

---

15. If a value in the fourth column is negative, the percentage for the control group is obtained by
adding the third and fourth columns.

Table 12-1. *Effects of the School Choice Scholarship Fund Program on School Climate*[a]

Percent

Sample and report	Scholarship offered	Scholarship offer effect	Attends private school	Private school effect
Parents				
Serious problems				
Fighting	44	–20***	39	–29***
Tardiness	42	–15***	38	–22***
Kids miss class	38	–12***	35	–18***
Kids destroy property	32	–12***	29	–18***
Cheating	35	–7**	33	–10**
Racial conflict	32	–5*	31	–7*
School rules				
School uniform	82	49***	97	71***
Certain dress forbidden	85	35***	94	50***
Visitors must sign in	83	–11***	79	–17***
Hall passes required	74	–11***	71	–16***
N	817–32	. . .	676–91	. . .
Students				
Proud to attend this school	64	8***	66	12***
Behavior rules strict	68	6	69	8
Get along with teachers	60	5**	61	8**
Feel "put down" by teachers	21	–4	20	–6
Have four or more friends who use bad language	20	–3	19	–4
N	547–78	. . .	404–30	. . .

Source: Authors' calculations.

a. Weighted values are reported. The first column reports effects for all applicants offered a scholarship, the second reports differences in outcomes between those offered a scholarship and the control group, the third reports effects for those attending a private school, and the fourth reports differences between those attending a private school and the control group (see text for further details). Statistical significance at the 0.1 level (two-tailed test) is denoted by *; at the 0.05 level (two-tailed test), by **; and at the 0.01 level (two-tailed test) by ***.

Table 12-2. *Effects of the SCSF Program on Homework*[a]

Percent

Sample and report	Scholarship offered	Scholarship offer effect	Attends private school	Private school effect
Parent				
Child has more than one hour of homework	51	15***	55	21***
Homework too easy	10	–6**	8	–8**
N	834–39	...	693–98	...
Student				
Trouble keeping up with homework	25	2	25	3
Do all homework	83	4	84	6
Teachers return homework most of time	44	–9***	40	–13***
N	573–609	...	486–514	...

Source: Authors' calculations.

a. See table 12-1, note a, for interpretation of table.

Homework

Table 12-2 reports the program's effects on homework. According to parents, students in private schools are asked to do more homework. Of the private school parents, 55 percent reported that their child had at least one hour of homework a day, whereas only a third of parents in the control group reported as much homework. Private school parents were also less likely to say that the homework was too easy.

Students' assessments of their homework situation varied somewhat from that of their parents. However, the wording of the questions for parents and students is sufficiently different that the results do not directly contradict each other. Students were asked whether it was true that they "had trouble keeping up with the homework." Twenty-five percent of private school students said this was true, but 22 percent of the students in the control group gave a similar response. Students were also asked "how much" of their homework they "usually" did. If their answers are to be believed, they are model students: about 80 percent of both groups claimed to do "all" of their homework. Over half of the students in the control

Table 12-3. *Effects of the SCSF Program on Communication between School and Parents*[a]

Percent

Parent report	Scholarship offered	Scholarship offer effect	Attends private school	Private school effect
Receive grade information	90	8***	93	11***
Notified of disruptive behavior	87	6***	89	10***
Speak to classes about jobs	43	9***	46	13***
Participate in instruction	62	12***	66	18***
Parent nights	92	5***	93	7***
Regular parent-teacher conferences	93	3*	94	5*
Receive notes from teacher	88	9***	91	13***
Receive newsletter	82	15***	86	22***
N	816–31	. . .	569–764	. . .

Source: Authors' calculations.
a. See table 12-1, note a, for interpretation of table.

group were more likely to say that their homework was graded and returned to them "always or most of the time," but only about 40 percent of the private school students gave this response.

Parental Involvement and Communication with Schools

Private school parents report more extensive communication and involvement with their children's schools. The data presented in table 12-3 indicate that a higher percentage of parents of students in private schools reported that they were more informed about student grades halfway through the grading period, were notified the first time their children were sent to the office for disruptive behavior, spoke to classes about their jobs, participated in instruction, were at schools that held more open houses or back-to-school nights, received notes from teachers about their children, received a school newsletter, and were informed by school when their children were absent and had more frequent parent-teacher conferences.

The largest differences in parental involvement and school communication practices involve parents receiving newsletters, participating in instruction, receiving notes from teachers, and speaking about their jobs.

For example, about 90 percent of the private school parents reported receiving notes from teachers, as compared with just over three-fourths of the parents in the control group.

Continuing in the Program

It is generally thought that students do better if they remain in the same school throughout the school year and from one year to the next. Does school choice destabilize a child's educational experience? In his evaluation of the Milwaukee school choice program, John Witte expressed concern at the high rate of attrition from private schools.[16] A number of critics of school choice have raised questions about the readiness of private schools to expel students who do not "fit in."[17] But other studies have found that private school students from low-income families are more likely to remain in the same school throughout the school year and from one year to the next.[18] The SCSF pilot program provides an opportunity to examine this question. In general, our findings indicate that school choice does not disrupt the education of low-income students.

Table 12-4 reports program effects on students changing school during the school year. A very high percentage of all students in the study reportedly remained in the same school for the entire year, much higher than is typical of inner-city minority children.[19] No differences in school mobility rates are apparent between children in private schools and the control group: 95 percent of both groups reported that their children had remained in the same school throughout the school year.[20] Similarly, suspension rates were much the same for both groups: 7 percent of the parents in the control group and 4 percent of the private school parents reported that their children had been suspended.

Those who did change schools were asked to list their reasons. Among both groups, answers were fairly evenly distributed across the variety of alternatives provided in the questionnaire. The most frequently mentioned

16. Witte (1991).
17. See, for example, Murphy, Nelson, and Rosenberg (1997).
18. See Greene, Howell, and Peterson (1998).
19. Witte, Bailey, andThorn (1992, pp. 19–20).
20. These percentages may underestimate the actual rates of school mobility for both groups. The families that did not attend the follow-up sessions are probably more likely to have moved, making it more difficult for evaluation staff to locate them. If so, their children would be more likely to have changed schools.

Table 12-4. *Effects of the SCSF Program on Changing School during the School Year*[a]

Percent

Parent report	Scholarship offered	Scholarship offer effect	Attends private school	Private school effect
Child suspended for disciplinary reasons	4	–2	4	–3
Child attended same school throughout school year	95	0	95	0
Reasons for changing school[b]				
Moved away	2	–1	1	–1
School quality	1	0	0	0
Too expensive	1	1**	2	2**
Suspended or expelled	0	0	0	0
Prefer public school	0	–1	0	–1
Inconvenient location	0	0	0	0
Prefer private school	0	0	0	0
N	832–42	...	783–86	...

Source: Authors' calculations.

a. See table 12-1, note a, for interpretation of table.

b. Denominator includes responses of parents of both those who stay and those who leave.

were that the school was too expensive or that the family had moved away. No other reason was given by more than 1 percent of parents. School quality was cited by four scholarship parents and seven members of the control group. Seven scholarship parents and four members of the control group said that expense was a factor. Only three scholarship users and two members of the control group said that their child had been expelled or suspended. In short, school mobility was very low and virtually identical for both those in private and public schools. Expulsion was a trivial factor, affecting less than 1 percent of each group.

Table 12-5 reports program effects on students' plans for the following year. According to their parents, scholarship recipients are more likely to attend the same school next year than are members of the control group. Of the families in private schools, 84 percent said they expected their child to be back at the same school the following year, as compared with 67 percent of the control group.

Table 12-5. *Effects of the SCSF Program on Plans for Next School Year*[a]
Percent

Parent report	Scholarship offered	Scholarship offer effect	Attends private school	Private school effect
Child will attend same school				
next year	80	12***	84	17***
Reasons for changing school[b]				
School quality	5	−2	5	−2
Moving	5	−2	5	−1
Graduating	3	−11***	2	−12***
Prefer (other) private school	2	0	1	0
Inconvenient location	2	0	1	−1
Too expensive	2	1**	2	1**
Want to keep all children in				
same school	1	0	1	0
Asked not to return	0	0	0	0
Prefer public school	0	0*	0	0
N	823	...	768	...

Source: Authors' calculations.
a. See table 12-1, note a, for interpretation of table.
b. In these calculations, denominator includes both those who stay and those who leave.

Approximately 5 percent of scholarship parents said that they were changing schools because they did not find the quality of the school acceptable, and another 5 percent said that they were planning to move. The next most frequently mentioned reasons for changing school, given by less than 2 percent of scholarship parents, were expense and an inconvenient location. Less than one percent of all scholarship users said that their school had asked them "not to return."

The situation was much the same for the control group. Thirty-one percent of parents in the control group did not expect their children to be attending the same school next year. However, 14 percent of the parents in the control group said this was because their child was graduating—presumably from elementary to middle school. This institutional break is found in public schools but not in most private schools in New York. If these families are put to one side, the percentage of those in the control group who say that they are thinking of changing schools is about 19 percent, only slightly more than the 14 percent of scholarship parents who expected their child to change school (for reasons other than graduation). Seven percent of all families in the control group said that they were moving because the quality of their school was not acceptable. Less than 1 percent of the control group said that their children had been asked not to return to their current school.

Test Performance

Most previous school choice experiments have not conformed to the classic randomized experiment. Privately funded programs in Indianapolis, San Antonio, and Milwaukee admitted students on a first come, first served basis. In the state-funded program in Cleveland, scholarship winners were initially selected by means of a lottery, but eventually all applicants were offered a scholarship. In Milwaukee, vouchers were awarded by a lottery if schools were oversubscribed; however, the lottery was not conducted by the evaluation team and data collection was incomplete.[21] The evaluation of the SCSF program provides an improved opportunity to estimate the test score effects of a scholarship program.

Table 12-6 reports the average impact of a scholarship on a student's test scores in reading and mathematics for all students, for students in each of grades two through five, and, to increase the stability of the results, for fourth and fifth graders combined. Because baseline test scores were not collected from applicants then in kindergarten, we do not report first grade results. The estimated impact after one year of attending a private school on all students in grades two through five is small in both reading and mathematics: less than 2 percentile points in each subject, a statistically insignificant effect.

This picture changes when one examines the results by grade level. The effects of attending a private school for one year on students' math scores in grades two, four, and five are, respectively, 5 percentile points, 7 percentile points, and 5 percentile points. The effects on reading for the same grades are, respectively, 4 percentile points, 1 percentile point, and 6 percentile points. The impacts on math scores are statistically significant for all three grades; for reading, they are significant in fifth grade only. For third grade, the effects in math and reading are –3 and –2 points, respectively;

21. Results from these evaluations are reported in Peterson and Hassel (1998).

Table 12-6. *Effects of the SCSF Program on Test Scores*[a]
Percentiles

Test and grade level	Scholarship offered	Scholarship offer effect	Attends private school	Private school effect	Sample size
Math					
Grade 2	20.3	3.6* (2.1)	21.5	5.3* (3.6)	371
Grade 3	20.2	−1.9 (2.3)	20.7	−2.4 (2.9)	396
Grade 4	30.5	4.8*** (2.3)	32.3	6.6*** (3.3)	395
Grade 5	29.0	3.9* (2.5)	29.4	5.1* (3.2)	294
Grades 4 and 5	29.9	4.2*** (1.7)	31.1	5.6*** (2.3)	689
All grades	24.6	1.2 (1.2)	25.3	1.6 (1.6)	1,456
Reading					
Grade 2	26.0	2.9 (2.4)	26.4	4.2 (3.6)	371
Grade 3	22.2	−2.4 (1.6)	23.0	−3.1 (2.1)	396
Grade 4	28.1	0.6 (1.7)	28.9	0.9 (2.5)	395
Grade 5	26.6	4.4*** (1.8)	26.9	5.8*** (2.4)	294
Grades 4 and 5	27.4	2.5** (1.3)	28.2	3.4** (1.8)	689
All grades	25.6	1.1** (1.0)	26.3	1.5 (1.4)	1,456

Source: Authors' calculations.

a. Measure is score on Iowa Tests of Basic Skills. Scores have been adjusted for students who either were "held back" or "skipped" a year in school. Weighted values are reported. For interpretation of first through fourth columns, see table 12-1, note a. Statistical significance at the 0.1 level (one-tailed test) is denoted by *; at the 0.05 level (one-tailed test), by **; and at the 0.01 level (one-tailed test) by ***. Bootstrapped standard errors are shown in parentheses. Conventional tests of significance yield the same results.

Table 12-7. *Effects of School Choice and Class Size Reduction on Test Scores*
Standard deviations

Program and grade level	Effect of being offered scholarship		Effect of attending private school		Effect of smaller class	
	Math	Reading	Math	Reading	Math	Reading
New York scholarship[a]						
Grades 4 and 5	0.15	0.11	0.22	0.16	. . .	. . .
Tennessee class size[b]						
Grade 1 (S)	. . .	. . .	. . .	. . .	0.32	0.30
Grade 1 (T)	. . .	. . .	. . .	. . .	0.15	0.25

Source: Authors' calculations; Mosteller (1995).
a. Measure is score on Iowa Tests of Basic Skills in reading and math.
b. Measures are Stanford Achievement Test (S) and Tennessee Basic Skills First Test (T).

the math results are not statistically significant. We do not know why results differ for grade three.

The results for fourth and fifth grade students combined are worthy of special attention because they are based on a larger number of observations, and thus are more stable. For these students, the effect of attending a private school is 6 points for math and 3 points for reading.

Effect Sizes

The magnitude of the effects of attending a private school can be assessed by comparing them with the results of the evaluation of another randomized experiment: Tennessee's Project STAR. As discussed by Frederick Mosteller in chapter 6 above, this program reduced average class sizes from approximately twenty-five students to fifteen. Table 12-7 presents results from the interventions in New York and Tennessee in terms of effect sizes; that is, effects expressed in standard deviations. In this way, one can compare the sizes of programmatic effects on different outcomes, even though raw measures differ.

In the case of the class size evaluation in Tennessee, no statistically significant effects were identified for students beyond the first grade. Among first graders, effect sizes vary between 0.15 and 0.32 standard deviation, as shown in table 12-7. Of these effects Mosteller observes, "Although effect sizes of the magnitude of 0.1, 0.2, or 0.3 may not seem to be impressive gains for a single individual, for a population they can be quite substantial." He also notes that "an increase of one-fourth of a standard deviation can amount to a considerable gain in performance."[22] The Congress has apparently been persuaded by the effect sizes observed in Tennessee. In 1998, after extensive policy deliberations in which the Tennessee evaluation was frequently mentioned, the Congress enacted legislation authorizing an expenditure of more than $1 billion for the purpose of reducing the size of elementary school classes across the country.

The fourth and fifth grade effect sizes observed in our evaluation of the scholarship program in New York do not differ materially from the first grade effects observed in Tennessee, the largest effects observed in that evaluation. As can be seen in table 12-7, for grades four and five combined, the effects of using a scholarship to attend a private school on reading and math achievement were, on average, about 0.16 standard deviation for reading and 0.24 standard deviation for math. These are not much different from the first grade effects found in the Tennessee study, where observed effect sizes varied between 0.15 and 0.32 standard deviation. In short, substantial private school effects on test scores of fourth and fifth grade students were observed after just one year in the program.

The Tennessee class size study finds that initial gains are sustained in subsequent years, but it does not find any incremental gains after the first year. It will be interesting to see whether the gains observed in the first year of New York's school choice program are sustained or enlarged in subsequent years. The evaluation is scheduled to continue for at least two more years.

Conclusion

Until now, there has not been a well-implemented randomized experiment on school choice, and as a result high-quality information about the effects of such programs has been limited. We find that low-income New York City students in grades four and five who attend private schools score higher in math and reading tests after one year than do students in the control group. In addition, parents report that the climate in the schools at-

---

22. Mosteller (1995, pp. 119–20). On the effects of reductions in class size, see also chapter 6 by Mosteller and chapter 7 by Eric Hanushek in this volume.

tended by scholarship recipients is, on average, better than that in the schools attended by the control group—for example, there were fewer disruptive events, there was more communication between school and parents, and teachers required students to complete more homework.

Although the effects are promising, it remains to be seen whether they will continue and grow. If gains are observed over the next couple of years, and if the results from these scholarship recipients can be generalized to all disadvantaged inner city students, then school choice may constitute a mechanism that will help achieve equality of educational opportunity. Further research needs to be done to assess the long-term effects and the systemic impact of school choice initiatives. Evaluations of systemic impact should address questions such as how private and parochial schools respond to the resulting increase in demand, how public schools respond when large numbers of students chose to leave, and what happens to the students who choose to remain in the public schools.

References

Angrist, Joshua D., Guido W. Imbens, and Donald B. Rubin. 1996. "Identification of Causal Effects Using Instrumental Variables." *Journal of the American Statistical Association* 91(June): 444–62.

Ascher, Carol, Norm Fruchter, and Robert Berne. 1996. *Hard Lessons: Public Schools and Privatization*. New York: Twentieth Century Fund Press.

Blue Ribbon Panel on Catholic Schools. 1993. "Report." Prepared for the Office of the Commissioner, New York State Department of Education.

Bonsteel, Alan, and Carlos A. Bonilla. 1997. *A Choice for Our Children: Curing the Crisis in America's Schools*. San Francisco: Institute for Contemporary Studies.

Brandl, John E. 1998. *Money and Good Intentions Are Not Enough, or Why a Liberal Democrat Thinks States Need Both Competition and Community*. Brookings.

Carnegie Foundation for the Advancement of Teaching. 1992. *School Choice: A Special Report*. Princeton, N.J.

Chubb, John E., and Terry M. Moe. 1990. *Politics, Markets, and America's Schools*. Brookings.

Cobb, Clifford W. 1992. *Responsive Schools, Renewed Communities*. San Francisco: Institute for Contemporary Studies.

Coleman, James S., Thomas Hoffer, and Sally Kilgore. 1982. *High School Achievement*. Basic Books.

Cookson, Peter W. 1994. *School Choice: The Struggle for the Soul of American Education*. Yale University Press.

Coulson, Andrew J. 1999. *Market Education: The Unknown History*. Washington: Cato Institute.

Deyette, Rachel. 1999. "Selection into Voucher Programs: How Do Applicants Differ from the Eligible Population?" Unpublished paper. Harvard Uniersity, Program on Education Policy and Governance.

Effron, Bradley. 1982. *The Jackknife, the Bootstrap, and Other Re-Sampling Plans.* Philadelphia: Society for Industrial and Applied Mathematics.

Fuller, Bruce, Richard F. Elmore, and Gary Orfield, eds. 1996. *Who Chooses? Who Loses? Culture, Institutions, and the Unequal Effects of School Choice.* New York: Teachers College Press.

Goldberger, Arthur S., and Glen G. Cain. 1982. "The Causal Analysis of Cognitive Outcomes in the Coleman, Hoffer, and Kilgore Report." *Sociology of Education* 55(April–July): 103-22.

Greene, Jay P., William G. Howell, and Paul E. Peterson. 1998. "Lessons from the Cleveland Scholarship Program." In *Learning from School Choice*, edited by Brian C. Hassel and Paul E. Peterson, 376–80. Brookings.

Gutmann, Amy. 1987. *Democratic Education.* Princeton University Press.

Hill, Jennifer L., Donald B. Rubin, and Neal Thomas. 1998. "The Design of the New York City School Choice Scholarship Program Evaluation." Unpublished paper. Harvard University, Department of Statistics.

Levin, Henry M. 1998. "Educational Vouchers: Effectiveness, Choice, and Costs." *Journal of Policy Analysis and Management* 17(Summer): 373-92.

Mosteller, Frederick. 1995. "The Tennessee Study of Class Size in the Early School Grades." *Future of Children* 5(2): 113–27.

Murphy, Dan, F. Howard Nelson, and Bella Rosenberg. 1997. *The Cleveland Voucher Program: Who Chooses? Who Gets Chosen? Who Pays?* New York: American Federation of Teachers.

Neal, Derek. 1996. "The Effects of Catholic Secondary Schooling on Educational Achievement." Unpublished paper. University of Chicago, Harris School of Public Policy, and National Bureau for Economic Research.

Peterson, Paul E., and Bryan C. Hassel, eds. 1998. *Learning from School Choice.* Brookings.

Peterson, Paul E., and others. 1997. "Initial Findings from the Evaluation of the New York School Choice Scholarships Program." Occasional paper. Harvard University, Program on Education Policy and Governance (November).

———. 1998. "An Evaluation of the New York City School Choice Scholarships Program: The First Year." Occasional Paper 98-12. Harvard University, Kennedy School of Government, Taubman Center for State and Local Government, Program on Education Policy and Governance.

Rasell, Edith, and Richard Rothstein, eds. 1993. *School Choice: Examining the Evidence.* Washington: Economic Policy Institute.

Stine, Robert. 1990. "An Introduction to Bootstrap Methods: Examples and Ideas." In *Modern Methods of Data Analysis*, edited by J. Fox and J. S. Long, 325–73. Newbury Park, Calif.: Sage Publications.

Wells, Amy Stuart. 1996. "African-American Students' View of School Choice." In *Who Chooses? Who Loses? Culture, Institutions, and the Unequal Effects of School Choice*, edited by Bruce Fuller, Richard F. Elmore, and Gary Orfield. New York: Teachers College Press.

Wilms, Douglas J. 1985. "Catholic School Effects on Academic Achievement: New Evidence from the High School and Beyond Follow-up Study." *Sociology of Education* 58: 98–114.

Witte, John F. 1991. "First Year Report: Milwaukee Parental Choice Program." Upublished paper. University of Wisconsin–Madison, Department of Political Science, and Robert M. Lafayette Institute of Public Affairs (November).

Witte, John F., Andrea B. Bailey, and Christopher A. Thorn. 1992. "Second Year Report: Milwaukee Parental Choice Program." Unpublished paper. University of Wisconsin–Madison, Department of Political Science, and Robert M. La Follette Institute of Public Affairs (December).

SUSAN E. MAYER
PAUL E. PETERSON

13

The Costs and Benefits of School Reform

THE DEBATE OVER SCHOOL REFORM in the United States is often cast in black and white: either resources should be increased or the structure of schooling should be changed. The studies in this volume suggest that both strategies could enhance the cognitive skills of young Americans. In this concluding chapter, we roughly estimate the costs and benefits of the reforms considered in previous chapters. While these are little more than back-of-the-envelope estimates, they provide a way to think about the relative costs and benefits of the reforms. Although scholars are beginning to learn more about alternative reform strategies, more careful research is needed, including the use of randomized experiments, before one can obtain exact estimates. To emphasize the uncertainty of our estimates, we round off both costs and benefits.

Several factors introduce uncertainty into the estimates we provide below. First, since some of the findings are from data that are not nationally representative, it is uncertain the extent to which they can be generalized. Second, we estimate the effect of reforms only on test scores and earnings, mainly because these are the benefits for which estimates are available. Others may think that goals such as producing well-adjusted, tolerant citizens are equally or more important. However, the acquisition of cognitive skills is undoubtedly a central purpose of a formal educational system.

Furthermore, schools that do well at enhancing cognitive skills and preparing students for future careers probably do well in other domains as well.

Third, policies may have both positive and negative effects. For example, a policy may increase average test scores while exacerbating disparities in scores between advantaged and disadvantaged students. More academically oriented math courses may improve students' math scores but increase stress and reduce self-esteem. Yet when researchers have looked for potential negative effects, they have found little evidence of them. Caroline Hoxby, for example, finds little evidence that more school choice results in greater inequality in test scores or educational attainment. John Bishop finds that students subject to external exams do not focus exclusively on studying examination subjects; instead, they watch less television, do more homework, and are more likely to think that science is important. Robert Meyer finds that academic math courses also improve the test scores of both college-bound and non-college-bound students.

Fourth, reforms are often proposed in general terms, but costs and benefits can only be calculated under specific assumptions. For example, those favoring reductions in class size seldom specify the ideal number of students in class. Yet costs vary enormously, depending on the size of the reduction. Also, it makes a great deal of difference to costs whether one reduces class sizes in kindergarten and first grade only or in all grades from kindergarten through twelfth.

Fifth, neither the studies in this book (nor any others of which we are aware) try to estimate the effects of interactions among policies. It is not clear whether students who began school at a younger age and then were offered a more academic curriculum in smaller classes would reap the combined benefits of each reform. Nor is it clear what would happen if students and families were given a choice of schools in a statewide system governed by rigorous substantive external examinations. When reforms are implemented simultaneously, the total benefit might be the sum of the two separate benefits. Or the reforms might reinforce each other, creating a benefit greater than this sum. Alternatively, the reforms might overlap, so that their joint effect is less than the sum.

Sixth, our estimates do not take into account the potential spillover effects of a better educated population. Would crime rates fall? Would more children be raised in intact families? Would relationships and communications among better educated citizens yield still higher rates of return on educational investments? If the answers to these questions are positive, the results reported below underestimate the benefits of the reforms.

Finally, it is not known whether the benefits that are observed in these studies would be realized if the reforms were introduced on a nationwide basis. For example, students who take math courses beyond geometry earn more, but would they still earn more if many more students took these advanced courses? Would an additional year of schooling yield as large an economic return if everyone else also remained in school a year longer? If the answers to these questions are negative (as they may well be), our results are overestimates.

Methods for Estimating Costs and Benefits

We estimate the impact of reforms on both children's test scores and their future earnings. We describe the effects of a reform on test scores in terms of a standard deviation. (To obtain a sense of the size of reform impacts on test scores, one might keep in mind that a 1.0 standard deviation is approximately the difference between average black and white test scores in the United States.) We also provide estimates of total monetary costs. We leave it to future research to sort the costs to individuals and families from the costs to taxpayers or society as a whole.[1]

We estimate a rate of return for each reform by calculating its effect on future wages. In most cases, the studies in this book estimate the effects of reforms on test scores but not wages. As Christopher Winship and Sanders Korenman point out, previous research has found that a one standard deviation increase in cognitive test scores is associated with an increase in earnings of between 3 and 27 percent. Their own estimate is in the middle range, showing that a one standard deviation increase in test scores corresponds to a wage increase of about 16 percent. Christopher Jencks and Meredith Phillips suggest that a one standard deviation increase in test scores increases wages by about 20 percent. In our calculations, we assume that a one standard deviation increase in test scores increases wages by 18 percent, midway between these two estimates.

---

1. Until this task is performed, it will not be clear whether the taxpayer should foot the bill for any particular reform. If the incremental costs of education are borne by the taxpayer, they would represent a shared cost for which society would want a shared return.

To estimate the monetary benefit of a school reform, we assume that the average annual future wage of students would be $30,000 in today's dollars, if nothing else changed.[2] Therefore if a reform increases test scores by a fifth of a standard deviation, and hence wages by about 4 percent, the corresponding monetary gain would be $1,200.[3]

This estimate assumes that the only effect of a reform on wages occurs through its effect on test scores. However, the growing literature estimating the effects of school policies on children's test scores and their future wages suggests that school reforms may affect wages in other ways as well. For example, while the requirement of an advanced math course probably does affect wages mainly because it increases test scores, class size reductions and school choice programs affect many aspects of schooling, including socialization and parental and child attitudes. Thus such reforms are likely to affect wages both by increasing test scores and by affecting other characteristics of children. Unfortunately, one cannot test this hypothesis with the available data. Because in this chapter we estimate only the effects of reforms on wages that occur via their effects on test scores, we may underestimate the wage returns to most reforms.

When estimating rates of return, we discount the return from investments made for students in elementary school by 30 percent, because about a decade will elapse before these students enter the market place. We do not apply this discount rate when estimating the return from investments made in high school, because we assume that these students will soon be working or will be making the calculated decision to defer work until obtaining further education.

Results

Our estimates are presented in table 13-1. The first point to note is that all of the interventions apparently increase test scores by approximately 0.2 standard deviation. Assuming that a standard deviation increase in

---

2. In 1995, the average annual pay for American workers was $27,845 (U.S. Bureau of the Census, *Statistical Abstract of the United States, 1997*, table 669). To account for inflation and for ease of computation, we round this to $30,000.

3. Assuming that a one standard deviation increase in test scores increases wages by 18 percent, the percentage wage increase is calculated as 0.2 x 18 = 3.6.

test scores results in a wage increase of 18 percent, this means that each reform increases wages by about 4 percent. The similarity of the effects is partly a result of rounding off the estimates and summarizing the findings from individual studies. But in our judgment the results would not differ materially if we used a more precise and detailed procedure. Given the diversity of authors, perspectives, data sets, and analytic techniques in the original findings, the similarity of the estimated effects on test scores seems remarkable.

But perhaps the convergence is not quite so remarkable as at first sight. We have included reforms that are of general interest because they have been part of the school reform debate for a long time. In general, a reform that has a very large effect on test scores would not be a subject of debate because it would already have been implemented. Conversely, a reform with little or no detectable effect probably would not win enough advocates to become part of the general discussion. It is precisely those reforms with detectable but modest effects that are likely to spark controversy and demand careful research on whether their benefits are worth their costs, both fiscal and political.[4]

Effects of 0.2 standard deviation may seem modest to those eager to transform American education. It would take an effect of a full standard deviation to achieve a truly major educational transformation. But as Frederick Mosteller has observed of the effects of class size reduction, "although effect sizes of the magnitude of 0.1, 0.2, or 0.3 may not seem to be impressive gains for a single individual, for a population they can be quite substantial."[5]

Table 13-1 also shows that the reforms that are politically more acceptable have lower rates of return than those that have engendered greater political controversy. Reforms with very high benefit-to-cost ratios are subjected to intense opposition from well-positioned interests with strong stakes in the present organization of public education. But those reforms that generate less political opposition can only be introduced at considerable cost, which generates taxpayer opposition. We return to this dilemma below.

4. Given the sample sizes that are generally available to social scientists, effects much smaller than 0.2 standard deviation are not likely to be statistically significant. Thus, perhaps not surprisingly, the effects observed here are all in what might be called the modest range.
5. Mosteller (1995, pp.119–20).

Table 13-1. *Estimated Benefits and Costs of Selected School Reforms*
Units as indicated

Reform	Test score gain (standard deviations)	Wage gain[a] (dollars)	Monetary cost[b] (dollars)	Rate of return (percent)	Political feasibility
Additional year of schooling					
High school or college	0.10–0.20	600–1,200	18,000	4–6	High
Elementary school	0.10–0.20	420–850	5,000	8–17	High
More rigorous math or science courses (additional salary costs)					
Targeted pay increase	0.20	1,200	1,540	81	Low
Universal pay increase	0.20	1,200	19,200	6	Low
Class size reduction of one-third					
Kindergarten and first grade only	0.20	840	1,980	50	Low
Kindergarten through sixth grade	0.20	960	11,620	8	High
External exam	0.20	1,200	200	600	Low
School choice	0.20	1,200	None	Infinite	Low

Source: Authors' calculations based on data from studies reported in this volume.
a. Calculated at 4 percent for each 0.2 standard deviation increase in test score.
b. See text for details of calculation.
c. Wage gain divided by monetary costs.

Additional Schooling

For over two centuries, the most common type of school reform in the United States has been simply to add a year to the time that students are in school. Such a reform does not threaten vested interests, because it does not alter the current system. On the contrary, it adds more resources to the system, giving new opportunities to those working within it. With each passing decade, more and more young people have remained in school for longer periods.

The upward trend in the number of years students spend in school has paid off—both to individuals and to society as a whole. Based on the findings reported in this volume, an additional year of schooling increases cognitive skill, as measured by standardized tests, by between 0.1 and 0.2 standard deviation. Assuming that this increases adult wages by between 2 and 4 percent and that adult wages are $30,000, the increase in wages due to an additional year of schooling is between $600 and $1,200 annually. Per pupil expenditures in elementary and secondary schools averaged about $6,600 in 1997. Thus it would seem that the potential return—between 10 and 20 percent—is worth the investment.

However, this estimate assumes that the return to each year of schooling is the same as the return to any other year. We do not know if this is true. It also assumes that the costs of each year of schooling are the same. This is not true: per pupil expenditures are greater in high school and college than in elementary school. Consequently, if students get additional schooling by staying longer in high school or attending college, the costs would be higher than $6,600. Also, high school and college students forgo earnings and work experience while they are in school. If entry-level workers earn $9,000 over a nine-month school year and the cost of secondary and postsecondary education is one-third higher than the average cost for secondary and elementary schooling, then the "true" cost of an additional year of education at the high school and college levels is $18,000. But assuming that this investment results in a 4 percent increase in wages ($1,200), the resulting return of 4 to 6 percent is still acceptable.

However if, as Susan Mayer and David Knutson suggest in this volume, the same gains in cognitive skill and wages can be obtained by reducing the age at which children begin school, the returns would be much higher, because elementary school education costs less per pupil and young students do not forgo earnings. One might reasonably assume per pupil costs as low as $5,000 per year for elementary school. Assuming a discount rate of 30 percent over the period between the additional year of schooling and the economic return, the increase in wages is reduced to about $850, a 17 percent return on the investment.

These comparisons suggest that one would need compelling evidence that either gains in cognitive test scores or wage returns were much higher for an additional year of high school or a year of college attendance than for an additional year of elementary school before one chose to extend schooling among older rather than younger students. Given these cost differentials, it is ironic that more has been done in recent decades to extend the number of years of schooling upward than to extend them downward.[6]

Curricular Reform

If the returns to an additional year of schooling seem pretty good, they are less than can be achieved by curricular reform. Jencks and Phillips, Robert Meyer, and Jay Girotto and Peterson separately estimate that students who take a couple of advanced math courses score approximately 0.2 standard deviation higher on math tests. This is about the same gain in cognitive skill as is obtained from an additional year of schooling, implying that students who take advanced math can be expected to have wages that are on average $1,200 higher than students who do not.

The political and financial obstacles to introducing more rigorous math and science courses in the high school curriculum are greater than is usually understood and make it hard to estimate the monetary costs of such a reform. Qualified teachers in these subject areas are in short supply, mainly because adults with the requisite skills can earn more in other occupations. Math and science teachers could be paid more, but this would require that school boards either pay all teachers higher salaries or else deviate from the uniform salary schedule. Teachers' unions have usually rejected the latter alternative in collective bargaining negotiations.

If additional advanced math courses could be taught by current teachers, and students substituted advanced math for other courses, there would be no additional monetary costs to requiring advanced math courses. But this assumption is probably unrealistic. If schools currently provide as many advanced courses as they can with available teachers, courses can only be added if they are taught by less qualified teachers, so that the gains

6. These estimates are averages. The cost of a year of schooling varies greatly across states and school districts, and the benefits may vary as well.

might not be as high as predicted in the studies in this book. To assure that additional courses are taught by qualified staff, schools would have to recruit new teachers. To attract qualified teachers, schools would probably have to offer higher wages. The least expensive way to do this is to offer higher wages only to math and science teachers, but if collective bargaining agreements require that the salaries of all teachers increase, the costs of offering additional advanced courses would be much higher.

Assuming that it is possible to increase only the salaries of those teaching high school math and science, the cost of such an intervention depends on the amount by which teacher compensation has to increase. Suppose that it would take a salary increase of a third to attract enough qualified math and science teachers, and assume a student takes two such courses (out of six) per year, then one-third of the personnel costs would have to increase by a third, for an overall increase of 0.11 in personnel costs (which we might assume are 50 percent of per pupil costs). Based on these assumptions and the further assumption that high school costs are $9,000 per year, the cost per student of this intervention would be $1,980.[7] If students gain $1,200 per year in wages from these changes, then the rate of return from requiring additional math and science courses would be a spectacular 81 percent.

However, the political costs of this intervention might be high, because the intervention violates the uniform salary contract to which teacher unions are deeply committed. To forestall opposition from teachers' unions, the salaries of all teachers might have to be increased by one-third. If that were the case, the per pupil cost of this curriculum change would be $19,800 over the twelve years a student is in school. Taxpayers are likely to resist this sharp increase in costs.

---

7. We base our calculation on the following reasoning. Assume that schools require students to take two additional advanced courses during their four years of high school and the schools must pay a third more to the teachers they hire to teach these courses. Assume, also, that the children take six courses a day for the year. Every year a third of the courses (two of six) will require a third more in personnel costs. Thus every year personnel costs are about 11 percent (0.33*0.33) higher. Assuming that personnel costs are 50 percent of per pupil costs, the increase in per pupil costs is 5.5 percent. If average high school per pupil costs are $9,000, the per pupil increase in costs equals $495 per year. Over the four years a student is in high school, the additional cost equals $1,980. If maintenance of a uniform salary schedule in high school requires that all high school teachers' salaries be increased by 33 percent in order to get qualified teachers to teach more rigorous math and science courses, per pupil costs would increase by 0.50*0.33, or about 17 percent—approximately $1,530 per year. Over four years this is an additional $6,120 per student. If the salaries of elementary school teachers must be raised by a similar amount, the cost over twelve years rises to $19,200.

However, it might be argued that higher salaries would improve teaching across the board—even though few studies have identified significant test score gains as a result of general increases in teacher salaries.[8] If the gains are limited to those achieved by means of a more academic high school curriculum, then the return from the investment would be about 6 percent, an acceptable but no longer a spectacular rate of return.[9]

In short, the variation of this curricular reform most likely to produce a high rate of return can be expected to provoke opposition from teachers' unions, while the variation acceptable to teachers is likely to encounter opposition from taxpayers.

Class Size Reduction

While curricular reform seems problematic, quite the opposite is true of reductions in class size. The pupil-teacher ratio has fallen from 28 to 19 in the past fifty years. In 1998 the Congress passed and the president signed into law a $1.1 billion program authorizing heads to reduce class sizes further in elementary schools. At the state level, California is implementing a similar policy.

Tennessee's Project STAR has shown that reducing classes from between twenty-two and twenty-five students to between thirteen and seventeen students in kindergarten and first grade increases sixth grade reading scores by about 0.2 standard deviation and sixth grade math scores by about 0.16 standard deviation. If the payoff in future earnings is 4 percent annually, the resulting annual wage gain is $1,200. When this amount is discounted by 30 percent to take into account the fact that earnings gains will come a decade in the future, the economic return from reducing class size in kindergarten or first grade is about $840 per year.

The Tennessee experiment found no additional gains in test scores for children in small classes between kindergarten and third grade after the treatment ended—in fact the initial gains declined a bit over time. Thus it

---

8. For an excellent discussion of the evidence, see Burtless (1996).

9. This analysis assumes that school districts are responsible for the education of both elementary and high school students. In some parts of the country (for example, Illinois), elementary school districts are separate from high school districts. Under these circumstances, the cost of this intervention without violation of the uniform salary schedule in each type of district would be much less. Since the separation of elementary and high school districts is an organizational form, we have ignored this factor in the estimates reported in table 13-1.

is unlikely that further gains can be achieved by maintaining smaller classes in subsequent grades. It is unclear whether class size must be reduced through all grades to maintain the effects observed in kindergarten and first grade. But the costs associated with maintaining the increase in test scores depend directly on the number of years that the class size reduction must remain in place.

To reduce class size by a third in a particular grade would require an increase of 50 percent in expenditure on the salaries and benefits of teachers for that grade. For example, if a school has six first grade classrooms, each with twenty-four students, and the school reduces class size by one-third, nine first grade classes will be needed instead of six. The per pupil cost of this increase depends on teachers' compensation. Assuming annual compensation of $44,000, we estimate a cost of about $1,250 per student for each year that elementary school class size is reduced by a third.[10] Decreasing class size also requires an increase in other resources, such as classrooms, which might represent roughly a third the cost of additional personnel, bringing the total cost to approximately $1,660 per year. Therefore, if a school reduces class sizes in seven elementary grades (including kindergarten), the additional cost would be $11,620 per student over the course of seven years. The rate of return on this investment is 7 percent. But if class size were reduced only in first grade and the same benefits were realized, the rate of return would be around 50 percent. This latter option is unlikely to win political support, however. Proposals for class size reductions that have passed in Congress and in the California legislature are directed toward reducing class sizes in all elementary grades.

---

10. The computation of the percentage increment in personnel costs associated with reducing class size in a year is as follows:

$$P_e = [(S_1 * C_1)/S_2]/C_2,$$

where S is the number of students, C is the number of classes, and subscripts denote time 1 or time 2. Thus if a school had three first grade classrooms (C_1), each with twenty-four students (S_1), and the school lowered the number of students per class to sixteen (S_2), it would require an increase in personnel costs of $[(24*3)/16]/3 = 1.5$. That is, the number of classes would increase by 50 percent.

If personnel costs were 50 percent of total costs, the increase in per student expenditures per year would be $0.50*0.50 = 0.25$, or 25 percent. If per pupil costs in elementary school are $5,000, then the additional pupil cost is $1,250. Thus if class size is reduced by a third in only the first grade, the overall increase in per pupil expenditures is $1,250. If class size is reduced for all students in seven years of elementary school (including kindergarten), then the increase in per pupil expenditures would be $8,760 per pupil over the course of the seven years.

National and State Examinations

It has proven to be extremely difficult to establish rigorous, substantive national or statewide examinations. Many states have minimum competency examinations. But the standards are so low that they do not motivate student learning in desirable directions. More rigorous exams threaten many entrenched interests. School boards worry that their students might not perform well; teachers' unions fear increased parental pressure; high school students do not want the pressure of examinations; and ideological groups fight over exam content. The Bush administration's proposal for noncompulsory national examinations met with intense opposition, and the whole issue became bogged down in disputes over content. The only state with anything like a substantive examination is New York, whose regents exam is not as demanding as the national examinations of many European countries or some Canadian provinces.

Despite this political situation, Bishop's results suggest that an external exam taken during the senior year increases eighth grade math scores by 0.2 standard deviation, which is about the same as the estimated effect of an additional year of schooling. These test score gains, if maintained through high school, would result in a 4 percent wage gain, or about $1,200 more per year.

While the benefits of such examinations are high, the costs are minimal. It would probably cost no more than $200 per pupil to develop, update, and administer the exam, plus any costs that schools incur in preparing students. If so, the return on the investment would be extraordinarily high: somewhere around 600 percent.

School Choice

School choice is as controversial as a national examination. School boards, superintendents, and teachers' unions are adamantly opposed to vouchers and typically oppose other choice proposals as well. The Congress passed a small pilot voucher program for the District of Columbia in 1998, but even this experimental initiative was so controversial that it provoked a presidential veto. Only two states, Wisconsin and Ohio, have conducted small experimental voucher programs; both have been the subject of intense litigation, strongly supported by teachers' organizations. Despite the popularity of school choice among parents, especially inner-city, minority parents, it is not clear whether additional voucher programs will be introduced.

Moreover, the opportunities for choice have been reduced over the past fifty years by the decrease in the number of independent school districts caused by combining smaller districts to form fewer larger ones.

Yet there seem to be important benefits from giving parents choice in their children's schools. Peterson, David Myers, William Howell, and Daniel Mayer report that, for fourth and fifth graders combined, the effect of giving vouchers to students from low-income, inner city, minority families is to raise test scores, after one year, by between 0.1 and 0.2 standard deviation. Hoxby finds that giving parents more choice by increasing the number of school districts in a metropolitan area shifts test scores upward by 0.2 standard deviation.

These gains come at virtually no long-term cost, because in the long run the cost of facilities and personnel do not depend on whether families and students are able to choose among schools. There may be costs of communicating alternatives to families, and there may be start-up costs as new schools supplant existing ones that are perceived as ineffective. But these are probably more than offset by the estimated 10 percent reduction in costs that Hoxby finds to be associated with a more competitive education system.

Combining School Reforms

As noted above, the estimated effects on test scores of the interventions discussed in this book tend to hover around 0.2 standard deviation, yet only a full standard deviation could be characterized as a major transformation. If these findings are sustained by future research, they suggest that no single reform can transform American education. To achieve that objective will probably take some combination of the reforms considered here.

The reforms with the greatest payoffs—national examinations, school choice, and curricular reform—are the most controversial politically, and therefore the least likely to be implemented. Those with more modest payoffs—class size reduction and additional years of schooling—have been adopted in the past and can be expected to be elements of school reform in the future.

For more than a century the United States has emphasized quantity over quality in its educational system. Historically, the country has led the world in number of years of schooling completed by an age cohort, amount of money spent on education per pupil, and teacher-student ratios. On quality measures, the United States has always lagged behind. The curriculum is not as demanding as in most other industrialized nations. Its examination system is more incoherent, fragmented, and unconnected to experiences in school. Students and families in the United states are not given the choice among state-run secular schools and privately administered religious schools that their counterparts enjoy in almost all other industrialized countries.

Although almost all who debate the future of American education express a strong commitment to improving the system, very few endorse all the reforms found to be of value in the chapters in this volume. But since all these reforms have at least some positive benefits, it is tempting to suggest that the current stalemate in the politics of American education be replaced by a great political trade-off: more resources to reduce class size and extend education, on the one hand, and the introduction of national examinations, a more rigorous curriculum, and choice for parents and students, on the other. This might be a win-win compromise acceptable both to those who demand more taxpayer dollars for education and to those who demand a more efficient, more effective educational system. If these reforms were implemented together, a major transformation of American education would indeed take place.

References

Burtless, Gary, ed. 1996. *Does Money Matter? The Effect of School Resources on Student Achievement and Adult Success.* Brookings.

Mosteller, Frederick. 1995. "The Tennessee Study of Class Size in the Early School Grades." *Future of Children* 5(2): 113–27.

Contributors

John H. Bishop
*New York School of Industrial
and Labor Relations,
Cornell University*

Jay R. Girotto
*Homestead Technologies,
Menlo Park, Calif.*

Eric A. Hanushek
*Wallis Institute of Political Economy,
University of Rochester*

William G. Howell
Stanford University

Caroline M. Hoxby
Harvard University

Christopher Jencks
*John F. Kennedy School of
Government, Harvard University*

David Knutson
*Harris School of Public Policy
Studies, University of Chicago*

Sanders D. Korenman
*Baruch College,
City University of New York*

Daniel P. Mayer
*Mathematica Policy Research,
Washington, D.C.*

Susan E. Mayer
*Harris School of Public Policy
Studies, University of Chicago*

Robert H. Meyer
*Wisconsin Center for Education
Research, Madison, Wis.*

Frederick Mosteller
Harvard University

David E. Myers
*Mathematica Policy Research,
   Washington, D.C.*

Paul E. Peterson
Harvard University

Meredith Phillips
*University of California,
   Los Angeles*

Christopher Winship
Harvard University

Index

Ability bias, 23–26

Academic achievement values. *See* Studiousness

Achievement model: assumptions, 16, 18, 50, 170; control for aptitude bias, 7–8, 23–26; and cumulative learning theory, 156–57; heritability issues, 19–20; impact on policymaking, 3–4, 18–19; implications of testing age, 20–23, 27–28. *See also* Cognitive skills

Achievement patterns: family effects, 137–40; impact of teacher quality, 163–64; international comparisons, 105–06, 146–47; NAEP test scores, 135–37, 246; per pupil spending, 133–35; pupil-teacher ratios, 132, 133, 145. *See also* Cognitive skills

AFQT. *See* Armed Forces Qualifications Test

Alberta: Catholic schools, 271; curriculum-based exams, 253, 267

Alberta Teachers Union, 244

Alexander, Karl, 174, 207, 211

Altonji, Joseph, 208

American Federation of Teachers, 242–43

Anderson, Ronald, 173

Angrist, Joshua, 25, 84, 87–88, 97–98

Aptitude bias, 7–8, 23–26

Aptitude model: assumptions, 5–7, 15–16, 18, 49, 54–55; control for aptitude bias, 23–26; heritability issues, 19–20; impact on policy-making, 3–4, 18–19; implications of testing age, 20–23, 27–28. *See also* Cognitive skills

Armed Forces Qualifications Test (AFQT), 50, 57–58

Armed Forces Vocational Aptitude Battery (ASVAB), 22, 57–58

Ashenfelter, Orley, 54, 58, 207

Athletic achievement values, 240, 241–42, 307–08

Atlantic Monthly, 15
Attendance policies, 79, 80
Attrition rates, 330–33

Baker, Linda, 140, 144
Baker, Regina, 87
Bargaining theory, exit opportunities, 300–01
Becker, Gary, 4
Behavior Problems Index (BPI), 88
The Bell Curve (Herrnstein and Murray): cognitive skill–earnings correlation, 6–7, 56; cognitive test predictors, 15, 44, 63; costs of schooling, 44; Head Start assessments, 207; intelligence measurement tool, 50; on schooling control in economic models, 73; schooling effects on cognitive skills, 49, 53, 54–55, 207, 222–23
Biddle, Bruce, 106
Birth quarter associations, 25, 87. *See also* Enrollment age
Bishop, John, 22, 24
Black-white student achievement gap: family effects, 138–39; impact of school resources, 144–45; patterns, 136, 137
Bloom, Benjamin, 26
Bound, John, 87, 98
Bracey, Gerald W., 106
British Columbia, curriculum-based exams, 253, 267
Brown, Marsha, 21
Bush administration, 352

California, class size reductions, 124, 160, 350, 351
California Achievement Tests, 245
Canada: nonpublic school characteristics, 270, 271, 274–75, 277–78; school governance structure, 254–55.
Canada, curriculum-based exams, 252–54; controls for selection bias in effects, 270; estimates of effects, 113, 224, 257, 260–61, 266–67, 270–71, 352; impact on nonpublic schools, 274–75, 277–78; research methodology, 255–57.
CBEEES. *See* Curriculum-based external exit examinations (CBEEES)
Ceci, Stephen, 55
Chambers, B., 251
Chubb, John, 251, 274, 275
Class size: Congressional funding for reductions, 336, 350, 351; costs of reductions, 107, 110, 124, 160–61, 162–63, 350–51; measurement, 140
Class size effects: international comparisons, 147, 161; limitations for policymaking, 158, 161–64; limitations of research results, 117–18, 124–26, 131–32, 160–61; model of, 118–19, 126–28, 161; research bias factors, 108–09; summary of econometric studies, 132, 147–53. *See also* Class size; Prime Time project; Project Challenge; Project STAR; Pupil-teacher ratios
Cleveland, Ohio, school choice, 317–18, 333, 352
Clinton, Bill, 318, 350, 352
Cognitive skills: achievement-aptitude model assumptions, 5–7, 15–16, 18, 49–50, 170, 207; and schooling length, 38, 39–40, 53, 54–55, 59, 61–65, 73, 344–46; children's receptivity to learning, 80–81, 82;

course selection effects, 40–42, 211–18, 222–25, 344–46; and curriculum, 205, 206–07, 208, 224; and enrollment age, 10–11, 25–26, 82–83, 88–96, 98–100; human capital theory, 4–5; influence of school choice, 115, 333–37, 353; student effort effects, 111, 220–21, 222–24. *See also* Cognitive skills–earnings relationships; Math curriculum model; Project Challenge; Project STAR

Cognitive skills–earnings relationships: with aptitude bias controls, 8–9, 38–39, 42–44; enrollment age, 10–11, 25, 79–80, 82–83, 95–98; family effects, 55–57; schooling length, 9–10, 11, 50, 51, 53–54, 65–73. *See also* Costs of school reform

Coleman, James: influences on student achievement, 5, 138, 147; peer group culture, 239, 240

Coleman report, 5, 138, 147

College choice, correlation with student effort, 221–22, 223

Compulsory school laws, 79, 80

Congress, U.S.: class size reductions, 336, 350, 351; voucher program, 352

Cook, Michael, 145

Corcoran, Jill, 57

Costrell, Robert, 244, 246

Costs of school reform: class size reductions, 350–51; with combined strategies, 353–54; estimation, 341–46; for math and science curriculum expansion, 348–50; national exams, 352; school choice programs, 353; schooling length

increases, 11, 82, 347–48. *See also* Spending, education

Course selection effects: on cognitive skills, 40–42, 211–18, 222–25, 348; on college choice, 221–22; research methodological issues, 205, 206–07, 208, 224; role of driver education classes, 213; role of extracurricular classes, 215–16; on wage levels, 208. *See also* Math curriculum model

Crouse, James, 21

Curriculum and Evaluation Standards for School Mathematics, 170

Curriculum-based external exit examinations (CBEEES): achievement hypothesis, 224–25, 247, 261, 266–67, 276–78; administrative incentives hypothesis, 248–50, 260–61, 276–77; costs, 352; incentive assumptions, 244–47; motivations, 112–13, 232, 242–44; nonpublic school performance hypothesis, 251–52, 274–75, 277–78; parental involvement hypothesis, 247–48, 257, 276–77; teacher behavior hypothesis, 250–51, 261, 276–77. *See also* Canada, curriculum-based exams

Deyette, Rachel, 324–25

Dickens, William, 50, 53, 72

District choice. *See* School choice behavior

District of Columbia, school choice, 318, 352

Dominance by insult game: consequences for peer culture, 236–42; described, 231–32; victim choices, 233–36

Early childhood education benefits, 5–6, 95, 207

Early enrollment. *See* Enrollment age

Earnings. *See* Wage levels

Education, U.S. Office of, 147

Educational Testing Service (ETS), 24

Education Subcouncil of the Competitiveness Policy Council, 243

Enrollment age: and cognitive skill levels, 10–11, 25–26, 82–83, 91–96, 98–100; changes in, 79, 80; and wage levels, 10–11, 25–26, 79–80, 82–83, 85–88, 95–96; cost issues, 11, 82, 347–48; research methodology, 81–82, 83–85, 88–91, 96–100

Enrollment statistics, 107, 142

Ethnic achievement gap, patterns, 137. *See also* Racial achievement gap

Evans, William, 145

Extracurricular classes: course selection conflicts, 215–16; influence of school choice, 307–08

Fagerlind, Ingemar, 22, 24

Family effects: and economic success, 56; and student achievement, 172–74; and test score patterns, 108, 137–40

Fischer, Claude, 50, 53, 57, 63, 73

Fleming, M., 251

Florida, school choice, 318

Funding. *See* Spending, education

Gardner, Howard, 58, 106

General intelligence (*g*), 15

Gilman, David, 119

Gissmer, David, 138

Glass, Gene, 118, 119, 125, 128, 153–54, 162

Grade inflation: indexing, 288–89; influence of school choice, 302–05, 312

Grade point average (GPA) as measure, 208, 219–20

Graduation rates, international comparisons, 105

Gresham's law, 252

Grogger, Jeffrey, 145

Gummere, Richard, 246

Hanushek, Eric, 6, 172

Harassment. *See* Dominance by insult game

Harris, Linda, 173

Head Start evaluations, 5–6, 207

Heritability issues, 19–20

Herrnstein, Richard. *See* *The Bell Curve*

High School and Beyond (HS&B) study, described, 28–29, 171

Hirschman, Albert, 284

Hispanic student performance, 137

Homework comparisons, 115, 328–29

Human capital theory, 4–5

Incarceration theory of education: described, 207–08; funding process, 206, 224

Income levels. *See* Family effects; Wage level correlations

Indiana: class size experiments, 119–20; school choice, 333

Indianapolis, Indiana, school choice, 333

Individuals with Disabilities Education Act *(1976)*, 141

Inequality by Design (Fischer and others), 50

Inequality (Jencks and others), 49

Insult game. *See* Dominance by insult game

Intelligence: achievement model
assumptions, 16, 18, 50, 170;
aptitude model assumptions, 5–7,
15–16, 18, 49, 54–55; measuring,
50, 57–58. *See also* Cognitive skills
Iowa Tests of Basic Skills, 245
Iowa Test of Educational Development (ITED), 209, 210, 245
Ireland, class size reductions, 124

Jaeger, David, 87, 98
Japan: class size impact, 147; fourth
grade science achievement, 105–06
Jencks, Christopher, 5, 21, 49, 52, 53,
55–56, 58, 72

Kane, Thomas, 50, 53, 72
Korea, fourth grade science
achievement, 105–06
Krueger, Alan, 25, 58, 84, 87–88,
97–98, 152, 207

Lasting Benefits Study (Tennessee),
121–23, 125–26, 157–58. *See also*
Project STAR (Tennessee)
Learning, children's receptivity, 80–81,
82
Lewit, Eugene, 140, 144

McGaw, Barry, 118, 119, 125
McGiverin, Jennifer, 119, 120
Madeus, George, 248
Mainstreaming. *See* Special education
sector
Manitoba, curriculum-based exams,
253
*The Manufactured Crisis: Myths, Fraud,
and the Attack on America's Public
Schools* (Biddle), 106
Math curriculum model: controls for
prior achievement, 111, 172,

175–76, 182–87, 195; course
variable definitions, 175–76,
200–03; data sources, 171, 177–82;
estimates of course effectiveness,
111, 187–94, 348; research
methodology, 175–76; review of
related research, 110–11, 172–75.
See also Course selection effects;
Math skills
Math requirements, 170
Math skills: estimated impact of
Canadian national exams, 261,
266–67, 270–71; improvement
strategies, 169–71, 194–95,
348–50; influence of advanced
courses, 40–42, 110–11, 171,
173–74, 181–82, 190–92, 193,
218; influence of science courses,
40, 111, 171, 192–94; international
comparisons of fourth grade,
105–06; vocational education, 111,
170, 192, 193–94. *See also* Math
curriculum model
Mayer, Susan, 138
Milwaukee, Wisconsin, school choice,
317–18, 330, 333
Mincer, Jacob, 4
Minimum competency examinations,
245–46
Minnesota, school choice, 293
Moe, Terry, 251, 274, 275
Mosteller, Frederick, 156, 336, 345
Murnane, Richard, 172
Murray, Charles. *See The Bell Curve*

National Assessment of Educational
Progress (NAEP): eighth grade
achievement levels, 246; high
school performance patterns,
135–37; international comparisons
of fourth grade, 105–06; testing
ages, 43

National Council of Teachers of
Mathematics, 170
National Education Longitudinal
Study (NELS), described, 287
National examinations. *See*
Curriculum-based external exit
examinations (CBEEES)
National Longitudinal Survey of
Youth (NLSY), 57, 58
New Brunswick, curriculum-based
exams, 253, 254, 267
Newfoundland: curriculum-based
exams, 253; nonpublic schools, 271
New York state: math performance,
113–14, 270; regents exam, 352
Nigeria, studiousness values, 242
Nova Scotia, curriculum-based exams,
253

Ohio, school choice, 317–18, 333,
352
Ontario: Catholic schools, 271;
curriculum-based exams, 253

Pallas, Aaron, 174, 207, 211
Parental involvement: effects of public
school choice, 299–301; with
private-public school choices,
329–30; school choice assumptions,
281, 284. *See also* School choice
behavior
Parent education, and test score
patterns, 108, 137–38
Path model. *See* Schooling path model
Peabody Individual Achievement Test
(PIAT), 88
Peer culture, male middle school:
effect of relative performance
ranking, 112–13, 240–42, 276;
insult game process, 231–32,
233–36; popularity values, 236–40

Poverty rates, relation to test score
patterns, 108, 137–40
Preschool attendance, social benefits,
95
Prime Time project (Indiana), 119–20
Private schools: Canada, 270, 271,
274–75, 277–78; discipline, 326;
test performance, 206. *See also*
School choice effects, New York
City study
Project Challenge (Tennessee),
121–22, 123, 125–26
Project STAR (Tennessee): compared
to school choice program, 335–36;
costs, 121, 160, 162–63; design,
109, 121–22, 123, 132–33,
153–54, 159–60; limitations of
research data, 125–26; purpose,
120–21; results, 109–10, 122, 126,
133, 154–59, 161, 319, 350–51
Project Talent, 21
Pupil-teacher ratios: compared to class
size, 140; as comparison standard,
131; decline in, 107–08, 132, 133,
350; impact of special education
enrollment, 143–44; and international test score comparisons,
146–47, 161; and student
achievement, 132, 133–37, 145;
summary of econometric studies,
147–53, 161. *See also* Class size
effects; Project Challenge; Project
STAR

Quebec, curriculum-based exams,
253, 267

Racial achievement gap: family effects,
138–39; impact of school resources,
144–45; patterns, 136–37

Random assignment experiments, 10, 109, 160–61, 319; and aptitude and achievement test bias, 26. *See also* School choice effects, New York City study; Project STAR

Reading skills, international comparisons, 105–06

River City, Iowa: curriculum administration, 210; driver education courses, 213; school performance, 209, 225; socioeconomics, 209–10. *See also* Course selection effects

Rivkin, Steven, 141

Rock, Donald A., 29, 177

Rogosa, David, 27

Rouse, Cecilia, 54

Rowher, William, 251

San Antonio, Texas, school choice, 333

Saskatchewan: Catholic schools, 271; curriculum-based exams, 267

Schmidt, William, 173

Scholastic Aptitude Test (SAT), 24, 113, 246–47

Scholastic Assessment Test. *See* Scholastic Aptitude Test

School choice behavior: data sources, 286–90; with district and school comparisons, 308–11, 353; Gresham's law, 252; influence on academic standards, 114–15, 285–86, 302–05, 311–12; influence on curriculum, 114–15, 285–86, 301–02, 311–12; influence on disciplinary atmosphere, 114–15, 305–07, 311–12; influence on extracurricular activities, 307–08, 312; and parental involvement, 114–15, 299–301, 312; research

difficulties, 282–83, 290, 292–94, 308–11; research methodology, 283–84, 295–99; theoretical assumptions, 114, 281, 284, 318. *See also* School choice effects, New York City study; School choice programs

School choice effects, New York City study: applicant characteristics, 324–25; disciplinary atmosphere, 326–27, 336–37; homework, 115, 328–29; parental involvement, 115, 329–30, 336–37; research methodology, 320–24, 325–26; school mobility, 330–33; student test performance, 115, 333–36, 353. *See also* School choice behavior; School choice programs

School choice programs: costs, 353; District of Columbia, 318, 352; Florida, 318; Indiana, 333; Minnesota, 293; New York City, 319–20, 325; Ohio, 317–18, 333, 352; Texas, 333; theoretical assumptions, 114, 281, 284, 318; trends, 352–53; Wisconsin, 317–18, 330, 333, 352. *See also* School choice behavior; School choice effects, New York City study

School Choice Scholarships Foundation (SCSF): applicant characteristics, 324–25; application process, 320, 321; eligibility criteria, 320; program description, 115, 319–20; student test performance, 333–35, 353. *See also* School choice effects, New York City study

Schooling length: and achievement gains, 38, 39–40, 55, 61, 63–65, 82–83, 344–46; and enrollment

age, 10–11, 79–80, 83, 87–88; as
    reform strategy, 11, 79, 82, 347–48;
    and wage levels, 3–5, 9–10, 53–54,
    65–73, 205, 347–48
Schooling path model: components,
    51–52; methodology, 57–59,
    74–75; reciprocal effects of
    schooling and cognitive skills, 50,
    51, 59, 61–65, 73; and education
    theories, 52–53, 63, 72–73;
    schooling and cognitive skill effects
    on income levels, 50, 51, 65–73
School mobility, 330–33
Schultz, Theodore, 4
Schultze, Charles, 50, 53, 72
Science skills: influence on math
    proficiency, 111, 171, 192–94;
    international comparisons, 105–06
*Setting the Record Straight: Responses to
    Misconceptions about Public
    Education in the United States*
    (Bracey), 106
Shopping mall schools, 206, 207–08,
    224
Signaling theory, 6, 260
Single-parent families, and test score
    patterns, 108, 137–40
Smith, Mary Lee, 118, 119, 125, 128,
    153–54, 162
Special education sector: growth,
    141–43; impact on pupil-teacher
    ratios, 108, 143–44
Spending, education: for
    disadvantaged students, 144–45;
    locality share, 255; per pupil
    patterns, 107, 133–34; student
    quantity approach, 206, 224; *1997*
    totals, 106–07. *See also* Costs of
    school reform
Sports. *See* Athletic achievement values
*Stability and Change in Human
    Characteristics* (Bloom), 26

Sternberg, Robert, 58
Student effort: correlation with college
    choice, 221–22, 223; GPA as
    measure, 219–20; influence on
    cognitive skills, 111, 220–21,
    222–24. *See also* Studiousness
Student population characteristics,
    and test score patterns, 137–40
Studiousness: and athletic
    achievement, 240, 241–42; effect of
    relative performance ranking,
    112–13, 240–42, 276; international
    comparisons of peer values, 242;
    peer group culture, 232, 237–39.
    See also Student effort
Success model: ability and aptitude
    bias controls, 8–9, 23–28;
    achievement-earnings relationship,
    9, 35–39; achievement estimates,
    28–33, 39–42, 45–46; aptitude
    defined, 19; benefits for policy-
    making, 18–19; error correction
    methods, 33–35; heritability issues,
    19–20; testing age implications,
    20–23; variables in, 17–18
Sweden, math and science
    enrollments, 270

Taiwan, studiousness values, 242
Tannenbaum, Abraham, 238
Teacher quality, 163–64
Television watching, 270–71, 277
Tennessee, class size experiments. *See*
    Project Challenge; Project STAR
Testing age, and adult success, 20–23
Texas: class size effects study, 152–53;
    school choice, 333
Third International Mathematics and
    Science Study, 146
Thomas, John, 251
Tiebout choice, 294. *See also* School
    choice behavior

Tillitski, Chris, 119

Virginia, enrollment age, 80
Vocational education: academic skill
    integration, 170, 194–95; influence
    on math proficiency, 111, 193–94
Vouchers. *See* School choice behavior

Wage levels: and enrollment age,
    10–11, 25–26, 79–80, 82–83,
    85–88, 95–98; and national exams,
352; and schooling length, 3–5,
    9–10, 53–54, 65–73, 205, 347–48.
    See also Cognitive skills–earnings
    relationships
Welch, Wayne, 173
Wells, Amy, 324
Who Gets Ahead? (Jencks and others),
    55–56
Willet, John, 27
Wisconsin, school choice, 317, 330,
    333, 352
Witte, John, 330